Observations on "The Spiritual Situation of the Age"

Observations on "The Spiritual Situation of the Age"

Contemporary German Perspectives

edited by Jürgen Habermas
translated and with an introduction by
Andrew Buchwalter

The MIT Press, Cambridge, Massachusetts, and London, England

First MIT Press paperback edition, 1985
This translation © 1984 by the Massachusetts Institute of Technology
All of the essays in this collection are taken from *Stichworte zur 'Geistigen Situation der Zeit'*, © 1979 by Suhrkamp Verlag, Frankfurt.

This book was typeset in Baskerville
by The MIT Press Computergraphics Department
and printed and bound by Halliday Lithograph
in the United States of America.

Library of Congress Cataloging in Publication Data

Stichworte zur geistigen Situation der Zeit. English.
   Observations on "the spiritual situation of the age".

   (Studies in contemporary German social thought)
   Translation of: Stichworte zur geistigen Situation der Zeit.
   Includes bibliographical references and index.
   1. Germany (West)—Politics and Government—Addresses, essays, lectures.
2. Germany (West)—Civilization—Addresses, essays, lectures.
I. Habermas, Jürgen. II. Title. III. Series.
DD259.4.S83313   1984   320.943   83–16180
ISBN 0-262-08132-6 (hard)
      0-262-58074-8 (paper)

Contents

Perspectives on the *Geisteswissenschaften*

Perspectives on German Affairs

Unconcluding Reflections

Translator's Introduction

I

After years of economic prosperity, political stability, and general social peace, there are indications that all is no longer well in West Germany. The most obvious sign may be the widespread protests against the deployment of Pershing 2 and cruise missiles, reflecting a fear that Germany might some day become the shooting gallery of the superpowers. Others include the widespread expression of anxiety about environmental contamination, the acceleration of social change, an increased dependence on anonymous foreign forces, and the lack of a meaningful future. These are all symptoms of a growing sense of unease, isolation, and rootlessness that has recently come to color Germans' perceptions of living conditions in their country.

Angst is difficult to gauge, but other developments suggest that there is a solid basis for German discontent. Problems have arisen in the economy, the political system, and the realm of culture. In the economic sphere the problems are twofold. On the one hand, the vaunted German economic system—until recently still referred to as the *Wirtschaftswunder*, the economic miracle—is now beset with unrelenting recession, record high unemployment, bankruptcies of major firms, fiscal crises of towns and municipalities, slippage of the deutsche mark, an inability of German companies to remain competitive with foreign counterparts, problems of export-dependent industries confronted with limited world demand, and an environment increasingly unable to cope with the ravages of industrial and commercial devastation. Moreover, the structures put in place to protect Germany from forces that have destabilized other Western industrial countries are themselves now plagued with difficulties. The extensive system of welfare-state capitalism that was launched by the Social Democrats and known as the *Modell Deutschland* [the German Model]—comprising such key elements as Keynesian state interventionism, a generous network of social services, and a program of close cooperation between government, labor, and industry—has foundered on the reefs of rising deficits, austerity measures, and general socioeconomic retrenchments. These difficulties are felt all the more acutely by a population that has come to expect growth, full employment, and the bountiful provisions of a social welfare state as its natural legacy.

On the other hand, the West German economy has come under attack by critics who question the basic values of Germany's postwar social and economic life, in particular by those individuals and groups directly or indirectly connected with *die Grünen*, the ecologically oriented Green party that in 1983 gained a place in the federal parliament. They include environmentalists, urban squatters, feminists, counter-cultural youth, and members of an increasingly influential peace movement. Rejecting the so-called materialist or acquisitive values of discipline, industriousness, careerism, frugality, competitiveness, and achievement, these individuals and groups embrace a host of "post-materialist" or "postacquisitive" values: solidarity, self-realization, and the quest for a meaningful life. Provoked by the adverse consequences and negative side effects of the economic miracle—destruction of the natural and urban environment, deteriorating housing conditions, neglect of social services in favor of the arms industry, intensification of the division of labor—the Greens and related groups reject central tenets of economic growth, technological progress, militarism, welfare-state government, and in some cases industrial society itself. In their place they propose a radical reordering of social and economic priorities: disarmament, termination of reliance on nuclear power, a systematic as opposed to a piecemeal approach to environmental protection, development of small-scale industries, reduction of the division of labor, decentralization, creation of more livable human spaces, production of more societally useful products and services. Although much is still unclear about these programs, the challenge they pose to the postwar German status quo is unmistakable.

A second set of problems concerns the country's system of legal and political institutions, which many have considered to be its real postwar miracle. Two radically different challenges are discernible, each demonstrating the extent to which some Germans see *eine andere Republik*, a different political system. First, some governmental policies and initiatives, together with a general tendency toward state expansionism, have raised questions about the seriousness of the country's oft-professed commitment to democratic values and institutions. Of particular significance in this regard are the legal and administrative measures taken in the past decade to secure the state against the presumed threats emanating from the left. Thus a computerized police security network has established an extensive system of state surveillance. A provision known as the *Radikalenerlass* [Decree against Radicals] requires that all applicants for state employment (approximately 20 percent of the population of the Federal Republic are state employees) pledge their loyalty to a "liberal democratic basic order" that in content is hardly distinguishable from the status quo. Through a practice known as *Berufsverbot* (roughly translatable as "professional proscription"), this provision also bars from civil-service employment individuals whose utterances or actions are deemed "inimical to the constitution." Other measures involve changes in criminal and judicial procedures that severely restrict a defendant's right to counsel and allow, at the discretion of the Ministry of Justice, for the defendant's solitary confinement (*Kontaktsperrgesetz*). Finally, there have been proposals that the German Criminal Code be revised to prohibit demonstrators from concealing their identities (*Vermummungsverbot*) and from taking part in a demonstration that turns violent, a charge that is refuted only when the accused proves that he or she was not actively involved in violent acts. The first three provisions were products of the now-defunct coalition between the Social Democrats and the Free Democrats, largely in response to the actions of rebellious students in the late 60s and early 70s, and of terrorists as well as terrorist "sympathizers" in the mid-70s. The changes in the Criminal Code are proposals of the recently elected Christian Democratic/Free Democratic coalition, largely in anticipation of the civil disobedience expected from groups intent on blocking the stationing of American nuclear missiles on German soil. These measures have given renewed relevance to the question often asked during the Federal Republic's founding years: Is Bonn Weimar? Has the second German republic embarked on a course whose final destination will in some way resemble that of the first German republic?

A different but still related challenge has come from the Greens and the groups they represent. In becoming the first new party since 1958 to sit in the *Bundestag*—the national parliament—the Greens have markedly altered the West German political landscape. They have also contributed significantly to the acute identity crisis currently being experienced by the Social Democrats, who must also deal with massive defections from their right-center flank into the ranks of the ruling Christian Democratic Union. The success of the Greens gives pointed expression to a pervasive dissatisfaction with the basic structures of West German political life and with a system of political representation that, for an increasing number of voters, not only has lost touch with, but is actually inimical to, citizens' everyday needs and their demands for political expression and involvement. The Greens question the current channels and mechanisms of political engagement and participation—oligarchically and corporatistically structured political parties, impenetrable and inflexible labor unions, and an anonymous state bureaucracy increasingly dependent on experts and specialists. They also articulate a challenge to the prevailing assumptions that politics consists in bargaining and compromise among parliamentary factions, that the central state is the sole repository of political power, and that the legitimacy of political decisions rests with institutionally sanctioned procedures. They advocate instead a new type of direct, radical democracy, one that would remove power and political decision-making procedures from the state and its various appendages and connect them more directly to the will and interests of the populace. The instruments of this "new politics"—commonly referred to as democracy of the base [*Basisdemokratie*] or "democracy in the first person"—include citizens' initiatives, direct political action, large-scale demonstrations, popular referenda and plebiscites, and a parliamentary strategy which, through the rotation of representatives and binding mandates, seeks to bridge the gap between formal political activity and input from the social base. All are components of a general program oriented to the creation of a public sphere free of state monopoly and institutional sclerosis.

It remains to be seen whether members of the Greens can maintain their commitment to the principles of direct democracy and still function effectively as a parliamentary party. Can this antiparty party, as Green leader Petra Kelly has called it, successfully mediate between the demands of Fundamental Opposition and Realpolitik? And in a different vein, their critics ask whether they have properly assessed the value of formal and representative democracy for complex, pluralistic, heterogeneously constituted societies? In any case, it is clear that in gaining a foothold in parliament the Greens have presented a profound challenge to the structure, methods, and values of postwar German political life.

A third problem-area revolves about the question of German "identity." In increasing numbers Germans have become involved with what is commonly known as the national question, the thorny tangle of issues concerning collective identity and the legal, political, and cultural status of the West German nation-state and the larger German nation. For the greater part of the Federal Republic's history, such concerns did not command much of an audience. The national question was discredited by Nazi ultranationalism and was forgotten, or repressed, in the postwar retreat into privatism and personal achievement. The assimilation of American culture pushed such concerns into the background, as did the socialist internationalism of the student movement. Moreover, the partition of the former Reich and postwar developments such as the Federal Republic's integration into NATO, its entrance into the Common Market, and an *Ostpolitik* predicated on formal acknowledgment of the destruction of the Reich as a territorial entity, impeded a national focus. While postwar Germany was never without sources and symbols of collective identity—the economic miracle, Europeanism, cosmopolitan consumerism, and cold-war anticommunism all provided acceptable surrogates—such concerns were not fashioned into a revivified national question.

In the past several years myriad phenomena attest to the rebirth of a "national" consciousness. What merits special attention, however, is not the increased animosity toward foreign "guest" workers, the appearance of youth groups that glorify the Nazi past, or the present chancellor's declaration that historical German virtues are the foundation of the present political order. Nor is it the fact that among young people the search for ways to express a sense of national identity is so pronounced that soft drinks are now promoted as "the German alternative." A more significant indication of the changing climate is the fact that the national question is now being discussed by liberals and leftists, for whom such concerns were long anathema. Thus liberal journalists bemoan the "absence of a national milieu"; liberal political scientists suggest that a functioning democracy must be supplemented by a consciousness of historical roots, tradition, and identity. Some leftists speak of a new feeling for the homeland (*neues Heimatsgefühl*), while others stress the uniqueness of the German identity by counterposing German culture to Americanism and Western civilization generally. In response to the prospect of NATO missiles stationed on German soil, members of the peace movement, and now Social Democrats, raise questions about the nation's "political sovereignty" and broach the topic of reunification. Some even espouse a return to Germany's historical equidistance from East and West. These developments should not be construed as evidence of a new consensus on the national question or as signs of a resurgent German nationalism. Nonetheless, for a country nurtured on national abstinence, even a muted posing of the national question must be regarded as a challenge to the postwar status quo.

These changes raise numerous questions about the nature and trajectory of contemporary West German society. Are they merely transitory phenomena, indicative only of what has often been characterized as a German inability to respond with composure to changing living conditions? Or do they indicate deeper tensions and broader historical tendencies? And if the latter, how are they to be interpreted? Is the Federal Republic of Germany experiencing a new phase of sociopolitical evolution, is it undergoing a process of cultural and political regression, or is it drifting aimlessly? On a different level, is there any single conceptual or theoretical framework in which the myriad of trends and currents can be adequately understood, or does the complexity of the situation obstruct and defy comprehension? Finally, are the changes and crises facing West Germany today unique to that country? Are the challenges issued to the postwar social, political, and cultural order a manifestation of what the French call *la malaise allemande*, a romantic impulse to defy imposed limits and to give in to what Nietzsche termed the "magic of extremism"? Or do these developments merely represent a sharper expression of problems being faced by other Western industrial societies and indeed the modern age generally?

II

German intellectuals have always shown a special inclination to pose questions like these. Social theory, reflection on the direction of the *Zeitgeist*, a sensitivity to issues of national and collective identity, evaluations of modernity, and a willingness to engage in a type of *Kulturkritik* focused less on literature and the arts than on the general domain of cultural reproduction have always been something of a German specialty. In recent years, however, the flow of books and articles addressing West German "political culture" has been unusually large even by German standards.[1] Provoked by present tensions and by the perceived divergence between social norms and social reality (which Hegel called the source of philosophical reflection), German critics and intellectuals have felt increasingly compelled to assess the nature and direction of their society. In this developing genre one book has stood above the rest: the two-volume collection of essays conceived, organized, and edited by Jürgen Habermas and published in 1979 as volume 1,000 of the *edition suhrkamp*, postwar Germany's most celebrated series of books dealing with culture and society. This collection, *Stichworte zur 'Geistigen Situation der Zeit'* [Observations on "the spiritual situation of the age"], consists of contributions by thirty-two of Germany's most prominent leftist intellectuals. The date of publication was not incidental, for in 1979 the Federal Republic of Germany marked the thirtieth anniversary of its founding.

Stichworte, as the book has come to be known, offers an unparalleled portrait of the state of West Germany today. The essays provide comprehensive accounts and penetrating assessments of German social, political, and cultural life. The economic crisis, the changing nature of social values and assumptions, the problems associated with welfare-state capitalism and the postwar modernization, the diverse challenges to political institutions, the new social movements, the problem of terrorism, the burden of the Nazi past, and questions of cultural and political identity are all discussed in uncommon breadth and depth. The book supplies a highly sophisticated framework for understanding German society. And because many recent political disputes are the culmination of currents and trends fully diagnosed by Habermas and his colleagues, *Stichworte* (which has gone through several printings) is still indispensable for an understanding of the German *Zeitgeist* today.

The book's essays are concerned not only with West Germany's political culture or, as it has also been called, its "political nonculture and nonpolitical culture." They also address themselves to at least four other aspects of "the spiritual situation of the age": religion and theology; the present state of the *Geisteswissenschaften*, the academic disciplines concerned with investigating meanings, values, traditions, and historical and cultural productions in general; the "voices" of the age, that is, those intellectuals who, by interpreting social trends and meanings, not only contribute to the actualization of the *Zeitgeist* but in many cases shape its development; and the nature of Western culture and, indeed, of the "present age" as such. It is owing to this comprehensive focus that *Stichworte* can well be taken as an expression of the epoch.

The present English-language edition consists of essays selected by Thomas McCarthy and myself from the two-volume German edition. We have attempted in our selection to provide readers with an array of perspectives on life in Germany today and also to convey the richness and vitality of contemporary German academic and intellectual concerns. Additionally, we sought to include essays that would be of value to an analysis of the cultural and political situation in other Western nations. While it was not possible to include all the essays that met these criteria, it is our hope that this selection will convey to readers something of the breadth and insight of the German original.

III

In soliciting essays on the spiritual situation of the age, Habermas set no specific requirements for his authors, but he did provide them with a focal point: Karl Jaspers's 1931 essay in cultural criticism, *Die geistige Situation der Zeit* (published in English as *Man in the Modern Age*), an overview of the social, political, cultural, religious, and intellectual condition of late Weimar Germany.[2] In appealing to Jaspers's work, Habermas was motivated in part by ceremonial considerations: *Die geistige Situation der Zeit* was also published as volume 1,000 in an important literary series, the Sammlung Göschen of the de Gruyter Verlag. There were, however, more substantive considerations behind the choice. Habermas felt drawn to Jaspers's brand of cultural criticism, which combined a theoretical analysis of the main features of the age with a normative assessment that was intended to influence the *Zeitgeist*.

He was also mindful of the tense and turbulent situation that confronted Jaspers, whose book appeared two years before Hitler took power.[3] In both respects Jaspers's assessment of life in the first German republic seemed a fitting backdrop for the engaged diagnosis Habermas hoped his colleagues would provide for the second German republic.

But the differences from Jaspers's approach are equally essential to Habermas's project. To begin with, Habermas rejects the ontological assumptions that informed Jaspers's analysis, assumptions rooted in the Hegelian notion of the unity of metaphysics and politics. In particular, he repudiates the view that the age expresses an underlying essence or spirit (a view as evident in Lukács's equation of *Zeitkritik* with an objectivistic philosophy of history as in Jaspers's equation of it with *prima philosophia*). Similarly, he criticizes the belief that a general philosophical theory can fully apprehend its time in thought, and he dismisses the notion that a single individual can adequately grasp the complexities of an age. Accordingly, Habermas proposes a far more modest approach to cultural criticism, one fully conscious of its empirical base and its hermeneutic relativity. This is signaled by the quotation marks around the term "the spiritual situation of the age," by the use of the word *Stichworte* or "observations" rather than "general theory," and by the fact that the project as a whole was designed as a collaborative undertaking.[4]

More important than the methodological distinctions, however, are the normative differences between the two projects. For Jaspers, cultural criticism had a decidedly conservative cast.[5] Like his contemporaries Spengler, Heidegger, the early Thomas Mann, and their Iberian kinsman Ortega y Gasset, Jaspers assailed modernization, technology, bureaucratization, and mass society; like the German academic mandarins portrayed in this collection by the historian Hans-Ulrich Wehler, he repudiated Western social science and "Anglo-Saxon" positivism; and in language reminiscent equally of Ferdinand Tönnies and Carl Schmitt, he dismissed democracy, pluralism, and liberalism. In the tradition of Novalis, Schiller, and Schlegel, he lamented the modern world's loss of meaning and substantive value and its general "despiritualization" — his term for what Max Weber called "disenchantment." It is true that the position advanced by Jaspers in *Die geistige Situation der Zeit* defies easy classification. His existential individualism is hardly compatible with conservative German social romanticism, while his nostalgia for substance and meaning cannot be easily reconciled with the irreverent antimodernism of Nietzschean young conservatism. Moreover, he is not an inveterate foe of progress. Still, his thought is imbued with the elitist, anticivilizational pessimism so characteristic of traditional German cultural criticism.[6]

By contrast, the intellectuals whom Habermas approached all came from the "left" side of the cultural-political spectrum, including liberals, left-liberals, liberation theologians, radical democrats, social democrats, socialists, and neo-Marxists. Roughly speaking, all espouse views committed to the values of modernity, Enlightenment, humanism, and democracy.[7] To be sure, they display little unanimity in their approaches, and several are quite willing to adopt themes more traditionally linked with conservative cultural criticism. Not only do they advance criticisms of bureaucracy, social reform, and scientific-technological civilization; they also call for solutions that employ a "conservative" rather than a "progressive" terminology.[8] At the same time, none of the contributors embrace the cultural pessimism that has led some conservative critics of modern culture to suggest that progress and Enlightenment are illusory and mystifying, that the modern world is a fall from a more glorious past, that salvation is achievable only through some romantic retreat inward. Nearly all of the authors remain loyal to the basic tenets of leftist cultural criticism, according to which contemporary ills are attributable to specific social conditions and solutions are to be found in a more rational organization of social reality. And those who do adopt conservative themes seem to act less out of disenchantment with leftist thought than with the conviction— already enunciated by Ernst Bloch and Walter Benjamin—that the problems of the present might best be confronted through an appropriation of themes too often conceded to the right.

Why did Habermas restrict potential contributors to intellectuals on the left? He did, after all, acknowledge that the cultural-political diagnoses of "young conservatives" such as Ernst Junger, Gottfried Benn, Martin Heidegger, and Carl Schmitt were particularly timely. One reason lay in his attempt to include only essays consonant with the aims and intentions of the *edition suhrkamp* series. This meant essays by intellectuals associated with the undogmatic left—individuals who, as he put it, "stand committed to the traditions against which a German regime established itself in 1933." For it was precisely this "resolute affiliation with Enlightenment, humanism, bourgeois radical thought, and with the aesthetic and political avant-garde of the nineteenth century" that informed the edition's preceding volumes.

A second reason was provided by the *Zeitgeist* itself. For much of the postwar period writers associated with the *edition suhrkamp* set the tone of cultural and intellectual life in West Germany. Indeed, for a society eager to distance itself from a regime opposed to humanism, democracy, and the precepts of the Enlightenment, the "suhrkamp culture"—George Steiner's apt characterization—was understood by many to be the conscience, guardian, and repository of the new republic's values. In the mid-70s, however, the climate changed. The position of the left as the arbiter of the nation's values was challenged, and attitudes, theories, assumptions, and behavior commonly associated with the traditions against which the second republic was founded were revived. Thus, in assembling a group of undogmatic leftists to assess the spiritual situation of the age, Habermas particularly wanted to reassert the values of the left and the principles of the suhrkamp culture at a time when they were under attack. At the very least he sought to determine the spirit of the left when the *Geist* itself no longer stood on the left.[9]

A number of striking indications of this changed climate of opinion occurred in the fall of 1977, which quickly became known as the German Autumn (a title that has also been earned by the fall of 1983). Partly in reaction to such terrorist actions as the abduction and execution of industrial leader Hans Martin Schleyer and the hijacking of a Lufthansa airliner to Mogadishu (undertaken to secure the release of terrorists in the maximum security prison at Stammheim), the German parliament, urged on by the public, the media, and many intellectuals, passed laws that were hardly compatible with the principles of the country's "liberal-democratic basic order" (*freiheitliche-demokratische Grundordnung*). The events also triggered attitudes and behavior that were disquietingly familiar, such as a friend-foe mentality that became increasingly evident both in the populace and on the part of the state. One example of this was the growing tendency to brand as "enemies of the state" not only lawbreakers (who in a constitutional order should of course be judged strictly as criminals) but also individuals (labeled "sympathizers") who merely questioned the wisdom and propriety of the state's conduct. One of the more scandalous episodes of this period is discussed in this collection by Albrecht Wellmer and Karl Heinz Bohrer. A contributor to an anarchist student newspaper at the Uni-

versity of Göttingen, writing an obituary under the pseudonym "Mescalero" (after the name of a group of Italian urban "Indians"), admitted
feeling a "secret delight" at the news of the terrorist assassination of
Chief Federal Prosecutor Siegfried Buback. This acknowledgment was
phrased as a confession in the context of a larger argument repudiating
terrorism and violence as legitimate tools for effecting social change.
Yet it was only the admission of "secret delight" that caught attention.
The paper was censored by the government with little protest from
the general media. A university professor who attempted to clarify
the real intent of the obituary was suspended from his position.

What led Habermas to focus on the changing cultural and political
climate was not the German Autumn per se, although he has likened
the time to a "pogrom."[10] His attention was drawn more by a general
swing to the right, of which the events of 1977 were one particularly
dramatic manifestation. Called the *Tendenzwende*, this "shift in ideological currents" was a reaction to developments in the late 60s and
early 70s, among them the antiauthoritarian movement, the "cultural
revolution," the increased popularity of countercultural life-styles, and
the welfare-state reform measures enacted by the Social Democrats.
The shift was quite evident at the political level, as the reform policies
of the Brandt government gave way, in 1973–74, to the technocratic
statism and crisis-management pragmatism of Helmut Schmidt (and
more recently to the conservative and in many respects antiliberal
administration of Helmut Kohl). Additional evidence was discernible,
as Hans Mommsen argues in his essay, in the emergence of radical
neofascist groups, a "Hitler Wave," and a swing in attitudes to the
"statist-authoritarian conceptions of the late Weimar period." In discussing the state of contemporary scholarly research in theology, academic literary criticism, and historiography, Jürgen Moltmann, Peter
Bürger, and Hans-Ulrich Wehler chart the conservative backlash that
took place in the *Geisteswissenschaften*. On a similar plane, Habermas,
Wolf-Dieter Narr, Ulrich Preuss, and Albrecht Wellmer document the
emergence of neoconservative ideologues determined to dislodge the
left from its position as the nation's arbiter of values and to reorder
the cultural and political agenda of the republic. More than anything
else, the ascendance of this aggressive New Right intelligentsia marked
the decline in influence of the suhrkamp culture.

German neoconservatives attributed all of the problems that emerged
in the late 60s and early 70s to "left-inspired" cultural and political

developments: welfare-state reforms as they overburdened governmental steering mechanisms, increased demands for political participation as they hampered governmental and corporate decision making,
the antiauthoritarian movement and cultural revolution as they radically
questioned the prevailing norms of West German society, and the
aesthetic counterculture as it encouraged a libertinism incompatible
with professional life. In the neoconservative view all these phenomena
interfered with the efficient functioning of state and economy and
threatened to render the country "ungovernable"—a theme analyzed
here by Claus Offe. Accordingly, the neoconservatives' response was
to call for measures that would counter these developments: dismantling
the welfare state, depoliticizing governmental steering mechanisms,
and restoring such values as obedience, discipline, and authority.

In many respects the position of German neoconservatives is not
markedly distinct from that of neoconservatives in other countries.[11]
Today virtually all neoconservatives are committed to the enhancement
of systems of economic growth, technological progress, and efficient
state administration. As underscored by many authors in this book,
neoconservatives seek to affirm societal modernization while challenging
cultural and political modernism.

At the same time, German neoconservatives are unique in that their
challenge to cultural and political modernism invokes the illiberal, anti-
Enlightenment arguments associated with the authoritarian elements
of the German historical tradition—arguments that were in disrepute
for much of the postwar period.[12] Three main variants of this "specifically German" neoconservatism are discussed in this volume. First,
some German neoconservatives respond to the crisis of authority and
the problem of ungovernability by appealing to a German constitu-
tionalism that separates the rule of law from democracy. An especially
subtle version of this thesis is discussed by the legal scholar Ulrich
Preuss, who shows how conservative constitutionalists manipulate concepts seemingly central to the principles of constitutional democracy
and subordinate them to the needs of state and economy. (This has
the consequence, Preuss notes, of rendering unconstitutional any behavior that deviates from these needs.) Second, there is a revival of
a concept of politics based on the friend-foe distinction, a concept that
was given systematic expression in the work of Carl Schmitt.[13] Albrecht
Wellmer discusses one component of this thesis in his analysis of
attempts to link social critics with terrorist "enemies of the state," a

strategy that relieves the state of any obligation to justify itself in response to criticism. Third, some neoconservatives respond to the crisis of values and institutions by turning to traditionalist morality and the pessimistic anthropology of a political Lutheranism.[14] Thus, as Habermas notes, some seek to stabilize German society by promoting an uncritical acceptance of values such as religion, nation, and historical consciousness; others aim to counter excessive individualism, hedonism, and mass democracy with an antihumanistic institutionalism supportive of "secondary values" such as industriousness, obedience, discipline, and love of order. It is clear, then, how criticism of German neoconservatism can be said to entail a defense of the republic against the burden of the past.

At the same time, the challenge to the values of the suhrkamp culture did not arise solely from the ranks of conservatives. There also emerged forces on the left that opposed certain principles and assumptions of "Enlightenment" traditionally espoused by the left. Habermas in fact now recognizes a "new *Tendenzwende*,"[15] one that joins members of the left and the right, despite their differences, in a common attack on "all that should be saved in Western tradition and inspiration."[16]

This shift was in part a response to disappointments arising from domestic and international developments, including the demise of the antiauthoritarian movement of the late 60s and the failure of the Social Democrats to "dare more democracy," as they had pledged upon Willy Brandt's election as chancellor in 1969; the oil and economic crises of the early 70s, which called into question the notion that social change could be linked unproblematically to the development of the forces of production; and the increasingly repressive conduct of socialist countries, which, as Wolf-Dieter Narr notes, deprived leftists of any established *point d'appui* for political protest.

The left *Tendenzwende* took the specific form of a romantic turn inward and a willingness to entertain themes more commonly linked to the tradition of counter-Enlightenment irrationalism.[17] Karl Heinz Bohrer generally characterizes this change as one from the Enlightenment objective to realize history toward a more romantic move to historicize reality. On a philosophical plane, this shift was manifested in a poststructuralist repudiation of universalism, utopianism, and rationality and a willingness to embrace a *Lebensphilosophie* that placed emphasis on the uniqueness of everyday life. In literature there was a movement away from the engaged social criticism of the 50s and 60s and a turn to "subjectivity" and the "new irrationalism," marked by a romantic fascination with topics drawn from the personal and emotional realm. In cinema the situation was reflected not only in the work of Hans-Jürgen Syberberg, whose *Our Hitler* paid homage to the Germans' "creative irrationality," but in the films of Rainer Fassbinder, Werner Herzog, Wim Wenders, who, while clearly critical of West German society, had abandoned avant-garde utopianism and had begun to explore themes taken from what Bohrer calls the mythic and anthropological sphere. The changing climate could also be felt in the willingness of some leftists to exchange their concerns over socialism and internationalism for concerns over reunification and nationhood.[18] And it was even perceptible within the *edition suhrkamp* itself, which after volume 1,000 introduced a new series (*Neue Folge*) that was designed to address topics not fully consistent with its past affiliation with "Enlightenment, humanism, bourgeois radical thought, and the aesthetic and political avant-garde of the nineteenth century."

The importance of this development is not to be found in its critique of the Enlightenment per se—this would hardly constitute a challenge to a cultural tradition that counts Theodor Adorno among its most prominent representatives. Rather, it consists in the fact that the dialectic of Enlightenment is now invoked in order to repudiate critical rationality and to glorify counter-Enlightenment values.[19] It is this Nietzschean gesture—described in this volume by Peter Bürger in connection with academic literary criticism—that has been characteristic of the German *Zeitgeist* since the late 70s, a *Zeitgeist* that gives prominence to such thinkers as Bataille, Foucault, and Derrida. And it is this same "destruction of reason," as Lukács once called it, that leads Wolf-Dieter Narr to suggest that certain leftists have signed "the pact of intellectual submission."

A similar shift was apparent in the political sphere. Rather than effectively promoting a more rational organization of society, some individuals engaged in irrationalist, existentialist behavior that in some cases spurned politics altogether. One of the first manifestations of this "depoliticization" was the emergence of a host of Marxist-Leninist sects and splinter groups posturing as a proletarian vanguard. Their political irrelevance was shown by their inability to address the real issues of the day: civil rights, feminism, ecology. A similar development was visible in the increasingly desperate behavior of the terrorists, who were politically significant only in that they served as a pretext, as Albrecht Wellmer notes, for conservatives and reactionaries to vilify and intimidate the entire left.

Meanwhile the alternative culture, while continuing the interest in reforming personal life-styles that emerged in the 60s, now abandoned one essential ingredient of the "cultural revolution," namely, the goal of linking personal and cultural transformations with the greater transformation of social and political reality.[20] In addition, certain environmentalists, as Mommsen observes, combined a critique of capitalist modernization with a romantic dismissal of industrialization, while some feminists completely dismissed modern culture as patriarchal. Despite their heterogeneity, all of these phenomena reflect a trend toward depoliticization that led away from the route championed by Rudi Dutschke as "the long march through the institutions."[21]

IV

As Habermas indicates in his introduction, there is little uniformity in his contributors' diagnoses of the *Zeitgeist*; indeed, the essays are so dissimilar in both method and substance that a single framework can scarcely accommodate their variety. Nonetheless, certain themes and issues are unmistakable, and three are particularly noteworthy: (1) the burden of the past; (2) the problems of capitalist modernization, particularly in postwar Germany; and (3) questions of the dignity of modernity and the legitimacy of the modern age. It is not possible here to summarize specific arguments in any detail, but it might be helpful to situate the different contributions in relation to these themes.

1. The German Autumn, the *Tendenzwende*, and the ideology of German neoconservatives have all raised questions about the persistence in the Federal Republic's "political culture" of the authoritarian, monarchical attitudes that have historically been so much a part of the German tradition, and about the consequences of that tradition's combination of economic modernization, political backwardness, and lack of democracy.

The authors who address these issues do not minimize the differences between the Federal Republic and other social and political structures that have been erected on German soil. For instance, Hans Mommsen, while drawing parallels between the political culture of the Federal Republic and the "statist-authoritarian" phase of the Weimar Republic, emphasizes that West Germany's democratic institutions are better established and that the Federal Republic is relatively free of the "political irrationalism" characteristic of the first German republic. Nonetheless, it was the tendency of the state, the media, and large segments of the populace to interpret the Federal Republic's values and institutions in ways inimical to the concept of liberal democracy that led Mommsen to follow other intellectuals in questioning the radicalness of the break that occurred in 1949. And in a similar vein, Wellmer speaks of the "continuity between a republican form of government and an authoritarian past."[22]

In the view of many German intellectuals, the Federal Republic bore the imprint of its past even in its very inception. Albrecht Wellmer argues that a certain continuity was ensured because the present order was not the product of a process of emancipation but resulted instead from the defeat of fascism—that it was not the product of popular will but was imposed from without, in this case by the victorious allies. Dieter Wellershoff suggests that continuity was nourished by a rebuilding process that not only buried the wounds and the memories of the past, but in a new way reaffirmed the opposition between economic modernization and political backwardness—an opposition that, as Horst Ehmke points out, was characteristic of the German *Bürgertum* under Bismarck and a key to Hitler's rise to power. Jürgen Moltmann discusses the continuity of a friend-foe mentality that was prominent during the Nazi period and was recycled after the war into cold-war anticommunism and later deployed against domestic "enemies." Others argue that continuity was fostered by the "chancellor-democracy" of Konrad Adenauer, who in policy and personality represented not a "new beginning" but a restoration of the status quo ante Hitler, and who further assured continuity by his elevation of former Nazis to high governmental positions.[23] Still others argue that continuity was nurtured by the partition of the nation and the integration of the two substates into the major power blocs—developments that dissipated any possible focus through which a mourning nation could come to terms with its past.[24]

Since the 1950s the Federal Republic has undergone many changes. Germany is, as Wellershoff suggests, a "state of flux." The change in generations, the antiauthoritarian movement, the reform measures of the Social Democrats, and, not least, the rise of left intellectuals to a position of moral authority (certainly a novelty in German history) all

testified to an altered cultural and political climate. With reference to
German historiography, Hans-Ulrich Wehler goes so far as to suggest
that a "paradigm shift" occurred in the 60s, one that signaled a radical
break with the traditional conservative statism still so prominent in
the early postwar years and an incipient adoption of themes and
approaches more common to the Western tradition. Yet the events
of the 70s demonstrated to many that the past still lingers on in West
German political culture, that its effects were never resolved but only
repressed, and that, as Mommsen argues, little "critical working through
of the past has taken place."

What would it mean to work through the burden of German history?[25] There are complex issues here apart from the problem of
whether people can ever fully free themselves of their heritage and
traditions and whether ruminations on the past can ever result in
anything but present and future paralysis. The 1979 broadcast in West
Germany of the television film *Holocaust* triggered a massive debate
on a number of these issues.[26] For some, the incredulity that characterized reactions to the film revealed a dearth of knowledge about
anti-Semitism and Nazism and seemed to suggest that an effective
approach to a coming to terms with the past (*Vergangenheitsbewältigung*)
might require fortified efforts at civic education—particularly in the
schools where, as many contend, these issues are insufficiently addressed. For others the film was significant for the profound outpouring
of grief it elicited and the residue of guilt it revealed. In this view the
burden of the past and its legacy becomes a problem of collective
psychopathology, which is to be treated less through rational means
and "antifascist enlightenment" than through acts of mourning and
other emotional means more appropriate to phenomena of psychological repression.[27] Still others maintain that efforts like *Holocaust* can
actually impede *Vergangenheitsbewältigung*, because they deflect attention
away from the sociopolitical causes of National Socialism and thereby
obscure the manner in which the weight of the past can continue to
exercise an influence on the political culture of the present. In the
present collection, this view is represented by Hans Mommsen. He
argues that "mastery of the past" can be achieved less through acts
of "historical enlightenment" or processes of emotional catharsis than
through "persistent confrontation with the causes and operating mechanisms of fascist domination." In particular, he claims that the illiberal
and authoritarian attitudes, structures, and traditions that gave rise to

Nazi fanaticism can be tackled and eliminated only through further democratization of society and through "active participation" in the public sphere. For Mommsen this process should be carried out not only on the institutional plane but at the sociopsychological level as well: Only through a liberalization of attitudes and modes of behavior might it be possible critically to work through the burden of the German historical tradition.

2. For a number of authors in this volume, the chief issues raised by the shift in ideological currents derived from specific arguments advanced by German neoconservatives in their analyses and assessments of German discontents. In particular, Offe, Preuss, Habermas, and, less directly, Narr and Wellmer seek to debunk the tenets and assumptions underlying the New Right's attempt to bolster the systems of economic growth at the expense of democracy. In one way or another, all defend the "dignity of modernity" and put forward a conception of the modern age based not merely on societal modernization but on cultural and political modernism as well.

We shall look more closely at the issue of modernity below; but it is important first to discuss the manner in which our authors diagnose current German discontents. They do not reject *in toto* the neoconservative appraisal of the current situation. On the contrary, there is much agreement, as Claus Offe shows, regarding some of the main features of the problems confronting Germany today. The critics all agree that the chief symptoms of the social crisis are "cultural" in nature, involving questions of life-styles, value orientations, attitudinal and motivational considerations, and what is called the legitimacy of the social-political order. There is also a structural similarity to their analyses, namely, the tension and interplay between the functional requirements of state and economy and the cultural-political action orientations of citizens. The two approaches differ, though, in identifying the source of the malaise. For neoconservatives the problems are rooted in the cultural sphere itself. Conferring normative status on the structures, processes, and "objective exigencies" of capitalist modernization, they attribute the difficulties to an aesthetic-political hedonism, social reforms, and a militant social criticism, all of which, they maintain, hinder the operation of the system of economic growth and its administrative complement. It is for this reason that they call for institutionalism, for a strong state, for dismantling a social-welfare system that levels differences, and for a return to religion and traditional values.

For the authors in this collection the situation is entirely reversed. They see the cultural dislocations identified by neoconservatives not as the *cause* of current discontents but as the *result* and the inevitable *by-products* of the very capitalist modernization that New Right ideologues want to defend and bolster. (It is this apparent inversion of cause and effect that impels Claus Offe to ask whether the neoconservative crisis literature, and specifically the "ungovernability" thesis, is a serious attempt to address present social ills or whether it merely represents an ideology based principally on political considerations.) Thus the diagnoses presented in this book focus not on the cultural sphere but on adverse consequences of capitalist modernization— unrestricted economic growth, the unchecked acceleration of technological innovation, and the increasing bureaucratization of welfare-state societies.

An obvious example of the ill effects of capitalist modernization is the commercial and industrial destruction of the natural environment, evocatively described here by Dieter Wellershoff. Equating West Germany's postwar economic history with advancing inhumanity, he shows how questions of ecology and environmental protection have for many Germans become questions of human survival. Habermas makes a similar point when he suggests that fears about nuclear waste, water and air pollution, acid rain, and gene manipulation have activated an awareness of basic sensual-aesthetic needs that cannot indefinitely abide an untrammeled devastation of the organic foundations of life.

A more common concern in these essays is the devastation wrought by capitalist production on the sociocultural environment. In particular, several authors are concerned with the manner in which the systems of state and economy in contemporary societies erode and destroy what Habermas calls the sphere of symbolic reproduction—the domain of identity formation, social integration, and the transmission of traditions and value orientations. This destructive process is discussed at length by Wolf-Dieter Narr, who graphically demonstrates how the agencies of capitalist modernization disintegrate the cohesive integrity of the self and thereby prevent individuals from making sense of their world. Narr focuses on changed performance demands that, together with a growing division of labor and rampant professionalization, sever occupational activity from personal life-experiences. He also discusses technological innovations such as those in the communication sphere: Without entirely dismissing their potential for enhancing orientation and social intercourse, Narr argues that such innovations are currently employed in ways that actually promote isolation and disorientation. On another point he outlines how the bureaucratic structures central to welfare-state societies not only formalize and segment more and more spheres of life, such as family, school, and education, but also define the relation between state and society so abstractly that meaningful political self-organization is practically unattainable. In all these dimensions it is the dynamic of capitalist modernization that fosters anomie and individual psychopathologies—the same features decried by neoconservatives when they defend this process.

To be sure, the German welfare state attempts to treat these maladies with a vast network of social services; but, as Narr demonstrates in his analysis of some of the "modernist reforms" enacted in Germany (and elsewhere) during the 60s and 70s, such measures are bound to fail. For one thing, they are ineffective in addressing the problem. Inasmuch as they seek to reintegrate individuals into the existing order, they fail to deal with the dehumanization endemic to a society that recognizes and values individuals only as they perform their segmented roles. Second, these measures are counterproductive. Narr develops this point, as does Habermas, in connection with the concept of legal regulation or juridification (*Verrechtlichung*), a concept that has recently received increased attention from critical intellectuals in Germany.[28] *Verrechtlichung* refers to the technocratic and legalistic response to social needs and problems, involving the formal restructuring of social relations. Like other features of welfare-state social policy, legal regulation is understood as a means of coping with difficulties that develop in late capitalist societies; but in actuality, Narr emphasizes, it exacerbates and even reproduces these problems. Not only does *Verrechtlichung* introduce ever more formal and impersonal structures into informal and personal spheres of life, thus abetting rootlessness and disorientation; by treating citizens as clients and as objects of administrative care, it extends the ubiquity of a bureaucratic paternalism that prevents individuals, either singly or collectively, from autonomously handling their problems. Juridification and the state expansionism with which it is connected undermine integrity and identity, heighten individual helplessness, and contribute to the danger Narr sees in the handwriting on the wall (his dismissal of Marcuse's "one-dimensionality" thesis notwithstanding): a Skinnerian society of bureaucratically produced conditioned reflexes.

What concerns our authors is not the mere fact that capitalism attacks the cultural environment. Some share with Marx and Enlightenment thinkers the view that this process has benefits, for instance, the abolition of habitual forms of thought, dogmatic traditions, and encrusted power relations. What does concern them is the destructiveness that occurs in late capitalist societies, where the economic-administrative system assumes such potency that it destroys not only outmoded traditions and forms of orientation but the very conditions for reproducing norms, traditions, and value orientations. It is this development that Albrecht Wellmer refers to as a "loss of ethical life" (*Verlust der Sittlichkeit*) more drastic than anything perceived by Hegel in the emergence of civil society; it is what Wolf-Dieter Narr has in mind when he suggests that advances in "economic concentration and political centralization" result in an "almost epochal change" definable as a "loss of inwardness." It prompts Dorothee Sölle to assert that the consumerist and functionalist redefinition of "unmarketable components of life" endangers the very possibility of expressivity and communication, and Habermas to warn of a "colonization of the life-world by an economic and administrative system that has assumed a life of its own."

On the basis of this general characterization of contemporary society, our authors shed light on some of the developments occurring in contemporary West Germany. For instance, their recognition of the devastations wrought on the cultural sphere by capitalist modernization provides them with a framework in which some of them explain the political withdrawal and subpolitical protest behavior that emerged in Germany during the 70s. Narr takes this perspective in his discussion of the retreat of many into the enclaves of the alternative culture. And Wellmer does so as well in discussing the terrorist violence that haunted West German society during the past decade. He argues that the deluded and desperate acts of urban terrorists were merely the fruition of the "structural violence" endemic to late capitalist societies, the violence "that permeates the social relations of individuals as well as their psychic constitution." The short-circuited manner in which terrorists react to problems and their willingness to opt for irrational, actionist, and existentialist forms of political behavior are manifestations of a social structure that destroys the conditions for the formation of "strong identities" and severs the link between "political decision-making processes . . . and individuals' experiences, needs, and possibilities for action." This is the basis for Wellmer's contention that terrorist violence is closer to what is considered normal in West German society than many of its "professional defenders" would believe. And it also provides the ground for his view that any attempt to come to terms with terrorism must fail unless one criticizes the "social matrix within which terrorism could first arise as one of many possible forms of reaction."

For our authors, Habermas in particular, the negative side effects and the "colonization of the life-world" are key to understanding the "new social movements" that now flourish as part of the West German social and political landscape. These include environmentalism, the Green alternative parties, the antinuclear movement, urban squatters, the youth culture, tax-protest parties, activist school parents' associations, and religious fundamentalism. These movements are new in two respects. First, they are distinguishable by their populist, subinstitutional methods of protest. They operate outside of and in opposition to the formal channels of political power and political representation. Second, they are distinguishable by the substance of their protest. They do not aim to exact socioeconomic or "materialist" compensations from the existing state. Rather, their protests are in defense of cultural or "postmaterialist" values, including rights and liberties, natural and culturally inherited resources, and the conditions that would foster autonomy and individual self-realization. Habermas marks this difference in suggesting that the new movements are motivated less by "questions of distribution than by concern for the grammar of forms of life."[29] He interprets them accordingly: Arising on the "border separating system and life-world," these movements are a response to an economic and administrative system that, in assuming a virtual life of its own, not only denies real political participation but ravages the natural and cultural environment.

Not all the authors view German affairs in these terms. Several advocate the "old politics" characterized by traditional welfare-state reform policies. Hans-Ulrich Wehler implicitly does so in his essay,[30] and the Social Democratic theorist Horst Ehmke explicitly reaffirms the notion of social democracy advanced by Kurt Schumacher, the party leader during the initial postwar years: "the economic liberation of the moral and political individual."[31] In the 1983 federal election, such views came under political attack from both the neoliberalism of the victorious Christian Democratic/Free Democratic coalition and the "postmaterialism" of groups and individuals associated with new social movements. Despite such opposition, these views continue to have considerable support. It has in fact been argued that prolonged economic crisis, coupled with neoconservative challenges to the progressive legacy of welfare-state reformism, could well turn the German leftist focus back upon these more traditional Social Democratic issues of social and economic justice.[32]

3. The primary aim of the essays in this volume is to analyze the basic tendencies of the Zeitgeist They do, however, suggest various therapies for the contemporary problems of both Germany and the other advanced industrial countries. One group of solutions concerns the problem that has assumed center stage in German intellectual and political disputes—the issue of "the legitimacy of the modern age." Two different positions are represented in this collection. One challenges and even repudiates basic elements of modern culture and Enlightenment rationality, elements traditionally deemed part of the leftist arsenal of concepts. Thus Dorothee Sölle's existential-religious notion of life contains an implicit critique of the notion that social ills can be cured through a more rational organization of social reality. Sölle appears to believe that rationality as such is so inextricably intertwined with the instrumental or functional rationality she criticizes that any attempt to preserve life's intrinsic, nonfunctional meaningfulness must have recourse to the nonrational, indeed to Lebensphilosophie. Johann Baptist Metz also challenges modernism when he suggests, largely against others on the left, that the problems of the present might best be confronted through a constructive appropriation of the notion of noncontemporaneity (Ungleichzeitigkeit). A Catholic theologian, Metz sees the basis for a "new mediation of public and private affairs," for a "new culture of solidarity in political life" in the noncontemporaneous and indeed "anachronistic" notion of churchly religion. A third author, Karl Heinz Bohrer, brings a Nietzschean antimodernism to his critique of both Enlightenment conceptions of reason and progress and avant-garde attempts to combine art and politics. Like anarchist members of the alternative culture, Bohrer argues that any promesse de bonheur is achievable only outside of the scientific-technical and moral-political structures of modern culture—within the private-aesthetic sphere of emotionality, self-experience, spontaneity, and what Habermas terms

Translator's Introduction

the "chauvinism of the imaginative ego." These three writers clearly
differ from one another; but each illustrates a view current in Germany
today that the institutional, normative, and intellectual resources of
modernity are not fully adequate to handling the problems and discontents of the present.

To be sure, the arguments of Sölle, Metz, and Bohrer are distinct
from the conservative analyses of contemporary culture and society
that also include a critique of modernity and Enlightenment rationality.
Although they challenge the values and assumptions of modernity,
they still adhere to basic tenets of leftist thought. While Sölle develops
the notion of "life" using Karl Jaspers's concept of "existential unconditionedness," she construes this concept not in the "repressive-
elitist" sense characteristic of Jaspers's *Kulturkritik* but with an "emancipatory-humanistic" emphasis common to left cultural criticism. Similarly, Metz does not base his paean to noncontemporaneity on a
nostalgia for the past. Rather, like Ernst Bloch—who in his *Erbschaft
dieser Zeit* [Heritage of our time] first formulated this notion—he sees
noncontemporaneity as a "trenchant and ultimately revolutionary way"
of criticizing existing social conditions and of illustrating how they
might be positively transformed.[33] His call for a new culture of solidarity
in political life, for instance, does not reflect a fascination with regressive
forms of community; it is an attempt to shed a new and different
light on a concern long of interest to the left, namely, the notion of
a postbourgeois form of individuation in which the privatism of civil
society might be superseded without renouncing such bourgeois
achievements as rights, liberties, and popular sovereignty.[34] As for
Bohrer, his invocation of the primacy of aesthetic experience against
the rationalism and utopianism of the left is not an affirmation of the
artistic traditionalism supported by conservative critics of culture. Instead, appealing to Heinrich Heine and the "now indefeasible discoveries of early German romanticism," he seeks to redefine leftist
notions of freedom and emancipation so that they might more adequately accommodate sensuality, humor, momentary fulfillment, and
the right of the "present."[35] In short, the challenge to modern culture
raised by Sölle, Metz, and Bohrer represents in large measure an effort
to broaden the parameters of leftist cultural criticism. And if these
authors do indeed adopt themes more commonly associated with
conservatives, their acceptance stems less from a disenchantment with

leftist assumptions and principles than from the conviction that these themes should not be abandoned to the right.[36]

A contrasting position is taken by Narr, Offe, Preuss, Wellmer, and above all Habermas. In his essay Habermas touches on themes he develops more systematically in *The Theory of Communicative Action*.[37] He argues that an acknowledgment of modernity's discontents does not mandate criticism of the basic norms and structures of the modern age. Such a dismissive response to the project of modernity ignores its real achievements, just as it places too great an emphasis on its deforming power. Habermas develops his theory of modernity in evaluating and expanding upon the concept of rationalization that Max Weber introduced to interpret the modernization process.[38] Like Weber, Habermas understands modernity in terms of the destruction of the traditional world-views of myth, metaphysics, and religion and the subsequent "disenchantment" and rationalization of all spheres of life. In his view, though, rationalization must be used not only in the restrictive sense employed by Weber—in terms of purposive or goal-directed rationality, the rationality that finds institutional embodiment in the economic and administrative subsystems that regulate the material reproduction of social life. Instead, Habermas also speaks of the separate rationalization that takes place in the domain of the communicatively structured life-world, the domain in which the functions of symbolic reproduction are fulfilled. The destruction of traditional world-views, he argues, increasingly frees processes of cultural reproduction, social integration, and socialization from imposed and inherited traditions, allowing for the development of institutions based on communicatively *achieved* consensus. For instance, communicative rationalization allows the emergence of democratic and constitutional forms of government, whose legitimacy relies not on imposed authority but on the informed and active consent of the governed.

Habermas and others argue that the discontents of the modern age are rooted not in the process of modernization or rationalization itself, but in the "one-sided" or "selective" form it takes in the actual history of capitalist development. One-sided modernization involves a growing independence of economic and administrative subsystems and their increasing domination of and intrusion into areas of life that are organized communicatively. As institutions embodying purposive rationality become more complex, they subordinate more and more spheres of life to the monetary and bureaucratic exigencies basic to the material reproduction of life. This depletes the stock of communicative structures on which the life-world must rely in carrying out symbolic reproduction. As suggested earlier, the pathologies of the present can be explained precisely in terms of this "colonization of the life-world."

Through this perspective Habermas suggests that current discontents can best be treated by completing rather than challenging the project of modernity. The problems caused by a one-sided rationalization process can be redressed only by the continuous, balanced development of all the forms of reason introduced with the modern age. This approach calls for a rationalized or modernized life-world, for institutions that set limits to an autonomized system of state and economy and that subordinate it to decisions reached on the basis of communicatively achieved consensus. Among these institutions Habermas would include mechanisms of democratic participation in which questions on the goals and values of society would be submitted to public discussion and be anchored in the agreement of societal members. Only by establishing a functioning public sphere can the evisceration of the communicative infrastructure of everyday life be arrested. Habermas makes this point by citing Albrecht Wellmer: "The loss of ethical life generated by the reproductive process of industrial systems can be compensated for only through democratic forms of organization that would again bring the total societal process into an intelligible connection with everyday reality and the needs of individuals." This is asserted against neoconservatives who react to current discontents by turning to counter-Enlightenment traditionalism; but it can also be advanced against those individuals on the left who respond to the problems of contemporary life by questioning modernity itself.[39]

V

Our authors argue that contemporary Germany is faced with two not unrelated problems: first, a one-sided modernization or rationalization process that destroys meanings, value orientations, traditions, and "the infrastructure of symbolic reproduction"; second, an illiberal political tradition that retains its hold on the country's political culture. These problems are not unique to Germany. Although the unparalleled rapidity of postwar German modernization and the particular burden of the Nazi past give them a special significance in that country, the challenge they represent confronts the left in all advanced industrial societies: to defend traditions and cultural resources that are being eroded by capitalist modernization and yet to avoid the traditionalism espoused by conservatives. In this respect the perspectives this volume offers on the German situation can illuminate our own. And if, as Jürgen Moltmann suggests, one's own situation is accurately understood only through the eyes of others, then these specifically German reflections on common Western problems may well provide us with insights that are otherwise unattainable.

I would like to thank Thomas McCarthy for his many comments on the translation and introduction; Jürgen Habermas for responding to my questions and making available to me some of his more recent manuscripts; those of the authors who reviewed draft versions of their essays; Seyla Benhabib, Nanette Funk, Elfriede Rosbach, and Katharine Rowe for their assistance; Stephen Slaner for his careful typing of much of the manuscript; and my parents for their encouragement. December 1983

Notes

1. See, for instance, Josef Becker, ed., *Dreissig Jahre Bundesrepublik: Tradition und Wandel* (Munich, 1979); Peter Brückner, *Versuch, uns und anderen die Bundesrepublik zu erklären* (Berlin, 1978); Heinz Brüggemann et al., *Über den Mangel an politischer Kultur in Deutschland* (Berlin, 1978); Volker Gransow and Claus Offe, "Political Culture and the Politics of the Social Democratic Government," *Telos* 53 (fall 1982); Martin and Sylvia Greiffenhagen, *Ein schwieriges Vaterland: Zur Politischen Kultur Deutschlands* (Frankfurt, 1979); Jürgen Habermas, "Modernity versus Postmodernity," *New German Critique* 22 (winter 1981); Habermas, "Neoconservative Cultural Criticism in the United States and West Germany: An Intellectual Movement in Two Political Cultures," *Telos* 56 (summer 1983); Joachim Hirsch, *Der Sicherheitsstaat: Das "Modell Deutschland," seine Krise und die neuen sozialen Bewegungen* (Frankfurt, 1980); Josef Joffe, "The Greening of Germany," *The New Republic* (February 11, 1983); Wolfgang Kraushaar, *Autonomie oder Getto? Kontroversen über die Alternativbewegung* (Frankfurt, 1978); Jürgen Leinemann, *Die Angst der Deutschen: Beobachtungen zur Bewusstseinslage der Nation* (Hamburg, 1982); Richard Löwenthal, *Gesellschaftswandel und Kulturkrise* (Frankfurt, 1979); Michael Naumann, "German Neonationalism," *Partisan Review* 1 (1983); Oskar Negt and Alexander Kluge, *Geschichte und Eigensinn* (Frankfurt, 1981); Wolfgang Pohrt, *Endstation: Über die Wiedergeburt der Nation* (Berlin, 1982); Richard Saage, *Rückkehr zum starken Staat? Studien über Konservatismus, Faschismus und Demokratie* (Frankfurt, 1983); Peter Sloterdijk, *Kritik der zynischen Vernunft* (Frankfurt, 1983); Reinhart Steinweg, ed., *Die neue Friedensbewegung* (Frankfurt, 1982); Hans-Ulrich Wehler, *Preussen ist wieder chic* (Frankfurt, 1983). See also the contributions to *Kursbuch* 71 ("Berichte über die Lage der Nation": March 1983).

2. Karl Jaspers, *Die geistige Situation der Zeit* (Berlin, 1931); *Man in the Modern Age*, translated by Eden and Cedar Paul (Garden City, NY, 1957).

Translator's Introduction

3. For a contrasting approach to "the spiritual situation of the age" consider the thinkers of the early and middle nineteenth century, for whom, as Karl Löwith has pointed out, "this phrase became the watchword of progress." See Karl Löwith, *From Hegel to Nietzsche*, translated by David Green (Garden City, NY, 1967), pp. 200–207. See also John Stuart Mill, "The Spiritual Situation of the Age," in Gertrude Himmelfarb, ed., *From John Stuart Mill: Essays on Politics and Culture* (Garden City, NY, 1962).

4. For a model of the type of nonmetaphysical, intersubjectively pursued approach to cultural criticism here employed, consider the notion of critical social theory programmatically formulated in the 30s by Max Horkheimer. The present relevance of Horkheimer's position is discussed by Wolfgang Bonss and Axel Honneth, "Zur Reaktualisierung der kritischen Theorie," the introduction to the book they edited: *Sozialforschung als Kritik* (Frankfurt, 1982).

5. For an overview see Karl Mannheim, "Conservative Thought," in Kurt Wolff, ed., *From Karl Mannheim* (New York, 1971).

6. In the original edition of *Stichworte*, some of these issues were discussed in the essays by Ralf Dahrendorf ("Kulturpessimismus vs. Forsschrittshoffnung: Eine notwenige Abgrenzung") and Klaus von Beyme ("Der Neo-Korporatismus und die Politik des begrentzten Pluralismus in der Bundesrepublik").

7. From this standpoint the views of the authors might better be viewed not in terms of *Die geistige Situation der Zeit* but through Jaspers's 1967 *Wohin treibt die Bundesrepublik?* [English: *The Future of Germany*, translated by E. B. Ashton (Chicago, 1967)], in which he criticizes the Federal Republic from the perspective of radical democracy.

8. It is owing to the present topicality of these issues that one of the original contributors to *Stichworte* went so far as to suggest that "all motifs of contemporary cultural criticism" are contained in Jaspers's 1931 analysis. See Peter Glotz, *Stichworte*, volume II, p. 474.

9. Cf. Eberhard Knödler Bunte, ed., *Was ist heute noch links?* (Berlin, 1981).

10. Jürgen Habermas, "The Dialectics of Rationalization," *Telos* 49 (fall 1981), p. 13.

11. For the situation in the United States see Peter Steinfels, *The Neoconservatives: The Men Who Are Changing America's Politics* (New York, 1979); Andrew Kopkind, "A New Political Culture: The Return of Cold War Liberalism," *The Nation* (April 23, 1983).

12. Habermas, "Neoconservative Culture Criticism in the United States and West Germany"; Richard Saage, "Neokonservatives Denken in der Bundesrepublik," in *Rückkehr zum starken Staat?* (Frankfurt, 1983), pp. 228–282.

13. Richard Saage, "Rückkehr zum starken Staat? Zur Renaissance des Freund-Feind-Denken in der Bundesrepublik," in *Rückkehr zum starken Staat?* (Frankfurt, 1983), pp. 7–42.

14. Habermas, "Neoconservative Culture Criticism in the United States and West Germany," p. 88.

15. Habermas, "Modernity versus Postmodernity," p. 14.

16. Habermas, "Dialectics of Rationalization," p. 15.

17. Some of these issues have been discussed by Russell Berman, "The Peace Movements and its Critics' Critics," *Telos* 52 (summer 1982).

Translator's Introduction

18. A great deal has been written on this question. In the original edition of *Stichworte* it was addressed by Iring Fetscher, "Die Suche nach der nationalen Identität," in *Stichworte*, volume I, pp. 115–132.

19. See Jürgen Habermas, "The Entwinement of Myth and Enlightenment," *New German Critique* 26 (spring/summer 1982).

20. One writer close to the alternative scene has characterized this as a commitment to an existential principle of life rather than a Blochian principle of hope. See Peter Sloterdijk, *Kritik der zynischen Vernunft*, volume 1 (Frankfurt, 1983), p. 199. In the present collection it is referred to as a yearning for "humanity in one's lifetime."

21. Of course, this period was not marked by a total absence of political activity. On the contrary, the late 70s also witnessed the rise of new social movements, neopopulist protest parties, and the emergence of the Greens as a national political force. But this new politicization was distinctive for its subinstitutional avenues of expression. This point will be discussed below.

22. It is in this context that some left intellectuals reaffirmed the validity of a statement by Adorno: "I consider the lingering traces of National Socialism *in* democracy as potentially more dangerous than the lingering traces of fascist tendencies *against* democracy." See Adorno, "Was bedeutet: Aufarbeitung der Vergangenheit," in *Eingriffe: Neun kritische Modelle* (Frankfurt, 1963), p. 126.

23. Jaspers, *The Future of Germany*.

24. Brückner, *Versuch, uns und anderen die Bundesrepublik zu erklären*.

25. For the classic statement of this question see Adorno, "Was bedeutet."

26. See the three issues *New German Critique* devoted to this topic (nos. 19–21).

27. Alexander and Margarete Mitscherlich, *The Inability to Mourn*, translated by Beverly R. Placzek (New York, 1975).

28. For Habermas's discussion of the notion of *Verrechtlichung*, see *Theorie des kommunikativen Handelns*, volume 2 (Frankfurt, 1981), pp. 531–534. For a discussion of this issue in connection with the reformist policies of the Social Democrats, see Gransow and Offe, "Political Culture and the Politics of the Social Democratic Government," and Otto Kallscheuer, "Philosophy and Politics in the SPD," *Telos* 53 (fall 1982).

29. Jürgen Habermas, "New Social Movements," *Telos* 49 (fall 1981), p. 33.

30. See also Hans-Ulrich Wehler, *Preussen ist wieder chic* (Frankfurt, 1983).

31. Contrast this "materialist" position with that of one leading proponent of a "postmaterialist" politics, Green leader Rudolf Bahro. For Bahro, social policy must now be focused on "the liberation from economics itself." See *Socialism and Survival* (New York, 1982), p. 13.

32. Andrei Markovits, "Reflections and Observations on the West German Elections," *New German Critique* 28 (winter 1983). For an emphatic defense of traditional Social Democratic policies see Richard Löwenthal, "Identität und Zukunft der Sozialdemokratie," in *Die Zeit* [overseas edition] 51 (December 18, 1981).

33. Ernst Bloch, *Erbschaft dieser Zeit* (Zurich, 1935). For a discussion of this work see Anson Rabinbach, "Ernst Bloch's *Heritage of our Times* and Fascism," *New German Critique* 11 (spring 1977).

34. In this respect there are strong resemblances between the Christian Base Communities (*Basisgemeinde*), here praised by Metz, and the Greens' program for democracy of the base (*Basisdemokratie*).

35. See also Bohrer's introduction to the collection of essays he edited: *Mythos und Moderne* (Frankfurt, 1983).

36. This point is made by Horst Ehmke, who links the national question to the general values and principles of the Enlightenment and bases this coupling on the conviction—also evident in Hannah Arendt's *The Origins of Totalitarianism*—that this issue should not be allowed "to fall into the wrong hands for a second time in German history."

37. In addition to Habermas's work, see Albrecht Wellmer, "Kunst und industrielle Produktion: Zur Dialektik von Moderne und Postmoderne," in *Merkur* 2 (March 1983), pp. 133–145. For discussions of Habermas's conception of modernity see Seyla Benhabib, "Modernity and the Aporias of Critical Theory," *Telos* 49 (fall 1981); Thomas McCarthy's introduction to his translation of the first volume of Habermas's *Theory of Communicative Action* (Boston, 1984); James Schmidt, "Jürgen Habermas and the Difficulties of Enlightenment," *Social Research* 49, no. 1 (spring 1982); Albrecht Wellmer, "Reason, Utopia, and the Dialectic of Enlightenment," *Praxis International* 3 no. 2 (1983).

38. Jürgen Habermas, *Theorie des kommunikativen Handelns*, volume 2 (Frankfurt, 1981), p. 449ff.

39. See Jürgen Habermas, "Konzeptionen der Moderne," manuscript from a work in progress tentatively entitled *Philosophical Discourse on Modernity*.

Observations on "The Spiritual Situation of the Age"

Introduction

Jürgen Habermas

With the consent of Siegfried Unseld and Günther Busch,[1] I sent a letter in the middle of 1978 to approximately fifty critics, writers, and social scientists; it read as follows:

Dear Friends and Colleagues, Ladies and Gentlemen:

Volume 1,000 of the Göschen Collection [of the de Gruyter Publishing Company] was published in 1931 under the title *Die geistige Situation der Zeit* [*The Spiritual Situation of the Age*];[2] it had *one* author: Karl Jaspers. In the fall of next year volume 1,000 of the *edition suhrkamp* (*e.s.*) will appear. It will bear the same title, though certainly in quotation marks; for who would still want to adopt the absolute perspective of the great philosopher? And it will have many authors—for who still entrusts himself with a general theory of the present epoch?

But don't worry: I too am unable to share the publisher's fascination for round numbers. As one of its authors, I do feel myself bound to the *e.s.* (and to its editor, Günther Busch). Yet this genuine sentiment would not in itself be sufficient reason for me to associate myself with a ceremonial ritual marking the occasion of the appearance of the thousandth volume in a literary series. I was intrigued rather by the historical association, viz., the recollection of Jaspers's publicly influential diagnosis of the age and the fact that it appeared two years before Hitler's assumption of power. In what follows I shall briefly outline the considerations that induced me to recommend to you a project for which Jaspers's book should serve as an (ironic?) reference.

All promotionalism notwithstanding, the first thousand volumes of the *edition suhrkamp*—which since the end of the late 1960s has frequently been imitated but today is no longer at the forefront of political developments—will constitute a document of historical importance. You will recall that the *e.s.* began in the early 60s as a literary series with philosophical relevance. Adorno, Beckett, Benjamin, Bloch, Brecht, Enzenberger, Frisch, Grass, Hesse, Szondi, Walser, Weiss, and Wittgenstein are among the authors of the first fifty volumes. Later such names as Abendroth, Barthes, Chomsky, Foucault, Hobsbawm, Kirchheimer, Laing, Lévi-Strauss, Marcuse, Mitscherlich, B. Moore, Sohn-Rethel, and Sweezy were added, as were many of the younger social scientists who located themselves within this tradition. With a certain excessive poignancy the *e.s.* represented an aspect of the intellectual development that, one can say, was dominant in postwar Germany. I refer to the resolute affiliation with the Enlightenment, humanism, bourgeois radical thought, and with the aesthetic and political avant-garde of the nineteenth century. If there ever was anything (in Germany, that is) to the slogan, "The spirit stands on the left," then it was during those years when, despite the massive social restoration, the memory of Nazism and the tradition with which it had broken was kept alive— and by an intellectual left that could place its stamp on the cultural milieu with a certain conviction that it had been entrusted with this task. All this, however, is now over.

That with which we identified, if I may put it so generally, and still can identify has been militantly called into question in the past half-decade. All things considered, the left is reacting meekly to a New Right that now constitutes itself more through educational policy and teacher training, philosophy and the social sciences, cultural politics and the mass media, than through literature and art. And its manifestations have shown the right to be more interested in displaying a mentality than in altering the state of the argument. Nonetheless it seems to me meaningful to test, in a not altogether trivial fashion, our ability to react—that is, to determine the state today of an intellectual left which into the 70s had, as we say, "made" the cultural life in Germany. Hence I am writing to a group of intellectuals with the request that they allow themselves to be stimulated by Jaspers's treatise into taking a position with regard to our own situation.

As for the circle of addressees, here I am open to suggestion. My selection is based on informed arbitrariness. It would be interesting to learn how informed and how arbitrary it is. With this letter I am appealing to German writers, critics, artists, social scientists, and philosophers who combine the following three attributes: those whose identity was formed only after the end of the war; those who have exercised a certain intellectual influence in the Federal Republic of

Germany; and those who stand committed to the traditions against which a German regime established itself in 1933.

In the event that the last point should be unclear, I submit it as a type of litmus paper: the *e.s.* can serve as a test instrument. Its short period of influence has already made it into an institution over which ideologies part ways. One need not admire or even approve of the series to reject the view that it has produced more political harm than good.

After this preface it may seem somewhat less peculiar when without further ado I request from you an essay on the topic: "The Spiritual Situation of the Age." The essay should not exceed fifty typewritten pages. I am counting on an average length of twenty to twenty-five pages. The relation to Jaspers's work can be as strict or as loose as you wish. When you read it, you will notice how great the distance has become in the meantime. Here one of the great German mandarins expresses himself. Jaspers speaks the language of haut bourgeois cultural criticism, and with the pathos of a nation's instructor. Undaunted by the traps the social sciences could set, he dares to confront the totality directly. All this has become obsolete. What has not become obsolete, however, is the duty of intellectuals to react with partiality and objectivity, with sensitivity and incorruptibility, to movements, developmental tendencies, dangers, and critical moments. It is the task of intellectuals to make conscious a murky reality. We should not concede this to people for whom the word "intellectual" is itself a term of abuse.

Jaspers's book is envisioned only as a stimulus. Some may wish to deal with its contents, either philosophically with the general project, or critically with the ideology underlying the intellectual approach and its conceptual framework, or social-theoretically with the basic principles of the analysis. Others may want to respond to a single sentence; for some even the title might be sufficiently provocative to serve as a source of inspiration. I can imagine the following possibilities: a diagnosis of the times through a reassessment of the political, social, and intellectual developments during the German postwar period; an analysis of the decisions of the Federal Constitutional Court or the roots and causes of terrorism; commentaries on "Autumn in Germany,"[3] on "Dare to Teach!" (*Mut zur Erziehung*),[4] or on the significance of neo-populist tendencies in politics; theses on the "end" of avant-garde art and on the Russell Tribunal,[5] etc. For my part I am concerned, when I look around within my own generation, with the peculiar discrepancy between a productive, or at least conceptually stimulating literary scene, and a largely sterile discussion in philosophy and the social sciences, one dependent on Anglo-Saxon models and oriented to reception. Perhaps you will take your theme merely from some singular phenomenon, an observation, or a symptomatic expression such as the exhibition of historicism in contemporary architecture. A book recently found its way into my hands, one published by the Seewald Verlag and advertised in the economic section of the *Frankfurter Allgemeine Zeitung*: *Kritische Theorie und ihre Folgen* [*Critical theory and its aftermath*]; this denunciatory blow impels me to want to preserve for posterity the memory of an ethical document (*Sittendokument*) of our time.

With these remarks I only wish to indicate what occurs to me as the range of possible responses. Yet the project would not merit the effort if my imagination could adequately anticipate your reactions. You have much time to ponder the topic. I must receive the manuscript by the beginning of February 1979. Please let me know if you wish to contribute.

With best wishes,

J. H.

The essays contained in this book are the responses to my inquiry. Those who refused usually did so for trivial reasons. One respondent clearly no longer wanted to be labeled a leftist intellectual. Others viewed the spectrum from Jaeggi to Johnson as too vapid.[6] Still others regarded the entire undertaking as inappropriate: at these levels the *Zeitgeist* engenders only vegetative reactions. Certainly the selection of contributors, as it originally occurred to me, was subjective, determined by the contingency of my circle of acquaintances. Yet what has resulted from the filtering process of invitation, consent, hesitation, and decline is an appropriately diverse collection of individual authors: they cannot be styled a "group" and indeed are perhaps of one mind only in that they would not agree on theses regarding a commitment or lack of commitment to any particular issue. Incidentally, despite frequent urgings to do so, I have not permitted myself to make assignments, that is, to distribute themes. No one was aware of anyone else. My editorial function consisted merely in looking through the articles as they arrived and putting them in some sort of order. I had two reasons for this restraint.

The attempt to repeat cooperatively the task that Jaspers dared to undertake by himself involves a claim that can no longer be seriously entertained. The diagnosis of the times is not an affair that can still be pursued with impunity *intentione recta*; Freyer's impotent *Theorie des gegenwärtigen Zeitalters* (1955) attests well enough to this. Of course novels like *The Tin Drum* and *Halbzeit*, plays like *Marat*, or films like *Kaspar Hauser* or *Messer im Kopf* all have high seismographic value for such considerations. Certainly, an interpretive perspective for diagnosing the times is incorporated into Wittgenstein's *Philosophical Investigations* and even more so into Horkheimer and Adorno's *Dialectic of Enlightenment*. Historical expositions and theoretical theses in the social and behavioral sciences have a core that is diagnostic of the times. Such works are symptomatic of the *Zeitgeist* and define the perspective from which its diagnosis must proceed. But as soon as they are advanced as diagnoses, one becomes painfully aware of the subjectivity of the gesture with which the author seeks to pull together the richly pleated garment of existing realities—with which he attempts to locate a more than merely subjective unity in the latter's multiplicity.

In Germany until 1933 there were two quite distinct ways of pursuing the diagnosis of the times. Jaspers himself is a good example of the first variant. Although philosophy in his view could no longer be accorded the status of a fundamental science, it was nonetheless regarded as possessing a cognitive dimension both different from the course of the empirical sciences and able to illuminate the nature of existence. Accordingly Jaspers regarded himself as singlehandedly capable of philosophically apprehending his own time in thought. This connection of time-diagnosis and first philosophy is clarified in the postscript [the foreword in the English edition] that Jaspers wrote after World War II for *Die geistige Situation der Zeit*, itself written in 1930 and published a year later:

The manuscript was put aside for a year, for I did not want it to appear without my *Philosophy*, which was to be published a few weeks later (in 1931) as a three-volume work. In elucidating the temper of the age I made use of facts which belonged to an earlier period. On some pages the book is tinged with the mood of its time. Yet in terms of its general philosophical stance and world-outlook, it seems to me to be as valid today as it was then, in spite of the events which have taken place in the time between its first appearance and its present reissue.[7]

An altogether different variant of diagnostic activity originated, as in the case of Lukács, within the context of the workers' movement. As long as unions and parties felt themselves bound to the Marxist tradition, they were faced with the task of a continual mediation of theory and practice. Their understanding of politics was rooted in Marx's critique of Hegel and called for a systematic interconnection of critical social theory, consciousness formation, and organization of class struggle. When tactical questions were to be judged on the basis of strategy and strategies on the theoretical analysis of historical developments, politics had to be sifted through the filter of a constant diagnostic reflection on the times.

In postwar Germany neither of these variants could be revived. The individual diagnoses of self-assured philosophers were replaced by the popular syntheses of nimble physicists, behavioral researchers, and social scientists. In place of the organizationally bound, theoretically informed interpretive activity of party intellectuals, one now found short-term prognoses and middle-term projections for planned administration. Whether it be popular scientific syntheses regarding the deadly sins of mankind or projections for 1984 or the year 2000, these made-for-the-media surrogates had the virtue of innocuousness, since they were outmoded within a short time, often in a matter of months.

My other reason for dispensing with a more precise prestructuring is simple and indeed more methodological than substantive. Authors who must respond to an unspecific stimulus such as "the spiritual situation of the age" will, in addressing the topic, betray something about themselves by the manner in which they define and pursue it. And as a group they will also betray something about the state of the left in this country. It is my impression that this collection presents a pensive left, one without militancy but also without sentimentality or resignation, one removed equally from certainty and uncertainty. In almost conventional clarity, this generation has developed an awareness that our republic, even in the thirtieth year of its existence, still stands on feet of clay and must be defended against those who are no longer too timid to complain openly of a surfeit of democracy. As to this point, it cannot be said that the essays contain any surprises. But it is equally clear that the authors share an awareness that interpretations fashioned for the decades immediately following the war no longer apply to the situation in the 70s. Incidentally, none of the authors addresses in any detail the staged efforts that engaged the public's attention during the 70s: the shift in ideological currents (*Tendenzwende*) and the awareness of ecological crises. The one is more or less ignored; the other is respected, but without acknowledgment of its epochal significance. In short, the reader is confronted with unpolemical essays, with honest, unpolished, and unguarded reflections. They may not draw one into the fray, but at least they provide a forum for discussion.

I shall break off here, for it is not my intention to write a review. However, I would like to add a few remarks from the metaperspective of an editor. The first two relate to the political-intellectual context in which we express ourselves here and now. The others are concerned with a theme that permeates many of the essays: the new prominence attained by the "life world," that is, the realm of everyday communicative life, and the increasing significance of "culture," that is, the safeguarding of realms of experience and forms of life that are threatened with being eroded, undermined, and washed away by the dynamics of economic growth and bureaucratization.

1. It is obvious that the authors in this book speak for themselves. What is less obvious is that they do so without reference to a common context. This is equally true for those who, as active politicians, stand in a clearly defined context of action, yet, as intellectuals, are no less free-floating than their colleagues. Ten years ago the protest movement created a reference system of aims, themes, and outlooks, in terms of which ideological viewpoints parted ways. This is not to say that variegated positions would not have been possible or that one was compelled to subordinate oneself to the rhetorically imposed definitions, to the friend-foe schemata, to the rash alternatives. But there was no question as to which definitions of the situation one had to confront. In the intellectual-political forcefield in which the authors of the present collection move, each must first formulate his or her own definition of the situation.

This constraint results not from a deficient structuring of the field but rather from a structure that is only too clear. This structure has taken shape in a circular process of closing in and closing out and has rigidified in the fatal interplay of combatants who reciprocally confirm each other's particular projections. I refer specifically to the self-imposed isolation of those who retreat into the ghettos of dogmatism or alternative life-styles, and to their active self-removal from the political public sphere, achieved with the aid of self-appointed guardians of a notion of democracy that is more militarist than defensible. The barriers that have thus arisen are not demarcated by monstrous edifices, yet they divide cities such as Frankfurt and Hamburg no less effectively than does the Berlin Wall. It is for this reason that we members of the left float somewhat less freely than usual. Viewed from the perspective of the ghetto, we are certainly not "inside," but we are also not willing to allow ourselves to be pushed altogether "outside" either. To be sure, there are attempts to break out of the ghetto, such as the two projects for leftist daily newspapers.[8] Some events have repercussions beyond the walls of the ghetto, such as the Hölderlin edition of the Red Star Press. And there are borderline cases, like *Kursbuch*, the Wagenbach Press, and so on. But even the history of the *edition suhrkamp* documents how the left, determined not to be cut off from the communicative network of the general literary, scientific, and political public, discovered itself one morning *extra muros*, or at best *inter muros*.

The upper limit of the age group from which the authors of this book were recruited is dictated by the nature of the undertaking: the authors must have matured intellectually in the Federal Republic of Germany. But the lower limit, the restriction to those in their forties and fifties, was not planned. After Peter Schneider canceled at the last minute, no one remained of the generation from whose midst the protest movement of the 60s had emerged. Certainly one or another of the authors had played a part in the protest movement; but at that time we all had to react to motives that were, at least initially, foreign to us. To be sure, the age distribution also results from the fact that the most active groups have split up, segmented themselves, and withdrawn into the delusive autarchy of their own private milieu, one cut off from both the general literary and scientific establishment and the arena of the public media.

It is not easy to explain the development of this situation in which we need to fend off the one side while avoiding being boxed in by the other. Part of the explanation lies in the apparent failure of those members of the left who, after the "wheel-spinning" of the protest movement, managed to keep an open mind.[9] Either they formed a temporary influential opposition within one of the existing parties, as was the case with the Young Socialists; or, as with the *Sozialistische Büro*, they explored new forms of organization to free themselves from the constraints of "instrumental politics." This latter course was taken by those determined to establish contact with Eurocommunism, those interested in founding a left-socialist party, and others. While the organizationally oriented continuation of antiauthoritarian politics remained unsuccessful, a new potential for protest emerged around the issue of environmental protection. In a certain sense this new potential resembles the old. Hardly capable of organization, it asserts itself by engaging in threatening activities outside the sphere of parliamentary politics. But its heterogeneous composition and diffuse objective have made the ecology movement an ambiguous force, one thus far un-receptive to socialist orientations. It is against this backdrop, I think, that one must view the battlefront mentality that has taken hold of the remnants of the protest movement and has led them along com-plementary paths into irrelevance, be it the path to party Communism and neo-Stalinism or the path to the counterculture. Both have led equally to isolation. W. Kraushaar interprets the neo-orthodox groups and the *"spontis"*[10] as "products of the decomposition of the extra-parliamentary opposition":

A short phase of activism was followed by what now is a long period of traditionalism. The various husks of identity were virtually crossed with one another: here Leninism, there Maoism; here Stalinism, there Trotskyism; here anarchism, there Castroism. One false role gave rise to the next, one supplanted the other, and there was no dearth of individuals who in this exchange of roles marched across the entire historical stage. And even today—ten years later—there are those who no less obdurately refuse to put their spurious costumes where they belong: the museum. One was at home everywhere, be it in China or Albania, in Cuba or in the Soviet Union; only here—between Hamburg and Munich, Cologne and Berlin—was it scarcely possible to run into anyone.[11]

But the immunization against experience is no less in evidence at the other extreme:

The mere fact that in the shadow of the university ghetto—from which the student left has for a decade been trying to break out—an alternative has been constructed, changes nothing; in fact it amounts to nothing but a reaffirmation of total political isolation. That ghetto remains ghetto and that nothing is altered by propaganda, however loudly it is proclaimed, is demonstrated by the structures which have developed there in the course of the past few years. In an almost uninterrupted transition from a continually available reservoir of *spontis*, ever on call for mobilization, to an alternative movement founded on economic self-sufficiency, character forms as well as authority structures were cemented; these became increasingly anonymous, and thus increasingly unassailable, the further the range of influence of this antieconomy— autonomized through a logic of its own—was extended.[12]

And as regards the Frankfurt scene, Kraushaar writes further:

This is also clearly apparent in the present state of projects. The social centers which were established to make possible a continual cooperation with migrant workers have become meeting places in their own right. Printing offices, instead of producing leaflets, work almost exclusively on contracted orders. Workshops have revived a trade guild condemned to extinction, and printing houses produce books that are little more than self-presentations. It is no longer possible to take seriously the project of effecting a social connection with other social strata and classes, something that in any case had occurred only sporadically at best. Even the last structured contact with the outer world has been terminated. A means-ends relationship in the social-revolutionary sense has been dissolved. The means have become immediate, the ends have disappeared. They have been displaced by an end in itself. Thus the social unrelatedness is figuratively conjoined in the illusory identity of the individual who calls himself a *"sponti."*[13]

Kraushaar's theses regarding the retreat into the escapist bastions of dogmatism and alternative life-styles are overstated and have met with resistance, but most important, they require amplification through reference to their complementary appearances. The closing in of the ghetto only mirrors, after all, the process of closing out—a dialectic in which Alexander Kluge and Oskar Negt have discovered a very German motif.[14]

2. Until now there has been no convincing analysis of the short phase of reform before 1972 and the beginning phase of restoration thereafter, the so-called shift in ideological currents. This has been implemented concretely at the level of administration and legislation, and has manifested itself in a factual alteration of the constitutional structure of our republic.[15] The ideological shift should not be confused with the rhetorical Muzak of those who have proclaimed it. But as a symptom of this change in sentiment—which has detached the cold war mentality from its fixation on an external enemy and has mobilized it for the exclusion of the internal enemy—the pamphleteering of New Right professors merits attention, even though it has in the meantime shown signs of running out of steam. This shift literature (*Tendenzliteratur*) has lent support to those who are politically and administratively prescribing the left's retreat into its ghetto. I do not want to go into specifics, but I would like to make three general observations.

a. The perspectives advanced by the shift literature rest on the premise that everything in the Federal Republic is running smoothly. They suggest a conception of normality that aims at neutralizing an awareness of deviant phenomena, of all that escapes the mechanism of social and psychic integration: they serve the ends of desensitivity training. And as a matter of fact, the Federal Republic is not in bad shape, either historically, in comparison with other political systems that have taken root in German soil, or internationally, in comparison with other advanced industrial societies. A successful system of crisis management and a satisfactory scope of economic development; a network of social services that "cushions" a relatively high rate of unemployment; no significant conflict with labor unions, which themselves have their memberships more or less under control; a party system that commands the allegiance of the great majority of the electorate; all things considered, a halfway functioning constitutional state; and now even a president [Carstens] who assures German continuity—what more could one ask for? From a static perspective limited to the institutionally ordered reality, one may not be presented with a tranquil picture; yet it is a picture in which the apparent polarizations serve only as a source of animation—indeed, the "Sunday portrait"[16] of a society in which all vibrations are properly integrated.

When the vibrations in a few societal sectors, particularly in the sphere of cultural reproduction, reach cacophonous levels, however, they are regularly traced back to the subjectively distorted perception of leftist intellectuals who, owing to their supposedly towering influence, can turn their own crises of consciousness inside out and contaminate the general population with their diseased imaginations. As we have seen in the past, ideologies serve to conceal opposing interests rooted in real conflict. Today, if we are to believe Schelsky, the ideology of the purveyors of meaning has become a source, if not the only source, of social conflicts.[17]

What is new in the position is not the idealism that stands things on their head, nor the process of punishing the messenger for the unpleasant message. What is new is rather the implicitly inculcated definition of normality, according to which crises of consciousness are not crises, disturbances in socialization are not disturbances, privatized (psychically internalized) conflicts are not conflicts, susceptibilities to political culture are not susceptibilities, the erosions of value-orientations and forms of life are not erosions, constitutional violations are not constitutional violations—but instead merely leftist fantasies that have been blown out of proportion by the media. Thus one is permitted to desensitize oneself against the problems with which the essays in this volume are principally concerned, problems I would trace back less to subjective conditions than to the colonization of the life-world by an economic and administrative system that has assumed a life of its own.

b. The shift literature has not generated any new arguments. But it has reactivated an existing source of argumentation (one whose potency in the postwar period was initially spent) by removing it from politically discredited contexts. This rearrangement equips the liberals who have drifted into the neoconservative camp. It involves primarily three complexes, and although I shall not discuss them here, I would like to indicate their intellectual-historical setting.

First, a prominent role is played by Carl Schmitt's criticism of the undesired consequences of a moralization of politics. This line was pursued, for instance, by Johannes Gross and Joachim Fest [editors of the *Frankfurter Allgemeine Zeitung*] when, on the occasion of the fortieth anniversary of *Kristallnacht* [the night of broken glass], they urged the chancellor, before a television audience, to nullify or at least render innocuous the annoying moral debts from the Nazi period, which restrict the political freedom of movement of an economic power such as the Federal Republic (to no avail, incidentally). Included in the same line of discussion is the oft-repeated thesis that not only a dogmatic philosophy of history but even the ethical universalism of the Enlightenment results in the terrorism of intellectual elites.

A second complex revolves about Gehlen's institutionalism. In his view, as archaic institutions lose the power to determine actions automatically, as their authoritarian core is dissolved through reflection and as individuals become saddled with the burden of decision, individual spontaneity thus liberated presses in the direction of anarchy and boundless subjectivity. Individuals made insecure in this fashion become overwhelmed by the abstract demands on their autonomy, their pursuit of happiness, and their capacity to make critical judgments. This polemic against humanitarianism has been revived today on all fronts, particularly with respect to an "emancipatory pedagogy" that is not content with instilling in children such secondary virtues as industriousness and love of order.

Third, the neo-Hegelianism of Hans Freyer (and Joachim Ritter) has been fashioned into a theory of postenlightenment or *posthistoire*, which is also able to redirect scientific currents into the melting pot of a diffuse traditionalism. In this view economy and political administration, science and technology are combined in the iron cage of modernity to produce independent, lawlike spheres of regularity demanding of formal rationality. These regularities are disengaged from the sphere of cultural values, from natural traditions, and at the same time refer to them in a complementary fashion. The critical thorn is thereby removed from a notion of enlightenment which had sought to link the acknowledgment of tradition to the presence of good reasons. It is on this basis that—as recently in Bavaria and Baden-Württemberg—public libraries and school textbooks are being exquisitely purified of all elements that do not comply with the arbitrary division of labor of positivism and obscurantism.

When at the beginning of the 70s a new dogmatism spread through leftist student circles, I was at first unable to believe that our extensive critique of Stalinism, which in the 50s did not require a great deal of effort, should have been in vain. A bit later similar feelings arose when, from the other side, all the arguments resurfaced that we had, at about the same time, used in our critical debates with Carl Schmitt, with Arnold Gehlen, with the theoreticians of technocracy, and so on. What was surprising was not so much that all this should actually reemerge, but rather that arguments whose intellectual roots could be traced back to the Nazi regime, and which after the War could be resumed only at some distance from the intellectual milieu of the Federal Republic, could today be employed as sustenance for a clearly apologetic political theory. Should we in fact have obtained a *different* political system (eine *andere* Republik) after all?

c. Finally, it is remarkable that the literary genre of the pamphlet, which had never been properly cultivated in Germany, has found new life on the right. The shift literature is doing its best to comply with the demand formulated by Lübbe in the following manner:

Professional academic philosophy can assert itself as a relevant factor in the exoteric process of consciousness and ideology formation, i.e., a process obeying the laws of the literary industry and the politics of ideas, only if it minimizes, wherever possible, what remains its characteristically esoteric and scholarly mode of linguistic practice and only if it places a premium on literary-rhetorical potentialities.[18]

To be sure, this commendable intellectualization of the mode of presentation hardly springs from the conservative self-understanding of these authors. But what does find expression in the new linguistic mode is a peculiarly instrumental relation to the exoteric presentation of political-intellectual positions. Lübbe, Scheuch, Schelsky, H. Maier, Sontheimer, and other comrades in a "League for Academic Freedom" view "intellectual confrontation" as something of a paramilitary operation at the front of a semantic civil war. They declare an interest in the occupation of word-fields, in strategies of denomination, in the reconquest of definitional powers—in short, in the determination of ideology by means of the politics of language. It is true that in the course of the protest movement a shift occurred in the political register of concepts. But I have never understood how one can seriously believe that basic political-theoretical concepts can in the long run be altered unless they absorb complex argumentations and are shaped to reflect innovations and learning processes. The objective spirit can hardly be trimmed to the left or the right by linguistic-political advertising agencies.

In any case, the rhetorical, language-manipulative tendency of the shift's literati, who want in this way slyly to assimilate to what they take to be a cunning opponent, explains two specifically German phenomena. I refer first to the semantic liberation of sentiments that until now had been slumbering benevolently under the cover of a decidedly liberal climate of political opinion. The resentments of a Mr. Ziesel were in their day what they were;[19] today there's a Ziesel on every corner.[20] Second, I refer to the phenomenon of the grand coalition of philosophers of order, who unite the ununitable at the level of a shared liberal-conservative idiom. Here critical rationalists are reconciled with Aristotelians, skeptics with dogmatists, empiricists with rationalists, and all of them together with the Hegelians—naturally, the right-wing Hegelians.[21]

3. Were one interested in breaking out of the circle of exclusion and seclusion, one would be confronted with two main tasks. First, the resolute defense, radical interpretation, and offensive renewal of the principles and traditions through whose spirit alone a German republic can preserve its existence against what Hans Mommsen terms the "burden of the past." In this respect the contributors to this book move along a beaten path first cleared by the liberal intelligentsia during the Adenauer phase of restoration. But in the meantime the

constellations have clearly moved. The cynicism of bourgeois consciousness has progressed to the point that the neoconservative heirs to the bourgeois emancipation mistrust the latter's own achievements and entreat us not, please, to take too literally its acknowledged ideals. As Claus Offe suggests, the discussion regarding ungovernability is one indication of the fright generated in the face of a surfeit of social welfare, of autonomy, of mass democracy. With the shift literature, the fronts have been repositioned in the debate over normative orientations. The New Right warns against the discursive dissolution of values, against the erosion of natural traditions, against the overburdening of the individual, and against excessive individualism. Its adherents want to see modernization restricted to capitalist growth and technical progress while at the same time wishing to arrest cultural transformation, identity formation, changes in motivation and attitude—in short, to freeze the contents of tradition. By contrast, we must again bring to consciousness the dignity of modernity, the dimension of a nontruncated rationality. We must make clear that in the posttraditional understandings of law and morality, in the release of subjectivity, in the liberation of spontaneity, in what sociology since Durkheim has termed "institutional individualism," there is established a fragile autonomy (*Eigensinn*) of moral-practical and aesthetic-expressive rationality. Max Weber called this the inner logic of differentiated value spheres. Whoever is willing to sacrifice this autonomy to a combination of a one-sided rationality and a vapid traditionalism risks costly regressions: on German (blood and) soil we have already conducted the experiment of a modernization restricted to economic growth and technological progress.

Certainly the authors of this book are not content simply to continue the critical concerns of the postwar generation. They regard as their more important and more difficult task that of investigating the complex zone of those ambiguous symptoms of the times for which plausible interpretations are lacking. This holds above all for the modes of reaction and groping innovations that turn on the depletion of the nonregenerable elements of natural as well as culturally inherited resources.

Albrecht Wellmer recalls the emphatic passage in the *Communist Manifesto* where Marx hails the capitalist mobilization of life conditions as a "melting away of all that is solid" ("Verdampfen alles Ständischen und Stehenden"). And Marx does this without the ambivalences confronting us today in view of a far more accelerated mobilization. For centuries capitalism has lived off the fat of prebourgeois traditions. To be sure, this also had a consequence envisioned by Marx, and already reflected in the universalism of the Enlightenment, in the utopian contents of an art that had become autonomous, and in bourgeois ideals as such: namely, the liberation of a potential for rationality of action oriented to understanding. But under the conditions of an extensively rationalized life-world, the spent contents can no longer be regenerated *qua* contents of tradition. Thus in the most capitalistically developed regions, these are approaching the point of exhaustion. And the imperatives of an autonomized process of economic growth and the administrative controls of a hopelessly overburdened bureaucracy cut through the detritus of eviscerated traditional forms of life, encountering at the exposed foundations the communicatively structured life-forms themselves. From this perspective, one perceives the danger of a systemically induced destruction not only of life-forms nourished on tradition but of the communicative infrastructure of any humane form of communal life. If this is correct, then two reactions are most definitely false: the interpreting away of the symptoms of the times and the flight into traditionalism.

Both topics—the defense of the republic and the investigation of phenomena symptomatic for the times—recur in nearly all the essays. Both are joined in the practical hypothesis Wellmer formulates regarding the depletion of nonregenerable elements:

The "loss of ethical life" generated by the reproduction process of industrial systems can be compensated for only through democratic forms of organization that would again bring the total societal processes into an intelligible connection with everyday reality and the needs of individuals.

4. Phenomena symptomatic for the times are conflicts and shifts that indicate a transformation in deep-seated structures. At the level of social interaction such symptoms are most easily recognized in social movements. In the Federal Republic today we observe those neopopulist currents that induced Herbert Marcuse to speak of the "people" (*Volk*), "individuals from all strata" who have replaced an integrated labor force as the agent of social resistance.[22] Among the important constituents of such currents are the *ecology movement*, uncoordinated citizens' initiatives, and those potentials that, in the form of a tax

protest party, are now to be run through the mill of the Christian Social Union (CSU); the *alternative movement*, a development of the protest movement that is played out in urban "scenes" but also embraces projects widely dispersed according to region and function, above all rural communes;[23] and the *women's movement*, which reaches beyond the framework of the alternative culture and establishes ties with historical liberation movements.

Movements for autonomy, which have been sparked by ethnic, religious, and regional conflicts and which have occurred in virtually every European country—particularly in Belgium, Switzerland, Northern Ireland, and the Basque region—have not been able to develop in the Federal Republic. I suspect, though, that in our case the national question could form an equivalent for dispositions opposed to the central state. For us, as Horst Ehmke indicates, the nation is no longer to be equated with the sovereign state (*Staatsnation*). Given the background of German history, the concept of the nation preserves ties to regionally rooted folk cultures more strongly than is the case with older nation-states, even more so than in Italy. Whereas Pasolini, in his struggle against the elimination of regional differences through the culture of consumerism, invokes the peasant and subproletarian life-forms of the Italian countryside,[24] Martin Walser can relate similar sentiments directly to the heritage of a national culture—his alemannic and his national homelands being equally removed from Bonn.[25]

Less clear than the active forms of protest are those conflicts shunted off into the private and psychic domains. The growing number of hospital beds occupied by psychiatric patients, the epidemic proportions of behavioral disturbances, alcoholism, the phenomena of addiction per se, the rising suicide and juvenile deliquency rates are all signs of unsuccessful processes of integration and failed socialization. Particularly noteworthy are the social-bureaucratically administered, social-therapeutically cushioned, and psychologically redefined problems in family, school, and education. Generated in part by reforms and in part by parental protests, these problems, difficult as ever to measure, indicate society's decreasing ability to incorporate future generations into its institutionalized value orientations.

Less conspicuous than potentials for protest and anomie are, finally, the reorientations and attitudinal discrepancies reflected in a population's normal mode of behavior. This phenomenon has in the past few years drawn the attention of sociologists and opinion researchers investigating political culture and voting behavior. Inglehart speaks of the "Silent Revolution."[26] The materialistic values of affluence, economic stability, and security (in domestic and foreign affairs), as well as the classic bourgeois virtues of career and competition orientation, compulsion to achieve, self-discipline, industriousness, and so forth are displaced by the postmaterialistic values of self-realization, solidarity, freedom of opinion, participation, the preservation of cultural and natural resources—that is, by postbourgeois virtues no longer shaped by instrumentalism and privatism. Inglehart claims that the tensions and interests of a "new" politics have been superimposed on the lines of conflict and the themes of an "old" politics defined chiefly by economics. Yet his theory of the "transformation of values" rests on an exiguous theoretical foundation, namely Maslow's psychological notion of a hierarchy of gradually actualized needs. It seems to me that it would be more advisable to view the latent transformation of attitudes expressed in the entire population together with the manifest appearances of protest and anomie. These in turn could be traced back to the experiences of and resistances against the violation of basic communicatively structured forms of life. Such an intepretation is in any case recommended in the essay by Wolf-Dieter Narr.

This complicated picture comes into sharper focus if we proceed not from the behavioral syndromes but from their causes—for example, from the phenomena that today trigger protest behavior. Thus the destruction of the urban environment, the industrialization, contamination, and sprawling disfiguration of the landscape make apparent to the populace standards concerning limits to the deprivation of basic sensual-aesthetic needs. These needs apparently sit very deep, even though it is clear that they have developed historically. In the fear generated by atomic power plants, nuclear waste, or gene manipulation, there is certainly a good bit of justified anxiety. But this *Realangst* also reflects the terror of a new category of literally invisible, hardly controllable long-term risks that exceed the biologically programmed thresholds of sense perception and the limits of our historically developed cognitive capacities, such as those for anticipated time, for personal identity, or for the extent to which moral responsibility can be attached to the consequences of action. Both exemplify the overloading of the sense-centered spatiotemporal capacities of the lifeworld, capacities which evidently do not automatically grow with the abstractions of an extended technical mastery of external and internal nature.

Even more provocative are the phenomena engendered by a *dev-astation of the communicative capacities of the life-world.* The instrumentalization of professional life; the mobilization of the workplace; the extension of competition and performance pressures even into elementary school; the monetarization of services, relations, and life's stages; the consumerist redefinition of personal life spheres (impressively described by Dorothee Sölle); the bureaucratization and legal regulation (*Verrechtlichung*) of private and informal spheres of action; and above all the political-administrative incorporation of school, family, education, and cultural reproduction in general—these developments make us aware of a new problem zone that has arisen on the borders separating system and life-world.

Through the historical example of the rise of the industrialized working proletariat, Marx revealed what lay hidden behind the category of wage labor or monetarized labor power: the shift from what hitherto had been a socially integrated sphere of life to the imperatives of an economic system regulated by law, formally organized, and steered through the medium of exchange value. This economic system stabilized itself in functional connections and could therefore reach through the normatively integrated action orientations of affected subjects. Today additional spheres of action have become systemically autonomized through the mediations of money, organizational power, and administrative decision; they absorb life connections, setting them free from outmoded and costly forms of social integration—an integration through values, norms, or communicatively achieved consensus. Many "modernist" reforms lead to an ambiguous legal regulation of life conditions. The ambiguity involved in reform-oriented intrusions into relations between parents and children, teachers and students, colleagues, or neighbors lies in the fact that these signify a detachment from traditionally established norms and, at the same time, also from value orientations per se. This detachment can and should promote an emancipation from encrusted power relations. But it carries the danger of a bureaucratic dessication of communicative relations, the danger of a deadening, as opposed to liberating, formalization of relations that in essence are not formalizable. It is this problem, for instance, that reigns in current discussions about the new regulations concerning parental responsibilities.

In investigating the factors that occasion the uneasiness symptomatic of the times, one comes across a problem zone whose comprehension is only too easily obscured by the clichés of cultural criticism. The encroachment of forms of economic and administrative rationality into life-spheres that in fact obey the independent logic of moral-practical and aesthetic-practical rationality leads to a type of *colonization of the life-world*. By this I mean the impoverishment of expressive and communicative possibilities which, as far as I can see, remain necessary even in complex societies. These are the possibilities that enable individuals to find themselves, to deal with their personal conflicts, and to solve their common problems communally by means of collective will-formation.[27]

5. If the depletion of nonregenerable elements, the colonization of the life-world, designates the sensitive zones of uneasiness in the *aporias* of modernity, how is this uneasiness culturally articulated, that is, how is it expressed in art, literature, and science?

In the autobiographical report of a young German scholar who depicts his "Life in Heidelberg," one finds a retrospective glance at the beginning of the student rebellions:

After 1967 everything was accessible only through systems of orientation and interpretations. Experiences were already conceptual. They were superimposed on the appearances. It was almost impossible to unearth literary correspondences, imaginative sentences, and images that stood next to the great events and that had not yet become clichés.[28]

The writer Urs Widmer has, in a similar context, given expression to the same experience:

Fantasy as such: somewhere, somehow fantasy should surely have been helped to attain power. But with us in any case a definite antipathy toward fantasy has prevailed since 1969 in favor of an absolute (if possible) conceptual comprehension of social reality.[29]

I do not know how accurately these utterances capture the situation at the end of the 60s. I do not recall that at that time very many felt themselves enlightened by Enzenberger's thesis that literature is no longer a socially legitimate undertaking. Nonetheless, these views definitely reflect the mood and scene in the final years of the 70s. Among the clichés gaining in popularity today is the abstract opposition between a literary experience that saves the nonidentical, is removed from concepts, and is directed to the concrete, momentary, spontaneous, and unique, and the leveling abstractions of science. In these considerations there is still a trace of Adorno. But the tendency extends further:

If individual myths are abolished (and after them perhaps even literature itself), then only science rules, as was the aim of the Enlightenment. That it is capable of doing so is beyond doubt. Society will then be regulated according to the laws of sociology, and psychology will tell people what and how they are. This they will be taught in group therapy, and those who choose not to believe will find themselves in psychiatric clinics. . . . This picture of Huxley's *Brave New World* does not differ significantly from Bloch's Utopia, for there too the thought of enslavement does not occur to people once their drives are satisfied.[30]

Ernst Bloch, the master thinker, and his pink-lemonade-tinted utopia are placed on the same plane as Skinner and behavioral therapy. Enlightenment is reduced to instrumental reason, so that literature, as the guardian of individual mythologies, can in an unimpeded fashion oppose both science *and* utopianism. The dialectic of enlightenment flips over into the Manichean world-view of the New Philosophers, which in the meantime has even penetrated the *edition suhrkamp.*

In the essays of this book, the changing state of the culture industry is conscientiously recorded: the mistrust of modernity's avant-garde movements, the farewell to functionalism and Neo Objectivity, the devaluation of grand theories, the retreat from the universalism of the Enlightenment. Against this, one now observes a turn to traditional forms and to the subjective in short stories and novels, a turn to the historical in urban planning and architecture, to everyday life in sociology, to late expressionism in film, to a new devoutness and piety in the churches, to narrative in the historical sciences, and to existential themes in philosophy. Cults of immediacy, the deflation of high standards, anarchy in the soul, celebrations of the concrete on all levels, relativism even in scientific theory, a shift of symbolic figures in culture criticism from Oedipus to Narcissus. I do not pretend to be able to distinguish between utterances that simply express new experiences and those that, while not necessarily conceptualizing such experiences, at least give them articulation. But this much is clear: it would be too easy simply to give in to the impulse to denounce features of a *Zeitgeist* that is obscuring itself in an irrationalist fashion.

Certainly the same features also reflect the need for concreteness, the desire for commitment and the determination to explore here and now the critical content of ideas, to consider seriously the significance of ideas for personal experience, to realize humanity in one's lifetime. The Hegelian heritage of Marxism, which has always distinguished it from utopian socialism, also consists in the insight recalled by Wellmer: "that theory must have an adequate concept of historically existing forms of freedom if it wants to anticipate emancipation not merely as a negation but as an 'overcoming' of this freedom." Perhaps the path inward that art, literature, science, and philosophy traversed in the 70s also sharpened the sense of and the sensitivities for existing forms of freedom. In this light the alternative movement and even the "province in the head"[31] acquire a significance that does not lend itself to short-term political assessments. In any case the alternative movement has already led approaches to the question of the reform of life conditions away from haut bourgeois elitism and the confines of Monte Verità.[32]

In the domain of social-scientific theory one finds approaches that seek to come to terms with phenomena symptomatic of the times. Recently Dahrendorf has been utilizing the conceptual duality of "options versus ligatures";[33] and Offe has returned to the conceptual duality of "social versus system integration" in order to comprehend imprecise phenomena that do not readily conform to the frameworks of Marxist, Weberian, or functionalist theories of development. Systems theory finds itself in the predicament of having to reinterpret the colonization of the life-world in such a way that hypercomplex social systems produce, as it were, external costs for overburdened personality systems. Within the Marxist tradition, and similarly among theoreticians of modernity, a decided about-face is taking place with regard to the historical theory of culture. Under the influence of E. P. Thompson, interest is now directed to "capitalism as culture." E. Knödler-Bunte, for instance, has characterized the scope of the problem in the following way:

One can say that all revolutionary movements of the past 150 years have been nourished on a potential that consisted of remnants of precapitalistic forms of life and production. Does this view stand in opposition to the Marxist concept, which, as is commonly known, subjectively and objectively connects revolution with the formation of developed relations of capital? Did the successful revolutionary movements in reality have an altogether different social class as their agent — namely, the peasant class? Wasn't it much less a matter of socialist revolutions than agrarian revolts against capitalism? And were not the revolutionary movements in the West European industrialized countries much more anticapitalist resistance struggles against the industrial factory system, characteristic indeed only of the painful and extremely deprivative transition from a predominantly agrarian to an industrial society? Do revolutionary potentials emerge only in the transitions from preindustrial to industrial-capitalist societies?[34]

These questions suggest the aforementioned perspective, according to which capitalist development appears as a parasitic intrusion into and gradual consumption of traditional forms of life; civil society (*bürgerliche Gesellschaft*) appears as parasitic upon prebourgeois (*vorbürgerliche*) cultures. Certainly this picture should not obscure the fact that (1) civil society was by no means culturally unproductive but first cleared the way for the independent development of cultural spheres of value and that (2) together with the capitalist economic system, it not only established an unpolitical form of class domination but also attained a new, evolutionarily significant stage of societal differentiation.

In the sphere of aesthetic theory, Peter Bürger sparked a fruitful controversy with his thesis regarding the failure of bourgeois art's attempts at self-criticism. He claims

that historical avant-garde movements negate the conditions essential for autonomous art: a removal of art from life, individual production, and an individual reception separated from it. The avant-garde had sought to overcome autonomous art by transferring art into life. This has not taken place within civil society, and indeed cannot take place, save perhaps in the form of a false overcoming of autonomous art.[35]

The attack of the classic avant-garde was directed not against specific artistic movements but against the institution of art itself. Since the institution has survived the attack, the neo-avant-garde moves today within a more or less nonbinding pluralism of artistic means and stylistic schools, while no longer able to enlist the force of an enlightening originality released in the violation of established norms, in the shock of the forbidden and frivolous, in irrepressible subjectivity. Attached to this skepticism is a feeling of remorse, resulting from Bürger's own identification with modernity.

Bürger's thesis has met with fierce criticism.[36] But all attempts to establish an unbroken continuity between classical and new avant-garde are problematic. In this respect it is more profitable once again to repeat, with Karl Heinz Bohrer, the dadaistic gesture and dismiss the entire matter as an internal controversy within the New Culture, which in turn is to be relativized against a Popular Culture that brutally renews the shock experiences from the midst of a trivial mass culture. Punk-anarchism strikes so accurately below the belt that sparks are sent flying in an aggressive desublimation, the likes of which one no longer would have thought possible. Yet such sparks hardly generate the profane illuminations Walter Benjamin once believed to be contained in the surrealist promises.

The spiritual situation is, as Johann Baptist Metz insists, characterized by noncontemporaneity. And social rejection—cultural noncontemporaneity—at one time nourished the specifically German outlook of the young-conservatives—Jünger, Benn, Heidegger, and Carl Schmitt. These thinkers existed in the tension between the remnants of unraveled traditions, the uncreative commotion of a ruthlessly exploitative present, and their own fanciful anticipations of a vaguely imagined past. Their diagnostic sensitivity to the times would have been suited to the ambiguous phenomena that today protrude into the foreground. One must also feel a twinge of regret that the intellectual line of this generation, one not only bewitched but instructed by Nietzsche, has been broken. This is the way things stand today: the old young-conservatives, like Armin Mohler and Rüdiger Altmann, scatter defiant words[37] in a well-oiled culture industry; it might have been possible for young young-conservatives to emerge from the failure of the protest movement, and yet the Federal Republic, unlike Paris, has produced almost no professed renegades. Günther Maschke only repeats what students of Schmitt and Gehlen were already whispering to one another in the early 50s. There are no Pasolinis. The only one today who has preserved, in a politically innocent and sovereign manner, something of the radicalness and neoromantic intelligence of a young-conservative is Karl Heinz Bohrer. In an article entitled "Germany—A Spiritual Possibility," Bohrer expresses his own profession of faith through the words of Hans-Jürgen Syberberg: "If we do not return to our innately grand style of imagination, metaphysics, indeed the style of the strictly forbidden, then we shall remain spiritually and psychologically colonized."[38] And then he enters into battle against those who in the name of reason, morality, logic, and sociology would make the so-called irrational taboo: "Nietzsche's 'everyday rationality'—the functionalist sociology, the technocratic idea of Europe; statistics instead of aesthetics, social-partnership instead of politics; right as well as left, many and yet one, the prohibition of conflict." No one can assume that I am citing these sentences purely affirmatively. For this I feel myself too much a part of the "West German intelligentsia" Bohrer here places on trial. But this is the only official context in which a statement from the alternative culture such as the following appears, a statement only too true: "Only if one dares to say 'I,' instead of referring to statistics, will perhaps that certain gray veil of West German boredom fade away."

Bohrer invokes the irrepressibly subjective, the shockingly inventive, "the rebellion against the normative"—the basic experiences of aesthetic modernity. His inconsistency begins at the point where, from the false transformation of surrealism into reality (and two forms of terrorism belong in this domain), he draws the conclusion of Stirner: "the dynamizing of culture is no political program. . . . No, one can only imagine such a culture, one can entertain it only in thought." Certainly, only at the level of symbolic systems—and therein consists the dignity of modernity—could the specific nature of the theoretical, the moral, and the aesthetic unfold so independently and so radically that Bohrer can today invoke the "chauvinism of the imaginative ego," the spheres of the basic experiences of aesthetic innovation purified of all theoretical and moral admixtures. Clearly, all attempts to reconcile, at the level of cultural symbolism itself, spheres that willfully follow differing paths must culminate in a pallid idealism. Yet beneath the threshold of the well-institutionalized orders of science and technology, law and morality, art and literature, beneath a politics reduced to administration, and on the periphery of a highly mobilized economic system, it is possible to detect processes of de-differentiation in praxis itself, new symbiotic forms in everyday life where the cognitive-instrumental once again touches upon the moral-practical and the aesthetic-expressive, with a garland of surrealistic appearances indicating perhaps not only regressions but also exploratory movements.

Notes

1. Siegfried Unseld is the president of Suhrkamp Verlag, which published the German edition of this book. Günther Busch was the editor of the *edition suhrkamp*, the series in which the book appeared (*tr.*).

2. Published in English as *Man in the Modern Age*, translated by Eden and Cedar Paul (Garden City, NY: Anchor Books, 1957).

3. Reference is to the turbulent period in fall 1977 following the kidnapping of the industrial leader Hans-Martin Schleyer by the Red Army Faction, chosen name of the terrorist group commonly known as the Baader-Meinhof Gang. Various aspects of both this affair and the general political climate were addressed in a film entitled *Deutschland im Herbst* [Germany in Autumn] released in March 1978 as a collection of short pieces by, among others, Fassbinder, Kluge, and Schlöndorff (*tr.*).

4. The slogan coined by influential conservative intellectuals who seek more authoritarian practices for the German education system (*tr.*).

5. A group of internationally prominent lawyers and intellectuals who in 1978 met at various sites in West Germany to assess the status of human rights there (*tr.*).

6. Reference to the authors of two of the original essays not included in the present translation (*tr.*).

7. Karl Jaspers, *Man in the Modern Age*, p. v. The translation has been altered (*tr.*).

8. The Berlin and Frankfurt *Tageszeitung* ("TAZ") (*tr.*).

9. "It almost seemed as though a movement had sprung out of the historical void, looked around, seen its own weaknesses, and again promptly collapsed back in upon itself. Out of fear of this fall into a bottomless pit, a near-instinctual attempt was made to grab whatever promised to provide political stability. Actually it was already before the end of the antiauthoritarian movement that the period of self-mimicry set in. Following the failure of the Springer campaign, the critical universities and, above all, the movement against the State of Emergency legislation, when the politically explosive content of the demonstrations had long since evaporated, actions became important for their own sake. One battled the forces of the state only to save what was still left to be saved: the purely formal principle of direct action. Figuratively stated, the movement had in effect spun its wheels: its deeds no longer held together, its groups ceased to take up issues, its slogans drifted aimlessly into space." W. Krauschaar, *Autonomie oder Getto* (Frankfurt, 1978), p. 57.

10. "Spontaneist" wing of the antiauthoritarian movement (*tr.*).

11. Kraushaar, *Autonomie oder Getto* pp. 57–58.

12. Ibid., p. 22.

13. Ibid., pp. 28–29.

14. Reference to an essay that is included in the German edition of this collection: Oskar Negt and Alexander Kluge, "Der antike Seeheld als Metapher der Aufklärung; die deutschen Grübelgegenbilder: Aufklärung als Verschanzung; 'Eigensinn,'" in *Stichworte zur 'Geistigen Situation der Zeit,'* vol. 1, pp. 135–163 (*tr.*).

15. See G. Frankenberg, Th. Krämer-Badoni, S. Meuschel, and U. Rödel, "Politische Tendenzwende," in M. Tohidipur, ed., *Der bürgerliche Rechtsstaat*, 2 vols. (Frankfurt, 1978), p. 136ff.

16. K. Sontheimer, *Die verunsicherte Republik* (Munich, 1979).

17. H. Schelsky, *Die Arbeit tun die anderen* (Opladen, 1975).

18. H. Lübbe, *Unsere Stille Kulturrevolution* (Zurich, 1976), pp. 94–95.

19. During the 50s and 60s Kurt Ziesel was one of the best-known right-wing German writers and journalists. His resentments stem from his relation to National Socialism (*tr.*).

20. Since "critical theory" functions in this context as a particularly effective source of provocation, I could have amassed a wealth of pertinent experiences. I am referring, however, not to the Sunday speeches of politicians, nor even to the waste from newspapers that stand to the right of the *Frankfurter Allgemeine Zeitung*. Instead I refer to the loss of emotional control in people who really should know better. Loss of control caused a well-known legal scholar to include idle tabletalk in what by law is the most influential commentary on the constitution. Loss of control caused a well-versed journalist to transform into a simple denunciation his "report" on a lecture by Albrecht Wellmer, a lecture that in expanded form is reprinted in this collection. Loss of control caused a noted philosophy professor to use the occasion of the ceremony marking the five hundredth anniversary of a university [Tübingen] to place the words of a philosophical colleague in the mouth of a blindly firing terrorist. See G. Düring, "Kommentierung zu Art. 3 III," Gloss-Nr. 116ff., 122 Note 2 (1973), in Maunz, Dürig, Herzog, and Schulz, *Grundgesetz Kommentar* (Munich, 1978); "Ist Gewalt Romantik Links?" *Frankfurter Allgemeine Zeitung*, May 17, 1978, p. 3; H. Lübbe, "Freiheit und Terror," *Merkur*, September 1977, p. 823.

21. A nice illustration of this is supplied by the "Congress for Academic Research," which, under the guidance of H. Lübbe, met in Munich in March 1976. Compare W. Raub, *Berichte der Projektgruppe Wissenschaftsforschung an der Universität Essen*, 11/76. [In the German text Habermas refers to an essay that is included in the German edition of this collection: Klaus von Beyme, "Der Neo-Korporatismus und die Politik des begrenzten Pluralismus in der Bundesrepublik," *Stichworte*, vol. 1, pp. 229–262 (*tr.*).]

22. H. Marcuse, "Postsozialismus und Spätkapitalismus," *Kritik* 19 (1978):18.

23. B. Leineweber and K. L. Schibel, "Die Alternativbewegung," in Kraushaar, *Autonomie oder Getto*, p. 95ff.

24. P. P. Pasolini, *Freibeuterschriften* (Berlin, 1978).

25. Walser's essay is to be found in the German edition of the present work: "Händedruck mit Gespenstern," *Stichworte*, vol. 1, pp. 39–50 (*tr.*).

26. R. Inglehart, "The Silent Revolution in Europe," *American Political Science Review* 65 (1971); for the Federal Republic: K. Hildebrandt and R. J. Dalton, "Die Neue Politik," *Politische Vierteljahresschrift* 18, issues 2, 3 (1977). An overview is provided by M. and S. Greiffenhagen, *Ein schwieriges Vaterland* (Munich, 1979), p. 236ff.

27. The difficulties involved in identity formation are intensified in milieus that in their communicative infrastructure are simultaneously demanding—because differentiated—and impoverished. An expression of such difficulties is the retreat in the search for identity into one's own inherent concreteness, the clutching onto natural, ascriptive attributes, like sex or skin color. Inasmuch as the two great recent liberation movements, the American civil rights movement and the international women's movement, appeal to natural categories (racial and sexual attributes), they furnish a context in which at least the temptation exists for purely concrete

forms of resolving an identity-problematic oriented to emancipation. In literary works one observes that several of the leading black and feminist spokespersons have in their search for roots indeed strayed into a biological glorification of race or femininity. Stephan Reinhardt concludes his essay, "Nach innen führt der geheimnisvolle Weg, aber er führt wieder heraus" (in W. M. Lüdke, [ed.], Nach dem Protest: Literatur im Umbruch [Frankfurt, 1979], p. 158ff.), with the following remark: "It cannot be denied that the new irrationalism, presented here as the narcissistic cult of inwardness and presented in parts of the feminist literature as biologism, is welcomed by those who view with mistrust and animosity programs to realize a humane society (itself, to be sure, an intellectual abstraction). . . . Segments of the women's movement adopt this ideology at the point where they brand reason and understanding as heretical and present themselves as the advocates of the true Nature; indeed, in some cases they even permit the revival of chauvinist and fascist mythologies" (p. 182).

28. Lüdke, Nach dem Protest, p. 42ff.

29. Urs Widmer, "1968," ibid., p. 21.

30. Karl Heilscher, "Über den Gegensatz von Kunst und Utopie," ibid, pp. 238–39.

31. "Province in the head" was a slogan used by certain membes of the left critical of escapist tendencies in the alternative subculture. An issue of Kursbuch (39 [April 1975]) was devoted to this topic (tr.).

32. See the catalogue to the remarkable exhibit at the Berlin Akademie der Künste, March 25–May 26, 1979 (Electra Editrice, Milan). [Reference is to an art exhibit devoted to a hillside retreat ("Monte Verità") in the small Swiss town of Ascona, near Lago Maggiore. Around the turn of the century Ascona was the southernmost outpost for a disparate group of predominantly upper-middle-class Northern Europeans engaged in exploring a variety of alternate life-styles (tr.).]

33. R. Dahrendorf, Life Chances: Approaches to Social and Political Theory (Chicago: University of Chicago Press, 1979).

34. Unpublished manuscript, 1977.

35. Peter Bürger, Theorie der Avantgarde (Frankfurt, 1974), pp. 72–73.

36. W. M. Lüdke, ed., "Theorie der Avantgarde." Antworten auf P. Bürgers Bestimmung von Kunst und bürgerlicher Gesellschaft (Frankfurt, 1976).

37. "One should not overlook the conservative camp's own contribution to the ideological shift. Under the leadership of a few wise old men—here mention need only be made of Arnold Gehlen and, more remotely, Carl Schmitt—an intellectual right of an altogether new style is developing: no longer quick to look back, little concerned with 'values,' a cold, aggressive intelligence with little respect for the moral imperatives which have accumulated around it. Its adherents show what man is in reality, how institutions originate, and once again they dare to speak of heredity and to suggest that a nation is in fact more than an invention of poets. And most of all: they do not drop a thought like a hot potato the moment it is declared to be 'fascist,' 'authoritarian' or whatever else." Armin Mohler, "Symposium," Der Monat 1 (1978):20.

38. K. H. Bohrer, "Deutschland—eine geistige Möglichkeit," Frankfurter Allgemeine Zeitung, April 28, 1979.

Perspectives on Politics and Society

Toward a Society of
Conditioned Reflexes

Wolf-Dieter Narr

No, Pavlov cannot be declared the winner. There is no reason to count on the arrival of a social pack of rats that awaits en masse the bell triggering a group plunge into feeding troughs or other social activities, a society cohesively and complacently allowing itself to be led by the nose. The technocrat's dream and the negative utopian's nightmare will not materialize, for there are too many cracks and contradictions that cannot be eliminated technologically without commotion. In this respect it is also unlikely that capitalistically developed societies could shrink to one-dimensionality, as Marcuse prophesied, allowing irrational-existential gestures of escape at most. Equally untenable is the notion that what remains of the dialectic of enlightenment is only the ideology become reality of indissolubly inhumane domination.

Yet it would be injudicious to terminate the old debate with more or less correct objections. One hardly need invoke a neohumanist form of cultural criticism to recognize the many signs indicating that the concepts of emancipation formulated in bourgeois terms and further developed by the workers' movement, concepts revolving about the notion of the cohesive integrity of the person, are disintegrating like moldy mushrooms. This disintegration, which is not the result of an inexorable process (even if promoted by powerful forces), is sustained both by careless modernist reforms of the jargon of emancipation and by prematurely abdicating intellectuals who, having grown weary of theory and strategies, prefer to concentrate on a form of praxis realizable in the here and now.

By way of a few experiences from and with the Federal Republic, I shall attempt—without furnishing in any detail the possible proof—

to elaborate somewhat on the topic of a society swinging back and forth between a progressive form of social organization and an absence of total societal planning. To begin with, I want to identify a change in behavior whose contours, after a long prelude, have now quickened into sharp focus. Then I shall specify certain features of this change. This will be followed by a critique of modernist reforms and abdicating intellectuals and, finally, by some observations amounting to a "rescue" of theory and its corresponding praxis.

Changes in Behavior: The Dismantling of Resistance

Hebbel's Master Anton was not the only one no longer able to make sense of the world. His experience typifies those that occur when an individual's surroundings and social orientation undergo rapid transformation. It finds expression in the conflict of generations.

The fact that contemporary transformations, those occurring within one's lifetime, seem so particularly significant and distinctive is to be explained by the closeness of one's perspective. Whatever we face directly and whatever touches us looms larger and more pressing than phenomena long habitual or internalized. Periods of tremendous disruption have always been coupled with disruptions in our perceptions. Societal occurrences strike us as alien, and what is alien appears dangerous. Occasionally this results only because we are forced to adjust and because our previous modes of behavior are no longer adequate. The student movement and the reactions to it, particularly within universities, illustrate this point nicely.

We of course know, on reflection, that as a rule social developments rarely take place in spectacular leaps and that they do not occur linearly and in unambiguous fashion. Hence it is difficult to pinpoint the actual crystallization of a new state of affairs so as to identify, both clearly and unequivocally, the emergence of a new society and its new modes of behavior. It is difficult to find a key or concept through which such a society could be understood. Nonetheless, it seems as though we have in fact been living through years, even decades, of an unspectacular, creeping, cold process of revolution, at whose yet indeterminate end the world, "our world," might no longer be depicted and comprehended in ways that at least seem possible today.

We are interested here only in one aspect of this process of cold and creeping revolution: the transformation of behavior. The change in behavior long observed by Riesman, Mitscherlich, Weber, and many others consists in a destruction of "inwardness," in a loss of the individual's mechanisms for reflection and for the processing of experience. What has been formulated by behaviorist psychology (rightly criticized on theoretical grounds) now seems to become reality. Stimuli and expectation engender responses, which individuals can neither process for themselves, choose of their own accord, or refuse to accept. Behaviorist psychology seems to be fundamentally mistaken—as regards empirical observation as well—only in its contention that this lack of individual and/or collective reflection and processing engenders no additional conflicts and problems. The mechanism of the stimulus-response schema in fact produces continuous costs and conflicts, which of course are borne individually and, in the appropriate circumstances, are cushioned by education and psychotherapy.

Norbert Elias, whose work has met with belated but widespread acclaim, has advanced the thesis that the "civilizing process," the process underlying modern, capitalist-bourgeois society, was characterized by two interrelated processes of unification. The first of these involved the formation of a political center. Following a long struggle with resistant forces, primarily those protecting estate interests, the political center, which we call the (modern) state, succeeded in securing a monopoly on the physical use of violence, the levying of taxes, and the generally valid promulgation and implementation of norms. This process of monopolization, borne, advanced, and shaped by an expanding bureaucracy, subordinated all local and regional authorities to a central authority. From autonomy sprang dependence. The internal civilizing of society was achieved, as Hobbes had already made clear, at the price of a statist monopoly on violence and its demands.

Second, the macrosocietal nationalization of social violence was accompanied by a microsocietal process that produced new patterns of psychic behavior. Corresponding to the large-scale process of monopolization, a transformation occurred within the logic of the individual psyche. An internal process of regulation emerged, which can be described as a psychic form of structuralization and monopolization. Traditional forms of spontaneity and immediacy were abolished; a superego representing social norms and a disciplined and disciplining ego were ceded a priority and placed above the id of drives. The individual now possessed within himself a model of state monopoly, an ever-present psychic ruler. The external discipline of the statist monopoly was supplemented by an internal one. It was in this internally disciplining process that individual behavior was civilized.

There is merit in the thesis of a homogeneous historical process that unfolds at the mutually implicative levels of large-scale politics and the interior of psychic reception and reaction. Still one must ask how these two interrelated processes were actually mediated, how the "external" and "internal" forms of policing complemented or reciprocally influenced each other, and how they came into conflict with each other. One must also ask whether the social disciplinary apparatus was ever fully established within the state monopoly on violence and within the superego/ego, whether the external monopoly on violence in essential social strata has in fact always corresponded to a regulating psychic structure of motivation and behavior, or whether it was not rather the case that motivations and behavior have again and again been externally constrained without further internalization. In support of the last supposition, reference can be made to the role always played by physical violence not only in the workplace and the legal system but even within formally private spheres. Further support is provided by the fact that the state's monopoly on violence, through its various representatives, cannot for an instant renounce its social presence without risking "chaos."

However these questions are answered, which indeed depends upon whether one is concerned with "citizens" or with "workers," progress is in fact being made in the external process of monopolization, a process that has always claimed priority. Yet this process (evidenced by economic concentration and political centralization) does not today sustain or require an "old bourgeois" regulating structure as in the Freudian model of socialization—a Mosaic superego and a disciplined, self-regulating ego that only rarely permits the inappropriate. On the contrary, an almost epochal change in motivation and behavior seems to have occurred. This change has the following features:

1. Economic concentration and political centralization assure an increasing abstractness of social conditions, which leave the individual powerless. At the same time the demands of production and its political manifestations control the living conditions of the individual down to the last detail.

2. The processes of economic concentration and political centralization, which have not yet reached their conclusion, not only entail the legal regulation (*Verrechtlichung*) and bureaucratic mediation of all

spheres of society; they simultaneously eliminate, as actually or potentially irrelevant, more and more social spheres that are no longer
economically or politically necessary. An example of such legal-
bureaucratic seizure can be found in both the educational and the
professional employment sectors. Illustrating the elimination of social
groups and even social spheres are the problems of youth and of the
elderly, as well as the manner in which municipal districts are removed
to the periphery and left there in isolation.

Contemporary society could be ordered on a scale of social relevance;
the margins, reserved for debris, would be designated for "wayward"
youths and parents, "ordinary" and political criminals, the homeless,
and alcoholics. On the now normal extremes, one would place children,
adolescents, and the elderly. In the center, arranged in a self-differ-
entiated and hierarchical manner, would be situated individuals in the
prime of professional and occupational life, people ranging in age
from twenty-five to fifty-five.

The arrangement of roles according to age and occupation and its
resulting social significance have direct consequences for the entire
welfare and public health care sector, just as they shape social and
individual consciousness.

The regional inequality that emerged in the process of capitalist
industrialization, resulting from the contiguity of premodern regions
and those already structured capitalistically, must be clearly distinguished from the regional inequality that arose as a result of capitalist
industrialization itself. With the latter we are indeed concerned with
postcapitalist domains. We can disregard the ghettos, as they are not
required for production. (Compare this with the particularly striking
examples from the United States.) Attempts are being made to satisfy
socially whole regions by converting them into vacation resorts and
mollifying their sense of lost significance with town beautification con-
tests and new festivals. The economy is concentrated away. Provoked
by such factors as jurisdictional reforms, politics has migrated to sites
far from the center.

3. The industrial-capitalist mode of production and the state (including its "extraeconomic" force), always interwoven in shaping each
other, have in the course of the industrialization process directed society
back upon itself, thereby profoundly altering the motivations and the
interests of individuals. The performances necessary for production
not only stand in the unquestioned social center; they also generate

a wave of professionalization and enforce a continually revised and expanded division of labor, even in those spheres not directly subordinated to industrial production. They create a society of roles, where the individual is important only as a bearer of attributes—with reference to this or that attribute but not to what these attributes constitute: the person. This role distribution is visible even in the division of cities into residential, occupational, recreational, and administrative zones. It also reappears in the age-specific division of lifestyles.

A one-sided "achievement society" was established with the aid of resources not directly produced in capitalist development. Disregarding the role that colonized countries have played (and not only for the British Empire), mention must be made of the preindustrial agrarian and handicraft sector; that remarkable product and motif of bourgeois-liberal society, the intimate nuclear family; and, finally, the collective organization of workers. The performance requirements were nourished on these behavioral elements, which were not directly produced by capitalism even if in large measure they went hand in hand with capitalism. In them, capitalist society found its social balance. The preconditions satisfied by these behavioral reserves can scarcely be overestimated. At the same time resistance potential was developed here, as capitalist development had not yet abolished the self-sufficiency of these domains.

4. Capitalist industrial society has always been characterized by the fact that it destroys its own presuppositions. The capitalization of agriculture has had a long history, but it is now nearly complete. Handicraft shops still exist but are themselves part of larger units or are viable only as dependent, marginal constellations. Although the bourgeois nuclear family continues to exist, it has nonetheless ceased performing any further functions internally or externally; its influence on behavior continuously declines. Workers' organizations have lost their strong formative and integrative power, not because they have failed as organizations (which is also the case) or because they have become large organizations on the traditional model, but because they no longer appeal to the workers who at one time embraced them.

5. What has changed is not the character of capitalist society itself but the fact that the consequences of its "logic" have now become apparent, consequences that arose from the successful establishment of capitalist society. (Even fascism was a product of its belated and

incomplete establishment.) These consequences flow from fully developed capitalist society and reflect its uniqueness.

The performance imperatives oriented to production remain. Yet they have attained such technological perfection that only in part do they impose specific occupational demands; above all, changes of behavioral requirements are exceedingly rapid. Permanent qualifications, which were acquired over long periods of time and were characteristic of the classic model of the skilled worker, are less desirable today. What is stressed first and foremost in contemporary training is the performance attitude itself, irrespective of the nature of the specific performance. Flexibility and mobility are valued as central postulates; or, in the jargon of the abstract performance ethic: always be prepared. Even the acquisition of internal plant experience is rarely required today. Reschooling and training are the new watchwords.

The organization of the occupational sphere and the provision for extraoccupational spheres intensify social isolation and the irrelevance of personal experiences both inside and outside the sphere of an individual's profession. Bureaucracy, in whose educational and regulatory net everyone is entwined, deals with clients. Whether in the factory, the school, the drug treatment center, the hospital, or elsewhere, individuals are reduced to subjects, subordinates who must relinquish their civil rights at the door. The abstract and complex character of bureaucracy has increased in large part because the possibilities for a politically meaningful form of self-organization have been nearly eliminated.

Performances demanded by production and the corresponding requirements of discipline are of central social significance. At the same time there are increases in those spheres and individual shares that are only indirectly needed. Sharing in consumption is often more desired than sharing in production. The technical logic of production frees both time and people, yet through consumption and general discipline it keeps individuals tied to the production process. The recreation industry, welfare and educational policies, and psychotherapy care for those who have fallen from the framework of established roles. Only by misunderstanding the logic of performance and regulation within production and bureaucracy could one assume that private spheres, free time, and autonomous personalities might be left to themselves. What is left to itself is only what is left over, what is no longer needed. Yet these individuals and groups are left to themselves only as long as they do not conspicuously appear to be anomalous. Anomaly is not allowed to reach the level of articulation.

A Résumé of Behavior

According to Elias, the civilizing process has two poles: the forceful construction of a statist monopoly on violence, and the emergence of an apparatus for psychic discipline coordinated with it. Both of these forms of unification are fundamentally ambivalent. To a certain degree the state monopoly on violence has ensured peace in society. But it has created as well a superpowerful Leviathan demanding constant demonstrations of respect in both word and deed. Moreover, the monopoly on violence permits the implementation of one-sided interests, as long as they coincide with those of the monopoly. Yet the psychic self-disciplining of the individual not only has resulted in a disciplining of behavior commensurate with the requirements of the external monopoly but has also constantly demanded sublimations and repressions.

Much as these two poles ought to be comprehended in terms of their interrelationship, it is important not to underestimate the relative autonomy that has been created by the capacity for self-discipline. Precisely because the individual, owing to his socialization, became competent as a subject and agent, he also became capable of resistance—resistance even against the external monopoly and its demands.

Owing to the way in which the external monopoly, together with the capitalist organization of production, has developed, and the way in which, with its regulations, it absorbs and, when necessary, destroys other societal spheres, the subordinate pole of psychic self-rule is being dissolved. Economic and political concentrations do indeed release social space and social aims; they eliminate economically irrelevant areas and considerably reduce the amount of socially required labor. Yet they set free these forms of space and time only as irrelevant waste products. Furthermore, they absorb the energies that would allow citizens in the full sense of the term—citizens also as workers— to develop themselves. For this, no isolated nooks exist. Self-determination is undermined in the very conditions of its possibility, even if, as a rule, it is fully required and desired as a form of self-discipline. Personal autonomy (*Integrität*) is deemed undesirable if it militates against its use in segmented roles and does not consistently favor a mobility and flexibility unaffected by considerations of space and time. It is severed from its roots, from its own space and time, from the conditions nurturing personal maturation and orientation. What is required and what is created is a self-righting buoy without mooring. Naturally this is not accomplished without costs. Left to their own devices, people react vulnerably, unable to protect themselves. Yet such costs are not only borne by individuals. They are also borne by all forms of social aid, because the stimulus-response mechanism leads or can lead to withdrawal symptoms in the affected persons, thereby confirming Negt and Kluge's assumption regarding the existence of an "emancipatory minimum." In addition, the destabilized individual's ability to perform is diminished, at least where self-sufficiency is at issue. It is evident, however, that this performance capacity is only partially required. The debate about the humanization of the workplace, which has again subsided, commences with the issue of the adverse consequences of a one-sided rationalization. The debate also demonstrates the minimal room left for a different kind of workers' organization within the framework of the ruling system of reference. In Lordstown, Ohio, and elsewhere, "unmotivated workers"—unmotivated because of good pay and sumptuous indulgences (even swimming pools are provided for their leisure time use)—rebelled against their working conditions; or, to be more precise, they obstructed (by staying away, calling in "sick") the job requirements which were supposed to satisfy completely Taylor's operational recommendations for increasing work performance.

Those who fall from the production sphere or who are still not enmeshed in it are caught only by the social-bureaucratic safety net. Since they lack means to articulate and organize themselves, they are left with little more than a helpless vulnerability and a vulnerable helplessness, which is without power save for what they use to harm themselves.

Indications of Instability

These are nothing more than symptoms. Yet the symptoms seem to indicate an illness, even if its diagnosis still leaves something to be desired. I would like to supplement my remarks on subjective states of mind (*Befindlichkeiten*) with examples that call attention to a fundamental transformation in the structure of communication. This transformation cannot be understood without the aforementioned economic-political requirements.

Subjective States of Mind

"States of mind" is the appropriate expression. Individuals intuitively sense and experience themselves, and yet are unable to gain generalizable insights from the sum total of these experiences. They feel isolated, even within and as a group. And they flee from work and behavioral difficulties by getting "turned on," taking drugs, in some cases even resorting to violence.

These observations refer primarily to that part of society not yet incorporated into the occupational sector. But it would be wrong to trivialize the phenomenon into a "youth" problem. Certainly it is most in evidence there. Nonetheless, one need only note the helplessness of "grown-ups" when for some reason the regular pace of everyday life begins to falter to recognize how much more prevalent are the actual difficulties in finding one's way, in orienting oneself, and in acting self-sufficiently. "The collective inability to interpret the transformed situation is currently the most striking feature of the worker's social consciousness." As Michael Schumann writes in his summary of more recent investigations into the social consciousness of the individual worker: "An attitude marked by individual impotence and absence of perspective predominates."[1]

Even if one takes into account that such observations themselves derive in part from an altered awareness, the proliferation of announcements about behavioral disturbances in children, adolescents, and students must be assigned great significance. Persons not involved with children and adolescents can scarcely imagine the number of work-related and behavioral problems even among those not held back in grade school or placed in special-needs programs. And those who succeed do so only as long as no unusual situations arise. They certainly do not possess any special capacity for orientation and self-definition. They are merely able to deal with their lack of orientation in the usual ways.

The deep-seated nature of these general disturbances in behavior is illustrated by the widespread literature on the topic of angst, which, notably in the case of students and teachers, reflects the consequences of one-sided stress and the inability to cope with it. It is particularly where adolescents, among others, search for different life-styles and working conditions, for "alternatives," that expressions of social suffering, helplessness, and a lack of a capacity for resistance can be seen. It is not so much that individuals get pushed out of social institutions as that they never get in or that they can't make it. The enemy consists not of persons but is found in institutions, in schools, in social work, and in the factory. The enemy is insufficient participation, insufficient integration, and unattainable, abstract requirements. Because the enemy remains essentially anonymous, because it is not clear how to deal with it, people attempt to withdraw from institutions entirely. Thought is not even given to a march through the institutions; this would presuppose perspective, endurance, and the ability to tolerate ambiguous situations. It is elsewhere that they hope to find what is missing: in communal households, in an urban "scene," in "alternatives" well-stocked with possibilities for immediate gratification.[2] People are searching for the "social backbone"[3] not developed in the family and never replaced on a collective basis.

These claims are apparently as valid for the traditional proletarian family and its relation to the workers' movement as they are for the bourgeois, fatherless family, which has never been constructively superseded in new forms of socialization. Public schools, which take the place of proletarian and bourgeois structures of socialization, and all the other institutions within youth, recreational, and professional spheres do not exactly offer opportunities for social growth.

The working-class family has suffered a visible loss of influence as regards the cultivation of a political disposition. Disappearing rapidly is the type of proletarian family that once gave children, prior to any explicit formation of political judgment, secure roots in a proletarian life context and that provided them with the collective self-perception of workers—a self-perception that often bound them emotionally to the organized workers' movement. This type of education through family and milieu, still typical of the Weimar period, safeguarded a stable organizational loyalty that was virtually independent of experience; for the postwar generation, for people of thirty today, it has almost no significance. The political socialization of the worker has shifted, on the whole, more emphatically into the secondary and tertiary phase of education: school, workplace/factory, and even the mass media.[4]

Technological Transformations Accelerating Rootlessness

At first glance the situation appears paradoxical. Orientation problems and an oft-lamented absence of "perspective"[5] stand over against a flood of information and a wealth of possibilities for communication that are in fact unprecedented. These possibilities are increasing rapidly.

But the contradiction disappears quickly. Information and communication do indeed open up new areas and regions. It is possible to become informed about matters of fact faster today than ever before; contact with others can be established more quickly than in the past. Distances can be bridged, time abbreviated. The opportunities for information and interaction rise. Yet the production of information and the possibilities for communication are characterized by features that heighten the individual's helplessness and intensify a sense of isolation.

Pieces of information or, to be more accurate, data are collected and disseminated by specialists. What is not developed is the ability to deal with these disparate data as forms of intelligible information. "A fact," as one of Pirandello's characters correctly states, "is like an empty sack; it does not stand upright if nothing is placed within it."[6]

Moreover, the data are disseminated with significant gaps. In the workplace information is not provided as to how and why decisions are made. Material bearing on an individual's personal situation is collected and stored; yet it exists more for the use of the bureaucracy than for that of the affected individual, who would in any case have no idea what to do with it.

Neither of these features is new, not even in its present dimensions. Of increasing importance, though, are two developments that reduce the possibility for individuals to avail themselves of this mass of information. First, the social opportunities for individuals to accumulate personal experiences shrink although the disseminated stimuli increase. Second, the possibilities for active participation or simply taking a part decrease, since concentration and centralization press forward even in the sphere of information, with the result that individuals cannot process the disseminated data at a corresponding pace. The technical production and storage of information have formed one of the largest branches of economic growth.

One cannot speak of information without mentioning communication. The two overlap. As previously indicated, a decrease is occurring in the opportunities for forms of individual self-articulation and self-organization not mediated by the media. By contrast the possibilities for communication mediated by the media are on the increase. Wideband communication is the most recent catchword. Audience rating of radio and television stations intimates this.

This kind of communication, praised as offering a new potential for democracy, relies on and even intensifies the isolation of the individual. It is mindlessly institutionalized in a manner similar to much of contemporary human commerce, which is emancipated from the constraints of space and time. This commerce in people and the mode of its institutionalization not only help in moving mountains; they also cut through social connections, breaking them up and jamming them.

Information and communication tend to become spaceless. They operate, it seems, without social mediation, in the sense of a newly acquired immediacy of the overmediated. Only in this way does the medium become the message, and not simply because the nature of the mediation influences the mediated, but also because the medium develops into the space of a substitute reality, where one can relate without cost and commitment.

The social effects of these information and communication forms have not been properly investigated; nor have their developmental tendencies been even approximately sketched. Hence one can do little more than speculate about them. Nonetheless it is clear that the direction and the driving force determining the development of information, of the media, and of the various forms of communication—from the telephone to wideband communication to automated subways—are based not on the individual's needs, potentials, or social organization but on the imperatives of a logic of capital realization (ökonomische Verwertungslogik). It is also clear that what is at work is not an economic cunning of reason whose inventions serve the social whole. Rather, this type of development of informational and communicative techniques destroys the integrity of social spheres as well as that of individuals themselves. Individuals possess no controlling criteria, no controlling information, no controlling communication; they can in fact reduce the complexity in the quantity of information and communication only by placing trust in this complexity. That is its primary sense.

Economic-Political Requirements

It is astonishing how constant the institutions of liberal representative democracy have remained, even though social change has taken place in qualitative leaps ever since their establishment (or rather their belated transference in the case of the Federal Republic of Germany). It seems as though the liberal democratic form of government is forever *ab initio* placing its stamp on a transformed society. Economic concentration has assumed multinational dimensions; the world market can even be felt in the Swabian Alps. The grip of bureaucracy has become universal. Politics has been concentrated, specialized, and professionalized. And yet the institutions of liberal democracy, uniquely prescribed by the Federal Constitutional Court in our "liberal democratic basic order," possess the durability of deerskin riding breeches. Generations come and go, society transforms itself, the economy becomes concentrated; yet liberal democratic institutions continue to exist. Indeed they do; and yet they remain as manifestly fitted to the contents and real forms of the political-economic process as do deerskin breeches to their changing owners.

In view of the fact that new forms have not been sought and located that correspond to the requirements of liberal democracy, it must be said that the traditional process of articulating and organizing interests has come to a virtual standstill. Interests are articulated through procedures that only pretend to be participatory, through forms of symbolic action such as general elections,[7] where participation remains abstract and partial. The nature of contemporary political elections illustrates the type of demand our ruling political authorities (by which are understood not only those that are formally public) make on citizens: a role-prescribed mobilizability with no right of participation.

Again it is possible to observe a contradictory occurrence. The more centrally, intricately, and even instrumentally the ruling institutions are structured, the more they must use the least problematic procedures possible, and the less they can risk social conflicts—in functional domains (as an air traffic controller strike) or at the social base (the debates and discussions about citizens' initiatives). The more central and thus more abstract the ruling institution becomes, the more powerless and helpless are its employees and clients. Apathy becomes a behavioral and occupational elixir. If conflicts or critical situations arise, no normalized resolutions are at hand. Apathetic individuals, those mobilized only role-specifically, react in a manner irrationally wild and unpredictable. For this reason the centralized institutions are, paradoxically, ill-equipped to handle emergency situations and therefore must arm themselves with preventive devices.

The institutional deficit, the lack of institutional conditions that would make possible and indeed necessitate participation, cuts across the entire society: from schools that institutionalize negative learning to the administrative bureaucracy whose members can at most be motivated by competition for positions and seeming proximity to money and power. Yet the obstacles to participation, to the cultivation of personal experience, and to involvement in the various spheres of work are not of a technical nature; nor are they to be located in socially unmediated objective exigencies. Rather, they result from interests in capital realization and political domination.

It is precisely in a technical fashion that decentralization, the development of relative autonomy, comprehensible institutions, information about local events and their relations, and even participation in one's own administration might be directly possible. Instead, jurisdictional reforms and similar decisions for concentration and centralization are technologically justified (in the sense of professionalized reform) through such social "achievements" as consolidated schools and swimming pools. Despite all rhetoric to the contrary, the lack of participation is not the result of technical causes or of causes attributable to the "nature" of larger societies or to modernity as such.

A political-institutional "culture" based on the acquiescence as opposed to the participation of the citizens, on a system that is not actively legitimized but functions through its citizens' tranquility and proper role-playing, is today in a particularly precarious position, since the social balance is lacking. What exist are only municipal suburbs; gone are rural spaces. The functions of the bourgeois family, viable only as long as the family remained an intimate unit, are undergoing a process of technological evisceration. At any rate, forms of organization in which groups and principles other than those in the ruling society have a say, such as workers' organizations, are nonexistent on a total societal basis. They might exist, if at all, only in some isolated nooks. The giant Antaeus was strong only when he stood on the ground, from which he derived his strength. (According to the myth, his mother was Gaea, the earth goddess.) This myth should not be interpreted in a bucolic, agrarian-conservative, romanticizing, or even blood-and-soil manner; it must be taken as a parable of someone who, bereft of social place, can no longer breathe and so loses all strength. And in fact there are no forms of social organization that have replaced this principle of one's "own place," one's immediate orientation. Rootlessness and disorientation, intensified by these new information and communication media, and the professionalized, concentrated institutionalization of political-economic decisions complement, supplement, and justify each other. As a result, participation is possible only after individuals have undergone rigors comparable to a grueling cattle drive. The production and utilization of the information and communication media function according to spatiotemporal requirements distinct from those that would have to be considered were one interested in creating social spaces that accommodate the formation of personal integrity and identity. An administration that adapts to the large asocial spheres fulfills its functions by averting and by pacifying or privatizing social conflicts. Disoriented subjects, incapable of dealing with their vulnerabilities (which indeed are the results of social neglect), are forced to the periphery, unneeded, able at most to opt for "alternative" seclusion. The current vogue for group discussion, where isolated individuals take turns displaying their psychic wounds, illustrates this impotence, which now can only be "experienced." A society disintegrating into roles and role types also undergoes a disintegration within the individuals themselves.

Modernist Reforms as an Exacerbation of Psychic Impoverishment

The reform phase has long since come to an end. Restriction and repression are again the order of the day. For instance, the law enacted in 1969 to stimulate employment (*Arbeitsförderungsgesetz*) was followed by an amendment in conjunction with the 1975 budget balancing law (*Haushaltssicherungsgesetz*). The bountiful years of reform in youth, welfare, and health care spheres were followed by years of meager revenues and fiscal sobriety.

Were it just for this, it would be hardly worth the effort to recall what once were termed modernist reforms. Such reminiscences would at best belong in a retrospective survey of the episodic history of the Federal Republic.

At issue, however, are not merely short-lived fads or sudden shifts in the economy. While the death knell has sounded for the jargon of reform, the underlying calculus remains in force, precisely because the question has always been only one of jargon. This calculus, to which social scientists and educators have happily contributed, and its piecemeal realization bring out something that could be called social weightlessness. These conceptions are tied not to what is known of the individual's life potentials but to economic-bureaucratic possibilities and to anticipated constraints. It is precisely at the point where it seems they want to help solve the problems of individuals that these conceptions are infused with a dictating terrorism of liberation that prevents authentic renewal.

The following three examples will illustrate this policy, which intensifies and nurtures subjective impotence. In them I shall make no distinction between theoretical conceptions and political realization. My aim is only to call attention to certain critical points, not to do justice to the conceptions in their entirety. The examples are didactics and educational institutions, therapy, and "prevention" as the most recent principle of reform in general.

Learning, or the Pedagogical Art of Reducing the Human
Dimension to Naught in Order To Secure It Bureaucratically

It is no coincidence that formulas of (pseudo-)progressive pedagogies such as "learning to learn" are circulating today.[8] They give pronounced expression to the not particularly novel insight that personal life experiences are not sufficient to enable individuals to find their way. The complementary formula reads: "lifelong education." These slogans, which represent the ecstasy of modern pedagogical thinking, clearly express more than mere recognition of a lack in continuity. The authoritarian fanfare over substance and meaning, typical of older forms of pedagogy, is superseded by a process-oriented pedagogy: everything is in flux, and process pedagogics teach the art of permanent leave-taking. Education itself becomes a process without substance, or a process whose substance has already been supplied by the general societal development. The educational purpose is delegated, and the legacy of the Enlightenment is abandoned in favor of the ordinary diet of postmodern social respectability. Just as modern methodologies disdain epistemological considerations, banishing them to the realm of metaphysics or affixing them with the all-purpose adhesive of ideology, so this form of pedagogy disdains the discussion of ends and reference points. Emancipation is itself emancipated from the pedagogic subject, the lifelong pupil. "Only he who changes is my kinsman." Learning loses its appropriative character, which in certain circumstances could also inculcate resistance against new and different forms of learning. It becomes a multiple-choice exercise for which any instrument is acceptable. Such education does not instill an ability to process personal experiences (*Erlebnisse*) and expand upon them through the incorporation of general human experiences (*Erfahrungen*) taken from elsewhere; it makes the lack of general human experience (*Erfahrungslosigkeit*) into a pedagogical principle. Valid models no longer exist.

The problem is not addressed by speaking of "loss of a sense of reality."[9] Even in the past, everyday life experience (*Erlebnisse*) permitted no adequate general understanding (*Erfahrungen*) of reality, allowing at most the experience (*Erfahrung*) of a stably ordered impotence within the confines of an isolated nook. But we do not need the gilded image of the past. Its uses and abuses for normal behavior become clear only in the context of a systematic historical comparison. It is now apparent that everything was neglected that might have provided and rendered serviceable the experiential aids necessary for developing the ability to act in a transformed world. On the contrary, where conservative residues might still provide points of reference, they are being completely eliminated: tabula rasa is the pedagogical point of departure. The diluted and distorted reality, which the individual can experience only passively, is accessible within the educational system merely in segments and as a means for specifying roles: the idiocy coupled with expertise (*Fachidiotentum*), not unjustly criticized by the student movement, in which the intellect is limited to specialization and becomes idiotic the moment it quits the chemistry laboratory. What is systematically blocked is the concentric model of education, which instead of viewing general education as a package proceeds from the place of instruction, the place of work, the place of present life, and through participation and expansion makes possible the assimilation of general human experiences that are not self-experienced.

Such "functional" models of learning—one inquires in vain about the source of responsibility for the respective functions—correspond to the scant consideration accorded the social presuppositions and effects of school architecture and school organization. In the conceptualization and realization of Comprehensive Schools, the rational goal of eliminating social inequities was often pursued in disastrously abstract manner. It is particularly with regard to school organization and curricula, instituted equally for students and teachers, that the system loses touch with reality. Classrooms and teachers are abolished. Internally, the school is further divested of a sense of place; it becomes a nonlocality where, in the permanent "orientation stages," individuals become entirely disoriented. Guidance counseling becomes a new profession.

Therapeutic Inflation

For a long time mental illness was not properly acknowledged, not accepted as an illness — a state of affairs which, in terms of the legalities of medical insurance, still obtains today. Fully disparate sorts of psychological ailments, to the extent that they were treated at all, were shunted off into undifferentiated institutions and departments. Mental illness, behavioral disturbances in the stricter sense, whose endogenous causes are not unequivocal, were deemed moral problems to be "guarded against."

Today the picture has changed. The national inquiry into the state of psychiatry — whose recommendations were not acted upon, owing to financial considerations (see the characteristic response of the Federal Republic five years later)[10] — is filled with suggestions for the creation of a vast network of institutions that would span the entire Federal Republic and have a station in every town. Although the existing institutions and the number of trained physicians and social workers leave much to be desired, the "psychic dimension" has in the meantime been so fully discovered that it is heeded in tests and psychotherapeutic counseling of every description. The psychic suffering of the subject has become such a topic of discussion that what now causes concern is not the lack but the manner of its consideration. When attention is focused on the "subjective factor," social suffering is often ignored in favor of subjective suffering and the subjective mastery of suffering. The psychological patient, much like the pedagogized pupil, is no longer able to avoid therapy; the way has been cleared for a society of isolated and impaired subjects.

The critique of this inflation in the very different types of psychotherapy, an inflation that has not yet been successful in the sense of the aforementioned network of psychotherapeutic institutions, is not directed against the concern for psychic suffering, or the fact that such suffering is no longer suppressed in moralizing fashion, or that the patient is actually helped to adapt, sometimes even with the aid of psychopharmacology. Instead the critique takes issue with the therapy's lack of presuppositions and results. Psychotherapy is concerned primarily with problems stemming from the fact that various social institutions now make use of individuals only in specific roles, systematically ignoring their needs. Like the police—but frequently affecting the integrity of persons even more (although with different objectives and means)—psychotherapy dissolves the anomalous and attempts to resocialize (renormalize) it, as if the problem were eliminated the moment the patient did not return to the couch or therapeutic institution. In its conception and program, psychotherapy aims to prevent "psychological flipping out"; it commences at the "earliest possible stage."[11] Yet without a theoretical understanding of societal conditions (and one including their respective causes) or of what in every case are specific personal agonies, this type of psychotherapy threatens to render subjects even more helpless than they already are. Anomie is tending to become—and here arises the political issue—the problem of therapy; it is explained away as an individual problem. It is not only in the USSR that this problem exists, though it has emerged in particularly blatant fashion there. A psychotherapy that refuses to argue institutionally and to adopt an active social role becomes, like pedagogics, an instrumental aid that serves to make the demands of flexibility and mobility, demands psychologically difficult to meet, acceptable on a total societal basis.

Repression through Prevention

Reformers have long criticized the fact that the social safety net is always unfurled too late, that medicine has a curative and not a preventive function, and that the security authorities are impelled to act only after the child has already fallen into the drink, after juvenile X has become a criminal. Thus the watchwords are precaution, prevention, avoidance. One does not fall ill, one avoids illness through early detection; one does not become a homeless person, one is integrated into society in due time. Who could object to this?

It is fairly obvious that the strategy of prevention within the domain of "internal security," the police, is not without problems. To equip the police preventively, the current practice not only in the Federal Republic but also in other Western countries, involves allowing them to be present even where nothing has yet occurred, where grounds for suspicion do not exist. Moreover, it requires that the police be outfitted with instruments for surveillance and for securing information, enabling them to work within broad social spaces and permitting them to recognize dangers clearly. The consequences of such preventive policing are evident: it is necessary to destroy the integrity of spaces and persons if from the very outset—totally, as it were—they are to be protected against crime. Prevention involves the exchange of all civil rights for a guaranteed security, which certainly cannot be so thoroughly guaranteed.

Yet however much these considerations may shed light on police preventive strategy, however much they might convince us that the costs of such security are too high (even if realities currently indicate otherwise), the situation seems fundamentally different when we look to the health care sphere. Who would not do everything to avoid illness? Moreover, it hardly seems appropriate to compare the security interests of physicians with those of policemen. Surely we cannot, and surely we must. Prevention that is rational in and for itself cannot be considered—and this holds for the domain of internal security as well—"in itself," apart from its social realization, but only within a given context. It then becomes apparent that the situation in social and medical prevention is more problematic than that of either smallpox vaccination, which in its day was also resisted, or the wrongly disputed prescription that one fasten one's seatbelt before driving. In welfare and health care policy this form of prevention takes place at bureaucratic levels, by means of legal regulation and from a perspective that treats citizens as clients. (Here mention will not even be made of the dominance of natural scientific medicine and its technologized, professionalized dismemberment and social isolation of the patient.) Yet if prevention is pursued in bureaucratic fashion, it then not only becomes tantamount, like the avoidance strategies of the police, to a mode of control oriented to the destruction of integrity and identity; it also becomes unable, all pledges notwithstanding, to fulfill its avowed intentions. At most it can have a socially pacifying effect, fully repressing a residue that cannot be handled bureaucratically. The themes of expanding legal regulation (*Verrechtlichung*) and the repression (*Verdrängung*) or individualization of what proves to be unmalleable are interrelated.

One feature of modernist reforms is the continuation of the bureaucratic administrative state by other means. This is linked to the fact that the organizational problem, which is absolutely central, is suppressed and argued about only functionally, with regard to specific tasks. But argumentation from the perspective of these tasks remains without substance since the tasks are not directly related back to specific political objectives. Hence an extended conventionalism is guaranteed *ab ovo*, to the extent that "reform" is considered at all. The argumentation is weakened, moreover, since no adequate analysis is provided of the importance placed upon the tasks. "Learning to learn," the construction of therapeutic institutions, and prevention appear to be ends in themselves. The lack of referents (which permits hidden reference to the ruling institutions) and the deficient historical justification (the announcement of the interest-bound causes of certain problems and the interest-bound suggestions for their solution) parallel the jargon of innovation and the aspiration to professionalization. (A truly classic example is found in the numerous recommendations developed within the sphere of juvenile assistance, recommendations which, it is true, have thus far not been acted upon, largely due to financial considerations.[12]) Small wonder that social scientists are here the ones most active in advancing recommendations. It is of little importance that one concept after another fails, if the learning process itself comes to a fatal conclusion.

The suppressed political anthropology has become obvious. Only in this way can one understand why individuals, with the best of intentions and the clearest conscience, hold on to considerations concerning techniques for "resocializing" subjects while refusing to analyze the roots of the helplessness itself.

The Pact of Intellectual Submission

The contemporaneity of noncontemporaneous phenomena—a ploughing peasant here and a factory producing semiconductors there—is an intriguing topic. In varied forms such noncontemporaneity is always present. Even the topic of this essay is one of noncontemporaneity: on the one hand the claim and social fact of self-confident individuals, capable of motivation and self-direction, who are apparently obsolete, like the peasant behind his horse; and on the other hand the socially institutionalized adaptation requirements, in which only a "subjective factor" remains, leaving individuals to their own suffering, their own therapy, or their own socially irrelevant leisure time.

But even the contemporaneity of mutually corresponding phenomena is puzzling if one does not invoke a mechanical notion of connection. Vietnam attacks Cambodia, China attacks Vietnam; Eurocommunism is a pallid hope, and Eurosocialism is from the very outset compromised in statist manner; "crises of meaning" are indicated; TUNIX [Do-Nothing] congresses are held;[13] infinite richness is discovered in the realm of private relations and elevated to poetic heights; there is much talk of identity crisis and indeed the crisis of Marxism. It would thus be surprising, albeit altogether desirable, were devotees of theory in particular and intellectuals in general to remain unaffected by such developments. Today when theory, the comprehension of what is and what can be, is direly needed, its death knell tolls again, as if the specified events and their background had devalued or even rendered impossible theoretical work. Hans Magnus Enzenberger writes:

Instead of this, our theoreticians, bound to the philosophical tradition of German idealism, refuse to admit what every bystander has long understood: namely, that there exists no world spirit; that we do not know the laws of history; that class struggle is also a "nature-like" (naturwüchsig) process, which no vanguard can consciously plan or direct; that social as well as natural evolution has no subject and is, for that reason, unpredictable; that when we act politically we never achieve what we intend, but something else, something we may not have even imagined. It is here that the crises of all positive utopias have their base. The projects of the nineteenth century have one and all been falsified by the history of the twentieth.[14]

These are global statements. Nonetheless, Enzenberger is correct in his contention that a whole series of issues should have been comprehended by us ("leftist") intellectuals long ago.

Not only is no revolution waiting for us at the corner or even around the block; it is also impossible to assert convincingly that capitalist society, owing to its contradictions and conflicts, will dig its own grave. Certainly it does not itself create those who will "overcome" the system.

Within the womb of this society grows no socialist bastard who could lay the foundations for a new and more humane realm. The dialectic of history prophesied by Marx is halfway paralyzed. Capitalist society devours the revolution directed against it and pervasively brands its children.

In this is also implied that the socialist hope cannot be based on the proletariat, as if this were an indestructible touchstone. Instead of becoming a historicopolitical subject, this proletariat, despite exploitation and undeniable structural inequality, becomes a subjectum, fully incorporated into the capitalist process, a subordinate which, even in its conflicts, is flesh of the flesh of capitalist society.

There also no longer exists a country, a geographical-social place, a territory-occupying utopia that could provide reference and serve as a source of inspiration. This rootlessness of hope existed even before the Chinese-Vietnamese War or Deng's visit to the United States. Some time ago Michel Foucault had already formulated the problem in the following way:

Today, as the succession to Mao Zedong is being settled with weapons, it can be stated that for the very first time since, perhaps, the 1917 October Revolution or the great revolutionary movments of 1848, there is not a single place in the world through which a ray of hope could still shine. There no longer exists a point of orientation. There is no single revolutionary movement and even less a single "socialist country" to which one could refer in order to state: this is how things ought to be done. We have been thrown back to the year 1830; we must begin anew.[15]

Far and wide there is no adequate theory—unless one is willing to seal one's eyes and mouth with the honey of eternally juvenile inanities—which could point to ways out of the paralysis of dashed hopes, to solutions, to the means of gaining territory. Of course, easy explanations of the situation are in no short supply. Yet a theory that explains a totality and is nonetheless valid for the details as well, a theory consisting not merely of vague tendencies but of specific lines of development, a theory finally that would pave the way for action (and not just in a casual manner)—such a theory seems possible today only as charlatanry.

Thus what reigns is insight into the incomprehensible complexity of the situation; an everyday structuralism defines the feeling for time and "theory"; an active society is possible only as a technocrat's dream;

theory can at most be realized in fragmentary investigations of the particular aspects and moments of an insuperable complexity. A new modesty seems appropriate, a concentration of features of simple, everyday life. A romantic retreat to every possible alternative and all varieties of resignation is underway.

Yet the correct insights summarized by Enzenberger do not support his thesis as a whole. The fact that these insights must be reacquired once more only argues against those intellectuals who again have delegated their powers of reflection to a party, a country, or a grand theory. Most recently Stalinism—beyond any specific problems and disappointments, which always exist—was an irrefutable warning both against the sacrifice of political reason and against trusting any variety of a politics by proxy. Stated somewhat solemnly, history will not permit the regeneration of avoidable naiveté without cost; nor will it allow innocent acts of delegation. But Enzenberger's summary is wrong not on account of this historically avoidable repetition. It is wrong because it suggests an unavailable alternative, one Hilde Domin has termed "humanity in one's lifetime," that is, "concrete" politics in the here and now.[16] Disregarding those who require dogma for psychic stability, is there anyone who would want to deny that one cannot trust the grand "teachings" of the nineteenth century and that in this sense one must "take leave of the nineteenth century" (even this insight could long ago have been found in Kierkegaard, Nietzsche, Burckhardt, and Max Weber)?

It is here, however, that we have to stop. To discard altogether the theoretical insights of the nineteenth century, those of Marx and Freud and of Weber as well, is to engage in a type of analytic self-amputation. For in this case the world could be comprehended, in fact, only as a fate, a *Geschick*, one would just have to accept. Certainly it would be wrong to adopt these insights without question or to elevate them to the rank of a *Weltanschauung*, to relate to them in the manner of a discipline or as one would to a positivist-normative theory from which one need only draw "implications"; it would be wrong, in short, not to correct and further develop them. Yet to relinquish or renounce them would only be to surrender the human claim to understand relations in their connection, and to do so not out of necessity but only because the claim has become burdensome. For instance, is it true that Marx's analysis of capitalism—beyond the assertions about capitalism's collapse and the hope for revolution—has in its approach and its core really been refuted? And how are we to relate to Freud, even if it be acknowledged that he derived his model of socialization from Viennese society and that the Oedipus complex was perhaps simply a very bourgeois phenomenon?

Even if this were true, even if Marx and Freud and *tutti quanti* have nothing more to contribute to the "elucidation of the horizon" (to cite Jaspers briefly), even then theoretical work would not be as nonsensical and obsolete as Enzenberger wants to believe. The host of unresolved problems does not release us from engaging in theoretical exertion, from clarifying, in Faustian language, "what holds the world in its innermost structure together"—unless one confuses conceptual exertion (*die Anstrengung des Begriffs*) with being trusting. But even if we were able to explain the dominant connections, we would still lack the tools required for their destruction and transformation.

There is yet a second error in the arguments of Enzenberger and others. From ossified and dashed hopes—like so many shards of ice, to recall Caspar David Friedrich's painting—nothing has been learned but the need to abandon or to scale down the hopes vested in theory and practice, as if the errors and misguided actions of the master thinkers and the master builders were thereby overcome. Obviously, people fail to recognize that this modest approach to self-organization, even if pursued with thoroughly critical and constructive intent, must remain, precisely for the sake of "humanity in one's lifetime," an illusion, a form of wishful thinking at best. Today the danger exists that the innermost presuppositions of a humanity in one's lifetime are eroding away. Were one truly intent on taking leave of the nineteenth century, it would not suffice merely to erase the idealist X in front of the bracket while adhering to the bracket itself, namely the concept of the (bourgeois) individual, of integrity and identity, together with the concept of the liberal (bourgeois) state and corresponding society. Whatever one might want to criticize in the so-called master thinkers, it must not be their goal of providing an analysis of society in its entirety. A politics of small efforts, of small steps, of specifically limited actions can be pursued in a meaningful way only if one is simultaneously aware that this type of politics is in fact threatened by a fundamental crisis in the concept of humanity still so familiar to us all. This crisis has also gripped the institution of the liberal state. A politics of small efforts that fails to recognize this remains romantic in the pejorative sense, a cheap flight into a remote nook.

The intellectual pact of submission involves, it seems to me, privatizing one's intellect or applying it to concrete politics, now that one can no longer place it within grand theories or hide it under the hat of the nineteenth century. What must be criticized is by no means the call for humanity in one's lifetime. It is entirely correct to "leap" in this society, even if restraint and much patience are necessary. What must be criticized is the fact that people act as though this were a novel situation; the fact that the radical critique of domination is shunted aside, although today it is needed more than ever; the fact that people act as though the real possibility for a nonreal but existent socialism is a bluff or an unattractive relic. The intellectual pact of submission is tantamount to a monstrous form of self-effacement, a type of soul-searching (*Seelenarbeit*). This readily takes the form of bourgeois rectitude (*biedermännisch*) that secretly still entertains destructive fantasies (*brandstifterisch*).

Resignation or Morality: Against the Comfortable Absence of Conceptions

By way of coarse simplification, two forms of reaction are discernible today. The first, predominant in institutions, is that represented by neoideologues who, after the student movement, have been crawling out of their holes, clamoring for a return to what is time-tested yet resisting any fundamental change in institutional conditions. People must once again be "educated"—thus it resonates throughout the land from the lips of Tutzing, whose position is echoed by the president and the chancellor; and it also rings forth from Bonn, from the mouths of Lübbe, Maier, and others. This appeal, whose understanding of education is based on the motto found in old Greek school primers ("Whoever is not disciplined is not educated"), expresses nothing but helplessness. Nothing is offered beyond an "education" of prescriptions and proscriptions, of habitual inoculation and injection. There is no understanding of contemporary problems and behavior. These are seen as sources of annoyance. Thus in reactive fashion old miracle drugs are poured into new bottles. To be sure, this only exacerbates the problems. In contrast to Hebbel's Master Anton, who could no longer make sense of the world, people do know how these problems can be solved in case of emergency. Yet our concern here lies, first and foremost, not with this reactive form of helplessness, which is also apparent within the antiterrorist "struggle"; nor does it lie with this bureaucratic-repressive strategy for the programming of (self-) generated problems. What requires most consideration is the other form of reaction, that of professing liberals and leftists, the "adult" intellectuals.

For these intellectuals, theoretical resignation is supplemented by practical resignation. Have we not already seen, it is argued, where everything leads? Can it not be demonstrated why all solutions must necessarily fail? Theory can only show, so it is claimed, how new malicious deceptions always arise from new situations, despite good intentions. Thus people write novellas about personal conflicts, discover new forms of privacy, seek out rationality in a niche or in the "nation." I protest against these Münchhausen tricks, for I wish, without claiming any originality, to set in motion once again some theoretical-practical procedures. It is indeed a Münchhausen trick for individuals to adduce reasons as to why they cannot extricate themselves from the mire and why no helping hand is extended, and yet begin to make them-selves at home here, convinced that it will not consume them.

Theoretical-practical procedures have again to be set in motion for the reason that they were never subjected to proper intellectual scrutiny. Just because the powerful theoretical buttresses do not support as much as they were erroneously assumed capable of supporting, just because these theories do not land us with certainty upon the shore of praxis, does not mean that we should give up "history" and "class consciousness" altogether. Instead we must heed Hegel's warning and liberate ourselves once and for all from every metaphysics of certainty. The tide of history does not flow with certainty, nor can it be channeled with certainty. Even Troeltsch's historical wish, "Everything is in flux, give me a fixed point where I can stand," is in its methodological-existential uncertainty oriented to grand theories and their directives. In order to provide for a renewed theoretical-practical debate and its possible consequences, a few circumstances should be summarily noted.

1. The imperial theoreticians of the nineteenth century are certainly dead. One must give up the longing for such theories—*eritis sicut deus ipse* [you will be like God himself]—or for complete explanations as a peg on which to hang the entire world.

Yet the fact that the imperial theories (and their practical promise, laced with theoretical certainty) have been dethroned (an act that has long been obstructed by ideological anti-Communism) requires neither the abandonment of total societal analysis nor the dismissal of Marx's valid insights. Applied to the late-capitalist present, a developed form of Marxist analysis can even now generate more insights than all the prattling social scientific theories taken together. Applied in a modified way, Marxist analysis shows, for instance, that the modernist reforms of the 60s and 70s, with their promise of a Keynesian management of society, were wholly misguided, particularly on account of their logic of unlimited growth. If one wishes to reacquire forms of social experience and human self-understanding, if one wishes to resist the growing tendencies toward exclusion and seclusion in their manifold configurations, it is essential to protest against "total" reforms, against the mania for gigantic mobilizations and adaptations. In the mid-60s everyone spoke of an "educational catastrophe." Today the costs and consequences of an ill-conceived process of educational reform are scandalous. The case is similar with health care, and indeed with virtually every sector of this society. The real scandal, however, is that the continuous production of societal "scrap" is tolerated with a mere shrug of the shoulders or, at most, with regret by liberals and leftists, established intellectuals among them. Only rarely do these individuals express themselves, and then only cautiously, on such matters as the Decree against Radicals (*Radikalenerlass*), a clearly repressive measure that continues to be enforced.

The moral of the first story is that one definitely must not mourn bygone certainties; today unambiguous possibilities exist for both critique and engagement. It is clear, however, that considerable uncertainty exists about the criteria of critique, the social locus of critique, as well as about the criteria of what is to be considered "positive." Critics of the ruling society too long adhered to the conviction that it is enough to measure society by its own objectives. They became all too certain of the social locus of critique. Thus they were doubly neglectful. First, discussion of the criteria of critique was neglected. To what extent are they appropriate? What about the danger of surrendering the criteria of critique to the existing forms of social development—a danger to which the pseudoreformism at the end of the 60s, with all the phases of planning and total reform, had almost fully succumbed? Must one invoke judgmental standards that coincide, strangely enough, with conservative or reactionary ones? How are we to respond to those new pedagogues who speak as readily of a lack of education as they do of a lack of orientation? How is one to avoid affirming Gehlen's trust in institutions or Freyer's postulate of "orders established on cultivated ground," which oppose the "system of secondary education"? It cannot be denied that certain critical remarks in this essay also accord with utterances of conservative critics. But the radical difference is not just one of the direction of reference; nor is it adequately stipulated by indicating the object of reference: "state" and "order," here; "walking tall" and the "social nature of man" realized in a society without much domination, there. Rather, the distinction becomes fully apparent only when it is also understood as an analytical one. A critical analysis of domination and capitalism, a comprehensive critique of the form of bourgeois society, is absent among all those writers who invoke Hobbes or Thomas Aquinas, Montesquieu or Möser, among others. This analytic dimension has direct consequences not only for all the theses that criticize reality but also for the envisioned solutions to the observed problems.

The criteria of critique have not been adequately discussed even at those points where recourse is made to "negative" dialectics or "negative" anthropology. But equally grave is the second failing, namely, the inability to engage in a discussion of alternatives. Both directions provide possibilities for gaining ground.

2. Orientation is impossible if the hope for a "humanity in one's lifetime" is allowed to congeal into a meaningless farce. Not only is it unclear where one should begin; it is equally unclear how and in what direction one should proceed. If the Mescalero text is read as a critique of the present university system, its content and, above all, its form; and if, further, the story of Christiane F. is read as a critique of the present school system, its content and, above all, its form—and there are hundreds of such tests—it then becomes clear what is lacking and what must elude the reactive "grasp for education": namely, an involving, participatory cultivation of experience. At the beginning of this essay the danger of a society of conditioned reflexes was outlined with reference to Elias's *The Civilizing Process*: the danger of such a society appears as handwriting on the wall. This is a society of individuals incapable of resistance, who stew in the juice of their own irrelevant subjectivity and who, at best, can express themselves in irrational outbursts, a society that at the same time is undergoing a process of bureaucratic ossification. The motto to whitewash this graffiti cannot read: Let us search for a lost internal policing force and replace paternal repression with civic education. Instead, the goal can only

be to realize in a nonbourgeois form such bourgeois values as "emancipatory minima," self-sufficiency, and the capacity for orientation without fear. Thus a double leave-taking is called for: not only from the traditional form of bourgeois socialization, which is undergoing a process of disintegration, but also from those somewhat new (compensatory) forms of socialization which now can only encourage adaptation and flexibility (with the corresponding waste).

Yet it has still not been determined whether it is in fact possible to maintain such bourgeois values as the identity and integrity of the person in nonbourgeois fashion, with the aid of new and different forms of socialization, through participation, decentralization, and, to the extent possible, reduction of the division of labor. To be more precise, it has still not been determined whether such values can be achieved at all, for the notion of patricide inheres in the bourgeois identity. A radical discussion of precisely these orientational criteria is indispensable, and so is, in the interest of humanity, a radical adherence to definite values and to the specific and proper forms required to ensure their realization.

3. In order even to be able to take advantage of the present opportunity, one admittedly immensely difficult to actualize, a revitalization of theory formation is of the utmost importance. This presupposes two things. First, it is necessary, with Hegel, to comprehend theory as a development, as a process, and not as a grand orientation that is complete from the very outset. Theory serves to formulate experiences acquired both through interaction with others and through contact with the circumstances under investigation. A theory complete from the outset and prior to all analysis and action is an absurdity. But even after a concept (or theory) is formulated, it continues to require confrontation with reality. The process of theory formation never comes to a close.

Second, it is essential to oppose cognitive and work-related diversion.[17] This diversion is responsible for the failure of collective and concentrated theoretical exertion. Intellectuals, social scientists in particular, are too often contemptuous of form. They analyze in a critical fashion, warding off barbs here and there, yet they conduct themselves according to the forms developed within universities, in liberal circles, in political parties, and elsewhere—hectic, harried, and absorbed, dispersed in a myriad of pressing obligations. Forgotten is the fact that theoretical work takes years, especially if one does not wish to remain bound to conventions or to make fashionable reputation-securing discoveries, and that new social forms must be found for the sake of theoretical work. The "crisis of Marxism," a topic in vogue today, is understood not as an organizational crisis of "Marxists" but as a "crisis in thought" itself. Without a (counter-)organization, however, and without carefully considered institutional forms that observe the principle of organizational austerity, nothing can be achieved, either in theory or in practice. Leftist intellectuals are squandering their energies.

The tasks of theory formation are certainly not difficult to locate: the removal of continually produced ideological debris is by no means an unimportant component of the task. Political struggle is concerned not least of all with concepts, with what people tend to understand as reality; conceptual clarification with regard to the model of socialization as earlier outlined is another task. For instance, is it possible and not purely illusory to demand, as in this essay, an adherence to selected bourgeois values, while opposing others like the Lockean-Kantian "desire for possession and power," or even to postulate altogether nonbourgeois forms? It is in a twofold sense that we speak of "the limits of bourgeois society": not merely with regard to limits specific to bourgeois society itself—capitalism and traditional bourgeois society growing further and further apart—but also with regard to our own limits. Is there no qualitative transcendence of a radicalized citizenry (Bürgerlichkeit)? Is not the damage done to our being, apparent not only in the Federal Republic and not only in capitalistically developed countries, demonstrable proof of the presence of a considerable number of the fundamental conditions necessary for social organization and the realization of a humane life? Here it would also be appropriate to examine systematically, from the perspective of the "logic of collective action," the abundant studies on workers' consciousness (a consciousness clearly not to be restricted to that of industrial workers). What interests are constituted and under what conditions? How do the normal forms of reaction and action materialize? In order to clarify this logic of collective action and of individual acting or nonacting, it would be necessary to redefine, without the scholastic palaver about productive and nonproductive labor, the meaning and the limits to the meaning of the sphere of production.

4. If there is to be a farewell to the nineteenth century, in the sense of further emancipation, then by all means let it be a more radical farewell! The conclusion that a resigned modesty is in order, since no

comprehensively dominant theories are available to usher us into the land of redemptive practice, only reveals that, while we realize that the umbilical cord has been severed, we are still afraid of proceeding autonomously. Albert Schweitzer, far more radical than many who rashly reach for this or that theoretical or "alternative" tranquilizer, once said, "Resignation is the corridor through which we enter the realm of ethics." Walter Schulz drew from this the following conclusion: "The belly of the ethically acting individual is vulnerably exposed." He writes further:

Resignation, however, is connected to life in a practical way. . . . It implies that I must have attained the freedom that enables me to do what I am doing, even with regard to possible failure. Obviously, ethics would be little more than an intellectual game . . . if it did not strive for real success in optimizing the potential of humanity. Yet we shall never succeed in putting an end to the evil that has ruled history since its very beginning. Not to repress this insight and yet to act on the belief that a superior form of humanity will one day become reality is the paradox to which every ethic is subject.[18]

This way of speaking is quite common, being that of traditional philosophy. And yet the approach seems valid on anthropological grounds as well.

Bourgeois modernity is based on a contradictory image of man. This can be illustrated, on the one hand, by way of Hobbes and Luther and, on the other, by way of Erasmus. Human nature is perceived either as totally corrupt or else as *bene condita natura humana* (good human nature). Both positions are similar, however, in their early bourgeois foundations: they are based on the assumption of an asocial individual. Curiously enough, a large part of the history of theory, especially that of political theory in the more general sense, can be traced back to these explicitly, or at least implicitly, employed models of interpretation. The Hobbes/Luther tradition is comparatively stronger. Those theories—chiefly those of Marxists—which emphatically postulate a theoretical-practical "maker" relationship, maintain an optimistic position, even if Marx himself did so on the basis of a decided revision of the individualistic approach. Man becomes *animal sociale, zoon politikon*; the goal is now social sociability and not bourgeois asocial sociability. All the realism of the analysis of capitalism notwithstanding, the optimistic attitude vis-à-vis the agent and bearer of the "new" society, that is, the proletariat, remains unchanged. Herein lies the basis for the theoretical and practical failure of the thesis concerning revolution.

Now, instead of resolving the dilemma, people dismiss the theory-practice promise, reducing theory to piecemeal analysis and practice to what is individually expedient at the moment—the semblance of privacy held intact by the cushioning privileges of the Federal Republic. In this way they do not escape the nineteenth century; they actually fall into its clutches. Instead of viewing as undialectical the assumption that success is an all or nothing proposition, they give up both conceptual exertion and revolutionizing praxis, claiming that "conditions" are not favorable.

Real opportunities as well as the justified fear of a process, one able to hasten its own development, toward a Skinnerian society of bureaucratically produced conditioned reflexes and a multiplicity of self-disabling social wrecks make it imperative—I don't deny the moral gesture—that "old European" intellectuals shed their sullenness and their self-satisfied criticisms. This at any rate holds for those intellectuals who both reject cheap cynicism and are willing and able to address concepts of democracy and socialism on their own terms. But we should not overestimate the chances. Drug addicts, unemployed youth, and the many people flirting with the various alternatives, all clearly attest to the need for a radical departure from the ruling forms of education and politics. However, they are not the agents who would be able to set in motion discussion about new forms of society. Nonetheless, it is in these individuals and their suffering, in these groups and their difficulties that the proper reference points for the discussion of their form and direction clearly crystalize. Furthermore, it is precisely in and alongside the educational and sociopolitical institutions that untapped possibilities materialize. The adumbrated dangers need not be embellished to recognize the host of efforts that in schools, among social workers, and even outside institutions are engaged in exploring processes for a more humane cultivation of experience, processes providing for self-sufficient and even resistant action. Thus points of reference are to be found not only where the dominant societal procedures have failed but also where individuals or groups have altered, extended, or even transcended these social forms.

This discussion of form (and content) cannot be restricted to a critique of the existing forms of articulation and organization, the reality of an obstructed society. Such a discussion must explore alternative models. For this, the regulative principles include decentralization, orientation to concrete conditions, the elimination of role divisions or distinctions, and real as opposed to spurious participation in decision-making processes.

That individuals and groups be willing to engage in such undertakings is "most emphatically to be desired." At any rate, there is no excuse for those intellectuals, irrespective of the dictates of fashion, who belatedly find their humility while playing with fire in the haystack of the nineteenth century. Rather than engaging in such indulgences, intellectuals would do far better to break ground for that first or second vacation home. Yet only those should speak of humanity in one's lifetime who dare to subject ruling forms (and contents) to radical criticism and who dare to call for strongly contrasting measures here and now. Otherwise, only more clever or more foolish forms of rationalization will remain.

Notes

1. See the concise and pithy survey by Michael Schumann, "Entwicklungen des Arbeiterbewusstseins, Schwierigkeiten, die veränderte soziale Lage zu interpretieren," *Gewerkschaftliche Monatshefte* 3, (1979):152–59. I will deliberately make only sparse use of quotations, and then only to refer bibliographically to the source of borrowed thoughts and formulations. This essay is connected with a larger work on the limits of bourgeois society. Much of the empirical (background) documentation and experience is drawn from a recently completed project, the results of which have been published in *Verrechtlichung und Verdrängung* (Frankfurt, 1981).

2. See W. Kraushaar's perceptive overview of the problem, "Thesen zum Verhältnis von Alternativen- und Fluchtbewegungen," in Kraushaar, *Autonomie oder Getto?* (Frankfurt, 1978), pp. 8–67.

3. See the reflections on the problem of violence in the "scene," in "Verpisst Euch! Zum Gewaltproblem in der Szene," *Pflasterstrand* 49 (March 1979):22–23.

4. Schumann, "Entwicklungen des Arbeiterbewusstseins," p. 157.

5. Disorientation and the search for orientation, feelings of inferiority and the search for recognition or the uncontrollable need for attention run through Christiane F.'s report like a red thread. See *Wir Kinder vom Banhof Zoo*, transcribed by Kai Hermann and Horst Rieg (Hamburg, 1979).

6. This citation is taken from Ida R. Hoss, "Sozialplannung und die kontrollierte Gesellschaft," *Bauwelt* 63, no. 38–39 (September 1972):221–228, esp. p. 222.

7. For a normatively excessive confirmation, see Niklas Luhmann, *Legitimation durch Verfahren* (Neuwied and Berlin, 1968), and critically: Murray Edelman, *Politics as Symbolic Action: Mass Arousal and Quiescence* (Chicago: Markham, 1971).

8. See also Walter Schulz, *Philosophie in der veränderten Welt* (Pfulligen, 1974), p. 651ff.

66

Wolf-Dieter Narr

9. See Arnold Gehlen, *Man in the Age of Technology*, translated by Patricia Lipscomb (New York: Columbia University Press, 1980).

10. *Bericht über die Lage der Psychiatrie in der Bundesrepublik Deutschland*, Publication 7/4200 of the German Parliament, 2 vols.; *Stellungnahme der Bundesregierung zum Bericht der Sachverständigenkommission über die Lage der Psychiatrie in der Bundesrepublik Deutschland*, German Parliament Publication 8/2565.

11. See H. E. Richter's plea in the preface to *Wir Kinder vom Banhof Zoo*.

12. Cf. *Dritter Jugendbericht*, edited by the Federal Minister for Youth, Family, and Health (Bonn, 1972).

13. This is a reference to a meeting of a number of the groups comprising the "alternative" subculture, held in 1978 at the Technical University of Berlin (*tr.*).

14. Hans Magnus Enzenberger, "Zwei Randbemerkungen zum Weltuntergang," *Kursbuch* 52 (May 1978):1–8, here p. 7.

15. Cited by Ulrich Greiner, "Der Untergang der Titanic: Das Desaster der Linken ist nicht nur ein Desaster der Linken," *Frankfurter Allgemeine Zeitung* 231, October 19, 1978.

16. See the lecture by Hilde Domin under the same title, published in *Süddeutsche Zeitung*, July 29, 1978.

17. The central concept of diversion is discussed, albeit in a modified form, by Walter Benjamin in "The Work of Art in the Age of Mechanical Reproduction," *Illuminations*, translated by Harry Zohn (New York: Schocken Books, 1969), pp. 217–251, esp. p. 237ff.

18. Cf. Schulz, *Philosophie in der veränderten Welt*, p. 651ff. Also see Norbert Elias, *The Civilizing Process*, translated by Edmund Jephcott (New York: Urizen Books, 1978).

Ungovernability: On the Renaissance of Conservative Theories of Crisis

Claus Offe

A number of structural similarities exist between neoconservative theories of the "ungovernability" of state and society and the socialist critique of late-capitalist social formations.[1] For obvious reasons these similarities are not emphasized by either side. Such parallels become clearer when we compare the theoretical and practical constellations that determined the debate in 1968 with those ten years later. The comparison shows that in both macrosociology and political science, theories of crisis have undergone a radical change in their sociopolitical base.

In 1968–69 leftists were the ones who advanced the theoretical arguments and held the practical conviction that "it cannot go on like this." They assumed that class contradictions, in however modified a form, and the ensuing struggles must result in the dissolution of the basic structure of capitalism, together with its corresponding political constitution and its cultural-ideological system. In a perhaps overly enthusiastic "dismantling" of the corresponding basic assumptions, Koch and Narr have shown that the left today lacks a solid foundation in crisis theory, something they claim can be found at most in the efforts of a few manipulators of scholastic concepts.[2] At the same time the theoretical positions employed to defend the existing order, which was so strenuously affirmed in 1968, have been almost totally silenced. Today bourgeois consciousness is everywhere engaged in doomsday ruminations over its fate. The limits of growth and of the welfare state, the world economic, financial, and environmental crisis—including the crisis of legitimation or "the crisis of the authority of the state"—have become standard topics, presented in every conservative or liberal newspaper to characterize the national and international state of society. That "it cannot go on like this" is a conviction that today inspires conservatives, while the crisis theories stemming from the critique of political economy have themselves become questionable, or at the very least can no longer yield the optimistic political conclusions that once constituted their very essence. Certain members of the left, unable to rely on their theoretical certainties, are now displaying the withdrawal symptoms of a "new irrationalism." By contrast, theoretical and practical points are being scored, it appears, by those who have long considered political modernization in the direction of social democracy as a road to crisis.

Not only has the neoconservative crisis literature almost completely removed the remnants of its leftist counterpart from the sphere of public attention; it has also skillfully redefined and adapted for its own purposes certain positions and approaches that derive from the tradition of a critical theory of advanced capitalism (from theories of the fiscal crisis of the state, legitimation problems, conflicts associated with structural disparities and fringe groups, ecological crises). But what is most remarkable is that this literature, or at least a large part of it, identifies crisis causes that are directly or indirectly connected with the continuing explosiveness of class conflicts or their inadequate institutionalization, that is, with the problem of the base, which sociologists and political scientists during the 50s and 60s sought to deny or to provide with a definite solution. Much of this literature reads like a series of case studies confirming the Marxist thesis that bourgeois democracy and the capitalist mode of production stand in a precarious and immanently indissoluble relation of tension to each other. The difference consists only in the fact that the neoconservative theorists of crisis see the source of crisis, and what they wish to eliminate, not in conditions of capitalist wage labor but in the institutionalized arrangements of welfare-state mass democracy. "That which Marxists erroneously ascribe to the capitalist economy," writes Huntington, "is in reality a result of the democratic political process."[3]

I shall begin by addressing the political aspects of the crisis theory, which has shifted its base to the conservative camp (I), and will turn then to a presentation and critique of its analytic content (II). By way of conclusion, I shall return to the relationship between crisis and capitalist development (III).

I

The political aspects result first from the diagnosis of the problem of ungovernability, that is, its identification subject to specific pragmatic premises; second, from the prognosis, or the prediction regarding the probable course and the individual symptoms of the crisis; and third, from the recommended therapy and its variants. Neoconservatives, we note, often employ a medical-biological metaphor in presenting the crisis theory; this of course has the effect of modeling the structural problems of society on the patient-doctor relationship.

Let us begin by looking at the diagnosis. It details the immediate danger of a chronic or even acute failure of the state. This has two components: first, the expectation-overload to which state power is exposed under conditions of party competition, pluralism of associations, and relatively free mass media. This results in a constantly growing burden of expectations, obligations, and responsibilities with which government is confronted and which it cannot escape. But why is government unable to fulfill them? This question is related to the other component of the diagnosis: the intervention authority and the steering capacities of the state apparatus are in principle too limited to be able to process effectively the burden of these demands and expectations.

The first component of this diagnosis refers quite plainly to an overstretching of claims to welfare-state services and democratic participation—an inappropriate politicization of themes and conflicts, whereby expression is given to "the unbridled and mindless covetousness of the citizens."[4] The second component of the diagnosis is related to the economic and poitical guarantees of freedom: an effective processing of the avalanche of claims would be conceivable only with the annulment of some of the constitutional guarantees whose continued existence ties the hands of state power. "Whoever says A must also say B; whoever desires indivisible state responsibility must also be prepared to sacrifice many enjoyed freedoms."[5] Such formulations of the problem recall, down to the last detail, certain determinations of the political crisis network found in the Marxist tradition. From this viewpoint the concept of liberal democracy presents a deceptive unity of elements that in fact are not amenable to combination, indicating instead ruptures that are at most temporarily obscured under conditions of prosperity.[6] Unlike the "false apocalypse of the bourgeoisie" (J. Schumacher), which in the 20s accounted for the mass success of, say, Spengler's *Decline of the West*, the new crisis scenarios of the conservatives have proven resistant to the Marxist critique of ideology and to the suspicion of being mere propaganda and mystification. This is due not only to their clearly improved theoretical quality but also to the fact that they retain—albeit for opposing political purposes—a central component of the political-economic crisis argument that the theoretical left had long held to constitute its own theoretical superiority.[7]

Crisis symptoms are expressed, so the conservative analysis continues, in the frustrations caused by the disparity between the volume of claims and the government's steering capacity. This leads first to a noticeable loss of confidence in the relation between party organizations on the one hand and their voters and members on the other, which results from the fact that the parties must almost necessarily frustrate the expectations they generate in obtaining a governing majority.[8] The promises of a given party platform remain unfulfilled, whereas the blunt methods such as wage and price controls, increased taxation, added regulation, whose use the party had previously explicitly renounced, must nonetheless be put into operation.[9]

The disappointments accumulated in this manner may release their explosive force in one of two directions. Either they lead to a polarization within the party system, to a reideologizing and "fundamentalizing" of the praxis of a particular opposition, which then seeks to avoid the predicament of the tension between expectations and performance capacity through principled alternative programs; or, where such a polarization process does not occur, there is the likelihood of a decrease in the canalization capacity of political parties, in their capacity to articulate the electoral will and, conversely, to contribute to its formation. In this case it is further to be expected that the established parties will be opposed by political movements for which the goal of parliamentary struggle and the possible exercise of governmental power are not of primary significance. Both alternatives—polarization within the party system and polarization between the party system and social movements operating in a nonparliamentary fashion—must lead to a further exacerbation of the basic situation. The level and volume of articulated demands increase, just as the action capacities of the besieged state decrease. Thus in essence the prognosis implies that the basic discrepancy between claim level and performance capacity unleashes a dynamic ensuring that this discrepancy is reproduced in intensified form: an ungovernable system always becomes more ungovernable. One cannot assume the existence of built-in mechanisms or so-called self-healing forces, as in economic cycles, to reverse the trend (for the opposite view see Huntington[10]). Rather, at some unknown but possibly not too distant point in time, extensive breakdowns and even a disintegration of organized state power will occur.

This course of development is to be prevented by a therapy whose two variants correspond to the two components of the diagnosis. Either it can aim at diminishing the overloading of the system with claims, expectations, and responsibilities, or it can attempt to enhance its steering and performance capacity.

Let us begin by examining the first variant, claim reduction. If I am not mistaken, three forms of implementation are at issue here. They are of particular interest in the Federal Republic because they still seem to be mostly at the "testing" and development stages (although in part without clear connection to the aforementioned arguments of crisis theory). In classifying these strategies I am making use of Luhmann's assumption according to which there are in principle four societal media through which social claims and expectations can be processed: (1) political power relations, (2) monetary, exchange, and market relations, (3) cultural norms or socialization relations, and (4) the medium of truth or knowledge. Therefore if, as suggested by the crisis hypothesis of ungovernability, the political medium of processing demands is to be unburdened, then each of the other three media must be considered as the object of a possible strategy.

The proposal to redirect claims that go beyond the "boundaries of the social welfare state" toward monetary exchange relations, that is, markets, is on everyone's lips today. The watchwords are the "privatization" or the "deregulation" of public services and their transference to competitive private enterprise. Examples are the conversion of public service performances from the support of "objects" to that of needy "clients," as in transportation policy, or more generally the introduction of cost-covering fees for residual public services. Other key phrases are the West German Council of Economic Advisers' "minimum wage unemployment" or even Friedman's "natural unemployment"—diagnoses of employment problems that recommend the reestablishment of a functioning market mechanism to dispose of such problems. Included here is a liberal proposal for industrial policy that in essence aims at, or limits itself to, demolishing protectionist enclaves that shelter individual sectors of the economy from the innovation-promoting fresh air of national and international competition. Generally it is a question of strengthening the workings of the mechanisms of "exit" against those of "voice" (Hirschman[11])—specifically, of dismantling the mechanisms of welfare-state security, as well as the political and economic power positions occupied by the trade unions in their struggle to establish and defend these mechanisms. The solution to the problem of ungovernability is expected to come from a restoration of the mechanisms of competition, which are supposed to arrest both inflation in the narrow sense and political demand inflation in the broader sense. In this connection mention must also be made of the projects that in the Federal Republic are connected with the slogan "the new social question" and that, while initially directed to a "reexamination" of the social welfare functions of the state, in fact amount to their reduction.

By contrast, the second strategy, which of course can be combined with the first, goes deeper. It is directed to the institutions of social control, to the agencies that regulate the formation and preservation of social norms as well as cultural and political value orientations. This strategy aims to promote values like self-restraint, discipline, and community spirit, to fortify national and historical consciousness, and to contain the postacquisitive values elaborated in the progressive doctrines of educators and social reformers. This last aim is to be accomplished with an alternate pedagogy that confronts questionable social-political circumstances with the slogan "Dare to Teach!" (*Mut zur Erziehung*) and which proceeds pedagogically from the maxim "That's just the way it is" (F. K. Fromme). Operating in the realm of socialization, these strategies employ tactics—from praise for the "earnestness" (*Ernstfalls Lehre*) of vocational training on the shop floor to attacks on broadcasting freedom, from the strengthening of parental rights in schools to the political disciplining of social studies teachers—that are so well-known that they need not be described here in detail. What is important to emphasize is that in these strategies, "deviant" interests, claims, and sociopolitical orientations are to be brought under control at their point of origin, whereas the first strategy is concerned with transferring the modalities of their fulfillment into extrapolitical domains, namely markets.

Third and finally, those claims and demands that can neither be prevented at their source nor shunted into other domains can be throttled in terms of their impact on the political-administrative system through the installation of filter mechanisms that would decide which of the claims merit being heard—whether certain claims should even be taken seriously as political inputs or should be dismissed as unrealistic or inadmissible. These filter mechanisms perform the function of rendering cognitive judgments, which themselves stand above the specific claimants and the institutions of a democratic process of will-formation and are not to be attributed to them. In the Federal Republic the Federal Constitutional Court fills the role of an institution that, independent of, and beyond the influence of, intragroup conflict, renders judgments regarding the common good.[12] The striking functional gains made by the Court in recent years can be interpreted almost entirely as the functional aspect of a resistance to claims; the same is true for other authorities, such as the Council of Economic Advisers and other scientific advisory bodies. Incidentally, within political science and political philosophy increased attention has been accorded the notion of an authority that stands above parties, counsels moderation, and claims a privileged access to knowledge of the common good.[13] Its promoters are active journalistically as well, defending the state against an overburdening of claims by social groups or discrediting those claims.

I shall take up again the question of whether and under what conditions these three claim-redirecting strategies are realistic after I present the other main variant of the therapy that follows from the ungovernability diagnosis. This encompasses all the strategies that, in the conflict between the overburdening by claims and steering capacity, concentrate not on the reduction and warding off of demands but, on the contrary, on an increase in the state's steering capacity. With regard to this variant of therapy, I would like to distinguish between an administrative and a political version.

The administrative strategy for the improvement of governmental steering and performance capacities—as stated in, say, the first draft of the Social Democratic party's Orientational Framework for 1985— provides for an increase in the state's share in the gross national product. It seeks to expand quantitatively and fiscally the elbow room the state has at its disposal. Likewise the regulatory capacity of the government is to be improved qualitatively and organizationally in order to achieve a higher degree of efficiency and effectiveness in political-administrative actions. At this level are to be found jurisdictional and functional reforms, an increased use of social indicators, the techniques of program budgeting and of cost-benefit analysis, and especially the concepts developed by Scharpf for improving the representation and consideration of real relations and interdependency in the process of policy formulation.[14] This strategy of administrative modernization is based on the principle of expanding the horizon for conceptualizing and acting—in both an objective sense, through a consideration of real interdependencies, and a temporal sense according to the principle of active-reformative long-range planning and problem anticipation.

Reflection and experience demonstrate rather quickly that such expansion of horizons is possible only if the consensual basis or the ability of the political-administrative system to absorb conflict can also be expanded. In other words, interdependencies can be adequately considered and long-term policies adequately conceptualized only if the requisite basis of consensus is successfully consolidated. The objective and temporal expansion of the performance capacity of governmental policy can succeed only if this corresponds to an expansion of the social alliances and mechanisms of integration on which it is to be based. Thus consensus becomes the decisive bottleneck.[15] Consequently, Scharpf recently affirmed (albeit in a manner requiring fuller explanation) the need for "new interpretations of reality that more properly correspond to the changed situation."[16]

The political version of the increased-performance strategy draws the consequences from this insight, most clearly in those political systems dominated by strong social democratic and labor parties. The arrangements that underlie Swedish economic and labor market policy, the Austrian "social partnership," the German "concerted action," the National Economic Development Council used in Great Britain equally by Labour and Conservative governments, and later the "social contract" between governments and trade unions—all these are examples of the attempts, intensified in the 60s and 70s, to enhance the performance capacity and steering effectiveness of state actions. This was attempted not only through intraadministrative forms of coordination but also through an institutionalization of alliances and consultative mechanisms among government, trade unions, employee associations, organizations of managerial personnel, and even consumer groups.[17]

Yet such consultative mechanisms, which under the title "liberal corporatism" have recently stirred lively interest in political science circles, are highly unstable constructions from two points of view. First, they represent extraparliamentary forms of political representation and to this extent stand in competition with the "proper" channels of political will-formation, a relation that remains ambiguous in terms of constitutional law. Second, it is altogether unclear in which relationship and about which questions groups are entitled or even obligated to negotiate. Nor is it any clearer what binding force the results thus achieved could have on either the government or the association members.[18] The solution to these difficulties lies, paradoxically, in a type of organized formlessness: strict shielding from publicity, informal discussions, personal agreements, cultivation of an attitude of concern. These are the preferred means of attaining a paraconstitutional cooperation on which every effort to enhance the performance and steering capacity of state policies depends.[19] Decisive for the creation of such alliances is the question of whether the organized interests affected by state policy are prepared to renounce their *obstructional* potential (which they possess in great measure), even as the interdependencies resulting from a given policy become more and more extensive.

Given this brief summary the highly descriptive value of the ungovernability thesis should be obvious. In my opinion the two components of the diagnosis fully and correctly circumscribe the functional problems that now confront the capitalist welfare and intervention state. The prognosis appears to be confirmed by a wealth of symptoms, manifested in the development of both the party system and the social movements of these countries, particularly the Federal Republic. And the five therapeutic approaches appear to comprise almost fully the reorganization strategies being practiced, particularly in northwest European political systems, either in explicit or implicit reference to the ungovernability thesis.

II

Marxists also affirm the partial validity of the conservative crisis theory. A policy statement of the German Communist party (DKP) asserts that "the capacity of governments to function has once again been called into question."[20] Just as conservatives adapt certain leftist theorems, so their analyses are in turn appropriated in Marxist and socialist theory. (See the characteristic position adopted by Wolfe with regard to Huntington's "The United States": "one need not agree with the Trilateral Commission's conclusions to be sympathetic to the analysis."[21]) In view of such unanimity we must ask whether the theoretical differences separating the liberal-conservative and materialist approaches to the social sciences have actually evaporated and whether the differences result less from the analysis itself than from the normative criteria and political aims with which the analysis is pursued. In other words, in a situation where everyone is convinced of the facts of the crisis and where general agreement exists regarding its symptoms and course of development, one is faced with the question of the specific political-theoretical role of crisis theories. The accused, who is to be indicted by the conventional crisis theories of the historical-materialist tradition, surprises the accuser not only by confessing without qualification but also by asking for sanctions not even sought by the accuser. Thus it has to be asked if the heirs of the leftist crisis theory are still able to offer insights and points that will not immediately be stolen by adversaries who bend them to fit their own ideology.

If one seriously wishes to speak of a crisis *theory*, then answers must be provided—beyond current scenarios and the pragmatic search for therapies—for at least two questions thus far unmentioned. First, what is the causative mechanism that in societies of this type always allows for the reemergence of a discrepancy between expectations and the political-administrative steering capacity? What is, to continue with the medical metaphor, the etiology of the ungovernability phenomenon? Second, and analogously, what justifies the expectation that the individual remedying strategies I have distinguished would be appropriate, either alone or in some combination, to bring the problem under control? Can the therapy be justified as a causal therapy? The answers to these two questions will ultimately indicate whether the ungovernability thesis is a scientific social theory that must be taken seriously or whether it is rather a crisis ideology conceived out of pragmatic considerations.

We start by looking at the various hypotheses and approaches that attempt to explain the origin of the problem. They can again be subdivided into those that are directed to an explanation of the growing pressure of expectation and those directed to the (relatively) decreasing steering capacity. According to a social-psychological theory of Maslow, the level and type of desires and demands directed to the political-administrative system fit a developmental pattern in which each achieved level of need satisfaction allows for the actualization of a qualitatively new category of needs. The empirical investigations conducted by Inglehart into the change of values in West European social systems can be interpreted within the framework of this social-psychological theory: "material" needs, those directed to the economic and military securing of social life, will permit, as soon as they are nearly satisfied, a different category of needs to step into the foreground—namely, postacquisitive needs, such as those for an actualization of universal moral-political and aesthetic values.[22] An independent logic or an independent meaning in the development of world-views and moral systems has also been espoused by Habermas, who in his theory of motivation crisis lays particular emphasis on the irreversibility of a once-achieved level of moral consciousness.[23]

Various approaches in the field of the sociology of culture—which are best understood as versions of the secularization thesis—refer, by contrast, to a process of deinstitutionalization. Scientific rationality and the welfare state destroy the agencies of social control and the bearers of traditional values, a development resulting in the dissemination of a political-moral and aesthetic hedonism whose satisfaction in turn engenders a further extension of the welfare state.[24] The agencies of the welfare state therefore produce, through paradoxical, latent functions, the very problems they are manifestly concerned with removing.[25] Thus Klages observes a "systemic crisis of a fundamental nature" in the fact that "a chasm yawns between the self-confidence, the societal understanding, and the 'objective' achievements of ruling political elites on the one hand, and the social-psychological realities of the subjective state of mind of individuals in welfare-state democracies on the other."[26] In a narrower sense theories in political science lay particular emphasis on the demand-inflating effect of party competition: through their programs the parties suggest to citizens demands and expectations that subsequently prove unrealistic, causing a spiral of constantly reinduced forms of "relative deprivation."[27] It has also been asserted that the international transfer of the norms underlying such demands and the effects of the competition among systems will result in a steady and uncorrectable overburdening of the state apparatus. Recently a role has been played by a hypothesis developed in the sociology of organizations, according to which the officers of large organizations like trade unions, in order to maintain their organization's internal cohesiveness and to secure themselves vis-à-vis competing organizations, are structurally forced to advance particularly drastic demands. This is especially the case in the discussion of organized interests (and the desirability of taming them through legal means[28]). Thus, for instance, Margaret Thatcher has expressed the view that in reality the conflict is not between trade unions and the state but rather among the union leaders themselves. An additional factor in the crisis-engendering increase in demands is said to be found in the specific interests of the officials who administer the social welfare state. It is argued that, while supposedly concerned with the welfare of the citizenry, these officials are in fact pursuing their own egoistic claims to power and patronage. (In all seriousness, Schelsky ascribes to them the character of a class.[29])

Finally, advocates of systems-theoretical and welfare economic models offer the explanation that under conditions of high societal complexity—which, owing to high informational costs, cannot be adequately conveyed either to the individual voter or to the members of an interest organization—there is always a tendency for an increase of claims and an overstraining of the political system. This is said to result from the fact that the side effects of the demands (such as inflation) are diffuse and therefore will not be considered by the individual making the demands.

The complexity argument also plays a role in explanations of the relatively or even absolutely decreasing steering capacity of the state. Basic to these explanations is the claim that an exponential growth occurs in the number of strategic criteria that must be observed by state institutions when processing welfare-state demands. Also basic is the claim that there is a corresponding increase in the veto power of those whose cooperation is essential for the realization of such programs.[30] A widely disseminated argument that is found in democratic theory and that seeks to account for deficient governmental steering capacity asserts that party competition and periodic election campaigns obstruct governmental action and planning (which are necessarily long-term in nature) and through discontinuities constantly hamper both the conceptualization and implementation of governmental programs.[31] Incidentally, both arguments furnish, as one can see, a direct grounding of and functional justification for attempts to extend the system of "liberal corporatism" (and in this specific sense hasten the "socialization" of state policies). The partial delegation of political-administrative decision matters to "mixed," semigovernmental authorities has indeed an advantage, at first glance, in that the partner in the strategic planning and execution of policy can to a certain extent be bound and sworn to cooperation. And it has the further advantage that such decision procedures are relatively insulated against the rhythm of election periods, election campaigns, and their disruptive influence.

What is conspicuous in this certainly incomplete list of explanatory approaches to the question of the emergence of the ungovernability phenomenon is the fact that they say as little about the concrete objects of conflict that constitute the substance of the demands and expectations as they do about the character of those matters requiring regulation, on which the steering capacity of the state founders as it attempts to master them. Of course, the proposed remedies for the problem of ungovernability identify at least indirectly which categories of demands and expectations must be reduced and neutralized, namely the individual and collective reproduction needs of labor power. And they also identify the specific obstacle on which the steering capacity of the state founders, namely the fact that the social power and blackmail capacity of capital (its ability to abstain from investing) can repel state intervention. At any rate, no great interpretive effort is required to decipher the stated ungovernability crisis as a manifestation—one no longer amenable to political mediation—of the class conflict between wage labor and capital or, more precisely, between the political reproduction demands of labor power and the private reproduction strategies of capital. In this way, to be sure, no more is accomplished than an exercise in translation. One conceptual language is decoded with the aid of another. The satisfaction that might be derived from this is lessened, I believe, by the recognition that while this translation results in the loss of a few details that are explained quite convincingly by the theories advanced, no answer is gained in return for the second question on the conditions for the success or failure of the five reorganization strategies I have distinguished.

The claim and the strength of the Marxist counterposition to the ungovernability and state crisis theories, whose contours I have presented here, cannot be based merely on disclosure of the fact that the contradictions and discrepancies of political-governmental organizations are rooted in socioeconomic conditions or are capable of being described in class categories. Rather, the claim must be based on a demonstration that the opposition in capitalist societies between living and dead labor, between labor power and capital, is so basic a structural defect of these social systems, one established so obstinately, that the therapeutic repertoire employed by the ungovernability theorists must be regarded as being so hopelessly inadequate that it in fact aggravates the crisis.

What, then, do the ungovernabilty theories have to offer with regard to the causal character of the proposed therapy, as opposed to its symptom-suppressing or even symptom-intensifying property? To be sure, not much here deserves the name of social-scientific argument. Instead, what predominates is a resolute pragmatism or a simple utopianism. Friedman's doctrine of the restoration of market mechanisms and the defusing of political crises through depoliticization owes its apparent logic, as Macpherson and many others have shown, solely to the fact that it ignores the differences between labor markets and all other markets.[32] Those who would like to reactivate prepolitical cultural disciplinary practices already demonstrate their helplessness by their rabid tone[33] and by their complete lack of agreement as to which cultural and ideological traditions should furnish the norms that could hold in check the much-lamented demand inflation. The dilemma of the conservatives consists precisely in the fact that they can neither rescue nor create anew those traditions and rules of collective life in whose name they do battle against reform politics and other manifestations of so-called political rationalism. They are thus left with no possibilities—as Hanna Pitkin convincingly argues in her critique of Oakeshott—except to invoke elements of a tradition that has become fictional or to suppress, both in theory and in practice, forms of political conflict.[34]

The New Objectivity of those, like Schelsky and Biedenkopf, who place their trust in technocratic structures or in the Federal Constitutional Court becomes entangled in the difficulty of having to justify political domination through nonpolitical considerations. This is particularly the case with strategies that aim to increase administrative rationality and governmental performance capacity by simplifying the manner in which the state apparatus relates to its social environment. These strategies are recognized by their own proponents to be inadequate, for reasons having less to do with a failure in their methods of calculation than with an insufficiency in the consensual base upon which they depend—a point that is not, however, explained.

Finally, a self-reproach has been advanced against neocorporativist reorganization proposals that aim at eliminating the problem through a far-reaching socialization of state policy or through alliances between large organizational groups and the state. According to this self-reproach, an overly extensive deployment of the scaffold of organized interests by the state could bring about that scaffold's collapse. Organized interests would thus be devalued in their function as guarantors of stability in direct proportion to their institutional appropriation.[35]

It is clear that the conservative theoreticians of crisis—and, for that matter, their social democratic opponents—cannot, with any theoretically grounded certainty, get a handle on the causes of the stated crisis; nor can the proffered remedies be shown to be causal therapies. The eclectic quality of the explanations provided for the political crisis of ungovernability is matched by the arbitrary and incoherent character of the proposed therapies: on the one hand a diffuse lament regarding the societal conditions produced in the political and economic process of modernization; on the other hand an appeal to politicians and actors in the public sphere, urging them to leave their conventional scruples behind and to set out on the path back to stability and "order." In the conservative world-view the crisis of governability is a disturbance in the face of which the false path of political modernization must be abandoned and nonpolitical principles of order, such as family, property, achievement, and science, must again be given their due. Therefore the polemic against political modernization—against equality, participation, and socialism—requires no consistent justification, no political program, and no theory of a politically effected transition to other conditions. Its proponents are content to forge a negative political coalition of those who (actually or purportedly) are threatened by reform. They do so through nebulous appeals to authoritative powers, which serious theoretical consideration would show to be either without substance or altogether subversive of their own appeals and which therefore, following the "rule for the distribution of the burden of proof" (Lübbe), need not be considered here.

III

By contrast, leftist theories of crisis actually do take seriously the task of proving their claims. For them, crises are not only disturbances; they are also constellations that can be made historically productive.

Claus Offe

At the same time crises are not contingent events that, like accidents, could just as well not occur; instead they are manifestations of tensions and structural defects inherent in the organizing principles of a social formation. Finally, leftist theories infer that crises are problematic sequences of events whose outcomes cannot be dealt with by certain models of overcoming the crisis. The two most important questions raised by these theories can be stated as follows: What is the decisive structural defect of social systems laboring under symptoms of ungovernability? And, what arguments can be marshaled to provide a prognosis of failure for the reorganization strategies that are unfolding before our eyes?

I shall examine these questions by way of conclusion, but not in order to attempt, even in outline, an answer to them. I merely wish to indicate, through a few observations, how difficult it is today to provide a concrete answer from the perspective of Marxist and other critical theories of society. (It was of course in the context of these critical theories that the skeletal elements of crisis theories originated— elements now being employed for purposes other than those originally intended.) Such an answer would of course be necessary were one interested in opposing theoretically (and not just politically) the neo-conservative prophets and their pragmatic concepts.

Crisis theories can be constructed in either an objectivist or a sub-jectivist manner; they can apply either to the being or to the con-sciousness of a social formation. If we understand crises as more than suddenly erupting and threatening exceptional circumstances in a social system, and if, additionally, we include in their definition the notion that in a crisis the economic and political principles of social organization are called into question (for otherwise we would have to speak of either recessions or accidents), then we must judge as unsuccessful the exclusively objectivist and the exclusively subjectivist attempts to argue for the insurmountability of crisis tendencies in capitalist industrial societies. Even if scientifically promising theories did exist about the course of the accumulation process, the course of the rate of profit, and the course of technological change, it would from today's per-spective remain an entirely open problem where, if indeed anywhere, an economic crisis of this type would give rise to a consciousness able to call into question the foundations of the political and economic organization of society. For we know that economic crises promote not only the motivation to engage in fundamental opposition (though certainly they do this as well) but also the readiness to conform and adapt. It is likewise an open problem whether a far-reaching augmentation of demands, an increase in claims, and a drastic withdrawal of motivation would indeed seriously impede the functioning of the accumulation process. Objectivist and subjectivist crisis theories that claim a measure of certainty are undermined today by one historical example or another, for they do not adequately take into account the elasticity of the different subsystems of welfare state capitalism. Hence any crisis theory based on the conceptual model of ever-increasing valorization difficulties, or the growth of consciousness critical of the system, or an interplay between the two, no longer seems defensible. This is especially true if one takes into account not only particular periods and actual economies but the structure of the capitalist system as a whole.

By contrast, ungovernability is meant to refer to a special case of a general pathology of the system. All social systems are reproduced through the normatively regulated meaningful action of their members as well as through the mechanisms of objective functional connections. This distinction between social integration and system integration, between rules that are followed and subjectless, self-implementing regularities, is basic to the entire sociological tradition. Conceptual pairs like use-value and exchange-value, ego and id, action and structure, state and society, reasons and causes are expressions and applications of this fundamental distinction. By employing them we can also define more closely the nature of the pathology intended by the concept of ungovernability. Social systems may be said to be ungovernable if the rules their members follow violate their own underlying functional laws, or if they do not *act* in such a way that these laws can *function* at the same time.

Given this schematization, one may note two diametrically opposed sets of conditions under which a discrepancy between social and system integration, between acting and functioning definitely cannot arise. Social systems are reliably immune to pathologies of the ungovernability type if they control and determine their functional conditions themselves through actions guided by meanings and norms or, conversely, if they erect a completely impenetrable barrier between socially significant motives and systemic functions, thus assuring that the functional laws are reliably protected against disturbances originating in the domain of action. Neither alternative finds real or complete counterparts in the societies with which we are acquainted; they are hypothetical or "ideal" solutions, which in opposing ways are tantamount to an abolition of the discrepancy between system and social integration.

The peculiarity of capitalist industrial societies consists in the paradoxical fact that they pursue both ideal solutions, attempting to solve the problem of their reproduction in contradictory ways. Ownership of the means of production, markets, competition, and private use of capital are institutional means that serve to separate the problem of system integration from the process of will-formation, collective action, and societal control. In the process of capitalist industrialization, material production is uncoupled, step by step, from will-mediated (political, traditional) steering mechanisms and delivered over to the laws of exchange relations—"interests" take the place of "passions."[36] The political-normative neutralization of the production and market sphere is connected with the phenomenon of secularization. The validity of norms is refined and relativized by the causality of market laws. But this equation underlying the process of modernization will prove correct only if the norm-free self-regulation of the market process is adequate to guarantee systemic integration. This is not the case, however, for two reasons. First, markets can only function if they are politically institutionalized, that is, embedded within a framework of roles established by the state (such as the monetary system or contractual law). To use the classic metaphor, the clock still has to be set, wound, and occasionally repaired by a skilled—and at the same time consciously self-restraining—ruler. Second, the mechanism functions only by virtue of the action of those who are included in it as "living" labor power, whose normative claims and willingness to perform are the resources with which the accumulation process stands or falls. The institution of the labor "market" and "free wage labor" is a fiction, since what is of interest positively and negatively in the commodity called labor power is indeed what distinguishes it from all other commodities, namely, that it is in fact a "living" labor power that (1) does not arise for the purpose of salability, (2) cannot be separated from its owner, and (3) can be set in motion only by its owner. This inextirpable subject-rootedness of labor power implies that in wage labor the categories of action and functioning, of social and system integration are inextricably intertwined. Thus while the emergence of a differentiated and normatively neutralized or "private" market sphere tends to solve the problem of societal reproduction precisely by segregating the functional level from the level of action, the organizing principle of wage labor, which emerges as the other side of the privatization of capital, presses toward the opposite solution. Action orientations and functional conditions fuse into one another, because labor power is governed simultaneously by will and by market, and because the process of accumulation does not function without political regulation that requires legitimation.

Capitalist societies are distinguished from all others not by the problem of their reproduction, that is, the reconciliation of social and system integration, but by the fact that they attempt to deal with what is in fact the basic problem of all societies in a way that simultaneously entertains two solutions that logically preclude one another: the differentiation or privatization of production and its politicization or "socialization" (in the Marxian sense). The two strategies thwart and paralyze each other. As a result the system is constantly confronted with the dilemma of having to abstract from the normative rules of action and the meaning relations of subjects without being able to disregard them. The political neutralization of the spheres of labor, production, and distribution is simultaneously confirmed and repudiated. Developed capitalist industrial societies do not have at their disposal a mechanism with which to reconcile the norms and values of their members with the systemic functional requirements underlying them. In this sense they are always ungovernable, and it is owing largely to the favorable circumstances of a long-lasting period of prosperity prior to the mid-70s that they were able to live with this phenomenon of ungovernability. Only if one ignores these structural conditions of ungovernability can one allow oneself to be affected by the mood of alarm being spread by the neoconservative crisis literature. Only in this ignorance can one imagine that the problem could be attacked successfully by trimming to size the rules and norms proper to action so that they might again harmonize with the functional imperatives and "objective laws" underlying the system. In fact it is the potency of these imperatives themselves that must be curbed and rendered capable of being subordinated to political-normative rules. (This contrary conclusion is of course identical to the one drawn by the left from the same analytic scheme.) Only then would it be possible to mediate social norms and claims with existing imperatives—freed now from their rigidity.

Claus Offe

In the Federal Republic the neoconservative crisis literature performs the function of, among other things, blocking discussion of solutions to the governability crisis, a discussion that it pretends to initiate. Advocating the adaptation of consciousness to any and all traditions and of claims to lowered expectations constitutes a pseudosolution to the problem. In this respect the Anglo-Saxon (not to mention the Italian) political science literature is far superior, at least in its impartiality. In the past few years I have come across many references in this literature to the following statement by Gramsci (which, incidentally, also assigns a good part of the German ungovernability literature its historical place): "The crisis consists precisely in the fact that the old is dying and the new cannot be born; in this interregnum a great variety of morbid symptoms appear."[37]

Notes

1. Since 1974 the concept of ungovernability has become a standard topic in international political science and political journalism. In the meantime a number of prominent social scientists have participated in its scholarly exploitation. See the following collections: W. Hennis et al., eds., *Regierbarkeit: Studien zu ihrer Problematisierung*, vol. 1 (Stuttgart: Klett-Cotta, 1977); M. Crozier et al., eds., *The Crisis of Democracy* (New York: New York University Press, 1975); M. Th. Greven, B. Guggenberger, and J. Strasser, eds., *Krise des Staates? Zur Funktionsbestimmung im Spätkapitalismus* (Darmstadt/Neuwied: Luchterhand, 1975); G. K. Kaltenbrunner, ed., *Der überforderte schwache Staat: Sind wir noch regierbar?* (Munich: Herder, 1975); A. King, ed., *Why Is Britain Becoming Harder To Govern?* (London: BBL, 1976); D. Frei. ed., *Überforderte Demokratie?* (Zurich: Schulthess, 1978).

2. C. Koch and W. D. Narr, "Krise—oder das falsche Prinzip Hoffnung," *Leviathan* 4 (1976): 291–327.

3. S. Huntington, "The United States," in M. Crozier et al., eds., *The Crisis of Democracy* (New York: New York University Press, 1975), p. 73.

4. Quoted from p. 39 of B. Guggenberger, "Herrschaftslegitimierung und Staatskrise—Zu einigen Problemen der Regierbarkeit des modernen Staates," in M. Th. Greven, B. Guggenberger, and J. Strasser, eds., *Krise des Staates?* (Darmstadt/Neuwied: Luchterhand, 1975), pp. 9–59.

5. Ibid., p. 41.

6. A. Wolfe, *The Limits of Legitimacy—Political Contradictions of Contemporary Capitalism* (New York: Free Press, 1977).

7. H. M. Enzenberger, "Zwei Randbemerkungen zum Weltuntergang," *Kursbuch* 52 (1978):1–8.

8. The growing functional weakness of political parties as a medium for political articulation and integration in capitalist democracies is a finding that can throw light on parallel phenomena. In any case, "suspicion that in the developed societies of the OECD world traditional party democracy is no longer a viable means of effecting necessary changes" unites in striking fashion

observers from the right, the center, and the left. The quotation is from R. Dahrendorf, "Krise der Demokratie? Eine kritische Betrachtung," in D. Frei, ed., *Überforderte Demokratie?* (Zurich: Schulthess, 1978). The view from the right is typified by S. Brittan, "The Economic Contradictions of Democracy," in A. King, ed., *Why Is Britain Becoming Harder to Govern?* (London: BBL, 1976), and by W. Hennis, *Organisierter Sozialismus: Zum "strategischen" Staats- und Politikverständnis der Sozialdemokratie* (Stuttgart: Klett-Cotta, 1977) and "Parteienstruktur und Regierbarkeit," in Hennis et al., *Regierbarkeit*, pp. 150–95. For the view from the center see S. Berger, "Politics and Antipolitics in Western Europe in the Seventies," *Daedalus* (Winter 1979): 27–50, and from the left, W. D. Narr, ed., *Auf dem Weg zum Einparteienstaat* (Oplanden: Westdeutscher Verlag, 1977).

9. A. King, "Overload: Problems of Governing in the 1970's," *Political Studies* 23 (1975):283–96, esp. p. 285.

10. Huntington, "The United States."

11. A. Hirschman, *Exit, Voice and Loyalty* (Cambridge, MA: Harvard University Press, 1970).

12. See H. von Arnim, *Gemeinwohl und Gruppeninteressen: Die Durchsetzung allgemeiner Interessen in der pluralistischen Demokratie* (Frankfurt: Metzner, 1977).

13. Ibid; see also Hennis, *Organisierter Sozialismus* and "Parteienstruktur und Regierbarkeit."

14. F. W. Scharpf et al., *Politikverflechtung: Theorie und Empirie des kooperativen Föderalismus in der Bundesrepublik* (Kronberg: Scriptor, 1975).

15. See R. Mayntz and F. W. Scharpf, *Policy Making in the German Federal Bureaucracy* (Amsterdam: Elsevier, 1975).

16. F. W. Scharpf, *Die Rolle des Staates im westlichen Wirtschaftssystem: Zwischen Krise und Neuorientierung* (Berlin: IIMV, 1978), dp/78–71, p. 16.

17. J. Douglas, "The Overloaded Crown," *British Journal of Political Science* 6 (1976):483–505, esp. p. 494ff.

18. See pp. 86–87 of C. Offe, "Die Institutionalisierung des Verbandseinflusses eine ordnungspolitische Zwickmühle," in U. von Alemann and R. Heinze, eds., *Verbände und Staat* (Oplanden: Westdeutscher Verlag, 1979).

19. Douglas, "The Overloaded Crown," pp. 499–500.

20. German Communist Party, "Entwurf, Programm der DKP," 1977, p. 20; also see E. Lieberam, *Drise der Regierbarkeit—Ein neues Thema bürgerlicher Staatsideologie* (Berlin/GDR: Akademie Verlag, 1977).

21. Wolfe, *The Limits of Legitimacy*, p. 329.

22. R. Inglehart, *The Silent Revolution: Changing Values and Political Styles among Western Publics* (Princeton, NJ: Princeton University Press, 1977). See also K. Hildebrandt and R. J. Dalton, "Die Neue Politik: Politischer Wandel oder Schönwetterpolitik," *Politische Vierteljahresschrift* 18 (1977):230–56.

23. J. Habermass, *Legitimation Crisis*, translated by Thomas McCarthy (Boston: Beacon Press, 1975).

24. D. Bell, *The Cultural Contradictions of Capitalism* (New York: Basic Books, 1976).

25. N. Glazer, "Die Grenzen der Sozialpolitik," in W. D. Narr and C. Offe, eds., *Wohlfahrtstaat und Massenloyalität* (Cologne: Kiepenheuer & Witsch, 1978), pp. 335–51.

26. Quoted from p. 196 of L. Klages, "Wohlfahrtstaat als Stabilitätsrisiko?" in H. Baier, ed., *Freiheit und Sachzwang: Beiträge zu Ehren Helmut Schelskys* (Opladen: Westdeutscher Verlag, 1978), pp. 192–207.

27. Ibid.; see also M. Janowitz, *Social Control of the Welfare State* (Chicago: University of Chicago Press, 1978).

28. U. von Alemann and R. Heinze, eds., *Verbände und Staat: Vom Pluralismus zum Korporatismus* (Opladen: Westdeutscher Verlag, 1979).

29. H. Schelsky, *Die Arbeit tun die anderen. Klassenkampf und Priesterherrschaft der Intellektuellen* (Opladen: Westdeutscher Verlag, 1975).

30. King, "Overload: Problems of Governing in the 1970's," p. 290ff.

31. Brittan, "The Economic Contradictions of Democracy."

32. C. B. Macpherson, *The Life and Times of Liberal Democracy* (Oxford: Oxford University Press, 1977). For a critique see J. Goldthorpe, "The Current Inflation: Towards a Sociological Account," in J. Goldthorpe and J. F. Hirsch, eds., *The Political Economy of Inflation* (London: Robertson, 1978), pp. 186–214.

33. Hennis, *Organisierter Sozialismus*.

34. H. F. Pitkin, "The Roots of Conservatism: Michael Oakeshott and the Denial of Politics," in L. A. Coser and I. Howe, eds., *The New Conservatives—A Critique from the Left* (New York: Meridian, 1977), pp. 243–88.

35. Douglas, "The Overloaded Crown," p. 507; similarly F. W. Scharpf, *Die Funktionsfähigkeit der Gewerkschaften als Problem einer Verbändegesetzgebung* (Berlin: IIM, 1978).

36. Albert Hirschman, *The Passions and the Interests* (Princeton, NJ: Princeton University Press, 1977).

37. A. Gramsci, *Selections from the Prison Notebooks* (New York: International Publishers, 1971), p. 276.

Political Concepts of Order for Mass Society

Ulrich Preuss

I

The following considerations take up ideas advanced by Karl Jaspers in his 1931 book *Die geistige Situation der Zeit*, which dealt with the economic, social, and cultural conditions of mass existence.[1] The generation that experienced its political and cultural socialization in the years following 1945 was nearly satiated with the negative connotations of the concept of the "masses," of "mass man" or "mass society." I recall very clearly that Ortega y Gasset's *Revolt of the Masses* was the catechism of my school days. Intellectual conservatism cannot again afford this distancing gesture of cultural criticism, now that the economy of capitalist industrial societies is, for better or worse, connected with the functional laws of mass society. Concepts such as mass consumption, mass culture, or mass democracy suggest a victory for the principle of democracy, against which the appeal to individual experiences and the individual shaping of life seems reactionary at times. In fact the revolutionizing of the apparatus of production and distribution, and the powerful implementation of its functional imperatives in the form of standardized mass production, as well as the conformism of mass consumption, have rendered obsolete the early bourgeois ethic oriented to the individualistic shaping of life. It is an essential feature of mass society that a market-mediated connection between individual performance and an individual's share of essential social goods has been dissolved by the political order's allocation of shares of the social product. There is no reason to lament this situation, since the previous system was based on a disregard for the claim on the part of the mass of the population to share in essential social goods. Despite clear cultural critical undertones in the diagnosis of Western capitalist industrial societies,[2] people have apparently come to terms with the existence and outward manifestations of mass society. We recall Walter Benjamin's famous statement that fascism assisted the masses in attaining their expression but not their right. Do Western consumer societies now assist the masses in attaining their right? Does the political order in the Federal Republic of Germany assist the masses in achieving their right? What is the right of the masses?

In what follows I shall be concerned only with those political conceptions of order for mass society that find expression in categories of constitutional theory or forms of constitutional law.

Jaspers defines "the mass" as "the totality of persons who are organized into an apparatus of the life-order in such a manner that the will and the peculiarities of the majority must be the determining factor."[3] Clearly, this characterization does not capture what is essential, for it merely describes a phenomenon, while the social forces accounting for the formation and unfolding of mass society remain obscure.

Mass society is the child of a capitalist economy that mobilizes and makes available all societal resources. In mass society each has claim to all. In it the aggressiveness of an expansive individualism is combined with the irresistibility of a radical egalitarianism. Essential social goods await conquest and cultivation, and in the same way that the relations of capital know no restriction on the accumulation of wealth, so too the individual is without any limitations on needs; beyond all forms of individuality, he is a "limitless appropriator" of resources. Each has the same access to these resources, and neither the goods nor the appropriators are subject to a preordained obligation that would assign them a social function. Like a narrow bottleneck, the market is the sole regulator of this system's egalitarianism, because it allows access only via the medium of exchange. The key concept for this form of economy is scarcity, the insuperable disproportion between the unlimited need for resources and their limited supply. Without scarcity—or, going back a step, without the unlimited need for limitless appropriation—no need would exist for the complicated mechanism of distribution that we simply designate as the market and that underlies the principle of the exchange of equivalents.

What is noteworthy in this connection between scarcity and the exchange of equivalents is the fact that the exchange of equivalents is at once a rule for both appropriation and distribution. In other words it is simultaneously a functional mode of economic activity and a principle of justice for both the appropriative process and the distributive result. This means that in the act of exchange "factors involved in production" are combined with one another and products are distributed among members of the society in such a way that everyone retains through nonviolent exchange the equivalent of what he relinquished. No one is treated unjustly, since freedom and equality are realized in the act of exchange. It can be said that this principle of justice so pervades the manner in which market societies function that a functioning economy is, as it were, the vehicle for distributive justice.

The close connection between the functional mode of market society and its principles of justice forms the basis for constitutionalizing its political order. This constitutionalizing process is subjected to far-reaching disruptions at the moment when, as Claus Offe puts it in his essay, the regularities according to which it functions violate the rules embodying the principles of justice.

I would like to designate the constitutional principle of every actual or at least purportedly successful congruence of functional modes and rules of justice in market society as the principle of "justice through a disinterested third party" (*unbeteiligte Dritte*). The notion of the disinterested third party is an essential element in all definitions of an independent tribunal; it serves to make clear that justice between disputing parties can be established not by the parties themselves but only through a party indifferent to the dispute and to the interests underlying it. The disinterested third party stands above the parties to the dispute and applies rules to which they are subject and which, at least in the case of the dispute, they are unable to change. The *regularities* of the market are, as I mentioned above, simultaneously *rules* of distribution. Through this coupling, the rules are made into an objective criterion of justice that lies outside the sphere of individual influence.

The development of mass society is complete when the restrictions of the market that regulate access to essential social goods fall away. The bourgeois acquisitive society becomes a democratic mass society when, under conditions of scarcity, each has a claim to all without allocation having to be steered through the equivalence relation between individual performance and individual income. At this point the contradiction implicit in the formula, "each has a claim to all," becomes apparent. A contradiction exists between the aggressiveness of a functional mode directed to achieving control (*Beherrschung*) and general powers of disposition (*Verfügung*) on the one hand and the principle of justice, which incidentally encompasses not only the narrow sector of distributive justice, on the other hand. The functioning of the market conceals this contradiction, because the principle of equivalence is at once a functional mode and a principle of justice. If the allocative functioning of the market can no longer be identified with its justice, then the claim of each to all immediately confronts the scarcity of available essential goods, and this conflict must be resolved according to explicit rules of social justice. In this event there no longer exists a disinterested third party to apportion justice among disputing parties; instead they must produce it themselves and with one another.

The distinguishing characteristic of mass society is that the "will and the peculiarities of the majorities" define the rules of justice, and therefore that the problem of social justice falls under the jurisdiction of the majority principle. In mass society justice is not *given* but *taken*. This basic situation for the problem of the distribution of social resources has existed in Western capitalist industrial nations only since the beginning of the twentieth century, in Germany approximately since the beginning of the Weimar Republic. For at that time it was clearly apparent that the organized working class, with its claim to political power, had been accepted as part of the new political order in which the distribution of essential social goods had in large measure become a matter of political and administrative regulation.

II

It is no coincidence that the crisis of the liberal representative constitutional system erupted in the Weimar Republic. A constitutional system could not do justice to the socioeconomic and cultural conditions of mass society if it represented merely a continuation of the basic principles of liberal representative order deriving from the nineteenth century.

Yet the new problems consisted not in the mere fact that "the will and the peculiarities of the majorities must be the determining factor." The majority principle is first of all simply a rule that makes possible the unified decision of the multitude; it can find application as much in semifeudal and liberal representative societies as in plebiscitary–mass democratic ones. According to Scheuner, it even stands in a structural relation to representative democracy, since the latter is based on the possibility of divergent interests and opinions, explicitly protecting them in such a way that the outvoted minority has the possibility of subordinating itself to the decision of the majority.[4]

It is of decisive significance for majority rule in mass society that the majority principle is transformed from a principle of procedure to a substantive principle of order. As a principle of procedure it regulates the decision-making process of a majority of persons entitled to vote, irrespective of whether this exists in an assembly of the estates (Ständeversammlung), a representative parliament, or a factory council (Betriebsrat). In each case the social homogeneity of the assembly permits application of a decision rule according to which the opinion of the majority can be deemed a decision of the totality, since the outvoted minority possesses the same structural attributes as the majority and thus is itself also capable of becoming the majority.

The situation is altogether different when the majority-rule principle becomes a substantive principle of order. In this case the *content* of the respective decision should accord with the will and the interests of the majority of those affected by it. The rule of the majority is expressed not in the validity of the procedure through which, by virtue of the social homogeneity of those entitled to vote, everyone has a chance to belong to the majority; rather, it is expressed in the implementation of characteristic forms of life, interests, and longings on the part of the majority of the population, which serve as the criterion for the "justness" (Richtigkeit) of a political decision. Contained herein is the implicit assumption of a deficient social homogeneity in the population, for the circumstance of majority rule as a substantive principle involves the rule of a structural majority that is distinguished from a structural minority through established socioeconomic and sociocultural attributes.

As regards distribution the majority principle, in its significance as a substantive principle of order for the rule of a structural majority, functions as a vehicle for a "conception of justice oriented to end-results."[5] A given distribution is no longer recognized as just for the reason that it originated in the medium of free exchange and is protected and legitimized through a specific procedure of law formation.

Rather, it is so recognized because and insofar as it can be viewed as being justified in its *result*, a judgment that is pronounced in the political process by the will and peculiarities of the majority. Law no longer protects acquisition and the object acquired on the grounds that acquisition occurred legitimately, that is, on the basis of a private-autonomous commercial will. Rather, the order of distribution engendered by acquisition is subject, as it were, to a second evaluation and stands at the disposal of redistribution according to the will of the majority.

In this way two competing concepts of justice are established, each equally concerned with the distribution of social wealth. The first, represented by the constitutional principle of nineteenth-century liberal representative democracy, is oriented to the procedure for the acquisition of goods and thus to the bringing about of a specific distributive result: what is acquired in just fashion—without force on the scales of the exchange of equivalents—is also just in result.[6] The other concept of justice, oriented to the distributive result, subjects a given distribution to an additional evaluation according to whether the distribution corresponds to criteria of moral worth, social utility, individual effort, personal needs, and so on. The two concepts exclude each other, since no argument can be presented to correct, in the name of a justice of end results, a distribution that has been achieved in just fashion, except in the name of a "higher" justice. This means that the first distribution requiring correction is indeed not just. As a matter of fact, concealed behind this competition in concepts of justice is the conflict between the functional mode of the exchange of equivalents and the legitimizing notions of a just and good life.

On the basis of this opposition, one can understand which ordering function the nineteenth-century liberal representative constitution had to perform and wherein lay the reason for its failure in twentieth-century mass society. Its function consisted in immunizing a procedurally just distribution of essential social goods against being corrected according to the criteria of a justice oriented to end results, in preserving a type of justice by means of a disinterested third party, and thus in preventing the constitutional competition of two legitimizing principles for a given distribution.

III

I have already mentioned the formal principle of representation that accomplished this ordering function. Underlying it are fundamental distinctions whose internal logic to this very day claims adherents and admirers. I am referring to the distinctions between state and society, politics and economics, public and private, citizen and bourgeois. These result from the unfolding of capitalist economy and represent the contradictory conditions of its functioning: the system of nonviolent accumulation determined by exchange has violent presuppositions not determined by exchange, presuppositions that can be neither guaranteed in the forms of exchange nor made subject to the functional logic of exchange. As a monopolist of the legitimate exercise of physical force, the "state," as an indivisible unity, is removed from every disposition determined by exchange, just as it is subordinated to the logic of power in its action and in the specific organizational means available to it. The aforementioned distinctions between politics and economy, public and private, follow from these diverse modes of functioning.

We commonly designate this dimension of the social life of an exchange society as public; it circumscribes the conditions for exchange not determined by exchange, the forcible conditions for the absence of force, the noneconomic conditions of the economy—in short the conditions for internal and external peace in capitalist exchange society. Its fundamental constituents are public power and politics.

This network of conditions attains conceptual expression in the abstracting polarization of state and society. By this means light is shed on what is structurally constitutive for the legally constituted character of civil society—the autonomization of the economic process vis-à-vis acting subjects, whereby all fetters are to be removed from an unfolding of the limitless realization of capital through the limited aims of concrete subjects.[7]

All constitutional arrangements are directed to optimizing a functional correspondence between those dualistic feedback mechanisms related to one another by way of separation. With Reinhart Koselleck, we can designate their semantic configuration through the notion of "symmetrical counterconcepts"—concepts through which the elements of an opposition become related to one another and become factors in a comprehensive concept of order.[8] The limitation of public power through the separation of powers, through a legally regulated government bureaucracy, and through an independent judiciary is as much a component of this function of order as is the separation of individual liberties from the functional operations of public power. What is noteworthy in this dualistic structure of order is not the demarcation of these two dimensions as a basic problem in constitutional theory. Rather, it is certainly the historically singular fact that the contradictory conditions for the functioning of the bourgeois acquisitive society were explicitly institutionalized, with the result that its intrinsic logic was laid bare. "State" and "society" are not two spatially distinct spheres but forms of association in which the one is the negation of the other. The reciprocally negative relation of one to the other represents the principle of order for the bourgeois constitutional state; in this structural separation of two opposing modes of functioning lies one of the reasons for the remarkable flexibility and stability of the bourgeois order.

In order to clarify the nature of the relation in which the bourgeois order stands to the aforementioned types of justice, I would like to appeal to an analytic distinction developed in the social sciences that Claus Offe refers to in his essay, namely the distinction between system integration and social integration. The concept of system integration denotes the operation of objective functional relations, regularities, and functional laws, through which societal reproduction is secured. Social integration, on the other hand, is engendered through the observance of rules of ethics, morality, and law—in short, through subjectively guided behavior. Functional laws and functional imperatives operate independently of the will of social subjects, just as, for instance, the "laws of the market" represent functional laws and operating relations that are independent of the will of individual participants in the market. Conversely, the rule-directed behavior of subjects follows the criteria of ethics, morality, law, and religion—in other words, criteria of what is recognized as just or right. What is crucial is that the functioning of society according to regularities and functional laws need not necessarily harmonize with the normatively regulated actions of societal members.

It is by no means the case that these two modes of association stand side by side without any connection; they are in fact related in a specific fashion. Offe speaks of the tendency, inherent in bourgeois society, to separate the two types of integration; at a strategically significant point, however, this separation cannot succeed. In the system of wage labor, human labor power is the object of an exchange mediated by the market and to this extent is subject, as is every other commodity, to the functional laws of the market. At the same time, however, this commodity is the only one exchanged on the market that cannot be detached from the subject; to this extent it is inseparably connected with the system of rule-governed action and the normative orientation of the subject.

In the relation of wage labor we also see the dissolution of the contradictory unity, agreed upon in the exchange of equivalents, of the economic mode of functioning and the rules of justice directed to the principle of equivalence. Theoretically, in a system in which equal values are always exchanged, there should be no structural majority (or minority) with regard to the socioeconomic attributes of the population, for everyone always receives a value equivalent to what he has relinquished. The problem of a distribution oriented to end results and of a "majority rule" defining it, in the sense of a substantive principle of order, arises solely on account of the exchange of labor power, its transformation into a commodity that produces more value than required for its own reproduction. In other words the majority principle, as a substantive principle of order, is, in contrast to its function as a procedural rule, the product of the wage-labor relation and of the deliverance of ever more domains into the status of wage dependency. This follows from the fact that wage labor is the condition for a structured distribution of essential goods and thus for the formation of a structural majority.

In this function as a substantive principle of order, majority rule is incompatible with the constitutional system of a social structure based on a separation of state and society, public and private, force and absence of force—in short the separation of social and system integration. For inherent in this separation is a functional guarantee for the exchange of equivalents wherein all people are free and equal. What the equivalence principle is to the sphere of exchange, universalism is to its nonexchange foundation in public power. In this latter context all citizens are equal; the constitution and legitimation of public power are based on the presupposition that all citizens have a share in it and that the ruling majority can therefore only make decisions that could be binding for all and accepted by all—hence, that every member of the outvoted minority could also be a part of the majority. This presupposition is destroyed, however, when public power is constituted and legitimized according to the nonuniversal rules of a structural majority.

We can also provide an economic definition of this functional connection between the exchange of equivalents and universalistic public power, and the limits of a politics of structural majority resulting from this connection. To do so we refer to the fiscal restrictions on the bourgeois constitutional state. A regulative and redistributive state is based on the functioning and prospering of a market economy, and the state must strengthen that economy by its own means so that it can, for instance, pursue allocative policies in the sense of distributive justice.[9] It must guarantee the functioning of the market to preserve the resources that enable it to act in accord with criteria of justness. In view of the modern problematic of the social welfare state, it was thus not unjustly recognized that

the modern fiscal state constitutes not only the foundation but also the limit of the social welfare state. If taxation overstrains the economic performance capacities of those subject to taxation, or if it weakens their will to perform, taxable income, the foundation of the social welfare state, will diminish.[10]

Thus politically the rule of the majority, as a substantive principle of order for the rule of the structural majority, removes the foundations from the majority principle as a type of procedural justice, in that it dissolves both the principle of justice for everyone and the universal compulsion of legal rules. Economically a collision takes place between a type of justice based on a disinterested third party and a structured, results-oriented justice favoring the structural majority. This follows from the permanent overstraining of the system of private economic activity and its functional processes, due to the imposition of aims that economic processes are supposed to fulfill; to related political and administrative impediments such as the participation of workers in management decisions, or the norms for the protection of juveniles, the environment, and labor conditions; and, not least, to an increasing sociopolitically motivated siphoning off of taxes, which allows the state to appear ever less as a guarantor of economic functional efficiency and ever more as a burden, a freeloader on the economy, introducing into the economic process subjective motives emanating from the political realm that are "foreign to the matter at hand."

IV

It would be illuminating to examine the Basic Law (*Grundgesetz*) or Constitution of the Federal Republic with the aim of locating in it attempts to preserve a concept of objective justice under the conditions of mass society. In what follows, however, I shall be concerned with principles of social and political life that in recent years have been drawn to the forefront of discussions in politics and constitutional law and that attempt to place the coordination of system and social integration on a new constitutional foundation. The central concepts are as follows: parity, neutrality, pluralism, consensus, and tolerance.

The traditional categories of the constitutional state revolved about the precarious relation between civil liberties and public power—a tense relation whose elements were to be mediated but not abolished in the conceptions of basic rights, law and the process of political will-formation. Freedom and coercion, subjective right and state jurisdiction, popular will and state will, designate in symmetrical concepts functional correspondences by means of oppositions, wherein the coordination of two opposing functional modes of social life are to be constitutionally regulated. It is apparent that these concepts, now drawn to the forefront of constitutional theory, are asymmetrical in Reinhart Koselleck's sense. Their negations do not imply, as do the symmetrical counterconcepts, a legitimate or even linguistically recognized opposite; rather, they designate exclusions from something that is illegitimate. The asymmetrical concepts are so comprehensive that they linguistically effect an exclusion of their negation. What is concealed behind this? Let us consider the individual concepts more closely.

1. The concept of *parity* derives from state-church law and denotes the equal treatment of a religion by the state.[11] Through the notion of parity the state gives voice to its religious neutrality. Today parity and neutrality characterize chiefly the relation of social associations—particularly trade unions and labor federations—to the state and to one another. Parity proscribes an unequal or even discriminatory treatment of social associations by public power, whether this be through direct confrontation or indirectly, through state regulations that inscribe the status of associations in social and political life. In this connection one speaks of the "social equilibrium of social partners" and of the "counterbalance principle," which the state is obligated to guarantee or to realize vis-à-vis social associations.[12]

Parity is not identical with the private-law claim to equal treatment, as set out in Articles 3 and 33 of the Basic Law. Here individuals are indivisible and equal in regard to their fundamental qualities as human beings. Parity pertains to organized interest groups (or at least interest

Ulrich Preuss

groups capable of organization) and thus to social units. According to the principle of parity, they should be treated equally in their relation both to one another and to public power, irrespective of the size, composition, and significance of the interests organized in them and of their organizational capability. Here we confront a peculiarity of this principle. Whereas according to democratic principles power is exercised and decisions are made according to the majority principle, the commitment to an equitable (*paritätische*) treatment of interest groups of diverse size by the state and their claim to an equitable participation in the important affairs of society as a whole imply that what is decisive is not the majority will of the population, given expression by means of law or governmental act, but one of the aforementioned conceptions of equilibrium. Obviously what is operative here is not the fundamental presupposition of the majority principle that the majority legitimately speaks for all since everyone is potentially a member of the majority. At the same time the parity principle is not a principle of minority protection, as it was within the context of the majority principle, especially for national minorities. (This is still the case today for the Danish minority in Germany's South Schleswig.) At issue is the question of a special right for structural minorities whereby, within the framework of a law valid for all, the peculiarities accounting for the minority status are to be protected against an assimilating type of equal treatment—without, however, relinquishing the claim, basic to the majority principle, that the majority is to decide for *all*.

The parity principle stands beyond the majority principle and the protection of minorities. It calls for the equal treatment of unequals. In contrast to a principle of equality based on individual rights as stated in Articles 3 and 33 of the Basic Law, which explicitly declares that differences of persons according to sex, ethnic heritage, race, and language are to be disregarded and asserts that only one's character as a human being is to count as a criterion, the parity principle allows religious and socioeconomic differences to be made into criteria for decisions. If, for instance, positions in public administration were to be distributed among organized religious denominations in accordance with the parity principle, it would be precisely the religious denomination—in contradistinction to the requirement, basic to the individual rights tradition, that the religion of the applicant be disregarded— that would serve as the determining criterion for employment.

The emphasis upon and observance of differences in organized segments of the population represent the acknowledgment of structural majorities and minorities (and the departure from the majority principle as a rule of procedure). In this way the presupposition is in principle created for the establishment of the majority principle as a substantive principle of order, since the condition no longer obtains according to which everyone, on the basis of socioeconomic and sociocultural attributes, could belong equally to the majority or the minority.

In fact, though, things proceed differently. The parity principle requires a relation of equivalence between participating groups, inasmuch as the interests of each are to be regarded as commensurable with those of the others. Distinctions in social priority and in the legitimacy of interests are leveled out, as are their diverse organizational capacities, so that, for instance, self-executing interests focused on property are equated with those first constituted in a democratic process of will-formation.

What is decisive for our question regarding the constitutional principles of order for mass society is the consequence that the demand for parity offers an independent criterion that, through a disinterested third party, is to regulate social order and the relation of groups and interests to one another. It can provide for justice, since it intervenes in disturbances of equivalence and reestablishes parity—as, for instance, the Federal Labor Court, applying the concept of the "parity of struggle," had done for years in dealing with the social disputes concerning the wage total that is to be distributed.[13] Analogously to the equivalence relation of contract, the parity principle is vindicated by a "justness" function, and the social disputes are resolved by an objective criterion of justice that is to provide for the objectification of justice. The state is to conduct itself neutrally with regard to the "justice" contained in the distributive struggle of groups if and insofar as it fulfills the conditions of struggle required of every guarantee of justness.

Thus neutrality requires . . . an active shaping of society through the establishment of parity. . . . The state exercises its social responsibility merely through the institutionalization of conditions that foster parity. Parity is . . . the standard for the neutral conduct of the state.[14]

Parity is thus demonstrated to be a social form of procedural justice, whose distributive consequences are justified according to an objective standard; it is a collective-law variant of the exchange of equivalents.

Thus one has to ask whether the "guarantee of justness" ascribed to it in relation to the distributive results also encompasses, as does the principle of exchange based on contractual law, functional processes whose integrity is to be protected through the medium of parity. In other words, are system and social integration conjoined in the principle of parity?

The idea of the guarantee of justice by means of the equilibrium and equalization of social competitors, on which the notion of parity is based, tacitly implies that the competition of many groups for re-sources on the basis of equal considerations of competition—parity— will lead to a "just" result corresponding to equilibrium. No one has thought of designating as just, in the sense of equalization and equi-librium, the distributive result of a game of chance—which of course also takes place under the conditions of competition—apparently for the reason that a game of chance is not a functional mode of distribution in a society where essential goods are produced and, recalling Nozick's formulation, do not fall from heaven like manna.

Thus the principles of distribution must stand in a relation of cor-respondence to the forms and functional laws of production. What is valid for the market economy is the "principle of equilibrium"—each according to his performance—a principle realized in the exchange of equivalents. For this reason the parity of social competitors in the struggle of economic distribution signifies more than a balancing of social powers under state sovereignty, more than an artificial technique of social organization. It is first of all an expression of the autonomy of social groups, which follow not the law of the political order but their own law, and which sustain the tension between the functional imperatives of the economy and the social claims of those subordinated to it.

Yet parity signifies not only the equal treatment of groups by the state, which the latter assures through an "active neutralization"; it designates equally a relation of groups to one another. When mention is made of the "counterbalance principle" or of an "equilibrium" of social partners that is to be realized on the parity model, an abstraction occurs from actually differentiated social power, from the priority and the character of the interests of groups, such that the specific group qualities and peculiarities are not considered but instead leveled out. This takes place in the interest of a superordinate justness guarantee, to which the relation of groups to one another is subordinated. As the social form of these relations, parity is thus a functional model for an optimal distribution that can serve as an objective standard— one initially unknown to the participants, but toward whose fulfillment they must orient themselves. Parity should institutionally ensure the achievement of these goals; thus it designates a functional network into which real social antagonisms and conflicts are fed and in which they are transformed into the functional elements of a preexisting structure of order.

In this way the social autonomy of groups is unexpectedly subsumed under a concept of order according to which parity becomes a tool for equal treatment with regard to a common object (*Sache*). In wage disputes the power of the participating organizations is not the criterion for the justness of the distributive result achieved. The wage model is organized according to a type of justice based on a disinterested third party and demands that justice be given and not taken. The power of organizations has thereby been abstracted and transformed into an equalizing equilibrium relationship. The criterion is justice in relation to the common object, and this is the "object domain of the economy" (*Sachbereich Wirtschaft*).[15] "Objective justice" (*Sachgerechtigkeit*) is the specific category of justice underlying the parity model; it is the equalizing relation between the functioning of the economic process and the social claims made against it, the optimum coupling of operating relations and normative expectations, which is to be achieved through the functional model of a parity principle oriented to equilibrium and balance.[16]

2. It is no coincidence that, in the context of clarifying the concept of parity, reference was made to *neutrality*. Originally a concept of international law, neutrality in its multiple connotations is now recognized as a domestic political principle, having become a central concept in constitutional law. Not only is the neutrality of the state vis-à-vis social groups postulated as a result of their parity with one another, but a multiplicity of other constitutional relations is also circumscribed with this concept. The place of the professional civil servant, the judiciary, the accounting office, the electronic media, schools, and even the law vis-à-vis interested parties are all characterized as neutral— one even speaks of a "neutral" interpretation of basic rights.[17] We seem to stand before a grand process of the neutralization of important spheres of life. With the concept of neutrality a magic formula seems

to have been unearthed that allows for the securing of "a highest axiom or principle, namely, freedom."[18]

It may be, however, that we are simply confronted with a variety of meanings for a concept that must be characterized quite differently in each application. Carl Schmitt noted eight different dimensions of neutrality, which might explain the multiple possibilities for its application.[19] Quite contradictory demands are grounded in the argument for neutrality. Thus, for example, the nationalization of the electronic media is seen as a guarantee of their neutrality, just as is the opposite principle of denationalization[20]—state activism as much as state abstinence.

If the most contradictory relations are subsumed under the concept of neutrality, this is obviously because they can draw on some common element that characterizes its function. This commonality lies in the "emergence of a standard for decision and action that is always generated by the object domain itself, and thus in the polemical repudiation of an alien standard."[21] Whatever may have been meant by the notion of "protecting something's own inherent standard" and object structures, it made clearly apparent a polemical thrust against concepts of order that placed demands on life-spheres that collided with their own modes of functioning. Neutrality effects a functional protection of life-spheres, which at one time can occur through active state actions, at another time through nonintervention, one time through identification and then again through nonidentification. Neutrality of the sphere of professional civil servants, the courts, or the Federal Bank ensures the fulfillment of a legally regulated function vis-à-vis social demands and thus preserves the state's integrity vis-à-vis citizens as the neutral authority par excellence. Neutrality of the schools and their educational objectives, as well as the administration of the electronic media and their programs, should protect the exercise of their function against governmental and social intervention and arrogation of authority. Neutrality of trade unions vis-à-vis political parties should protect the function of their purely economic struggle for the improvement of their members' work and wage conditions and at the same time limit them to this function. In all cases neutrality designates a depoliticization and restriction of partial social spheres to an object sphere (*Sachbereich*).

It is clear that neutrality is the formula, not only in constitutional theory but increasingly also in constitutional law, of a politics of order that is opposed to the principle of majority rule as a substantive principle of order for mass society and that attempts to neutralize its effects. Here, too, as in the parity model, a functioning order is presupposed, according to whose standards a neutral or nonneutral form of behavior can be measured. A just form of behavior is one that is functionally appropriate, and neutrality is the criterion by means of which this can be determined.

3. *Pluralism* is a concept that attempts to answer the question of the place of social groups and associations in the political community. The question is as old as the history of the modern state, whose historical achievement—the introduction of political unity into a society based on the separation of competing individuals—seems to be endangered by social associations with independent and even competing loyalties.

We shall not trace here the stages in the formation and legal-institutional recognition of associations in the modern state,[22] particularly since the concept of pluralism that informs constitutional law, while based on pluralistic theories of association, is also a general concept of constitutional theory. Pluralism is concerned with the constitution, legitimation, and method of operation of political domination in the democratic constitutional state,[23] grounding this concern in the free competition of organized interests with respect to state control. Rousseau's notion of a homogeneous, unified political will in the form of a *volonté générale* is as much repudiated by the pluralists as is the Hegelian conception of a homogeneous state as a substantial unity of what is "in-and-for-itself rational," an end in itself, "in which freedom attains its supreme right, and in which this final end has supreme right against the individual" (*Philosophy of Right*, §258). State politics is more the vector sum of the interests of social groups and their struggle for power. At the same time the organized groups must obtain the support of nonorganized parts of the population in order to be able to survive in the competition, so as to avert the danger, inherent in the pluralistic system of political will-formation, of an association-oligarchical form of domination.[24] A pluralistic democracy is open to diverse concepts of the common good, allows constitutional space for an opposition, protects minorities both through the toleration of divergent opinions and life-styles and through an ideologically neutral state, and presupposes the guarantee of the freedom to articulate and organize interests and to participate in the political process of will-formation.[25]

Ulrich Preuss

The criticism to which this pluralistic conception of democracy has frequently been subjected will not be repeated here.[26] Against it one can also raise an objection that was directed at the parity model: namely, that all interests—independent of their substantive character and independent, above all, of their varying degrees of organizational capacity—are drawn into a relation of equivalence. With the equalizing of all specific distinctions a decisive transformation occurs in the pluralistic conception's point of departure, which now consists in the recognition of social oppositions organized according to groups. Diverse interests organized according to groups are transformed into the functional elements of a pluralistic model of order, whose functioning specifies for participating organizations the limits of a "functionally appropriate" behavior. Pluralism is substantialized into a political functional order, with the consequence that a criterion of justness has now been attained, one that authorizes the exclusion of what is illegitimate (*Unrichtigen*)—as had also been explicitly foreseen in Articles 9 (paragraphs 2 and 18) and 21 (paragraph 2) of the Basic Law.

In addition to its significance for the theories of association, state, and democracy, pluralism has in recent years acquired yet another connotation, which serves as the substantive principle for specific life-spheres. As an expression for the constitution and legitimation of domination, pluralism includes the expectation that diverse interests are contained within the definition of the "common good" and that from this emerges something like a "pluralistic common good." This expectation is particularly apparent in the sphere of the electronic media, universities, and schools, that is, in institutionalized intellectual communication, where intellectual freedom and cultural claims to power confront each other and where the cultural manifold is, in particular measure, subordinated to the tendency toward hegemonic unification. When the Federal Constitutional Court, in its 1961 television decision, postulated an organizational structure for the management of the electronic media that ensured "that all affected parties shall have an influence on its organs and be entitled to a say as regards the entire programming, and that operational principles shall be binding for the content of the entire programming, so as to guarantee a modicum of substantive balance, objectivity, and mutual respect," it thereby clearly related plurality to the objective content of intellectual production and communication, without, incidentally, discussing the related question of whether this might not result in a constitutionally inadmissible restriction of specific—namely, "unbalanced"—views.[27]

In contrast to the management of the electronic media, schools and universities are not constituted in a pluralistic fashion. Rather, they belong, either directly (schools) or indirectly (universities), to the state administration, even though the universities possess far-reaching rights of self-determination that are recognized by the functional groups within them. Although schools and universities are not in a position to guarantee a breakthrough of organized plurality into the produced content, a substantive plurality has been demanded for them as well. For universities, academic pluralism has been postulated in terms of a pluralism of theories, based on the plurality of truths, where truth is defined as "not-yet-falsified knowledge";[28] as for schools, the commitment to pluralistic curricula has been claimed as a constitutional principle, that is, as the content of a "fundamental right to an ideologically tolerant school."[29] In both cases the concept has been fully disengaged from the process of the competition of organized groups for scarce resources, which from a systems-theoretic viewpoint also includes normative orientations.

The pluralistic balance of cultural norms and orientations mediated in these institutions designates for this reason an intellectual model of order in which an individual's intellectual freedom, already by definition indivisible and thus nonpluralistic, is at least relativized. Pluralistic radio and television programs, scientific theories, and school curricula are the product of a development that situates the individual, as the bearer of a function, within an intellectual order of equilibrium where he serves, as it were, as an organ of this order. Just as in the parity model of social groups, where the majority principle is sacrificed to an order of equilibrium ordained by groups, so in the sphere of cultural production the model of order of a pluralistic culture supplants a principle of intellectual freedom logically based on the autonomy of the subject. At the level of cultural norms, of knowledge, and of orientations, pluralism, as a substantive principle, should fulfill those "functions of justness" that pluralism has in constitutional theory for the constitution and legitimation of power.

The pluralism of social groups is transformed, as we have seen, from a political-economic model of competition into a substantive concept of order, in which only associations capable of pluralism are allowed to compete. It becomes a cultural principle of order only when balanced and pluralistic cultural contents may be regarded as legitimate. Thus here, too, an objective criterion for justness has been attained.

Pluralistic, tolerant, balanced norms and cognitions mediate the objectivity of life-spheres and situations, which are to be directed and controlled by orienting practical knowledge produced, for example, in the media, schools, and universities. Objectivity, so one may surmise, consists in mediating the immanent structures of order and the working mechanisms of social life-spheres with subjective claims, expectations, hopes, fears—in short, with the action orientations of individuals. It consists as well in reconciling them to such personal questions by means of an objective stance and, in the final analysis, in functionalizing the intellectual and ethical autonomy of individuals in the service of a cultural concept of order.

4. The founding of democratic rule on the *consensus* of the governed is so obvious an assumption that it would seem to require no further clarification. If even authoritarian and dictatorial regimes cannot survive without a modicum of popular consent (even if it is passive), then consensus belongs all the more to the constitutional principles of political rule in a democratic society, which is not based on a given substantial unity of the populace but is rather seen as a product of unification processes achieved in the populace itself. However, it is not these multiple attempts at grounding political rule in popular consent that concern us when we designate consensus as a central category among the newer concepts of order for mass societies.

It is clear that in the contexts where mention is made of the necessity of consenting views in the populace, there is typically talk not of consensus but of "basic consensus." Expression is thereby given to the fact that, beyond the differences and conflicts necessarily present in a pluralistic system of competition, a foundation must exist, protected from all groups and interests, consisting of rules according to which competition takes place. In this sense there exists in fact a close structural connection between pluralism and consensus.[30] Stated more precisely, it can be said that "basic consensus" is the medium in which the minority defeated in pluralistic power struggles comes to acknowledge the decisions of the majority and finds compelling reasons to submit to the majority.

This is now a constitutional novelty, inasmuch as, according to the classical rules of parliamentary democracy, the relation of every citizen and thus also the defeated majority to public power was defined by means of legality—or, to be more precise, by obedience to the law, wherein it is irrelevant whether those obeying agree inwardly with the law or whether they repudiate it. Nonetheless the supplementation of obedience to the law, which today is still the primary means of regulating citizens' behavior, by consensus is not without internal consistency. If the majority principle as a principle of procedure asserts that potentially everyone can belong to the majority as well as the minority since (with the exception of the aforementioned national minorities) it negates "structural majorities" or "structural minorities," there follows the subordination of the defeated minority to the majority on the basis of the structural homogeneity (implicit in the procedure) of the entire population. For this reason the majority can decide for all.

To the extent that this presupposition can no longer be implemented in constitutional forms—and this is the criterion for a mass society in which the majority principle becomes a substantive principle of order—obedience to law ceases to function as the sole legal-political administrative structure binding the minority to the decisions of the majority. Recourse to substantive principles of legitimation—to rules that, recalling the famous Kantian distinction between morality and legality in *The Metaphysical Elements of Justice*, make "an action a duty and at the same time make this duty the incentive"—indicates that in the present political system structural minorities and thus far-reaching latent conflicts exist, which in the medium of legality alone cannot be integrated into a political unity based on parliamentary majority functionalism.[31]

Paradoxically sociopolitical steering through consensus has one of the effects it was intended to prevent. The basic consensus should equip structural minorities—which can no longer be subordinated to the decisions of the majority with the argument that they too potentially belong to the majority or that every individual could belong to the majority—with compelling reasons for all to follow existing laws, in that they identify themselves with the functioning of the political system as such. In a certain sense the basic consensus provides a hedge against the appearance of structural minorities in the constitutional system for the legitimation of political rule. Yet now it itself produces a structural minority and excludes it from the functional network of the political order. These are the minorities who through their action do not orient themselves in terms of the functional laws of a pluralistic democracy, since they do not make its efficacy into an "internal incentive." These are also the minorities who accept the decisions of the majority not from the perspective of a majority *procedure* for a structurally homogeneous electorate but exclusively from that of expediency. Within the framework of the legal system, this is a permissible stance, for in it no inquiry is made into the motives for obedience to law. In an order grounded in basic consensus, however, this stance poses the threat of a fundamental disturbance of the political system, since legal behavior is not identical with behavior that is fundamentally just; this agreement is introduced only with the consensus.

We are led, finally, to the problem of the justness of the political decisions of a given majority. The justness guarantee of the majority principle as a principle of procedure consisted, as we have seen, not in the assumption that the majority "has right" as a majority but in the presupposition of the structural homogeneity of the electorate and the resultant principle: namely, that structurally the minority likewise belongs to the majority and can thus accept its decisions as binding. In an order governed by consensus, however, the guarantee for the justness of the majority decision lies in the "justness" of the functional laws whose efficacy is engendered by political decisions. Hence the protection of this justness becomes one of the central tasks of the political system, which, given a legal system that is agnostic vis-à-vis its foundations, is evidently unable to gain mastery by itself over the new situation that results from the intrusion of structured groups into the constitutional system and their demand for a justice oriented to end results.

5. The concept of *tolerance* complements the concepts of neutrality, pluralism, and consensus. No more than these can tolerance be grouped with the structural concepts of a liberal representative type of constitution. On the contrary, it derives from the conceptual world of the preconstitutional state, having emerged for the first time in arrangements where the coexistence of differing religious denominations was accepted by the state.

In the constitutional struggles at the end of the eighteenth century and throughout the nineteenth century, the concept of tolerance no longer played any role. It was replaced by the concept of civil liberties, in which freedom of conscience and religion assumed a central place. Tolerance presupposes "the presence of an opposition that in some way is perceived as evil" and signifies the "intentional guarantee of a specific measure of freedom, in terms of which this opposition can affirm itself."[32] As the foundation of a subjective right against the state not to interfere with expressions of freedom, civil liberty is based on the opposition between public power and the citizen subordinated to it; however, this is perceived not as an evil but as a necessary condition for the functioning of the nascent bourgeois order. Incidentally, for civil liberty there is a "rule of distribution" that differs from that for tolerance. Carl Schmitt's "constitutional (rechtsstaatliche) distribution principle" consists in the principled limitlessness of freedom and the limitation of public power,[33] whereas the "intentional guarantee of a specific amount of freedom" realizes precisely the opposite principle of distribution, namely, the principle of consensual order, which has recourse to preconstitutional institutions. For this reason it is remarkable that in recent years tolerance has been explicitly characterized as a constitutional principle.[34]

Tolerance—whose dimensions must be specified—represents the amount of freedom that surpasses the fulfillment of a function within the framework of a social order and thus activates an "opposition that in some way is perceived as evil," consisting in the noncorrespondence of this order's functional laws and action orientations. This "excess" (Übermass) is not legally secured and thus is not freedom in the legal sense; instead it is a privilege that is revocable at any time. The criterion for the "right amount" (rechte Mass) of freedom, whose violation can still be comprehended only with the category of tolerance, is the consensus regarding the functional conditions of the political order. The Federal Constitutional Court declared in its decision prohibiting the Communist party of Germany that the Basic Law has "consciously attempted to forge a synthesis between the principle of tolerance vis-à-vis all political persuasions and the affirmation of certain inviolable basic values of the political order"; it thereby gave explicit articulation to this connection.[35] For this reason Püttner's assertion that "democracy can guarantee no tolerance for the declared opponents of the system, those fighting against democracy" is imprecise (cf. Article 9, paragraph 2; Article 21, paragraph 2 of the Basic Law); what is correct is that the type of democracy constitutionalized in the Basic Law can confront "opponents of the system" with tolerance, but cannot guarantee them equal rights.[36] This is a consequence of a political order in which the specific functional laws of social life have been ordained to be un-

Ulrich Preuss

conditionally true; as regards the truth manifested in the basic consensus, those in error have no right and at most can expect tolerance.

This constitutional situation has the result that the political persuasions espoused on the basis of a consensus regarding the unconditionally true are all equally true or equally false, since the truth of the constitutionalized functional conditions lies in the fact that the democratic principle consists in the pluralism of opinions and interests, that is to say, in their equivalence. In the face of this truth all pluralistic opinions and interests have the same right, especially since, according to the pluralistic principle of equivalence, each is potentially capable of espousing every position and every interest (the perspective of the structural homogeneity of the majority principle). The recognition of this relativity of all positions vis-à-vis the unconditionally true makes the invocation of legally assured freedom, that is, legal behavior, into a loyal action. For with the application of rights, consideration is simultaneously always given to the functional conditions of the system in which they claim validity. The system of legality is transformed into an order of loyalty regulated by consensus, and in it freedom becomes tolerance.

The relation of positions to one another is likewise ruled by tolerance; it is the relation of the equal treatment of diverse opinions and interests in light of an independent power that keeps the functional conditions of the political system free from conflict. This second dimension of tolerance universalizes the principle from a relation between state and citizen (and groups) into a general principle according to which, for instance, school curricula, electronic media programs, municipal construction projects, or personal life-styles are governed by the principle of tolerance.[37] As a principle of law, this can mean nothing but the obligation on the part of all individuals and groups to recognize the universal truth according to which particular claims to truth, particular interests, and particular forms of life have equal right and thus are equivalent, although they forfeit this equal right if they are not commensurable. When a cognition is asserted to be true and all others false, an interest legitimate and all others illegitimate, a form of life valid and all others invalid, then this qualifies the true cognition, the legitimate interest, or the valid life form as intolerant and, in the sense of the functional conditions of the political system, false. They have then no right, because they deny the pluralistic foundations of their existence; but certainly they can be treated with tolerance in the sense of the aforementioned principle of consensus.

V

To summarize let me first recall that the delineated concepts of *parity*, *neutrality*, *pluralism*, *consensus*, and *tolerance* are asymmetrical. They are not elements of an opposition whose tension sustains the structure of a social and political order; rather, they are comprehensively structured, and in such a way that their opposition is somehow perceived as evil. At the same time it is clear that from a conceptual standpoint they continually thematize a relation to other persons and other things: parity designates a relation of equality with something else; neutrality connotes "neither the one nor the other" and establishes in negative fashion a relation between many; pluralism implies the equally protected coexistence of many; consensus is the agreement of a multiplicity of persons or groups; tolerance, finally, circumscribes "the acceptance of a not always agreeable other."[38]

The other and the others are not semantically excluded but are embraced in a totality and harnessed together conceptually. The peculiarity of these relational concepts consists not simply in the fact that the relationship between the partners is specified but also in the fact that the equalization of interests between them is simultaneously implied. In each case they also designate a function within the framework of this overarching setting of objectives that the specific forms of social relations should serve. None of these concepts proclaims a state of affairs that is legitimate in itself, and none is amenable to further grounding—as are the concepts of freedom and equality, the central categories of the bourgeois constitutional state. Freedom in the sense of this bourgeois understanding of the constitution establishes the individual as the *cogito* of all social relations, which are clearly not themselves expressed in the concept. Equality, conversely, seems to possess the structure I have employed in characterizing the asymmetrical concepts; it is necessarily related to others and for this reason is a relational concept. Yet in contrast to the concept of parity, which only seems to represent a latinized version of the term "equality" (*Gleichheit*), no independent third party emerges from the relation of equality with another, such that with equality an equalization (*Ausgleich*) between the two participants is also created. In contrast to equality,

Ulrich Preuss

parity encompasses a state of equilibrium from which justice among partners emerges.

Neutrality protects the inherent standard of a sphere of life, preserving the integrity of existent structures of order and allowing them to operate vis-à-vis an objective justice. Pluralism has the function of constituting a concept of the common good, not known in advance, from the competitive interaction of diverse views and interests, thereby creating a just order. Consensus regarding the functional conditions of the political order should guarantee their viability and thus stand at the service of the constituted order. Tolerance, finally, should guarantee the functioning of the pluralistic system of competition.

Of course, freedom, equality, and (public) power also have a function within the framework of the civil order, which operates through an interplay of market steering and the state's monopoly on violence. Yet in contrast to the new constitutional concepts they do not explicitly thematize this order; rather, they are related to their opposites, which are situated outside the framework of this order. They presuppose the order in which they function and, as it were, expect from the maintenance of this opposition a balanced order, the coordination of system and social integration. Conversely, the asymmetrical concepts already designate the conditions of equilibrium; indeed they themselves describe a state of equilibrium by incorporating the functional conditions of political order into the conceptual framework of the constitutional state.

I would like to clarify this important state of affairs by way of an example from the sphere of private law. As fundamental categories of the liberal representative state, freedom and equality are related to the new concepts of a social-political equilibrium here under consideration, just as the will (*Willensmacht*) of the subject in private law is related to the category of contract. The private, autonomous power of the will is the system of private law's point of departure, one that is not further divisible and not open to additional justification. "Contract" denotes the relation of two (or more) private legal subjects and serves as a legal form for equalizing interests between them. Now a contract, however precisely formulated, presupposes two things if it is to perform this function of equalizing interests. First, the contractual partners must have the will to act according to the contract. This is a functional requirement that underlies its viability and that can be guaranteed neither by the contract itself nor by its institutions. Even if in the contract the partners obligate themselves to fulfill its conditions faithfully, the performance of this obligation in turn presupposes that the will to do so preceded the contract's formation. The second, objective requirement for a viable contract is designated by the (assumed) basis of transaction (*Geschäftsgrundlage*). This denotes the general circumstances over which as a rule the contractual partners have no control; it circumscribes the economic, social, and legal framework in which the contract holds its social significance. Thus, for instance, it has long been acknowledged that the "removal of the basis of transaction" extinguishes the obligation to fulfill the contract. Both requirements pertain to the noncontractual conditions for contract.

In domestic contract law the first functional requirement is guaranteed by public power; the second cannot be guaranteed by anyone. This guarantee function on the part of public power fails entirely, however, if there exists no superordinate power (as normally does exist both in international law and with regard to the domestic constitution) that cannot also guarantee its own conditions of functioning. The reason why, in contrast to the private law of contract, public power possesses no independent guaranteeing power lies in the simple and fundamental principle of the democratic constitutional state according to which the supreme power and its instrument, the sovereign state, are first created by the constitution and therefore cannot themselves claim to be the constitution.

The nonconstitutional foundations of the constitution also lie in a twofold phenomenon: (1) in the regularities and functional connections of the social order, which provide the constitution with stable form and security, and (2) in a people's constitutional will (*Willen zur Verfassung*), that is, the will to create and to maintain the order established in the constitution. The first pertains to the process of system integration, the second to that of social integration. It is on the interrelations of these nonconstitutional conditions that the viability of the constitution is based.

A people's will to political formation finds democratic expression in the majority principle. This principle is the mode of political functioning by means of which the people can theoretically abolish or fundamentally alter the constitution, or at least express their lack of constitutional will (*Unwillen zur Verfassung*). The regularities—the other, system-integrating condition of the constitution—lie, as the fiscal structure of bourgeois constitutional states clearly indicates, in the functioning of the market economy, particularly in the laws of capital accumulation. These regulate the cycle of investment, production, and consumption and react with extreme sensitivity, through functional weakening of the system, to interventions of a social welfare state nature that attempt to subordinate this process to action orientations. Thus Böckenförde was right to point out that the "liberal secularized state . . . lives off presuppositions that it itself is unable to guarantee."[39]

When I mentioned earlier that the asymmetrical concepts of equilibrium here under discussion have integrated the functional conditions of the constituted political order into the conceptual framework of constitutional law, I did so to suggest the following: they determine the first, subjective functional condition of the constitution, the popular "constitutional will," in that they preclude what is always the simultaneously conceived possibility of a "lack of constitutional will." The focal point is the majority principle. In an order of asymmetrical equilibrium it functions neither in its procedural dimension nor as a substantive principle of order. The systemic goal of an equilibrium between system and social integration—which, according to the standards of parity, neutrality, and so on, is translated into relations of equilibrium between interests and groups—cannot be achieved on the basis of *counting* votes, but is based on *weighing* interests, from which an equilibrium is subsequently constituted.

Formally the majority principle is certainly still valid for the process of democratic will-formation in elections and in the legislative procedures of parliament. Yet the subordination of the law (resolved upon by the majority) to the supplemental control of a constitutional judiciary acting as a disinterested third party indicates that the majority principle is subordinated to the superordinate objectives of the political order. In parliamentary elections the practice of prohibiting parties in accordance with the Basic Law has the effect, for the pluralistic competition of parties, of eliminating parties that do not conform to the system's functional requirements; in this way the principle of electoral equality and the tabulation of votes have likewise been modified according to the criterion of the pluralistic functional order through the principle of weighing votes.[40]

Altogether incompatible with a system of constitutional equilibrium is the majority principle as a substantive principle of order for structural majorities, whose relations to structural minorities under the regime of this principle would have to be organized in accordance with the model of national minorities. Yet today they are integrated into the institutionalized equivalence relations, thereby constituting a latent crisis potential for the equilibrated political system.

With the limitation of the majority principle through the constitutionalization of states of equilibrium, a weakening occurs in the resistance potential of those action orientations that oppose the functional laws, particularly of an economic system based on market economy, in order to subordinate them to democratic control. We shall not concern ourselves here with strategies for democratization; what is decisive for this structural analysis is the circumstance whereby the operating laws, particularly of the economic system, are assured a sphere of development in which they can exercise their system-integrative function without disruptive interventions from the political and sociocultural system. This occurs, for instance, in the reinterpretation of the guarantee of private ownership of the means of production into a guarantee of "the capacity to function" of business concerns;[41] in the labor law principle of the "parity of struggle" between the interest groups of capital and those of labor; in "recognizing the inherent standards" of parts of the social order through state neutrality; in the transformation of constitutional freedom (which simultaneously also connotes the legally codified state guarantee of the inviolability of autonomous functional operations) into a constitutional principle of tolerance. Freedom now always falls under the provisions of legally prescribed concretizations and restrictions; that is, the guarantee of the autonomy of functional operations falls under the provisions of legally recognized political intervention. Tolerance, as the "acceptance of a not always agreeable other" (Püttner), requires the preservation of some functional modes that are historically obsolete but cannot be eliminated through legal "devaluations," such as those that were implemented when the residual elements of feudal privileges were eliminated in the interests of a bourgeois order of property and acquisition. In short, through the constitutionalization of states of equilibrium, a boundary is drawn, rooted in the functional imperatives of the social system, which demarcates action orientations from the political and sociocultural spheres of society.

Incidentally, with the reinterpretation of traditional liberal representative constitutional elements into relations of equilibrium between systemic and social integrational modes of association, an objective criterion of justness has been established for social development, which can be applied by a disinterested third party and implemented by public power. This is significant for several reasons. When there is talk of asymmetrical concepts declaring their opposites to be illegitimate, then it is possible to ground this semantic finding in a more precise manner. The constitutionalized order of equilibrium has in a certain sense inscribed in every social activity the entirety of the system of order, thus totalizing all legal-constitutional institutions so that all internal oppositions are abolished and are possible only as a total opposition: that between the order of equilibrium as a whole and its total negation, the "enemies of the system." Oppositions that cannot be integrated into this order of equilibrium are, with an internal necessity, processed by means of a totalized polarization of the legitimate against the illegitimate. That is the price for the functioning of an order that constitutionally autonomizes its functional imperatives, immunizes them to a large extent against the action orientations of its citizens, and deploys the might of the state to guarantee their efficacy.

In the power of the "will and the peculiarities of the majority," Karl Jaspers saw the distinguishing feature of mass society. We must make this more precise. Mass society consists not in the domination of the quantity over the quality of the individual personality, but in the appearance of a "structural majority" of those who are socially dependent within the network of legally constituted domination. In mass society this majority proclaims the right to control freely its social existence, not to have to have justice *given* to it by a disinterested third party, but to *take* justice themselves as participants. Herein consists the historical right of the masses. Does the political system of the Federal Republic assist the masses—to return to our initial question—in attaining this right? We have seen that the concepts of constitutional theory here under investigation tend to lead to a situation where the justification and legitimation of social power and political domination is made independent of the majority principle. Behind this is concealed the unstated hope of being able to escape from history. The price to be paid for this has already been mentioned. But an additional price derives from the fact that historical development, to the extent that this concept is still even conceivable in the abstracted relations of equilibrium, is disengaged from the principle of popular sovereignty and connected with the functional logic of a social system capable of processing meaning orientations exclusively as disruptive interventions. It is no coincidence that the Basic Law contains, in Article 79, paragraph

3, an "eternity clause" and thus a constitutional declaration of the end of history. Of course society continues to be subject to an immanent process of technological, economic, and social development. Consequently the eternity clause has bearing only on the historical force of action orientations; with regard to functional imperatives it is powerless.

The political order is becoming the habitat for a controlled release of the developmental logic of system-functional necessities. Whether one can thereby guarantee the existence of a free society and its developmental possibilities is doubtful; what is certain, however, is that the masses are in this way not assisted in attaining their right.

Notes

1. K. Jaspers, *Die geistige Situation der Zeit*, 7th printing of 5th ed., revised in 1932. Published in English as *Man in the Modern Age*, translated by Eden and Cedar Paul (Garden City, NY: Anchor Books, 1957).

2. See, for instance, in the collection of essays edited by A. Hunold, *Masse und Demokratie* (Zurich/Stuttgart, 1957), the essays by Hayek, Oakshott, Röpke, and Rüstow.

3. *Man in the Modern Age*, p. 37. The translation has been altered (*tr.*).

4. U. Scheuner, *Das Mehrheitsprinzip in der Demokratie*. Lectures of the Rheinland-Westphalian Academy of Sciences (Opladen, 1973).

5. R. Nozick, *Anarchy, State and Utopia* (New York: Basic Books, 1974), p. 149ff.

6. "Whatever arises from a just situation by just steps is itself just. . . . As correct rules of inference are truth-preserving, and any conclusion deduced via repeated application of such rules from only true premises is itself true, so the means of transition from one situation to another specified by the principle of justice in transfer are justice-preserving, and any situation actually arising from repeated transitions in accordance with the principle from a just situation is itself just." Ibid., p. 151.

7. O. Mayer, "Die juristische Person und ihre Verwertbarkeit im öffentlichen Recht," in *Staatsrechtliche Abhandlungen. Festgabe für P. Laband*, vol. 1 (Tübingen, 1908), p. 1ff. esp. pp. 25, 29. See also U. K. Preuss, *Die Internalisierung des Subjekts* (Frankfurt, 1979), p. 69ff. The concept of the juristic person—a central category in public and private law, and of direct significance for our topic (since in the field of law the state functions as a juristic person)—expresses this state function with dogmatic sharpness. Thus O. Mayer wrote in an 1887 essay: "The authentic juristic person can exist only when it is something other than the participating individuals, legally separated and demarcated from them. Proper to this, however, is also the fact that the juristic person has its 'substratum,' its 'reference point' outside of these individuals." And inasmuch as he was concerned primarily with juristic persons in commercial law, Mayer added: "And this can apparently be found only in business, only in the (stock) corporation itself." Stated more generally: "The juristic person is impossible and meaningless wherever the link to the original owner and the bearer of the rights vis-à-vis the disposal of real property is not severed." The bearers of legal property act as human subjects only to the extent that they intervene in the autonomous valorization process in order to eliminate functional disturbances while reducing their subjective aims, which are linked to economic activity, to the acquisition of profit.

8. R. Koselleck, "Zur historisch-politischen Semantik asymmetrischer Gegenbegriffe," in H. Weinrich, ed., *Positionen der Negativität* (Munich, 1975), pp. 65–66.

9. See R. Hickel and R.-R. Grauhan, "Krise des Steuerstaats? Widersprüche, Perspektiven, Ausweichstrategien," special edition of the journal *Leviathan* (Opladen, 1978).

10. Ch. Starck, "Die Grenzen des Sozialstaates," *Frankfurter Allgemeine Zeitung*, March 5, 1979, p. 9.

11. See M. Heckel's article, "Parität," in *Evangelischen Staatslexikon*, 2nd ed. (Stuttgart, 1975).

12. See K. Schlaich, *Neutralität als verfassungsrechtliches Prinzip* (Tübingen, 1972), p. 115ff., with further references.

13. The fundamental decision of the Federal Labor Court appears in *Amtliche Entscheidungssammlung*, vol. I, pp. 291ff., 308.

14. Schlaich, *Neutralität als verfassungsrechtliches Prinzip*, pp. 115–16.

15. U. Scheuner, *Das Mehrheitsprinzip* p. 49; cf. also Scheuner, *Die Rolle der Sozialpartner in Staat und Gesellschaft* (Stuttgart, 1973).

16. There already exists a dissertation by G. Girardet with the very promising title *Die Ausgewogenheit der sozialen Gegenspieler als Verfassungsgebot* [The balance of social competitors as a constitutional prescription] (Bonn, 1973).

17. Schlaich, *Neutralität als verfassungsrechtliches Prinzip*, p. 120.

18. Ibid., pp. 227–28.

19. C. Schmitt, *Der Begriff des Politischen*. Text of a 1932 lecture and three colloquia. Colloquium 1: *Übersicht über die verschiedenen Bedeutungen und Funktionen des Begriffs der innenpolitischen Neutralität des Staates* (1931; Berlin, 1963), p. 97ff.

20. K. A. Bettermann, "Rundfunkfreiheit und Rundfunkorganization," in *Deutsches Verwaltungsblatt* (1963), p. 41ff., against Federal Constitutional Court 12, p. 205ff., esp. pp. 262–63.

21. Schlaich, *Neutralität als verfassungsrechtliches Prinzip*, p. 219.

22. Cf. G. Teubner, *Organizationsdemokratie und Verbandsverfassung: Rechtsmodelle für politisch relevante Verbände* (Tübingen, 1978).

23. W. Steffani, introduction to the reader he edited with F. Nuscheler, *Pluralismus: Konzeptionen und Kontroversen* (Munich), p. 9ff.

24. For a report on the state of the pluralism discussion primarily in the United States (in relation, however, to the situation as of 1970), see F. Scharpf, *Demokratie zwischen Utopie und Anpassung*, 2nd unchanged ed. (Konstanz, 1972), p. 29ff.; see also, in addition to the studies published in the reader referred to in the previous note, C. Offe, "Klassenherrschaft und politisches System. Die Selektivität politischer Institutionen," in Offe, *Strukturprobleme kapitalistisches Staates* (Frankfurt, 1972), p. 65ff.; Teubner *Organizationsdemokratie und Verbandsverfassung*, pp. 63ff., 73ff.; U. Scheuner, "Konsens und Pluralismus als verfassungsrechtliches Problem," in *Staatstheorie und Staatsrecht: Gesammelte Schriften* (Berlin, 1978), in particular, p. 145ff.

25. In this normative version, see above all E. Fraenkel: "Der Pluralismus als Strukturelement der freiheitlichrechtstaatlichen Demokratie," printed in Nuscheler and Steffani, *Pluralismus*, p.

Political Concepts of Order for Mass Society

158ff.; K. Sontheimer, "Staatsidee und staatliche Wirklichkeit heute," in Nuscheler and Steffani, eds., *Pluralismus*, p. 199ff., as well as Scheuner, "Konsens und Pluralismus."

26. See the essays in the aforementioned reader, and also Offe and Scharpf.

27. Federal Constitutional Court 12, pp. 205ff., 263.

28. See M. von Brentano, "Wissenschaftspluralismus: Zur Funktion, Genese und Kritik eines Kampfbegriffs," *Das Argument* 66 (1971): 476ff.

29. G. Püttner, "Toleranz und Lehrpläne für Schulen," *Die öffentliche Verwaltung* (1974): 656ff.; cf. Th. Opperman, "Nach welchem rechtlichen Grundsätzen sind das öffentliche Schulwesen und die Stellung der an ihm Beteiligten zu orden?" Opinion C in the 51st German Conference of Jurists (Munich, 1976), pp. 37ff., 92ff.

30. Scheuner, "Konsens und Pluralismus."

31. I. Kant, *The Metaphysical Elements of Justice*, translated by John Ladd (Indianapolis, IN: Bobbs-Merrill, 1965), p. 19.

32. Scharnagl, Column 394.

33. C. Schmitt, *Verfassungslehre* (Berlin, 1965), p. 131.

34. G. Püttner, *Toleranz als Verfassungsprinzip: Prolegomena zu einer rechtlichen Theorie des pluralistischen Staates* (Berlin, 1977).

35. Federal Constitutional Court 5, pp. 85ff., 139 (decision prohibiting the Communist party of Germany).

36. Püttner, *Toleranz als Verfassungsprinzip*, p. 39.

37. Ibid., p. 48ff.

38. Ibid., p. 13.

39. E.-W. Böckenförde, "Die Enstehung des Staates als Vorgang der Säkularisation," in his *Staat, Gesellschaft, Freiheit: Studien zur Staatstheorie und zum Verfassungsrecht* (Frankfurt, 1976), p. 42ff., here p. 60; Böckenförde, "Das Grundrecht der Gewissensfreiheit," in *Veröffentlichungen der Vereinigung der deutschen Staatsrechtler* 28 (1970): 33ff., here p. 80; Böckenförde, *Der Staat als sittlicher Staat* (Berlin,1978), p. 37.

40. Thus, according to the decision of the Federal Constitutional Court, the representative of a party declared to be unconstitutional loses his mandate. "The voter of an eliminated representative is not disadvantaged, since the demand to be represented by representatives of an unconstitutional party would itself be unconstitutional." See Federal Constitutional Court 2, p. 1ff., here p. 74 (the decision prohibiting the [Neo-Nazi] Sozialistische Reichspartei).

41. Thus the Federal Constitutional Court in the Worker Co-determination Decision, March 1, 1979.

Perspectives on Culture and Religion

The Three Cultures

Karl Heinz Bohrer

It is revealing that since the 1920s the concept of culture, or *Kultur*, had never dominated West European self-understanding as much as it did during the late 60s. At that time cities like Paris, Berlin, Frankfurt, Milan, and even London bore witness to the radical form of cultural criticism that became known as the "cultural revolution." What was revealing in this transference of the notion of criticism onto that of revolution was the exclusive attachment of the concept of culture. This made evident, but not always to the parties concerned, the fact that what had been at issue all along was indeed a superstructural phenomenon, a movement in the minds of artists, academics, and the elite of an entire generation of students, as well as the masses of young people from urban centers who were without traditional attachments. This mental insurrection, much as it attempted to concern itself with matters of political and economic import, could in fact never claim a solid basis in reality. When, following the Sorbonne uprising in May 1968, the French Communist party agreed to a pact with de Gaulle, more than one precocious left-romantic illusion was shattered. Extinguished was the beautiful chimera captured by Novalis in the apothegm, "All power to the imagination!" and with consequences that even today continue to define the spiritual situation in Western Europe. Suddenly it became vulgarly apparent that the aggressive form of cultural criticism represented by the Parisian neo-Marxist Henri Lefebvre, the American economists Paul Baran and Paul Sweezy, the American linguist Noam Chomsky, and above all the Frankfurt School's Herbert Marcuse, Max Horkheimer, and Theodor Adorno, was not to culminate in political action. Two generations of West European intellectuals had by dint of sheer imagination anticipated something that was never to materialize. In this way what were then the last schools of radical culture criticism bequeathed a scandal that may prove even more significant than the rude awakening experienced by a host of prominent European Marxists over the Moscow trials of the 30s. Although at the time the trials could still be conceived as a divergence of the real and the ideal, such dialectical mollifications lost their effectiveness after 1968. The uncertainty of the leftist intelligentsia is therefore tragic, since its basis was not only moral and emotional but theoretical as well. The results of the 1978 French election against the left coalition not only superseded the trauma of 1968 but in a banal way made it definitive.

Thus if we place the concept of culture as a grid upon the past ten years of European history, the reality of two opposing yet overlapping epochs becomes apparent. The point of reference is 1968. If we view this year as the pivotal date separating a revolutionary "left" epoch from an evolutionary "right" epoch, then we can ascribe to it a significance similar to that of the revolutionary dates of 1848 and 1870–71. In 1848 Richard Wagner, after first standing at the barricades in Dresden with Bakunin, decided—following the failure of the revolution—to write his *Siegfried* myth; in 1870–71 Karl Marx, after first declaring his sympathy for the insurrectionists of the Paris Commune, distanced himself with strategic criticisms from London.

If what is at issue is a particular date, others can be recalled in stenographic fashion to shed light on the relations of *New Culture*, *Old Culture*, and *Popular Culture*, the concepts to be elucidated in this essay. Incidentally, it should be emphasized that these concepts, as well as the realities designated by them, are to be understood wholly within the framework of historical and ideological considerations; to interpret them in terms of aesthetic or anthropological structures would be sheer positivism.

1967   First serious student unrest in West Berlin, prompted by the visit of the Shah of Iran. Benno Ohnesorg, the student shot and killed by police, becomes the first martyr of the left-revolutionary student movement, with which the left-liberal and, to some extent, the haut bourgeois intelligentsia proclaimed its solidarity. Here mention can be made of, among others, the influential university professor and neo-Marxist sociologist Jürgen Habermas, the psychoanalyst Alexander Mitscherlich, and the liberal educationalist Hartmut von Hentig.

1968   Outbreak of the Paris student revolt, with strong West German participation (Cohn-Bendit) and expressions of solidarity from groups of automobile factory workers, until the agreement between the French Communist party and the government once again rescues the de Gaulle regime. Concurrently the so-called Prague Spring is being crushed by the tanks of the Warsaw Pact alliance. This parallel occurrence furnishes neo-Marxist West European leftists with additional reasons to distance themselves from the Moscow orthodoxy and envision the new utopia in terms of the concept of anarchism or Mao's cultural revolution.

1969   Under the leadership of Willy Brandt, first Social Democratic chancellor of the Federal Republic of Germany, and with the help of the left wing of the Free Democratic party, a program of cultural reform is enacted. Ten years later, under pressure from the conservative majority of the population, it is revoked.

The deaths of Adorno and Horkheimer left a vacuum in the sphere of cultural criticism that was not filled by their heirs. It was replaced by a different sort of strictly materialist exegesis: that of the orthodox Marxists of the German Communist party or the German Democratic Republic (GDR) and Louis Althusser's momentous critique of the reception of the "humanistic" Marx.

1972   High point of the new strategy vis-à-vis the Soviet Union, Poland, and particularly the GDR, a strategy that became known as *Ostpolitik*. This strategy eliminates a state of affairs that could have served as a rallying point for the West German left. Capture of the left-anarchist Baader-Meinhof terrorist group, whose trial in the mid-70s led to new urban guerilla groups in West Germany and Italy; supported by a relatively powerful minority in the universities, these groups had a dramatic influence on domestic politics in both countries.

1974   Shrouded in scandal, the resignation of Willy Brandt, a charismatic figure for more than just the West German socialists. With Helmut Schmidt as the new Social Democratic chancellor, a shift (in personality, as well) is announced, wherein categories of pragmatism and state order are accorded priority over those oriented to reform.

All this took place against the backdrop of three simultaneous developments: (1) The departure of American troops from Vietnam deprived the West European left of a central focal point for moral protest. (2) The oil crisis challenged the previously assumed permanence of the affluent society and its liberal submilieu, thereby diminishing the topicality of a theme favored by what was in any case an already enervated form of cultural criticism. (3) When viewed in terms of its once world-defining industrial revolution, England's economic decline appeared tragic. West Germany was placed in the forefront, both as an economic-political power center and as a spearhead for the NATO model.

1975   The death of Franco, in the wake of which Spain's future becomes a reality and many people discard their anarchocommunist anticipations. There thus arises the possibility of an Iberian socialism, which, in conjunction with the Eurocommunism of the French "Popular Front" alliance and the Italian "Historical Compromise," offers an alternative to the social democrats of the North European industrial countries, West Germany in particular.

1977   High point of the West German and Italian terrorist anarchism; strained transformations in the domestic political climate in the Federal Republic, with a slide to the right in regional elections. The jail cell death, never convincingly clarified, of leading members of the Baader-Meinhof anarchists leads to anti-German demonstrations in France and West Germany, substantially backed by the left-liberal elite paper *Le Monde*. The West European intelligentsia's new target becomes the conservative and reactionary segments of the West German middle class, whose attitudes appear to combine traits of former German fascism with features of American imperialism.

1978   The "united" French left narrowly loses the election with the result that, precisely ten years after the Paris May, the French left alliance is broken. The cultural revolution—that is, the left-radical bourgeoisie—in the end has no confidence in the aims of the base, namely, party communism, just as conversely the communists in 1968 were unable to place their trust in the Red Utopia of the Parisian students. Only at this point did the decade of the 60s finally come to an end, a decade called the era of radical negation. Eurocommunism remained far from power.

Correctly understood, the foregoing list reveals how the host of reform- and utopia-oriented ideas spawned by the cultural revolution of the 60s have, with the exception of a few remnants, been totally worn away. Henceforth promises about the future will be less credible: the spell of eschatological language has been broken, and "everyday life," to invoke a concept of Lefebvre, exacts its revenge on the revolution by consigning the latter to the status of mere literature. Yet this revision did not simply reinstate all that preceded the 60s. Of continuing significance for West German intellectuals was their rejection, in the late 60s, of the lies and taboos that a petit bourgeois, reactionary survival generation, intent on falsifying its own history, was leaving as a legacy for the children and grandchildren of the Nazis. They had gleaned features of this falsified past in the writings of the German-Jewish emigrants Adorno and Horkheimer yet had to await the Parisians Lefebvre and Althusser to ascertain the full extent of the barbarism of their cultural amnesia. Whereas in France the Marxist discussion, still relevant for the present situation, commenced in the 30s, discussion in the birthplace of Marxism was interrupted for more than a quarter century after it had begun so auspiciously following World War I in Bloch's *Geist der Utopie* and Lukács's *History and Class Consciousness*. That this hiatus lasted more than thirty years, far longer than the duration of the Nazi period, can be attributed to the fact that the secret civil war between West and East Germany and the new alliance with the Western democracies created a climate of repression vis-à-vis West Germany's intellectual resources. The economically industrious West German bourgeoisie and its spokesmen had no interest in witnessing the rediscovery of the leftist tradition that had existed prior to fascism. To this extent the purely existential and humanistic interpretation of the early Marx, typical of the 50s and early 60s, was also part of the suppression that was fully revealed only with the 1965 publication of Althusser's *For Marx*.

All this became clear only at the end of the 60s. It can never be forgotten again. A simple restitution of the old bourgeois forms of cultural piety as the cognitive status of the ruling classes is, according to all rules of intellectual chemistry, no longer possible. Yet if we interpret these years through the rubric furnished by William Blake, "The tigers of wrath are wiser than the horses of knowledge," then we can say with certainty that at the moment the horses of knowledge have been displaced by the tigers of wrath; or, at the very least, the tigers have simulated a wise appearance. For instance, whereas the furious effect Herbert Marcuse's cultural revolutionary message once had on European students has now been nearly forgotten, this same magnetism is still discernible in the cult persona of Antonio Gramsci, founder of the Italian Communist party. Like Marcuse, Gramsci also accords a social function to the intelligentsia. While Marcuse attempted to fashion the cultural-revolutionary student avant-garde into the new revolutionary subject, Gramsci assigned this role to the "organic intellectuals" themselves. Thus the displacement of the German-Jewish university professor by the Italian politician and martyr reveals the same attraction: it also provides a place in the revolution for the politically and socially isolated intelligentsia. And yet recourse to Gramsci only appears more political than appeal to Marcuse, for it also attests to how much wiser the tigers of wrath have actually become: Gramsci, after all, has also been philologized.

With this delineation of the historical-ideological framework of the three aforementioned concepts of culture, we now come to the problem that enables us to distinguish the 60s from the 70s, the revolutionary from the evolutionary epoch. This is the problem of the temporalization of time. Generalizing from the phenomenon just described, namely, that Gramsci has been fashioned into an object of philology, it is possible to characterize the 70s by way of an emphatic reconstruction of and reflection on contemporary history or, for that matter, its revocation. *Either historical contents are realized or reality is historicized.* On the basis of the predominance of these polemically exclusive yet categorially corresponding alternatives, one can define, and this is my thesis, the concepts of New Culture, Old Culture, and Popular Culture not only in a purely descriptive manner but theoretically as well. The alternatives of realizing history and historicizing reality would correspond roughly to the following intellectual positions: On the side of realized history one finds the French neo-Marxists Lefebvre and Althusser, the heirs of the Frankfurt School (Habermas), the West

German artistic avant-garde (Joseph Beuys), Peter Weiss's dramatic aesthetic, and Peter Brook's theater of cruelty, the theoretical reconstruction of surrealism, futurism, dada, the neo-avant-garde. On the side of historicized reality one finds the structuralists Lévi-Strauss and Michel Foucault, the later, ironic Harold Pinter, the linguistic psychoanalyst Jacques Lacan, art-historical conservatism, and the social-technological program of the West German sociologist Niklas Luhmann.

Stated in less esoteric terms, these alternatives can be characterized in terms of the distinction between history and structure, the question of whether Europe now finds itself in its *posthistoire*. This is a question the French structuralists have asked of the philosophical heirs of Hegel and their temporalization of tradition, especially as such concerns find expression in the existentialism of Sartre. These debates, originally understood merely as the literary disputes of the Parisian *haute couture*, have long since been academically thematized (Alfred Schmidt). In West Germany the main participants in this debate have been Niklas Luhmann, representing an Anglo-Saxon-inspired form of social technology, and Jürgen Habermas, proponent of a dialectical social theory understood as the former's antipode. What is of particular interest for us in this debate is simply the fact that Luhmann, distinguishing between evolution and history, has concluded that one must abandon the notion of a philosophically mediated unity of history whose nature can be definitively specified. Appealing to the contingency or complexity of developmental possibilities, he opposes such unity with the notion of the difference between possibility and reality. With reference to Althusser's concept of "overdetermination," which was intended to correct the contradictions in a dialectical theory of development in order to save the venerable unequivocality [in the meaning of history], Luhmann affirms, in opposition to Althusser, its definitive loss. At issue is the loss of a universally applicable theory of history, the renunciation of the European-Hegelian tradition as such. Thus, for instance, the emancipatory interest in revolution, the central theme of the 60s, is demoted to the rank of a special interest, for it is claimed to represent a formulation of the problem that is artificial, externally interjected, and lacking in structural viability. Yet what is thus demoted is also the concept of meaning that since Descartes and classical German Idealism has been associated with the concept of the subject. In opposition to Habermas, not to mention the humanist neo-Marxism of the *Paris Manuscripts*, to which of course romantic leftist radicalism made appeal,

Luhmann categorically refuses to define the concept of meaning in terms of the concept of the subject. For him the concept of meaning is logically prior, because the concept of the subject "qua meaningfully constituted identity" always presupposes that of meaning. Luhmann's repudiation of the transcendental questioning of objective realities, already prepared in Husserl's phenomenology and revivified in Gadamer's aesthetic, also entails an epistemological revision of the subjective aesthetic of the nineteenth century, whose legacy was bequeathed to West European aesthetic debates chiefly by the romantics, by Baudelaire, Nietzsche, Walter Pater, the surrealists, and Walter Benjamin.

The theoretical divergence involved in this alternative of history and structure, which to be sure can only be intimated here, is pragmatically mirrored by the cultural situation in the following manner: (1) as a reconstruction or repudiation of revolutionary Marxism and (2) as a reconstruction or repudiation of the classic avant-garde. Central to an understanding of the concepts of New Culture, Old Culture, and Popular Culture is the dynamizing of the concept of the avant-garde, which so suddenly appeared on the scene in the 70s, albeit only in theoretical form. Let us recall: the aesthetic practices of so-called pop art, in which elements of the still esoteric American Beat Generation were placed on the agenda for everyone, contained the entire cultural-revolutionary reservoir of the classic avant-garde. Techniques included happenings, underground films, spontaneous writing, the theater of "cruelty," and the pathos of the new "sensibility." Here special emphasis must be accorded the discoveries of Marcel Duchamp, Man Ray, Kurt Schwitters, Max Ernst, André Breton. Susan Sontag, the American critic best known to Europeans, correctly analyzed this renaissance of the West European avant-garde. But what she failed to address and what as a non-European she could not question has now been challenged by the historically scrupulous European debate: if what now is already yesterday's avant-garde—extending from Daniel Spoerri and Bazon Brock, from Richard Hamilton and Kitaj to Andy Warhol, with its *objets trouvés* and *readymades*—merely repeats, with the disintegration of the classical concept of art and the usherance of art into life, something that had already been invented long ago, then how can the shock it invokes still be effective? Was not the provocation sought by the avant-garde since the 50s from its very outset an illusion born too late?

The category of the "new," advanced primarily by way of formal innovation, has constituted, ever since the emergence of an aesthetic concept of modernism, the criterion by which contemporary art is to be comprehended. As a consequence it may well suffer the fate experienced by the hare in the fairy tale who imprudently entered into a race with the hedgehog only to discover that the latter was always at the finish line ahead of him. This, to be sure, was a deceptive maneuver: the cunning hedgehog had placed his wife there, who looked exactly like him. Yet the hare failed to notice this before he died of exhaustion. The argument for the formal identity of the neo-avant-garde and the classic avant-garde becomes even less compelling if one recognizes in it the symptom of a historically postautonomous situation in the arts, wherein the semantic contents of the old "new" have long since been spent and their subversive claim long since forfeited. Here the situation of contemporary art corresponds fully to that of the remaining American Indians, who are consigned to designated reservations. Avant-gardism would then be at best therapeutically defined in the social-psychological sphere as one form of aesthetic amusement available to a once historical subject now occupied with leisure activities. At any rate, this culturally pessimistic consequence plays a role precisely at the point where one becomes conscious of the concept of subjectivity bearing the imprint of the French Revolution and the German ego philosophy (Kant, Fichte, Schleiermacher, Hegel)— the two features of the European tradition that experienced a vibrant renaissance in the 60s.

Here the sudden realization of historical contents or the imminent historicization of reality becomes apparent, that is, either the vibrant or the melancholic renaissance of the nineteenth century. Both are indicative of the profound questioning of identity now occurring among West European intellectuals. As long as one adheres to the concept of the avant-garde—and this is done by all representatives of the New Culture—one need only act like Münchhausen, who was able to pull himself out of the mire by his own bootstraps. In this way reference is made to a strictly voluntaristic act that stands opposed to all forms of determinism. This is not accomplished, however, through a formal reconstruction of the avant-garde as aesthetic procedure. Rather it is only with the spiritual reacquisition of the surrealistic shock, only in a Benjamin-like ascertainment of the "instant," the here and now, that one can escape the paralyzing historicism of aesthetic forms. But this profane-historical dynamic is now accessible more through an act of thought than through aesthetic activities.

The crisis of the New Culture has in a negative way become explicit in discussions of the concept of the aesthetic avant-garde. The journalistic polemic, while having a symptomatic significance, has generated no real knowledge. Concurrent discussions in the field of literary theory, inherently without much influence on the general public, have nonetheless created something akin to an elitist and yet relevant public sphere. The fact that this discussion was carried out with such vigor demonstrates the extent to which the status of the problem has changed since H. M. Enzenberger's early essay, "Die Aporien der Avant-Garde" (1962), and Theodor W. Adorno's treatise, *Kriterien der neuen Musik* (1957): 1968 bore witness to a historical dynamic in which even then no one believed and which was coupled with the emergence of a neosurrealist emphasis in the arts dedicated to the realization of the unfulfilled claims and promises of classical surrealism. Since then the concern has no longer been exclusively, as Adorno and his immediate disciples believed, the criterion of the technical mode of production; nor has it only been the questions of function and formal innovation or their erosion and ideological paralysis. At issue, in other words, is not the reconstruction of the avant-garde as procedure. To allow such misunderstanding would obviously make it easy for cultural conservatives to appear to checkmate the artists and theorists of the neo-avant-garde. Cultural conservatives could say that an epigonic situation is conclusively reached when the destroyers repeatedly revert to Man Ray, Duchamp, and Schwitters, when they repeatedly return to the same gesture of surprise. Yet what cultural conservatives are obliged to suppress is the real criterion of every conceivable type of new art: the specific supersession of accepted concepts of value, the specific methods, the repudiation of any return to natural harmonies, the "burning of ships." They must suppress such nuances because their concern is primarily with values, natural harmonies, and ships that have not burned. By attacking the constructions of the avant-garde as epigonic, they aim to retrieve traditional elements. In formalizing the problem—and indeed it is precisely in this that the early avant-garde theorists made their strongest claims—cultural conservatives believe they have cornered the avant-garde. The extent of this method's success was initially indicated by the discussion within the very circles taken seriously by the neo-avant-garde. Thus in his *Theorie der Avantgarde*

(1974), Peter Bürger assigns to the neo-avant-garde a position of academic defeatism, a position that was countered, in *Antworten auf Peter Bürgers Bestimmungen von Kunst und bürgerlichen Gesellschaft* (1976), with the requisite arguments developed from a systematic perspective. This seems to have been executed most proficiently, that is to say, most consistently, by Dolf Oehler, who took on the totality and linked his demand for a "glance" at it with the question on which everything turns: whether it is even possible to dynamize the theory of the avant-garde. Oehler answers this question affirmatively, albeit decisionistically: "A dynamizing of the theory of the avant-garde entails a recovery of what had been rendered harmless by the para-aesthetic reception, namely, the intended or, more properly, actual meaning present in the work at the time of its composition." Oehler believes that the avant-garde will "founder" unless redeemed by the mass of "ordinary mortals." And the historical precondition for a renaissance of the avant-garde must be "the naiveté of all avant-garde movements, which perhaps shakily yet doggedly possess a truly ingenuous belief in the alterability of the world." This naiveté and belief can be invoked, yet today nothing indicates that such an incantation will be answered. Consequently one should rely not on the problematical category of alterability but on the laconic evidence of sensuous appearances manifested in the material fulfillment of experiences such as surprise, doubt, movement, and desire. One would thereby avoid in a credible way the *posthistoire* already proclaimed by Arnold Gehlen, according to which nothing more can be expected in the history of ideas. To this one need only reply that these ideas have for some time been of no interest to us! With respect to our fruitful cynicism regarding ideas, Oehler once again provides a nice example. Comparing the humor of Tünnes and Schäl with Hegel's dressing-down of sensual appearances as bare appearances, he writes: "Childish as it is, humor has much sense and has the advantage over Hegel at least in that it contains within itself knowledge of an essential element of sense certainty: that the drive, when strong enough, will itself constitute the object of its satisfaction." The conservative culture industry has deemed the repression and control of this drive its most important task. The identification of avant-garde desire and political anarchism by our reactionary cultural censors was made public so long ago that the attack on the neo-avant-garde was forced to become political.

Now if we ask contemporary art for the concrete answer that either consciously or unconsciously it gives to this dilemma, we can observe with the aid of the terms New Culture, Old Culture, and Popular Culture a general tendency. The New Culture of the 60s—by which is to be understood all experimental dissolutions of classical modernism from Peter Weiss and Peter Brook through the *nouveau roman* of Nathalie Sarraute and Alain Robbe-Grillet to the philosophy of art since Benjamin and Adorno—has either lost its fascination or has come to approximate the Old Culture. In the form of belletristic literature, which has never lost its popularity with the general public, the features of Old Culture have remained unchanged: whether it be Sartre or Malraux, Graham Greene or Doris Lessing, Moravia or Calvino, Böll or Grass, the best-known representatives of the European postwar literature are only superficially related to the avant-garde. They have always constituted the bulwark of Old Culture. But while New Culture is approaching Old Culture, a certain stability has become noticeable in the domain of Popular Culture. Under this category are to be subsumed not only all the transformations of Anglo-Saxon rock music, together with its attendant subcultures (New York and London punk being the most recent transformation) but also pornography, football, television, the occult, the increasingly aggressive feminist movement, the language of West German Mescalero anarchism, and all varieties of what, following Lefebvre, we term "everyday life," something which as a "dialectic of the concrete" (Kosik) has even been rediscovered within a New Left in Budapest. One could say that the authentic elements of the New Culture have in a manner devoid of theory been rescued in Popular Culture, while its theories have dissipated at the border of the aforementioned avant-garde discussion. The explanation—more sociopsychological than aesthetic—for this new constellation in the relation of the cultures to one another lies in the fact that the New Culture, a concept invented by bourgeois intellectuals, is weakening at the moment it must revise its progressive self-understanding. In contrast, the Popular Culture, borne by petit bourgeois and proletarian youths, is somewhat protected from such scruples of reflection. Beyond the objections of cultural criticism, it possesses the vitality of its own self-regenerating reality.

Before substantiating these theses in detail, we must clarify the nature of the dissolution of the New Culture in the domain where it is most directly affected: avant-garde prose and the theory of the literary avant-garde. In the late 1960s it was still assumed that one could accept as definitive the verdict pronounced by Nathalie Sarraute on classical modernists such as Virginia Woolf. In fact, this verdict as well as its aesthetic implications have nearly been forgotten: the *nouveau roman* is dead, while Virginia Woolf's prose has been rediscovered with a vengeance—albeit, interestingly enough, not by a new aesthetic school but by the "popular" interest of the women's movement. This is no argument for the eternal recurrence of the past, but it does show how false it is to combine, as literary modernism has done, formal progressiveness and existence-transforming qualities.

Such an intellectual illusion is exemplified by the late aesthetic of Adorno. The admirable consistency with which Adorno, in his last work, *Ästhetische Theorie* (published posthumously), attempted to summarize all preceding attempts to rescue the true in the beautiful gives characteristic expression to a pernicious circularity. With respect to the claims of concepts, ideology, and "alienation," he constantly stresses the incommensurability of the work of art. Yet he was able to do this successfully only because he still based his thought on a Hegelian concept of art, on the "sensuous manifestations (*Scheinen*) of the Idea" and not the aesthetic appearance (*Schein*) itself, whatever that might be. When Adorno assigns to art the function of articulating the truth of the future within a world of falsity—and here must also be included, in the sense of his "negative dialectics," the world of concepts—he elevates art, employing what is still an idealist argument, to the rank of a goal of material progress. The crux of an idealist form of pernicious circularity is contained in every attempt to transform life through literature. This was the great message of surrealism, to which Walter Benjamin in 1929 already ascribed a paucity of "materialist illumination," whereby a *contradictio in adjecto* inheres in the terminology itself. This was also the message of the Paris May of 1968, when the surrealists were rediscovered and the group associated with the journal *Tel Quel* actualized Artaud and de Sade. But all these efforts made clear that "alienation" is not to be overcome through literature and that in essence this claim represents merely the last phase in the revenge that the bourgeois intellectual subject exacts on the everyday life described by Lefebvre.

I now want to clarify the conservative revision or transformation of the European cultural scene by means of four examples, which either are particularly characteristic for the countries designated or have had the greatest international influence:

The transformation of the political theater of cruelty into aesthetic drama

The dissolution of shock and pop-concept art

The return of myth in West German cinema

Punk anarchism and terror anarchism as real forms of Popular Culture

Whereas the last example focuses on Popular Culture, the others are concerned with occurrences within New Culture. This distribution is indicative, for culturally relevant developments have taken place only within New and Popular Culture. Old Culture remains important as the ever-present foil for New and Popular Culture in terms of which the corrections of New Culture and the deviations of Popular Culture first become apparent.

The transformation of the political theater of cruelty: This theatrical form was a major discovery of the 60s. It is characterized by three names and two productions: Antonin Artaud, Peter Brook, and Peter Weiss, *King Lear* (1962) and *Marat/Sade* (1964). When Peter Brook, at the Royal Shakespeare Company, exposed madness as theatricality's chief manifestation, using the examples of Shakespeare's *Lear* and Peter Weiss's *Marat/Sade*, he simultaneously revived Artaud's visionary ideas, to which he had paid tribute in 1961. The scene of Cornwall's blinding of Gloucester, in which Brook for the first time confronts the public with an unbridled aggressiveness free of the standard moralistic mollifications, became the archetype for the new theatrical sadism. The sudden assault on the public, combined with the intellectual rediscovery of the great French surrealists, was so powerful that it provided sustenance for an entire epoch. In 1963 Brook, together with Charles Marowitz, founded an experimental company in London entitled Theatre of Cruelty. The artistic forms thus established played an important role in the production of *Marat/Sade*, which reproduced the ingenious Artaudian spirit of the new theatricality: suppressed acts of violence, somnambulism, madness as intensity, the theater of suprapsychological senses, pure action as opposed to morality, torture as a basic metaphor.

The subsequent major productions of the Royal Shakespeare Company are inconceivable without the theater of cruelty. They are also inconceivable without the phenomenally effective combination of Artaudian and Brechtian stylistic elements. The Elizabethan legacy of the English stage encouraged the method of Artaud. The Polish director Jerzy Growtowsky could write in 1967, at the height of the epoch: "We are now entering the era of Artaud." And in 1973 Susan Sontag still maintained: "The course of all recent serious theatre in Europe and America can be said to divide into two periods—before Artaud and after Artaud." But Peter Brook left England the end of the 60s and Peter Hall, founder of the obsessively experimental Royal Shakespeare Company, began to follow more traditional paths at the National Theatre.

These biographical developments coincided with a fundamental transformation of the contemporary British stage. The foremost playwrights of the era—Pinter, Orton, Wesker, Bond—had written, if not dreams of cruelty, at least those of hate, violence, and moral blasphemy. Thus such well-known plays as *The Kitchen* (Wesker), *Entertaining Mr. Sloane* (Orton), *The Birthday Party* (Pinter), and *The Narrow Road into the Deep North* (Bond) all contained central scenes of sadistic fantasy, fully equivalent to the hate orgies of Shakespeare's *Henry VI* which, with its "War of the Roses," served to inaugurate theatrically the Vietnam era. The new plays of the 70s lacked this viciousness and sociopsychological aggressiveness, however. While Edward Bond, with *The Fool* (1975) and *The Bundle* (1978), invented elegies to social martyrs, and while Wesker, after a long silence, resurfaced in melancholic tranquility with *Love Letters on Blue Paper* (1978), Harold Pinter in *No Man's Land* (1975) dissolved the overwhelming terror and the intrusion of the unexpected found in his earlier plays into an ironic music of words. With this graceful recourse to earlier themes, he undoubtedly moved closer to Oscar Wilde than to Beckett, who for his part, in the half-hour plays, *That Time* and *Footfalls* (1976), translated old commonplace horrors into poetic fantasy akin to the madness of William Blake. Wilde's Dorian Gray was the hero in the last play (1975) of John Osborne, who himself has now been playing the role of the conservative dandy.

The general tendency toward political abstinence in the once-aggressive English dramatic literature is nicely illustrated by the continuing success of the two playwrights who for years have presided over West End comedy: Simon Grey and Tom Stoppard. Interestingly enough, their plays have two things in common: formally, the return to a pure comic dialogue, free of Artaudian and Brechtian techniques;

substantively, the ironic dissolution of all ideological and moral messages. Stoppard's *Travesties*, tumultuously acclaimed in London, is paradigmatic for this state of affairs. The brilliant idea of setting the aesthetic and political avant-garde of Europe against one another, in the personages of James Joyce, Tristan Tzara, and Lenin, had, all comic implications aside, a malicious intent: Stoppard ridicules the utopian notion of the New Culture according to which the aesthetic avant-garde created or at least occasioned and accompanied the political revolution. This conservative answer, which in *Travesties* is to be read as a commentary on the 60s, is also reflected in the work of the leading directors: with Peter Stein in West Berlin and Giorgio Strehler in Milan, anthropological-symbolic elements supplant the political themes that were once so much in favor. Stein's production of *Peer Gynt*, as well as his *Prinz von Homburg*, attests to this. Strehler's program notes for his 1973 *Lear*, while demonstrating the extent to which the effects of the famous Brook production still linger, nonetheless stress the motifs of collective cultural consciousness and the antinomic physiognomy of the age. In this context it is significant that Brecht's conceptual and dramaturgical suggestions are, after twenty years, declining in influence. The "distancing technique," which became a common practice in the modern European theater, has lost its function; and it is precisely this development that encourages a new form of aesthetic-anthropological positivism.

The dissolution of shock and pop-conceptual art: Here, too, once-aggressive positions are swept away; here, too, a charming and intelligent attempt is made to ground the elements of tradition. This was demonstrated in 1976 by the intellectual spokesman for the English neo-avant-garde, the American-born R. B. Kitaj. In London's Hayward Gallery, he organized an exhibition of paintings and drawings on the theme of the human body under the title *The Human Clay*. In a programmatic essay for the catalogue he explains an apparent commonality between all the paintings on display and the "London School." Kitaj evidently wanted to call attention to a specific relation to given natural forms. This is now elevated to a criterion. Were one interested in providing a theoretical summation of Kitaj's thesis, it would be necessary to assign importance not to surrealism, or to the imaginative combination of artists and intellectual painters in the early twentieth century, all prior to Duchamp and Man Ray, but to the great French masters like Degas, whose paintings portrayed the natural figure, the female form.

As with dramatic literature, the fathers of the avant-garde are repudiated and a classical prototype is rediscovered.

This is the perspective of the mid-70s. Instead of a progressive decomposition of nature, instead of the brutally shrill or emphatic dissolution of elementary particulars taken from advertisements, photography, and the citation of reality, the search is now for natural form. Line, color, and form once again become substance and not merely function. A curious search for the elementary is underway. Examining the possibility of an anthropological revision in the general context of the contemporary English cultural scene, one must acknowledge, after distancing oneself from the intellectual origins of the concept and the aggression, its indifference and its weaknesses. It is of course true that the founder, Richard Hamilton, together with Dieter Rot, still manages to needle, with black humor, the general public and certain London critics. He does so, however, within the framework of the conventional technique of provocation, drawing encouragement from the reactionary mentality of the bourgeois observer. No artistic new world exists. As in the case of theater, the focus is on savage beginnings. Hamilton's 1975 landscape essays in the Serpentine Gallery were already lacking in aggressive force. They merely offered poised visions of beauty and melancholic-cynical inner images. Clearly there is a danger present in this hide-and-seek game of reverting to a frivolous, masked traditionalism, specifically to a decorative art. Hamilton, a conceptual artist, is aware of this and attempts to guard against it. But even in the most hardened artists, like Jones, Blake, and even Kitaj, one cannot avoid noticing a transformation from the severe to the soft, from assault to epilogue.

To understand the cynical-romantic defeatism which today characterizes English neo-avant-garde and conceptual art, one must contrast them to the work of the West German Joseph Beuys. Beuys exemplifies what remains of the neo-avant-garde in the 70s, for which reason he is subjected both to vulgar abuse by an uninformed press and to the institutional attacks of reactionary politicians. The vehemence of these attacks restores to Beuys precisely what has been lost by the English pop avant-garde: anarchist subversion. This is the classic weapon of the cultural-revolutionary artist, invented by dada and surrealism. In both his external appearance as a fool and a prophet and his ritualistic appearance, Beuys establishes direct contact with the provocative objects of the early surrealist exhibitions. Certainly in this sense he already serves as an example of the dilemma described earlier. But Beuys recognized the shallowness of the reconstructed avant-garde as purely formal procedure: "The innovations within the isolated cultural sectors, which lead to nothing other than new styles within the museums, galleries, and art markets, would be pernicious were they to last an eternity." Beuys realized that the avant-garde claim could be redeemed only through an extra-aesthetic inspiration, like that already attempted by surrealism. This means that perceptual intelligence rather than shock now becomes central: instead of responding to appeals and signals, one now acknowledges structures. Yet Beuys allows the progressive to appear as regressive, as archetypal. His much-discussed contribution to the 1976 Biennale in Venice, the *Strassenbahnhaltestelle* [Streetcar stop], gave occasion to compare this "conservative" development with Breton's postwar compositions: in both cases an interest is shown in staging ceremonies based on liturgical myths drawn from the ethnological sphere. Are we thus to conclude that here, too, we find only the weight of tradition, only a postfiguration of something already given? Quite the contrary. One has to acknowledge that Beuys's symbols of war and death, his iconography conceived in the stench of seedy catastrophe, are original inventions. It is here, in contrast to the practices of the "civilized" English, that the eschatological historicity of the Germans becomes apparent. Nonetheless the insight advanced before is confirmed: the neo-avant-garde is saved through the archaic.

The return of myth in West German auteur films: What in theater and the visual arts was announced hesitantly and was initially not recognized as a conservative or melancholic shift had been anticipated early on by the mythologizing fantasies of West German film directors. The unusual and abiding interest that since the early 70s has been displayed by the younger French and British intellectual public in the films of R. W. Fassbinder, Werner Herzog, and recently even H. J. Syberberg can be explained only in terms of a new atavistic romanticism. It is characteristic of this need for romantic-enigmatic messages that the real pioneer of new West German cinema, the intellectually disciplined rationalist and "leftist" Alexander Kluge, was not himself able to command the attention accorded his more exotic compatriots. This causality becomes even more evident when one recognizes that the appearance of the new West German cinema coincided with the departure from the scene of Jean-Luc Godard, master of the intellectual European auteur film. Fassbinder's fame is a chapter in itself, partially attributable to the public's fascination for a vital, primal talent. Like the films of Wim Wenders, Fassbinder's early films followed themes of social crit-icism, and as a result he acquired the image of leftist director. None-theless the explanation for his early vogue appears to lie not in his "leftist" message but in his stoically brutal investigation of anthro-pological conditions, his laying bare of the primitive instincts at the base of the nearly presemantic spheres of a postfascist petit bourgeoisie.

In Wenders's films as well one discovers a melancholic speechless-ness, a disturbed communication in which emphasis is placed more on the broader perspectives of romantic nature than on the sparse dialogue. Speechlessness, distance from ideological assertion, and a sensitive observation of movements, an existentialism of the insignif-icant—these are the typical elements of this style. Socially engaged critics have vehemently assailed the products of this "new sensitivity," which have been associated with certain leading representatives of West German avant-garde prose—Peter Handke, for instance. Wen-ders's withdrawal from political engagement led directly to the skep-ticism of Stoppard: "If only the political and the poetic could be one"—thus exclaims that very German hero in *Wrong Move* (1975), so consumed by his *Weltschmerz*. The homage paid Wenders, which quickly became audible in other West European cities, can undoubtedly also be at-tributed to the clear uniqueness of the German identity. Only since they have begun searching for themselves, for the "dead souls of Germany," have German artists, for the first time since the end of World War II, been able to influence the entire continent.

Wenders and Fassbinder have expressed themselves in a romantic melancholia, an inward path that has led them back to classic German literature (Fontane's *Effi Briest*, Goethe's *Wilhelm Meister*, Eichendorff's *Aus dem Leben eines Taugenichts*), a movement that has an accurate East German parallel. By contrast, Werner Herzog appears even more authentic, free of the tortured detour; his work evinces the intensity of a savage mythology in which the colors and motifs of German Romanticism are passionately reborn, as if created for the first time. What Peter Handke is for Wenders—a kindred literary spirit—the Bavarian anarchist Achternbusch is for Herzog. Often viewed as the most interesting and most poetic of the German New Wave Directors, Herzog has been feted in France as the romantic *génie allemand*, and he has had great popularity in London film circles as well. The French acclaim is symptomatic of the temper of the times, and one is almost inclined to see motifs of the Parisian New Philosophy presaged in Herzog's visions of catastrophe. This at any rate is the mood that introduced his specific combination of anarchism and a counter-enlightenment mentality. *Aguirre, the Wrath of God* (1973) became a cult film for West German and Parisian devotees. This and films such as *Kaspar Hauser* (1974), *Land of Silence and Darkness* (1971), and *Heart of Glass* (1976) announce an anarchosecretive gesture, which fully unfolds in the images themselves. His concern is always with myths of ruination, in which the history of humanity is redeemed and destroyed not only by magic, nature, crime, and madness but by prophesy and longing as well.

It is in *Heart of Glass* that Herzog most radically strips these interests of social-psychological and historical considerations. Turning to a fairy tale by Hauff, Herzog presents extreme situations in which people function in states of complete hypnosis and are left abandoned as useless ornaments, a condition deriving from hallucination, prophesy, and visionary and collective madness. The mystically shaded glow of the images recalls Caspar David Friedrich's visions of nature and the sea but is infused with an inhumanly cold beauty. The development from *Kaspar Hauser* (1974), where Herzog sought solutions, to this aesthetic prophesy of world destruction represents a deeper step into mystical darkness. Herzog's aesthetic, whose rudiments were formulated in Paris, corresponded fully to the late-70s *Zeitgeist*: "Psychology does not interest me, a priori. Sociology does not interest me. I am drawn more to the anthropological aspects of existence. To know what we are, what human suffering consists of, why we behave the way we do, why we suffer so." In other words, an aesthetic grief able to invoke Artaud became the objective moment of an anthropological curiosity unencumbered by extreme subjectivism.

It would be possible to view Herzog as the most prominent example of this extreme mythology were it not for the emergence of a kindred spirit in Syberberg, who in *Our Hitler* stages counterenlightenment romanticism in an even more scandalous fashion. In contrast to Herzog, Syberberg seeks this mythology not in self-created images but in material provided by literature and intellectual history. He had adopted this approach in his Karl May and Richard Wagner films, where he utilized a method of material-archaic reference and association similar to the theatrical style of Peter Stein. Yet where Stein pursues an objectification of the subject (by situating the specific dramatic figure,

Peer Gynt for example, within the sum those historical determinants responsible for his existence), Syberberg takes the opposite path. In his work one observes the dissolution of the objective material of psychology, politics, and intellectual history into the individual perspective of a thoroughly eccentric figure: Karl May, Richard Wagner, Hitler. This perspective on world history is further disrupted by secondary figures: Ludwig II's cook, Hitler's valet. At issue is the programmatic renunciation of "reason" and the irrational celebration of the mad outsider. The private mythology of this outsider, the most terrifying of whom is Hitler, is now taken seriously in the context of a rediscovered romanticism, one suppressed after World War II. Syberberg is more aggressive than Herzog, since his aim is not to present his own personal mythologies but to assault the taboos and conventions of postwar German society. The violated taboo: Nazism appears not as a gruesome perversion, as it was characterized by Thomas Mann in *Doctor Faustus*, but as the necessary heir of European imperialism, which implicates even the Kantian category of the sublime. Here again one can observe similarities to the conservative shift of certain Parisian leftist intellectuals.

Punk Anarchism, Terror Anarchism, and the New Cynicism: Popular Culture is a by-product of New Culture. Dating back to the invention of the Anglo-Saxon comic, attaining clear cultural critical consciousness with the rock and roll of the late 50s, it was in the 60s conceptualized by middle-class intellectuals in terms of the intentions of the cultural revolution. The borders between New Culture and Popular Culture thus remained fluid. Poetry and prose of the American New Culture, including texts by Frank O'Hara, Ed Sanders, Pinelli, Sparling, Cherrystone, Richmond, and others, developed a pornographic fantasy that renounced surrealist transformation and reverted directly to obscenities, porno magazines, and pissoir graffiti. Yet even this movement enjoyed the intellectual patronage of the highbrows and was soon to be imitated by European literati. The synthetic-fictive no man's land between New Culture and Popular Culture, between Chelsea, Hampstead, and Notting Hill, between Frankfurt's West and East Ends and the Free University of Berlin implies contradictory things: LSD, the London *International Times*, the Rolling Stones, the art center movement, left-radical squatters, terrorist cells, the soccer rituals between Liverpool, Inner Milan, and Borussia Mönchengladbach, where unemployed youth unleash their aggressions and where enthusiastic intellectuals literally rediscover the playground of lost spontaneity. Popular Culture and New Culture, one might say, were held together by the cultural revolution's concept of utopia. But when the leftist intelligentsia abandoned this utopia, when it terminated its "solidarity" with the masses and, in a way still defined by generational differences, retreated to the old notion of autonomous individuality, nothing remained as a proletarian element except that which did not require the complicated legitimation of the privileged—the genuinely authentic, truly popular element in Popular Culture. Yet this element could find expression only through the proletarian petit bourgeois base. As long as Popular Culture was still bound to the milieu of middle-class office workers, a banalization of "higher" themes took place. Symptomatic in this regard is the Swedish hit tune *Waterloo* or the favorite of a British season: *Wuthering Heights*. In both cases European myths are trivialized.

The transformation of a relatively artificial rock music, widely accepted even among academic youths, into proletarian punk is, together with its subculture, the best-known phenomenon of Popular Culture today. Even if the brutalized forms of punk, those attracted to a neurotic type of juvenile criminality, have lost their initial naiveté to commercialization, the contrast with the earlier New Culture remains clear. This contrast confirms the previously discussed utopian dive into regression. It can be summarized by comparing *Clockwork Orange*, an anarchic utopian fantasy, with *Jubilee*, an anarchic regressive fantasy. Both the stories and the films describe the terrorist domination of London in an imagined future. Both exhibit an excess of malicious violence. In *Clockwork Orange* this is presented diabolically, fictively, psychoanalytically, culture-critically, and as analytic science fiction. In the punk film *Jubilee* the following expressive equivalents are in evidence: naiveté, regressiveness, a documentary approach, neuroticism, cynicism, perverseness, as well as elements evoking medieval allegory.

What is expressed in the punk phenomenon, particularly in its use of sexual and parafascist emblems, is the perpetuation of anarchic forms of juvenile revolt beyond the semantic forms employed earlier. Despite its proletarian directness, however, it remains a symbolic action; it stops at a barrier ignored by the terrorist anarchism of a West German (and Italian) student minority. In both cases the process of proletarian action abolishing a once-privileged social status is linked with the loss of utopian hope. In both cases the bond is severed with an intellectual elite that includes the Italian publisher Feltrinelli and the now-dead founding figures of the West German Baader-Meinhof terrorists. The motivation for this anarchism, which derives directly from the utopian 60s, was highly theoretical. To the very end it required the constant repetition of moral legitimations and observed, even in situations having fatal consequences, thresholds of the intellectual environment (German philosophical and theological radicalism), a practice in which political discussion became a ritual of justification. In this sense the West German journalist Ulrike Meinhof and the Italian publisher Feltrinelli remained bound, even after their break with the bourgeois intelligentsia, to the framework of the cultural revolution. It is because this break with their intellectual background was effected only *abstractly* that they were able to maintain for so long their intellectual identity and draw from it anarchic energy.

These conditions have been transformed not only in the subsequent generation of terrorists but also in the anarchist student minority, which, while not actively terroristic, nonetheless belongs to the ideological and psychopathological periphery. Fantasies of action are now catalyzed not by a specific combination of cultural-revolutionary utopianism and moral rigor but by pessimism, despair, and hate. Typical of this despair is the language in the obituary published by the Göttingen student newspaper for Chief Federal Prosecutor Buback, who was mowed down by the machine-gun fire of nihilist assassins. The publication of this obituary is still an issue in the Federal Republic. The author, initially anonymous, adopted the name "Mescalero," after an anarchist group of urban Indians that originally surfaced in Italy. In the article he analyzes his own feelings about the death of the federal prosecutor, whom he despised, and contrasts them, perhaps ingenuously, with the terminology of the German media, whose response to this event demonstrated what he perceived to be a conspicuous lack of intellectual and moral consciousness in those who mold public opinion. Even though his article concluded that the left, as a representative of the people, is not entitled to "hate," let alone "liquidate," the "oppressors of the people"—that is, even though this obituary, in the name of a radical university group, distanced itself from terrorism it still triggered a wave of indignation that has only superficially subsided today. A climate of silence and deception resulted since the full text of the incriminating obituary was never published and no important "personality" could afford to interpret the text objectively without incurring public stigmatization or even personal ruin. The seemingly criminal expression, "secret delight," represents not only a contemptuous but also a critical commentary on the contradictory nature of the official (state) mourning over the murder. The entire text violates a linguistic taboo, not only in its brutal jargon ("bump off") or in its manifest insensitivity to a victim of terror, but also in the rawness of a consciousness frankly unaligned with collectively approved morality. Examples of such inverted morality (secretly feeling something alien to what is allowed by the majority) are known to everyone through the interior monologues of classical and modern drama. Scandalous deviation from moral normalcy is indeed a presupposition of theatrical effect. Yet this is always expressed only in aesthetic fashion, symbolically. The moment one departs from the symbolic level, and this is just what occurs in the Mescalero text, the ethical order of everyday life is forcibly disturbed.

One could certainly object that punk and Mescalero anarchism are expressive forms of a cultural and political fringe scene that in a cultural diagnosis should not be taken seriously in any systematic way. Indeed, this fringe is so subject to changes in fashion and to contemporary developments that it is now possible to observe a greasy-haired petit-bourgeois youth agitating in a manner lacking all political consciousness. It is precisely this objection, advanced by the aging representatives of the New Culture jealously watchful of their position, that I wish to refute. To this end the case of Florian Havemann can serve as an excellent example. Here again we can observe an eccentric form of verbal outrage, distinguishable from the foregoing examples, however, in that it is extremely well articulated and did not take place in the cultural and political milieu of the outsider. Nonetheless it generated an emotional reaction from the general public and the intellectual community on a par with the cries of fury leveled at the Mescalero text.

The twenty-seven-year-old son of Professor Robert Havemann, Florian Havemann (who fled to West Berlin in 1971 and has since been involved with literary and theatrical projects), published a scandalous piece in *Der Spiegel* (October 30, 1978) on aspects of his father's intellectual and personal life. In the present context this article is significant, aside from its patricide, for its combination of a natural, cynical (unbiased) realism and an intentional and systematic violation of central idealistic taboos, those of the academic bourgeois middle class (father figure, death) as well as those of the West German leftist and liberal intelligentsia. Without embellishment, but penetratingly and instinctively, even philosophically, this article—and this is its chief merit—debunks the cautious, idealistically grounded reasoning that so often typifies humanistic scholars, and of which the learned natural scientist and now speculative thinker Havemann certainly offered an inviting example (something a sense of piety does not prevent us from saying). I shall disregard the motivating problem of the father-son relationship as well as the son's empirical assertions (which I am not in a position to verify) concerning scenes and incidents among intellectuals in the East German opposition. Instead I want to focus on the text's most notable violation of a cultural taboo, namely, its attack on the notion that there exists an intellectual force of benificent thought beyond system and orthodoxy. It is an assault on the fashionable idea of a repression-free communism, an assault in fact on the notion that abstract thought can be revolutionary and original. Florian Havemann presents himself here not as a punk youth or a Mescalero student but as a young artist who, while not totally repudiating, at least discredits the illusion that the musing, nocturnal conversations of philosophical dilettantes can be productive. The artist recognizes that orthodox ideas cannot be controverted by general ideas unless one wants to revert to the humanistic essayism dominant in Germany during the 50s and 60s. Florian Havemann writes:

A partisanlike citation of the classics will cause despair not only in the dogmatist but in anyone involved in scholarly analysis. The dilettante remains conspicuous since something new is always occurring to him. To him citations carry the weight of proof. He derives great pleasure in demonstrating that his adversaries have not properly studied the classics. The dilettante is adept at taking everything out of context. This can be productive certainly, when the contexts are false. But it is impossible for the dilettante to form new concepts from mere fragments.

And then further:

I must concede that the other dilettantes are strongly motivated by assurances that the connections are really not so complicated. Simple connections, produced in thought, assume utopian dimensions in the face of reality. What emerges is not a utopia in the classic sense but a conviction, incapable of being revised by facts, that the world can be structured in accord with these simple ideas. One is repeatedly assured that all this is quite simple. Perhaps it is these ideas that are too simple.

Florian Havemann then takes an annihilating tack. The boy, nurtured in the German Democratic Republic on materialist thought, shows how his father, the idealist communist raised in a bourgeois manner, in fact merely repeats what the thinkers of the bourgeois Enlightenment said before him: society can be improved with a form of education aimed at the cultivation of the individual. According to the son, what is altogether absent in this naive scheme is the decisive factor: "The utopia of a different kind of work."

This is the systematically decisive point. It is also the criterion of Popular Culture. The young artist Havemann did nothing more than describe, using the personal example of his father, the cultural interest of a philosophizing science that long ago reached its limits. One can find parallels to the father's intellectuality in the dilettantishly philosophical writings of West German natural scientists, theologians, and pedagogues: here the same idealistic-pompous-capricious language is elevated into the "Western" context. Its highly privileged authors, so far removed from practice, think that ideas really are free. The harmlessness of our cultural philosophers, pedagogic idealists, and idealistic fanatics—yes, the shallowness of their supercilious conceptualizing— all this was first brought to light by a dark, nonideational pragmatism. Let me put it this way: the homosexual English playwright Joe Orton, the obscene street kid from Leicester, understands in each of his dramatic compositions more about the present than any German aesthetician in his system. The extent to which this pragmatism has been a source of discomfort even for the representatives of the New Culture is exhibited either in their own helplessly psychologistic or merely enraged reactions to young Havemann's text. Properly understood, the passages cited here make clear that very few West German intellectuals indeed can match this text's originality, laconic insight, cynical humor, and lucid penetration, for their language is too infected with sentimentality and leftist self-absorption. Of the published letters to the editor of *Der Spiegel*, only one understood, without bias, the essence of Florian Havemann's scandalous piece: that he had the audacity to undermine, with every available tactic of subversion, what is still, politically, the wholesome world of many intellectuals. That this is also a "psychic outrage" and "forcibly merciless," as Erich Fried wrote, does not detract from its truth. There is a special need to raise the question of whether a "liberating" text ever accomplishes more than a "self-destructive" one. For we now know that the term "self-liberation" belongs to the optimistic youth-movement-oriented arsenal of the New Culture, now at an end, whereas "self-destructive" acts continue to be linked to artistic productivity. Havemann's article is guided by a pragmatic aggressiveness that, undaunted by the sacrosanct taboos of the Old or New Culture, aims to ridicule the latter's idealistic fairy tales. Lurking in Havemann's work is an as yet unwritten blasphemous comedy about the German intelligentsia. The agitation precipitated by the text fully describes the senescence of the New Culture. It also indicates how dangerously and quickly sentimentality and intellectual mendacity can erupt within this camp—features long justifiably ascribed to the conservative and academic representatives of the Old Culture.

Were one willing to set aside all systematic arguments, one would at least be able to comprehend Florian Havemann's immense humor, his euphoric frivolity. For this, however, the aging representatives of the New Culture are too pompous, too humorless, too ponderous, and in some cases too stupid. Ironically it was not all that long ago that certain representatives of the New Culture themselves wanted to abolish culture. What are we to learn from the Havemann case? It teaches us that so-called nonconformist leftist artists are furious merely because a virtual unknown dared to attack one of their own, someone from the leftist culture establishment, thereby converting an intended tragedy to farce. Florian Havemann is a creative talent because he feels and thinks unfettered by the categories of Old and New Culture.

The aggressive texts of the cultural revolution of the 60s did not possess this *pragmatic* aggressiveness. When in 1967 Berlin anarcho-leftists used the American napalm war in Vietnam cynically to advance the idea of burning department stores in Western metropolitan centers, the language of their writing was highly formal and stylized, acquiring thereby a surreal, utopian dimension. Even when soon thereafter the future terrorists Baader and Ensslin set a Frankfurt department store ablaze, this was still understood as a symbolic act. Likewise the brutalized, vulgarized form of the West German pamphlet at the beginning of the 70s still demonstrated a style and intonation modeled on the polemic between Marx and the Young Hegelians. What distinguishes the extremely progressive form of Popular Culture from New Culture is this difference between symbolic and authentic language. In this sense the theater of violence of Pinter, Wesker, Orton, and Bond carried New Culture to its outermost limit. What was now possible was not an intensification at this level but only a qualitative transformation. The intellectual representatives of the New Culture, who soon attained a status of privilege, could not bring about this transformation. At this point symbolic language was itself disavowed. Thus the transformation to the form of Popular Culture described here is no accident but a necessary development. In the opposition between Popular and New Culture erupts one of the aporias of our civilization: the tension between symbolic and authentic actions. Theories, confessions, and cultural projects are symbolic actions with promise for the future. As long as the symbolism of linguistic signs made this promise credible, it remained autonomous and unthreatening. Since only actual practice can redeem a promise now, symbolic reflection abdicates in favor of authentic acts.

With this we return to the hermeneutically important distinction between the realization of history and the historicization of reality. It appears that realization now takes place only in the precultural, vulgar-anarchic milieu, although also without utopian assumptions. At the level of true culture, which is semantically mediated (it is insignificant whether this be understood in terms of New or Old Culture), artistic and conceptual pride of place has to be given to the historicization of the real. In France Foucault's ambivalent writings have decisively turned discussion against the emphasis on utopianism and the subject. If his discovery of "madness" in the age of rediscovered Artaud serves as a plea for the outsider against the terror of normality, his work *The Order of Things* transforms this message into its opposite: as a "recent invention," man vanishes into an infinite history "as a face sketched in the sand is washed away by the tide." A comparable situation has developed in West Germany, where the Frankfurt School's notion of enlightenment, specifically Habermas's optimistic program for rational discourse among individuals, must confront the contempt for the subject characteristic of the stoicism of Luhmann's social technology. In the pretheoretical, artistic sphere a revision has also occurred in what during the 70s became the standard conceptual themes of the intelligentsia. In Stoppard's *Travesties*, Syberberg's *Our Hitler*, Glucksmann's *The Master Thinkers*—diverse but representative references for West European culture—the Enlightenment, long taken for granted, was shaken and forced to justify itself in the face of thoroughgoing skepticism. These revisions were performed not so much by traditional "cultural criticism" as by images and aesthetic events unleashed against ideas. It was the same with the French New Philosophy: although no longer the focus of current fashion, it is nonetheless important as a symptom, more as theatrical action à la Heinrich Heine and Nietzsche than as a system of ideas. The avant-garde, abstraction through reason, "ideas" in general, are reincorporated into the refractory material of anthropology, psychology, and ethnology. Thus the liberating claim of ideas is "unmasked" as a claim of domination. From this perspective it is also possible to explain why the traditional center of culture, the province of belles lettres, has been shifted, comparatively speaking, to the periphery, whereas the more objective, nonverbal forms of art are deemed promising: things have become mightier than words. An almost inflationary confessional literature, found primarily in West Germany, cannot alter this state of affairs. Formally and intellectually insignificant though it is, this literature typifies the petit-bourgeois, sentimental core of the West German literary industry, against which only texts like Florian Havemann's can be effective.

It would be wrong to assume that this alternative has been theoretically decided in favor of things. Yet the cultural climate smacks of it. For Foucault or Stoppard or Luhmann this takes the form of a playing with fictions; for others it represents the end of "happiness." For this reason there has even been talk of a new pessimistic existentialism. It is illustrated in Robert Bresson's most recent film, where the young hero, a pre-Raphaelite student from a leftist milieu, is disgusted by the illusions in what remains of the cultural-revolutionary scene. In a stoic ritual he allows himself to be shot by a friend. For him distinctions between Old, New, and Popular Culture have become meaningless.

Jaspers, one of the last thinkers of "epochal consciousness" (that celebrated German category from early Romanticism upon which our initial differentiation is ultimately based), recalls in *Die geistige Situation der Zeit* an 1829 statement by Stendhal repudiating the repeatedly asserted identity of political and aesthetic progress: "In my opinion freedom will within a hundred years snuff out the feeling for art. That feeling is nonmoral, since it entices us into the delights of love, indolence, and exaggeration." Heinrich Heine, still the model of the politically committed German author and equally a man with a feeling for the pathos of the epoch, would have agreed almost completely. And yet our progressive aestheticians, extending even to Adorno, assumed the validity of an equation already contested at such an early date. A few years ago it was still scandalous to controvert it. The fact that it did not disappear, that after a hundred years it did not want to disappear, is doubtless a deeper cause of the crisis of the New Culture and even the crisis of the cultural-revolutionary left.

If now, in their morning after, some of its representative members are nursing quasi-chthonian experiences or substantive longings, this indicates only panic; it offers no shred of evidence demonstrating that the culturally conservative reaction is in the end to be vindicated. In distinguishing between the realization of history and the historicization of reality, we have found an alternate way of characterizing the now dominant epochal reaction. It is more in this than in ideological rhetoric that one can appreciate what is left and what is right. Let us term "left" history measured on the standard of the present and "right" the present measured on the standard of history. If Foucault allows the people of my time to disappear like grains of sand, then this idea can no longer interest me. If Luhmann declares the revolution of my present to be ephemeral, then this idea is also of no interest. And if an art collector or a philologue declares the avant-garde dead, then I couldn't care less about their ideas. Only as a scholar am I interested in structuralism, social technology, and antiquities; they have no interest for me insofar as I am I. But why are they uninteresting to me, since, after all, as ideas they are neither thoughtless nor malicious? The answer: I am not prepared to conceive of something outside my "present." I know that I have never belonged to the "cultural community" of those refined sophisticates who understand themselves and others in terms of cultural symbols. I do not belong to the Holy Family of Topos Research. I am not interested in universal loci. I am not interested, for instance, in H. M. Enzenberger's strongly associational collection of possible world endings. Instead I am interested only in the one end of the world in which he really believes. It was one of the now indefeasible discoveries of early German Romanticism to conceive the "present," to affirm the notion of the present against a falsely objectified tradition. This concept was systematically elaborated by Marx in his progressive account of history. But not even the Marxian reality is a point of reference for me; this I find only in my own epochal feeling. Without this feeling Marx, too, would once again be

Charlemagne, a figure in cultural space, not in my time. Explaining time as space, as a cultural specimen, as structure, is the conservative mode of thought found in the notion of the eternal recurrence; this notion is imaginable only if one remains true to "culture" and not to oneself.

Without relating culture to this imaginary "I," one quickly arrives, however learned and artistically disposed one might be, at the objectified concept of culture disseminated with good intentions by all stripes of cultural functionaries, Marxist ones included. Stendhal's assertion has proved this point. We have only to draw the proper conclusion: not the conservative one, which in the name of "art" wants to roll back freedom and emancipatory processes, but the conclusion of the "I" that identifies the oft-cited notion of "freedom" with itself. This is no flight into subjectivism. In this way I even conduct myself categorially, namely, for the present.

"Thou Shalt Have No Other Jeans before Me"

Dorothee Sölle

Upon rereading Jaspers I asked myself what might be implied by the category of "existential unconditionedness" (*Unbedingtheit*), what he may have meant by it, whether if even today there might be a need for such unconditionedness and whether we have a language capable of articulating it, how it might be possible to clarify the theological background of this question, what assistance could be provided by the language of religious tradition to permit a better understanding of the spiritual and political situation of the 70s.

In order to champion the notion of a "more human life-world," Jaspers criticizes the "universal apparatus of existence" that oppresses us:

But should the time come when nothing in the individual's real and immediate surroundings is made, molded, or handed down by that individual for his own purposes; when everything serves as nothing but the stuff for the instant gratification of needs, to be consumed and discarded; when living itself becomes mechanized and when the surroundings become despiritualized, when work counts only as a day's labor and ceases to play a role in shaping an individual's life— then the individual would be, as it were, without a world.[1]

These words, written long before the second industrial revolution, have lost even more of their subjunctive character. The number of people who through their work make, mold, and hand down something has undergone even further decline; a "spiritual quality of one's own surroundings" can now be conceived only in caricature, having become fully privatized in summer homes on the Mediterranean; the "continuity" of the individual self was already ridiculed by Gottfried Benn, who likened it to "those garments which, cut from quality cloth, are guaranteed for ten years." If one asked what could save people from the apparatus, what would make their world human again or could preserve its human character, one would find in Jaspers's discussion such hackneyed phrases as "the attainment of being," to "turn to human existence," and, most important, the "existential unconditionedness" that keeps alive the claim of existence. Today all these terms strike us as peculiarly impotent. Although once filled with meaning, they have now degenerated into elements of a cultural criticism that takes aim at Marxism and psychoanalysis, throwing them into the same pot as racism, the pot of "ideology." Apart from this unjustified and elitist critique of mass existence, it must still be asked whether there is something more concealed within Jaspers's formulations and his tumid prose ("will to destiny," "authentic human existence") than the fear of loss in prestige that mass culture had instilled in the German bourgeoisie of the 30s. For in the term "existential unconditionedness" an attempt was made to secure something that, while already suspected of representing a form of "irrationalism," seemed nonetheless to be more than a mere negation of critical rationality.

What is meant by unconditionedness? At the very least it signifies an interest in an existence that is not exhausted by the performing of functions defined by others, that does not consist in the means for externally imposed ends. Existence denotes what is irreducible, nonderivable, and incapable of being fashioned in terms of function. Existence is the basic category of a philosophy of liberation that struggles against precisely this functionalization of human life within the massive apparatus. "I exist" means that I am not an object for others. I am more than what they know of me, more than what they can use. Even when I experience myself as conditioned in every respect, the meaning of life continues to consist in being an end and not simply a means, in existing and not simply in functioning.

As conservative and even reactionary as Jaspers's conclusion may seem to be, the task remains, even within a philosophy of existence, to distinguish between features that are emancipatory-humanistic and those that are repressive-elitist. The claim to exist, to be an end and not a means, to fulfill existence and not merely a function, is one of the most profound of all human needs, and it cannot be dismissed as merely irrational. Unconditionedness and absoluteness may indeed be misleading expressions, since, after all, unconditionedness can itself be achieved only under conditions that lend themselves to research and derivation, just as absoluteness can be understood only in ascertaining its relativity. Nonetheless the essence of unconditionedness, of the nonderivative meaningfulness of human life, cannot be disposed of in this fashion.

This essence found historical expression in the language of religion. Jaspers's entire analysis is imbued with a sense of grief regarding lost religions. It is a philosophy after the death of God, which aims to supersede and translate into existential terms that which was once designated by the word "God." Religion was a specific historical form of this longing for absoluteness; in a postreligious age we must find another language to express the nature of unconditionedness, one that gives human life a sense of meaning. Jaspers made this attempt. The experience of and adherence to an existential unconditionedness led him to a "philosophical faith." Yet did not Jaspers, even with this notion of a faith that has been rendered autonomous and severed from the tradition and institution of the church, remain more under the spell of religion than he himself knew? Is not the exaggerated demand for meaning, however philosophically it might be cast, itself still a part of religion? Might it not lie in the deepest interest of an existential unconditionedness to actualize religious traditions? Is it not possible that we cannot afford to dispense with those congealed experiences of meaning present in scripture and tradition, when the presentation and conveyance of existential immediacy is at issue?

Jaspers lived at the end of the age of bread. Plastics had not yet become the primary means of sustenance. Religion was in a process of decay, but the need for meaning had still in no way been rendered superfluous. By contrast, the situation in which we find ourselves today can be described as one in which there no longer exists a language to express the notions of meaning, existential unconditionedness, and faith. The age of bread (Brot) is over, and so too is the age of philosophical nourishment (Brötchen). We have been exposed to a manipulation of needs that has also transformed the need for uniqueness, novelty, and meaning into an obsession with possessions. Domination, the manipulation of consciousness, schooling in the destruction of one's own interests are no longer performed by religion and the church but by production and advertisement. The new religion is consumerism.

At the beginning of the 70s an advertising jingle appeared rec-
ommending "Jesus Jeans." The Italian author and filmmaker Pier
Paolo Pasolini applied to this jingle a form of linguistic analysis in
which he makes a comment on the spiritual situation of the age.[2]
Pasolini sees a "revolution from the right," which by the beginning
of the 70s had reached Italy as well. This revolution is profound,
fundamental, and absolutely new, invested with sufficient power to
destroy all existing institutions: family, culture, language, and church.
He calls this new state of affairs "hedonistic fascism" or *consumismo*
(consumerism). With regard to the theme advanced by Jaspers, this
consumismo represents the perfect and inexorable repression of every
form of existential unconditionedness. "There is indeed no longer
anything religious in the idealized image of the young husband and
wife propagated and ordained by television. They are just two people
whose lives gain reality through consumer goods."

What is implied by the expression, "no longer religious"? Did the
ideal of a young couple at one time have a different significance? Was
the subject matter different? Was there a promise of happiness filled
by something more than consuming with each other? "It is futile to
want to preserve an unconditioned truth without God" (Horkheimer).
The mythical basis for a life incapable of being made or being given
as a thing was designated by the word "God." "Without God" was
therefore illusory, since—incidentally, as much to the Frankfurt School
as to Jaspers—the danger was apparent that mundane, partial, conditioned, and particular ends might expand into universal, unconditioned, and divine ones. To live meaningfully and yet without God
would appear unintelligible, as it is only *with* God that false gods and
obtruding idols could successfully be repudiated. In fairness it must
be conceded that in Horkheimer's philosophy as well God is in danger
of being reduced to a mere function, a purifying and iconoclastic
function oriented to the critique of ideology. Here, too, it is not possible
to make positive statements about what God wants, where God
stands—illuminating myths capable of instilling hope. Unconditioned
meaning could be attained only in a leap from the conditioned. It was
not the exodus from Egypt but the prohibition of idols that was incorporated into Horkheimer's philosophical position. Hence this approach is equally incapable of solving the difficulty that beset Jaspers's
position—preserving an unconditioned truth without God. Without a
"leap," without a decision for life over death, unconditionedness is

impossible. To cite one example of existential unconditionedness becoming a practical-political, there is no "rational reason" not to kill mentally retarded children.

In a 1975 article entitled "Herz" [Heart], Pasolini commented on the practice of abortion in Italy. He had been criticized for pursuing an irrationalist course and for seeing "something holy in life without reason." In his analysis of the situation of the age, Pasolini responds by posing a legitimate question: In whose interest does free choice for abortion really lie? His answer: "the new consumerist and permissive forces," a new type of domination, which, having no interest in the couple producing offspring (the proletarian model), requires a pair that consumes (the petit bourgeois model). Its sanctuary consists in the "ritual of consumerism and in the fetishism of commodities." In Pasolini's view the issue of existential unconditionedness is presented under the catchwords "heart" and "sanctuary." "To say that life is not holy and that feelings are dumb amounts to doing the producers an enormous favor." Today the ruling powers are no longer clerical-fascist but secular-consumerist. They assert themselves no longer in repressive but permissive fashion. The decision that must be faced and in fact is faced by the silent majority is that "between the sanctity of life and feeling, and capital and private property."

In this context I would like to make a personal comment on the question of abortion. I participated in the campaign calling for the abolition of Section 218 of the German Criminal Code [the law regarding abortion], yet I was neither willing nor able to support one of the essential features of this struggle: I could not sign the women's declaration, "I had an abortion." Instead I could only criticize the slogan, "My womb belongs to me," since it merely acknowledges, without surpassing, the moral level of capitalism, which is always aware of "what belongs to me."

With the Italian feminists, I would like to criticize Pasolini because he never once addressed the plight of those affected, the women; he de facto instrumentalizes them. Just as before! Nonetheless I am in agreement with his stance, which involves a certain tension between the bourgeois-liberal and the Christian positions. I support the legalization of abortion and women's freedom of choice; my commitment to life takes effect only after this liberalization. We are living not in a Christian but in a secular state where the ever-diminishing minority of Christians has no right to impose ideas on those who think differently.

The truly constraint-free dialogue about life, which indeed "without reason" I take to be "holy," can commence only at this point. I no more wish my daughter to visit an abortion clinic than my son an army boot camp. All training in killing destroys those who engage in it. Yet my existential unconditionedness with regard to life cannot assume the form of a legal norm; it can only be a call to life, an invitation.

"Set your hearts first on God's kingdom and righteousness, all these other things [intending: food, drink, clothing] will be given to you as well" (Matthew 6:33) This language of existential unconditionedness presumes the possible unity of our life. There are times when we see ourselves as undivided and free from dispersion, endowed with all capacities and dimensions (such as past and future). The oil in the lamp of the virgin awaiting her bridegroom is a symbol of this unity. Should she lack this oil, she lacks everything: she is "foolish," unprepared, dispersed into a thousand parts. If her lamp is filled with oil, she has nothing to fear; she is, to speak in jargon, "fully there."

Existential unconditionedness is drawn from that indivisible totality to which I commit myself. "Choose life" presupposes that there is "life" in this emphatic, unconditioned sense and that it can be chosen and accepted or rejected and abused. "I call heaven and earth to witness against you today: I set before you life and death, blessing or curse. Choose life, then, so that you and your descendants may live . . ." (Deuteronomy 30:19).

To choose life over death implies participation in the great affirmation of life. In the biblical context this means to remain alive and to multiply, life and procreation being things endangered in Egypt; it means to live in a country, to be blessed, to live in peace.

We tend to affirm life in specific circumstances, under given conditions, as when it is expressed in youth, beauty, strength. But the affirmation in the emphatic, biblical context is an unconditioned affirmation, valid in sickness and in death and above all for those lacking in self-esteem, who, after perceiving themselves negatively for so long, have become resigned to this state of affairs. To choose life involves precisely the ability not to resign oneself to the blatant destruction of life around us and to its accompanying cynicism.

In the Christian tradition this commitment to life is known as "belief"—belief in the existential sense of trust and not in the rational sense of holding something to be true. "Choose life, then, so that you and your descendants may live, in the love of Yahweh, your God, obeying his voice, clinging to him; for in this life consists; on this depends your long stay in the land which Yahweh swore to your fathers Abraham, Isaac and Jacob he would give them" (Deuteronomy 30:19–20). Within this tradition a language developed that recalls, represents, and thus makes possible the emphasis on life, its imperilment and salvation.

The integrative moment ("totality") and the voluntarist moment ("decision") constitute what Jaspers termed "existential unconditionedness." But even if we trace this language back to its theological origin, a certain uneasiness persists.

It is precisely in its comparison with biblical language that the formalized and depleted character of the philosophy of existence becomes fully apparent. Terms such as blessing and curse, home and exile, as well as the kingdom of God, lamps, and marriage contain more than what can be conceptualized in the notion of existential unconditionedness. In a certain sense this philosophical language is as impotent as that of those young people whose most important approbative terms are "real" and "tough." The philosophy of existence heightens the need for a nonfunctionalist foundation of life but cannot do much beyond that. The prevailing state of affairs is typified by the fact that we lack a language able to convey in comprehensible fashion something about life's assumed meaningfulness, about the human capacity for truth, about the unconditionedness and totality of existence. *Survivre n'est pas vivre*—thus it was written by students on the walls of Paris in 1968. But what is meant by *vivre*? Is it definable only in terms of its opposite, *survivre*? Are we only able to articulate what we do not want and what life does not mean? Pasolini grounds his critique of the reigning consumerism by referring to, among other things, the destruction of language, specifically the destruction of expressive language. Although we are still understood, we no longer say anything. People's expressive linguistic practices, especially apparent for Pasolini in dialect, are being extirpated along with the dialects themselves. The dominant language is the language of television, which suppresses and makes uniform regional, social, and group dialects. In this process Pasolini sees a loss of expressivity in language. No longer able to convey anything about oneself, one is no longer able to communicate with others. It is without detour, shall we say, that we make ourselves understood. The language of science has made expression taboo, and

Dorothee Sölle

it is for this reason that women, in their role as bearers of expressivity, have difficulty making themselves understood in it. One always feels that one is saying nothing at all when uttering normal male sentences. The uniform character of ordinary language, disseminated by television commercials, promotes the language of science.

Linked with the loss of expressivity is the isolation from all forms of transcendence. The young consumer couple, owing to the ruling mode of television programming, has no need for a language capable of expressing personal anguish or desire. Life itself is not at stake; it has value, in fact, only inasmuch and as long as it can be purchased. "The empty store windows, that drabness. What is life there good for anyhow?"—thus an American tourist commenting on his visit to the East bloc. Pasolini characterizes this consumerism as a new fascism; it destroys all humanistic values without physical force, with its new tools of information and communication. If the age of bread is over, why still share bread and wine with one another? "It is clear that superfluous goods render life itself superfluous."

Religious traditions have articulated the consciousness that life itself is at stake, that it can cease to have meaning. It is here that people's anxiety in the face of a loss of meaning and identity has been given voice—and of course also rendered manipulable. "Save us from hell" is a prayer centuries old. It enunciates something that today, simply in being felt, will guarantee entrance to the psychiatric clinic: the fear of a wasted life, of destroyed unity, of loss of self. Well-heated rooms are cold. "Things are dead" is the standard reply of young people asked how things are going here and there.

It is possible to waste one's whole life, to throw it away, to treat it as a disposable object. One can win or lose it; in any case one does not "have" it. Yet we lack a language sufficiently expressive and transcending to allow us to communicate with one another about it. Without this existential angst about life, however, the more profound love of life also cannot exist; what remains is only a quick and ever-frustrated aggressiveness that at any moment can be turned into diffuse melancholia. One can only love something that is threatened and endangered—something potentially changeable or potentially non-existent, something that could die.

Existential unconditionedness goes hand in hand with existential angst—the emphatic understanding of life as growth, being touched, touching, as the development of new qualities and experiences. This qualitative understanding of life contains an emphatic-traumatic relation to death. We are capable of dying. To know this is more important than repeatedly to acknowledge our mortality. Perhaps no one knows this better than someone suffering from mental illness. Life can be lost on the way to birth and before death. Were this not the case, it could not even be found.

Yet precisely this insight is expunged in the forgetful innocuousness of the blasphemy, "Though shalt have no other jeans before me." This slogan "contains the spirit of the second industrial revolution and the concomitant mutation of values." The cycle of production and consumption functions most efficiently when people are severed from the experience of nature and history, that is, when they live in a purely technical and secular world, free of all religion.

When people are fully severed from the experience of nature, they cease to be aware that life requires renewal; that after work we need rest; after day, night; after befoulment, purification; after commotion, peace. Instead everything continues on an even keel. Rhythm is no longer a part of our lives. Independent of body and soul, the bleeding ordained by the monthly pill symbolizes this destruction of rhythm.

Just as people are severed from the experience of nature, so they are also severed from a transcending experience of history. Consumerism has generated an entirely new culture of communication, dominated by such pressing questions as how to save taxes or where to get a good deal; class differences are reduced to a question of the geography of good values. It is as if all historical experience, especially that viewed through the eyes of the forlorn, has been forgotten, has vanished. Its reference point, God's kingdom and its new justice, is now inconceivable. The cyclical understanding of history has overpowered the eschatological-teleological one. Loss of continuity and planned amnesia are prerequisites for the hedonistic culture, since memory requires behavior inimical to consumerism. And since the loss of history is likewise the absence of a future, a sense of dramatic hopelessness sets in. Beckett's *Happy Days* is now being performed. One is buried in the sand, sitting motionlessly in one's hole and, in a perfect absence of all affect, awaiting sunrise and sunset.

What is blasphemous is not the use of the first commandment for an advertising slogan, but advertisement as such. Every attempt to direct my attention to hair spray, cat food, and trips to Ibiza is an attack on the one in whose image I was created.

Dorothee Sölle

Consumerism means eyes that are continually insulted, ears that are clogged, and hands robbed of their creativity. My relations with other people are subject to laws unimaginable to earlier generations. (I have the birthday party of an eight-year-old daughter in mind.) If everything is expressed and measured in terms of possession, then there remains no time, no energy, and no language for being with one another.

To believe means to struggle against the ruling cynicism. Yet the language of struggle is not adequate to conceptualize the courage and beauty of belief. We must learn to express more precisely the nature of the promises of happiness being made here, the nature of the experiences of happiness being discussed. To speak more precisely is to learn to speak in a more existential, more concerned, and therefore more coherent manner.

If life in the Judeo-Christian tradition has been concerned with what is at stake, with a thoroughly premortal hell and heaven-sent infusions of light, then we must assign the word "happiness" a definition different from that prescribed by consumerism. The latter's advertising agencies are trying to dismantle the traditional values of frugality, family life, and altruism with the slogan, "If it feels good, do it!" Yet the addressee of this ad is less and less the anal collector and the quiet enjoyer. The genital conqueror has now become the primary model. Happiness lies not in accumulation and consumption but in the seizure and taking possession of something previously seized and possessed by someone else. It is no longer the acquired item but the experience of acquisition itself that is the focus of advertisement; it is to be engaged in lustily. What thereby becomes even more incomprehensible is that essential element with whose aid religious traditions had attempted to define happiness: the experience of grace.

The young man and woman on television, no longer burdened by religion, are without grace. They do not need it, they do not expect it, and when we see them it does not occur to us to say, "May God give you grace." Yet it was just this promise, this hope, that in our culture once accompanied the idea of the young couple. Young people were once enveloped in an aura of frail happiness; it made them "touching," a word that at the time was still part of our vocabulary. Today we cannot even wish *mazel tov* to our television models. Why should we? Whatever they hope for they can buy. Thus wishes freeze on lips, and the icy chill of relations devoid of all longing seeps from the television into every room.

Grace illuminates the depth of our possible happiness. When I choose life with existential unconditionedness, as Jaspers would say, when integration and decision fuse, when I take part in the great affirmation of life and am trained in the struggle against cynicism, then I shall experience the moment that is the basis of all true happiness, at least to the extent that it can be articulated within the context of the culture handed down to me. I realize that it is not owing to my own efforts that I have been brought into the particular circumstance that first establishes the objects of my own desires. I have no control over my affirmation, I am not in charge and forget that I may have wanted to be. "Uncontrollability" (*Unverfügbarkeit*) is the other category employed by the philosophy of existence that cannot be ignored without deleterious consequences. Each true affirmation is an answer, a response, and this responsive nature is our very experience of happiness. Happiness means relating (*ent-sprechen*) to, not merely speaking (*sprechen*) to, someone or some situation. It is an integration into the process of give and take—not just taking, gaining, and appropriating and not just doing, making, giving. It is grace, and the more grace we experience in happiness, the greater its depth.

A young person untouched by religious tradition may ask how I know this. I would answer: the limits of my language are the limits of my world. The tradition in which I stand bequeathed to me a language that interprets, clarifies, makes transparent, and enriches my own experience. One of its words, "grace," contains a conception of happiness that seemed more enticing than anything otherwise offered me. In it I found respect for my capacity for desire, a way of addressing my fears, and a total acceptance of my need for meaning. My capacity for happiness grew with my capacity for meaning (and, for that matter, with my capacity for pain, although in my tradition this belongs to the category of repentance). Therefore I regard consumerism as an attack on my dignity and do not by any means consider the word "genocide" employed by Pasolini an exaggerated description of what occurs on a daily basis with consumerism. But the use of such terms presupposes the aforementioned emphatic understanding of life, which relies on the framework of heaven and hell.

What reason could exist to exchange this life between heaven and hell for a secular-trivial one? Why give up a tradition that regards

Dorothee Sölle

bread and wine, fear and guilt, coitus and birth, death and the justice of the Kingdom of God as the unmarketable components of life? A tradition that continually surpasses the limits set by the language of the social sciences in favor of a promise of life for all; a tradition in which one person could reclaim for others the unseen light: "He shall let his countenance shine upon you."

Notes

1. This is a modified version of the translation found in the English edition of Jaspers's *Die geistige Situation der Zeit*: *Man in the Modern Age*, Eden and Cedar Paul, translators (Garden City, NY: Anchor Books, 1957), p. 42 (*tr.*).

2. In P. P. Pasolini, *Freibeuterschriften: Die Zerstörung der Kultur des Einzelnen durch die Konsumgesellschaft* (Berlin, 1978).

Productive Noncontemporaneity

Johann Baptist Metz

I

What can a contemporary so noncontemporaneous as a theologian, and a Catholic at that, have to say about the temper of the age? Perhaps this; it is high time to develop a better understanding of noncontemporaneity. Above all, it is high time that the leftist intellectuals of this country develop a better understanding of noncontemporaneity. In so doing they might establish closer ties with a still noncontemporaneous people and thus will not be left to lament impotently about, among other things, a revived populism. And they might also free themselves from their all too many subjectless theories and from an abstract rigor that is not made "radical" by the fact that they so gladly label it that way. Only if the left sheds the nervous anxiety it experiences in the face of noncontemporaneous phenomena can it successfully counter the reactionary flight into a wholly noncontemporaneous life, a flight that—considering the increasing social conflicts in our country as well as, say, the United States—is characteristic of the present mood and tendency.

II

A Christian religion worthy of the name, one that has not yet been secularized into a utopia (which, as everyone knows, is not the object of anyone's prayers), is in the highest degree and almost irritatingly noncontemporaneous. It is indeed informed of this by all parties. For

the left Christian religion serves as a special example of a noncontemporaneous residue left from the period preceding the Enlightenment; it is perceived as professing a purely perfunctory interest in
universal justice and liberation. As for the right and the center, the
situation at first appears different. Indeed there is even talk of an
ideological shift (*Tendenzwende*) in society toward religion; and religious
terminology is once again appearing in political programs. Yet it must
be asked whether what is at issue here is really a matter of religion.
Is this shift a timely form of inspiration and imitation wrought by
religious noncontemporaneity? Or is it instead an indication of society's
interest in its own security, a type of protective ideology for affluent
bourgeois societies that, confronted everywhere by increasingly insistent
demands and challenges, refuse to alter their priorities and look to
religion as a supposedly reliable and time-tested accomplice in their
efforts to safeguard the status quo?

In any case there seems to be agreement on at least one point:
religion is a phenomenon of noncontemporaneity, a patina phenomenon, of which today even many who view themselves as religious
dare make only ceremonial and not serious or radical use. In fact a
religion that has not been rendered superfluous through the abandonment of its aspirations is permeated with this atmosphere of noncontemporaneity, with this scent of the anachronistic. It comes from
afar, from the depths of the history of humankind, which from a
standpoint of dialectics or of a logic of evolution, is now held to be
transparent or at least capable of being rendered transparent.

Of parallel significance is the way in which the major societal systems
of our day react to religious noncontemporaneity. In the West, in
bourgeois-liberal societies, this noncontemporaneity of religion is—
somewhat grudgingly—privatized: "To each his own noncontemporaneity!" In Eastern countries, those bearing the imprint of Marxist
socialism, that aspect of religion not regarded as bald alienation has
long ago been incorporated into and stood on its feet by the dialectical
process of a socialist history of liberation. Finally, we know from our
recent past that fascism has its own way of dealing with a noncontemporaneous religion; time and again it has attempted to politicize
and exploit in populist manner the cultural and political resentments
often bottled up in a religion owing to its noncontemporaneity, such
as a latent animosity toward enlightenment and democracy.

III

I would like to clarify the experience of religious noncontemporaneity first by way of a few autobiographical observations. Religious non-contemporaneity is not simply a position; it is a comprehensive way of life, a mode of presenting oneself, of learning and experiencing— a social-psychological life rhythm. I come from an arch-Catholic Bavarian village. One comes from far away when one comes from there. It is as if one were born not fifty years ago, but somewhere along the receding edges of the Middle Ages. I had to approach many things slowly at first, had to exert great effort to discover things that others and that society had long ago discovered and that had since become common practice, like democracy in daily political life, dealing with a diffuse public sphere, and rules of the game of conflict even in family life. Much appeared alien and in fact continued to be alienating. Only gradually did I adjust to urban life. (To this very day, it seems to me, Catholicism remains essentially a rural religion; I am referring to the Catholics who, in the diaspora of our fully secularized cities, are shaken almost to the core.) Later I was depressed by the cognitive isolation experienced by Catholic theology, especially within our universities. In general, I made an observation about the theoretical-theological domain similar to one I made about the domain of everyday religion: from a point quite removed, I had to work my way into the academic and social discussion fronts, had to learn to comprehend things that supposedly my theology and I had already discovered and compre-hended long ago, had to gain access to phenomena that my contem-poraries seemed to master through clichés: enlightenment, pluralism, emancipation, secularization, the critique of captialism, and Marxism. And I had to learn how difficult and problematic it was to connect these parameters of contemporaneity, or however one wishes to des-ignate the signals for the "height of the age," with that religion already so familiar to me before I had begun reflecting upon it.

IV

With reference to the situation in Catholic theology, I would like to distinguish three ways in which it deals with this experience of non-contemporaneity. I am making these distinctions with extreme caution and with the expressed recognition that they serve only as ideal types, for in reality we always confront only mixed forms. I am more interested in sketching out mentalities than positions.

First, there is theology as the systematic consolidation of noncontemporaneity. Here the tensive contradictions contained in the experience of religious noncontemporaneity are relaxed. The experience of noncontemporaneity is fashioned into an immediate expression of the intrinsic untimeliness and foreignness of religion and its message. This in fact involves a retreat to earlier theological and cultural-political positions. Without wishing to denigrate the merits of the so-called neo-Scholasticism of nineteenth- and twentieth-century Catholic theology, I must nonetheless characterize it as a prototype for the traditionalist approach to the experience of religious noncontemporaneity. It is sufficiently telling that this school's classic work during the last century was entitled *Theologie der Vorzeit* [Theology of the premodern period]. This fixation of theology on premodernity was accompanied by a process of spiritual and social isolation in which Catholics were consolidated into a firm and, not least of all, political *corpus catholicum*, a rather weak imitation of the great *corpus christianum* of the Middle Ages. *Kulturkämpfe* in the sociopolitical sphere and controversial theology in the confessional sphere testified to the strictly defensive character of the treatment of the experience of religious noncontemporaneity. Ecclesiastic religion, which adapted only with great difficulty to the conditions and requirements of the industrial revolution, appeared more rigorous than radical; dike-plugging strategies began to dominate the Church's pastoral practice. Ecclesiastic religion displayed features especially characteristic of a traditionalist welfare religion (*Betreuungsreligion*). Unfortunately this depiction of the historical situation is even today only too apt!

Second, there is the catch-up mentality in theology: the energetic attempt to shed noncontemporaneity and install theology "at the height of the age," with which it is not (or is no longer) identified. Here all forms of progress since the Reformation are painstakingly and meticulously incorporated into theology. The goal is a consciousness that is as contemporaneous as possible with bourgeois-liberal society and scientific-technological civilization. Thus even in Catholicism there has now emerged a type of bourgeois theology. In this country the model is not infrequently Protestant theology, which is always regarded as being more contemporaneous. Clearly this also has the consequence that this type of Catholic theology, while commonly viewed as particularly progressive or critical within Catholicism, has been accorded less attention by Protestant thinkers, who too often expect to find in it only a reproduction of the problems and questions with which they have already become familiar as a result of their own recent history. The churchly basis for this kind of theological treatment of a non-contemporaneous religion consists in the fact that in our society even Catholic Christianity is assuming more and more the character of a bourgeois religion, with a contemporaneity bonus similar to that long enjoyed by Protestantism.

Finally, there is the theological attempt to specify the creative character of religious noncontemporaneity. I would like to shed some light on the creative component in noncontemporaneity first by way of comparison. In a biography of Einstein I recently read that this great physicist was constantly asked how he had managed to arrive at his revolutionary insights. In reply he suggested that it might be connected with the fact that in school he had always learned more slowly and comprehended with greater difficulty than others; that even later he had experienced more difficulty with physics than some of his colleagues and that for this reason he had to devote himself to a problem for a longer time and with greater tenacity than did others, continuing to play, as it were, with the same ball long after others were already juggling new ones. The biographer noted that as a child Einstein had in fact so many learning difficulties that he could have been designated learning-disabled. People who are religiously devout, particularly Catholics, are like learning-disabled students in the school of progress! And indeed why not, if one bears in mind the "Einstein effect," thus viewing the noncontemporaneity of the devout not merely as a form of backwardness to be overcome as quickly as possible but as a trenchant and ultimately revolutionary way of relating to reality and its conditions, a form of timely inspiration and irritation through noncontemporaneous religion.

With reference to Catholicism, G. K. Chesterton once spoke of the "adventure of orthodoxy." I would like to refashion this phrase into the "adventure of religious noncontemporaneity." Certainly this adventure remains as removed from every progressive approach to religion as from every traditionalist one, the latter neither deriving strength from nor finding inspiration in the tension of noncontemporaneity. I see the impetus for a theological approach to religion, which attempts to make visible religion's creative noncontemporaneity for social life, in the theology of Karl Rahner, who as no one else has influenced the Catholic theology of our day. Rahner's thought is particularly apparent or at least invoked in the approach of the new political theologians and especially the liberation theologians, whose significance within Catholicism as a whole is far less marginal than the left's within West German society. For this theological left the Christian religion is primarily a messianic religion of emulation, certainly not in the elitist sense but in terms of impulses emanating from the social base. After many setbacks it has tenaciously taken root and asserted its presence within Church life as part of a process in which the entire ecumenical situation, with its tremendous tensions and challenges, has become an internal element in the individual situation of every Church. For instance, as a result of this process, the Church in this country, much more so than the society as a whole, has been forced to abandon a strictly European orientation and to view and judge itself through the eyes of the other—through the eyes of the victim, in this case through the eyes of members of the impoverished Churches of the Third World. So noncontemporaneous a notion as the community of believers, the Eucharistic fellowship of the devout, is ever more compelled to set free that kernel of radical praxis often concealed within the lawlike rigidity of Church life. Our Latin American brothers might also interpret for us the noncontemporaneous language of mortal sin in the sense of those sins through which quite literally we bring death to others as long as we fail to change ourselves radically.

V

And yet the question remains: Can talk of the creative noncontemporaneity of religion, of a religion that intervenes not just in our private life, be anything more than the creation of modern theology? Will it not founder on the reality of the church, on the practice, say, of "Catholicism" in this country? I am, of course, aware that there are sufficient grounds to pose these and related questions, and I myself have done so frequently and repeatedly to my Church. Of course, I understand what by now has become the near-constitutional distrust of those, particularly on the left, who no longer believe that ecclesiastic religion, with its notion of redemption, also pleads for the liberation of the oppressed; who no longer believe in its intention to combine prayer with struggle, love with a solidarity partial to the damaged life; and finally who no longer believe that its living faith can also give voice to a passionate opposition to that world of exploitation and consumerism that desecrates humanity's divine image. Not only must the Church be found wanting; there are also pitiful clichés about the Church that are sorely wanting. For instance, I regard as foolish and ignorant the view (held at times by Christians) in which the Church is seen only as a feudal relic that has since been refashioned into agent and advocate for the interests of monopoly capitalism.

But where is one to observe in the practice of ecclesiastic religion something of a connection between a noncontemporaneous religion and a form of political life that is creative and not oriented to backwardness and accommodation? Admittedly an answer to this question cannot go much beyond intimations and first approximations. In any case I would like to call attention to the Christian base communities (*Basisgemeinde*) that have sprung up primarily in the Churches of the Third World (although not only there); in the very terms used to define these communities one detects something of this connection. In them the noncontemporaneous social form of a cultic community has become societally differentiated, incorporating fundamental social conflicts and afflictions. In this way they reveal as a rule far greater orientational and integrational force than does a base oriented exclusively to strategies for socioeconomic transformation. To be sure, in this country these Christian base communities are not held in particularly high regard. Although their specific developmental validity for Third World Churches is affirmed in certain circumstances, this is done to stress their nontransferability and to reinforce the ideal of a "purely religious community" whose peace is only disturbed by the incorporation of conflicts emanating from the social base— as if love rendered social suffering and the suffering of the afflicted invisible, rather than making it all the more visible; as if in some meek way love were general and impartial! (Hate is selfish, individually as well as collectively, but love is partial.) The price our congregations pay for this type of social insouciance is high. It reveals only too clearly those features one would want to avoid in societal uniformization and in the political pseudo-neutrality of religious communities, such as relationlessness, lack of warmth, alienation, and lack of compelling and identificational force (especially among the young).

But, most important, our congregations renounce in this way the possibility of becoming a productive model in our society for a new mediation of public and private affairs. If today politics and morality can, in a clearly diffuse and rather helpless albeit ineluctable fashion, establish contact with one another (one speaks of renunciation and asceticism, of changing life priorities or abandoning consumerism, of conversion as a maxim of political survival), then the classic bourgeois distinction between public and private once again becomes a topic of discussion. And indeed not simply to dismiss it, which would be possible only at the price of a denial of the individual and ultimately of barbarism, but in order to constitute it in new fashion. In the form of base communities religion could and would have to intervene in this process, which is accessible neither through sound political pragmatism nor through selfless moral rigor. These base communities could become exemplary social localities, where political life becomes personal through its moral claims and where personal life, through the radical way in which it can be affected, nears political life. Here it could be demonstrated that a greater political potency and capacity for resistance can be found in the noncontemporaneous elements of Christian religion than in their purely secular counterparts. For in terms of their origin such notions as sin, conversion, sacrifice, and grace all clearly stand opposed to any pure internalization and therefore make more radical claims on individuals.

VI

In this context I would like to add a few remarks about the relation of noncontemporaneous religion to a question for which the left has evinced a special sensitivity. This question concerns the possibility for a new culture of solidarity in political life, a new principle of political individuation that does not renounce the achievements of a bourgeois principle (such as the basic political rights of the individual, the right to dissent, the right to popular sovereignty) but rather extends and surpasses that principle. Whence comes the forces for a new, quasi-postbourgeois principle of individuation, no longer based on the repression of others? Whence comes the power to resist a solidarity systematically distorted by hate or depersonalization without simultaneously jettisoning the hope for a solidarity that unconditionally enjoins individuals to assert their identity not against but with the meek, the socially and economically disenfranchised, the dependent groups and classes?

Who wants to place trust in the pure reserves of contemporaneity, in the exclusively contemporaneous man, who is in any case so horrified by his own future that, unlike members of all preceding generations, he no longer envies his successors? Is not a contemporaneity in which all the wrinkles of a noncontemporaneous life have been ironed out too narrow, too fortuitous, and too devoid of fantasy to generate any vision of a new individual that differs from the tiny unit of labor power, from the cunningly adaptive animal, from the smoothly functioning machine, or from the individual as a potentially criminal clog in a totalitarian grip?

The future, especially that of a new life dedicated to solidarity, is not nourished merely on the stuff of contemporaneity or on a noncontemporaneity rendered contemporaneous. The future of the village is not simply the urban center; the future of the cathedral is not simply the bank or the politically cultified mausoleum (as architecture may wish to insinuate); the future of childhood dreams is not simply the adult world of reason; and the future of religion is not simply a pallid utopia. Precisely for the sake of a future life of solidarity, noncontemporaneity demands more respect—and not only from traditionalists and conservatives, who, after all, only confirm themselves in it and who derive from it no spark of promise.

Why is it that on the left only artists and writers find sustenance in the tough, resistant stuff of noncontemporaneous religion? Does the left indeed deal with noncontemporaneity only in aesthetic fashion? I believe it is high time to think about this.

Perspectives on the
Geisteswissenschaften

Theology in Germany Today

Jürgen Moltmann

Perspectives

1. Whoever speaks about the spiritual situation of the age is always partial. One can be defensive or critical but never objective. One's own situation is never the object of disinterested contentment. We are affected by the suffering of our period. We are oppressed by the guilt of the past. We look forward to a better future.

Thus we must ask: Is it possible to speak *about* the spiritual situation of one's own present? Does one not always only speak *from* it? Indeed, if we wish to gain clarity about our situation, we must also transcend it. Otherwise we do in fact speak not about it but only from it. We must, as Helmut Plessner graphically put it, look at ourselves "over our own shoulders." Yet if we would be so eccentric as to observe ourselves reflecting upon ourselves, we must still do so with our own eyes, with our own customary prejudices and our own unconscious delusions. Must we not learn to view ourselves and our own situation through the eyes of others in order to recognize what we cannot recognize and acknowledge ourselves? How do we appear in the eyes of others? How do others view us? Which others?

2. It was a shock to many older Germans when in 1945 they saw themselves and the German situation of their time through the eyes of their victims—the Jews, the persecuted, the murdered. Germany mirrored in Auschwitz, and the silent Church in the eyes of Pastor Paul Schneider, slain at Buchenwald, or of Maximilian Kolbe, who sacrificed himself at Auschwitz, differed greatly from how they would have wished to see and present themselves.

It was a shock to many younger Germans to see themselves and the West German situation through the eyes of their spatially distanced victims in the Third World—the starving in India, the exploited in Brazil, the oppressed in South Africa. The Federal Republic, along with other affluent white industrial nations, appears differently in the eyes of its victims than it would want to appear to itself or to others.

"For us the whites are like a plague of locusts," a black South African said cautiously, after we had known each other for some time. "Once they have wiped out the game, plundered the mineral resources, and ruined us, they will most likely move on."

3. Those who remain confined only to their own situation become blinded by routine. Common prejudices and blindness prevent any real self-encounter. Nowhere do they question their own validity. Their self-knowledge and self-presentation are conditioned by the interests of their world, by the economic, political, and spiritual situation of the age. For the most part, self-knowledge and self-presentation are only the *conditioned reflexes* to the situation.

Those who see their own power and way of life through the eyes of others, particularly the eyes of their victims, transcend their own situation and enter a new one causally connected to their own. To be sure, no assurance exists that they will in this way find the essence of reality and exchange the reflected appearance for the true being. Nonetheless, as long as the "messianic light," discussed by Theodor W. Adorno in *Minima Moralia,* does not manifest itself directly, it shines most clearly from the eyes of the victim onto the "faults and fissures" of one's own situation.

4. In this essay I shall attempt to apply methods normally tested only in other situations to the theological situation of our age. These are the *historical method,* which examines inherited expressions of human experience in their "real place in life" in order to understand them in terms of their own situation or their "own time," and the *contextual method,* which attempts to comprehend the spiritual significance of these expressions from the standpoint of their own context. Involved in both methods is a reaffirmation of an existential hermeneutic that finds reflected in all expressions of human experience their own standards and conditions and that does not obscure them through abstractions or through an all-inclusive language. At the same time this reaffirmation expands earlier existential hermeneutics into a realistic *political hermeneutic.* With the emergence of "black liberation theology"

and "feminist theology" it is no longer possible to ignore one's own white, male, middle-class situation. Theology begins at home.

In this essay I wish to discuss in rough outline (1) the conditions of our society and the conditions of the Protestant Church within it, (2) the conditioned reflexes of theological theories that adapt themselves to these conditions, and (3) the liberations effected by suffering from alienation and by contact with new experiences. My restriction to Protestant theology and the Protestant Church is suggested by the conception of this book.

Conditions of Society

Political conditions

1. At the end of World War II the German Reich was decapitated and divided up by the victors. The Federal Republic of Germany (FRG) has not had a real capital since then. This means that no central forum exists for the public discussion and debate of political issues. Bonn has never become a true capital (*Hauptstadt*). The major demonstrations and debates take place frequently in Frankfurt, Hamburg, and occasionally Munich. The press, the arts, and the banking communities have all formed different centers of their own. To be sure, in view of the former Berlin centralism of the imperial government, there are advantages to this federalism, as demonstrated by the recent federalist tendencies in France and England. But this diffusion exacts the price of growing provincialism. Cultural autonomy rests with the regional states. Thus it is becoming ever more difficult to alter the policies and practices of schools and universities. Federalism has led to a denationalization of the Federal Republic that is without counterpart in the German Democratic Republic (GDR). For many young citizens the "brothers and sisters" in the FRG are no longer members of a real community.

2. Until the construction of the wall in 1961 the Protestant Church in Germany was a firm bond of unity for the nation and the community of people possessing a common language and history in both German states. The major Church congresses in Berlin and Leipzig clearly demonstrated this deep sense of community. With the construction of the wall, however, the Protestant Churches in the GDR were forced to organize themselves as the Alliance of Protestant Churches. They

Jürgen Moltmann

did this resolutely, acquiring therewith a new sense of autonomy. In contrast, the Protestant Churches in the Federal Republic still understand themselves as the Protestant Church in Germany. Owing to the lack of a common public forum, however, the laboriously crafted constitution for the Protestant Churches of Germany (EKD) foundered on the resistance of provincial Churches in southern Germany, particularly those in Württenberg.

If one looks at the map of the Protestant German Churches, one can easily recognize the political particularism that preceded the establishment of the Bismarckian Reich in 1871—regardless of whether one looks at Lippe-Detmold, Kurhessen-Waldeck, Eutin, or Oldenburg. Only the Lutheran Church of Nordelbein was successful in forming a larger alliance. This means, however, that while the Protestant Churches are strongly represented at the state level, they are poorly represented at the national level and are almost without representation at all at the European level. With the exception of the synods of the EKD and the Church congresses Protestant Churches have been unsuccessful in creating for themselves the common public forum not provided by society itself, a forum that tackles future tasks in their broader dimensions. The degeneration of Protestant faith into folklore mentality poses a real danger in this country.

3. Since the establishment of the two German states, the German people have been divided. The incorporation of old German traditions resulted in a "real socialism" in the GDR and a parliamentary democracy in the FRG. That the continuing East-West conflict materialized in Germany has spelled political and spiritual disaster for the German people. As a result, political opposition can be equated with and defamed as treason. Those in the West who criticize are suspected of being Communists. Those in the East who criticize supposedly betray secrets, are called CIA agents, and so on. Each state's need for security is evidently so great that low thresholds of tolerance are maintained. What this means is that the political partition of Germany continues to impede and paralyze political development in both parts of Germany. The situation in the Federal Republic was altered only by the student revolts of 1967–68, which violated ideological and linguistic East-West taboos. Yet it can be assumed that in this country these revolts disintegrated as a result of a political consciousness paralyzed by the partition.

The political and ideological division of Germany has caused the East-West conflict to touch almost every family. It has fixated public consciousness on alternatives that, leading nowhere, are condemned to stagnation. The simplifying either-or mentality, for which the Germans were already famous and infamous, has, through the division and the mutual contestation of the other's right to exist, been amplified in both German states to a mania. In it the old fascist friend-foe mentality was continued, as if the cohesion of the body politic depended on the evocation of a common, arch-evil state enemy. The fatal propensity for binary thinking and the unfortunate division of the world into either friend or foe is likely rooted in the identity insecurities of this "belated nation," to use Helmut Plessner's term. People who exhibit insecure, unstable identities often try to define themselves in demarcations and aggressions against others. But the puerile form of self-definition through negation is fatal to those negated. Opponents are always first dehumanized into hostile specters before they are physically exterminated. But this reveals angst rather than self-assurance. According to analyses of Germany conducted by English and American newspapers in 1978, the mood of the people in this economically successful country is one of angst, a general, diffuse attitude of defensiveness, constantly anticipating the worst. In the Federal Republic it is still possible to cash in on these insecurities, this repressed fear, this blatant aggressiveness, in both a political and a religious fashion.

Economic conditions

1. Politically, the German Reich had probably always lived beyond its economic means. Enthusiasm was enough to begin wars but not to win them. Today the Federal Republic lives politically far below its economic means. Externally this political restraint may appear wise. We must ask, however, whether it does not result in a renunciation of self-image and particularly of self-understanding, a renunciation that promotes and disguises a lack of morality in the political domain. When politics no longer determines the economy but economy the politics, then *Realpolitik* means economic power-politics (*Machtpolitik*). Indicative of the success of this *Realpolitik* are the annual advances in the rate of growth. Symptomatic of the extreme shortsightedness of this orientation is the dilemma between the billion deutsche mark

investments for the construction of nuclear power plants and the increasingly justified anxiety of the populace about such plants, as well as the progressive deterioration of the Federal Republic's reputation in the countries of the Third World. The fact that the FRG is prepared to spend on foreign aid only one-third of the 0.7 percent of gross national product regarded by the United Nations as a minimum, and the fact that this contribution is steadily declining reveal the blindness of a one-sided orientation to economic growth.

2. Economics, politics, and public consciousness are still so fundamentally fixated on the East-West conflict that the North-South conflict, virulent already for decades, is accorded only the most reluctant consideration, if indeed any at all. One is constantly aware of the East-West relationship, whereas the Third World remains far removed, television pictures and reports from abroad notwithstanding. East and West have now settled on a type of peaceful competition and coexistence. From the perspectives of the Third World, however, our societies—irrespective of their political systems—appear uniformly repressive. It is both painful and irritating to consider this truth: Are not problems only avoided and repressed in an irresponsible manner when German social conflicts are solved by higher growth rates achieved at the expense of impoverished countries?

The shortsighted economic and political policies in the North-South conflict cannot be deemed realistic, even if it is advantageous on a short-term basis. They destabilize the situation irreparably. In the long run it is more realistic to strive for an equalization of burdens and a more equitable world economic order than to dwell narcissistically on one's own rate of growth.

3. In this connection an all-inclusive language asserts itself in a particularly penetrating way: our growth constitutes a significant part of the growth of the world, our development stands at the forefront of progress, and what is good for us is also good for the rest of the world; finally, we live in the "modern age" and thus define the age of the world for other peoples, as if for them, too, the epoch is conditioned through European considerations. This all-inclusive language is the language of imperialism. Whoever is caught in its grip knows it immediately. Only those holding the grip pretend to be naive.

Historical conditions

1. Of all European nations Germany is the country of missed and miscarried revolutions of liberation. The German consciousness emerged out of the Reformation, whose partial success went hand in hand with the altogether unsuccessful German Peasant Revolt of 1524. Ever since Luther's decision against Thomas Müntzer and the peasants, the theme of "Reformation and Revolution" has always been present in the German consciousness, though constantly suppressed. Since 1524 all routes in Protestant Germany from Reformation to Revolution have been obstructed by fundamental anxieties, warnings, and the condemnation of heretics; here threatens, so it has been claimed, "fanaticism," "the politicization of the Gospel," "hubris," "insurrection against God," "the Spirit of the Antichrist" ("You really don't want a paradise on earth, do you?"). Confronted with the choice between revolution and dictatorship, the Germans have always opted for the dictator. Sins from above are more forgivable than sins from below, and violence from above is more bearable than violence from below, for the one is order and the other is chaos. This precedent was already apparent in Luther's pastoral letter to the peasants. It is for this reason that the French Revolution did not penetrate the German states. It is for this same reason that the bourgeois revolution of 1848 miscarried when the Prussian power of order destroyed democratic freedom. Even the decisions of 1919 and 1933 are to be seen against this historical background. It is owing to this sixteenth-century reformation without revolution that in the nineteenth century the French Revolution led with us only to a "revolution in thought." Its impulses were absorbed by German inwardness and preserved in a pure form by intellectuals through an "inner emigration."

2. Since 1789 the Christian Churches in Europe have opted for a conservative alternative to the principles of liberty, equality, and fraternity. Up to now only a few groups have been able to distance themselves from this attitude. According to official pronouncements, too much freedom still always leads to chaos, to the dissolution of the moral order, to anarchy. In the affected congregations "emancipation" is readily understood as a "moving away from the protection of God's hand," and "self-realization" is treated as a dirty word. The conservative religion of order, oriented to authority, family, and fatherland, can still be deemed the ruling political religion of the Christian Churches.

Jürgen Moltmann

3. A typical example of this can be observed in the discussion of the use of violence taking place in religious bodies. This discussion was occasioned by the antiracism policy adopted by the Ecumenical Council of Churches in Geneva. As early as 1971, at the time of the establishment of this policy, only a redistribution of power from the powerful to the powerless was considered to be a real solution to the problem of ideological racism. Yet the methods for this redistribution remain controversial. Are the powerless ever justified in engaging in passive or active resistance, in employing a liberating violence against their oppressors? To the disenfranchised, exploited blacks in South Africa there is near unison in the admonition from representatives of German Churches to renounce the use of violence. Liberation movements are categorized as terrorist. Christians must suffer injustice. Yet these voices were not heard during the conflict between Biafra and Nigeria, when blacks fought blacks. Is the German War of Liberation against Napoleon to be understood in retrospect as a terrorist undertaking? Were Andreas Hofer and Wilhelm Tell anarchists? The total silence about our own history and our own existence, manifest in the ringing pronouncements against the use of force by blacks in South Africa, is rooted in the aforementioned historical prejudice and in a guilt complex built on the lack of resistance to the dictatorship in Germany.

Conditions of the Protestant Church

1. "There exists no state Church," so it is declared in Article 137, paragraph 1, of the 1919 Weimar Republic constitution. Until then the Protestant Churches in Germany were *state Churches* as sovereign ecclesiastical governments. The Thirty Years War was ended in 1648 with the political separation of the religious faiths that had been in dispute: *cuius regio—eius religio* [Each state shall assume the religion of its prince]. Persuant to this maxim, the Protestant Church also became the state religion of its region in an internal-political sense: the sovereign was the Summepiscopus, his pastors political officials, and the Church the public institution of civil religion. Consequently obedience to the God-ordained public authority became according to *Romans* 13 a central element in the Protestant faith. Yet in 1919 this alliance of "throne and altar" was terminated only in a juridical sense. Essential elements of the state Church, the Church tax, and public privileges were left

intact. An actual separation of Church and state never materialized. Following World War I the lost throne was for many Christians replaced by the concepts of nation, fatherland, and the people (*Volk*). After the formal termination of the state Church the Protestant regional Churches conceived of themselves as *People's Churches* (*Volkskirche*). This term supposedly derives from Schleiermacher and was originally advanced in opposition to the Prussian national Church. Its critical tone, however, has long since died away. The term now is meant to signify a Church not of the people but for the people: a pastoral welfare Church (*Betreuungskirche*) or social service Church (*Versorgungskirche*), a public institution to administer the religion of society. Ministers, spiritual care stations, diaconical works, religious broadcasts in the media, and so forth furnish society with a religious network of spiritual security. In this way, too, the political direction of the Church is defined: a People's Church exists for everyone, albeit only in a religious sense. It is therefore said to stand above political parties and combatants in social conflicts. It is fundamentally neutral. Its ministers accept no political mandate. In this way the Church proffers a "third force" in conflicts, a platform for discussion oriented to mediation and reconciliation. One cannot expect it to adopt critical positions or engage in one-sided partisanship. This would violate its social constitution. For instance, money from Church funds should not be allocated to fight racism. The Church can comment on vital national issues only when certain that it speaks for all groups, strata, and classes of people.

2. In book 4, chapter 8, of *The Social Contract* Rousseau aptly characterizes the basic assumptions of civil religion:

There is . . . a purely civil profession of faith, the articles of which it is the duty of the sovereign to determine, not exactly as dogmas of religion, but as sentiments of sociability, without which it is impossible to be a good citizen or a faithful subject. Without having power to compel anyone to believe them, the sovereign may banish from the state whoever does not believe them. . . . The dogmas of civil religion ought to be simple, few in number, stated with precision, and without explanations or commentaries. The existence of the Deity, powerful, wise, beneficent, prescient, and bountiful, the life to come, the happiness of the just, the punishment of the wicked, the sanctity of the social contract and the laws; these are the positive dogmas.

The *Der Spiegel* opinion poll, "What Do the Germans Believe?" (1968), and the church poll, "How Stable Is the Church?" (1974), have shown that People's Church designates only the administration of civil religion. Rousseau distinguished between "civil" and "universal human" religion, subsuming the "pure spiritual religion" of Christianity under the latter. For him Christianity had made impossible the total integration of man as citizen into political society. "I know of nothing more opposed to the social spirit. Since the Gospel established no national religion, holy war among Christians is impossible"—so he overoptimistically believed. On the other hand, it is not overly pessimistic to ask how Christian the ecclesiastically administered civil religion in the Federal Republic really is. The more open and universal the People's Church becomes, the less binding is its offer. In this way it itself produces and reproduces the very identity crises and legitimation problems from which it chronically suffers.

3. A comparison of the ecclesiastical religious systems in the Federal Republic and in the United States can make partially clear Christianity's situation in West German society. Whether the Church is portrayed as a national Church, a People's Church, or an administered religion, the presupposition is that religion is involuntary, an act of providence, fate, and thus unavoidable. People's Churches are therefore available to all; they act on behalf and for the sake of everyone. They provide life with meaning, relieve people of the burden of fundamental decisions and aid them in times of crisis. Thus over 90 percent of the population "belong" to the Church, although only 15 percent are active participants. Church operations therefore depend primarily on membership and only secondarily on participation. People's Churches in the Federal Republic guarantee everyone the freedom not to attend Church, but find it difficult to guarantee everyone the freedom to attend the Church of his choice. Tradition, public institutions, and baptism have made Christianity a fate that even the atheist can escape only with difficulty. Church membership is involuntary; leaving the Church, however, is voluntary.

The situation is different in the United States. There democratic polity was established in opposition not to the European State Churches but to European monarchies and ecclesiastically autonomous congregations. The system of voluntary religion originated in the American republic: Churches are constituted entirely by the congregation, and the congregation is what its members—from religious services down to finances—want it to be. It is this fundamental congregationalism that enabled the various Christian denominations to avoid dispute over the control of the state religion. The struggle between orthodoxy and sects never occurred. Alternate communities and life-styles could exist side by side on a voluntary basis. The democratic respect for the freedom of the individual has promoted the congregations' voluntariness. The question arises, therefore, whether the principle of ecclesiastical autonomy is not the religious foundation of democracy. Nowhere else do state Churches and People's Churches create a climate favorable to democracy. Certainly the freedom "to worship in the Church of your own choice" does not preclude a lack of commitment similar to that found within established Churches of Europe. Churches and religious communities readily present themselves as religious supermarkets. Basic to the American notions of freedom, however, is not simply the voluntariness of decision but, with equal importance, the *covenant* of freedom as well. Only where congregations — originating as voluntary associations — are unified in reciprocal promise and mutual reliability can one speak properly of a Church. The association of congregations originates in freedom, but such freedom is secured and preserved only by this association. If the principle of covenant were lost, freedom would involve as little commitment as it does in the People's Churches of Europe.

4. Included within the German notion of "religion without decision" (H. O. Wölber) is the *Church without community*. Religion is viable as a managed institution and a social network of spiritual security as long as it is able to emanate an aura of beneficent indubitability. Since people still perceive themselves individually and socially as creatures in a precarious position, they require relief from the burdens of life. In this sense the religious question of the meaning of life is best answered by not even posing it. This avoidance of the question of meaning through concentration on relief from life's daily burdens is taken up by the administered Church in its rituals and symbols and in the theological wisdom of its authorities. As a managed institution, religion relieves people of the responsibility for their own decisions of faith. It is enough to accept the "belief of the Church," since one belongs to that Church. Yet if personal decisions are delegated to the institution of the Church and the latter is utilized as an institute of relief, then behavior assumes the form of institutionalized nonbindingness. "Christian" becomes a truism, something that cannot be called into question.

As a managed institution, religion is simultaneously made into a *private affair*, an object of subjective caprice. On the other hand the Church without community also means Christians without Church. The Protestant religion of conscience attempted to compensate for the Church's institutionalization, wrought in the emergence of the People's Church, through a corresponding privatization of faith. In this way the community of the congregation fell by the wayside.

The institutionalized nonbindingness of the People's Church in general and the privatized capriciousness of faith in particular reciprocally condition and effect each other. The religious administration in the People's Church privatizes religion, and the reclamation of religion as a private affair shapes a religious administration to which no one gains proximity. At issue are not alternatives but opposite sides of the same coin. In times of the oppression and persecution of Christians neither of these positions remained viable; the leadership of the People's Church submits to external pressure and is silent "for the sake of the people." The individual, pained by conscience, experiences powerlessness. One cannot depend on a willingness to resist by the People's Church or by individuals. They are constitutionally incapable of resistance. This at any rate was the doctrine of Church struggle in the period of the German dictatorship from 1933 to 1945.

Conditioned Reflexes and the Conflicts of Theology

Theories of integration

1. Shadowed by the alignments and controversies of the Church struggle, the immediate postwar period was still dominated by theological and denominational "schools." The scene was shaped by the disputes between Barth and Bultmann, between demythologization and ecclesiastical dogmatics, between the politics of the "Imperial Rule of Christ" and the political abstinence of the "two-world doctrine," between bible fundamentalism and historicocritical interpretation of the bible, between religious and religious-critical theology. Theology had a fundamentally denominational character. At the end of the 60s this founding of schools became less pronounced. Theological positions lost their distinctiveness. "Positional theology" as such fell into disrepute. Meta-theological theories emerged that sought to provide instruction for the interpretation and pragmatic utilization of various theologies. These

theories reduced the disputed theological standpoints to mere moves on the chessboard of Christianity. To be sure, with the dissolution of schools and the cleric's know-it-all manner, emphasis on the denominational character of theological knowledge also disappeared. The focus of interest shifted away from advancements in knowledge and fixated on the relativity of the totality.

Old and universal concepts long deemed useless were now taken as foundations for theological metatheory—concepts like Christianity, religion, meaning, history, and modernity. The ambiguity and indefinability of these universal concepts seemed to make them easily applicable to all forms of theology. The indefiniteness of these great placative concepts enabled them to be used to explain everything, thereby uniting all explanations, even those contradicting one another, in the greater community achieved at the Numinos. Christian theology demonstrates its significance no longer in actual critique of and real liberation from society's Godless bonds but in its integrational power vis-à-vis different positions, denominations, cultures, and religions.

Apparent here is the old German longing for unity—the unity of being in general, the unity of thought, the unity of human society, the unity of the Church. Early "dialectical theology" (Barth, Brunner, Gogarten, Bultmann), which opposed the Christian cultural syntheses of the nineteenth-century bourgeois world, was rejected and annulled as alternative thinking, as diastasis, as a self-isolation and a self-ghettoization of the Church. The combative theology of the "confessional Church" was declared obsolete. In its place the apologetic theology of the nineteenth century was invoked: Enlightenment and modernity are "Christian" (as if there had never been a Verdun or an Auschwitz), and "secularization" is in fact nothing but the realization of the Christian faith in a Christian culture (as if there had never been colonialism, slavery, and exploitation). However important the dissolution of clerical, sectarian, and narrow-minded positions within theology, the integrating metatheological unity of theory itself threatens to become delusive. Directing their attention to the universal totality, its adherents are notorious for overlooking their own conditions of existence, which, for this reason, are imperiously generalized.

2. The most striking form of such an integrative theology of unity is undoubtedly Wolfhart Pannenberg's theology of universal history. After Karl Barth's *Kirchliche Dogmatik* and Rudolf Bultmann's existential *Glaubenslehre*, the forgotten *weltanschauliche* aspects of theology are with

Pannenberg once again brought into the foreground. His theology of universal history again provides objective orientations and justifications for Christian faith. Kerygmatic claims and decisionist grounds for faith are unmasked as theological expressions of embarrassment. Theology is promoted and pursued as universal science. Here is not the place to address the specific difficulties involved in the assertion and justification of universals. The melting of one's own standpoint into the interests of one's society, Church, and politics makes it difficult to pursue a theology of universal history, for what is questionable is not the universal, the general, and the unifying as such but surely the right to specify what these are—that is to say, the right to specify these for everyone else. Theories of universal history have hitherto been Eurocentric and therefore have served, wittingly or not, the interests of European culture. Following Hegel the theology of universal history presents Christian religion as absolute religion. The corresponding theologians of religious history quite correctly relate Christianity to the other world religions and vice versa. But they overlook the primary question, namely: Who writes the rules of dialogue and the laws of these relations? Who has this right? Since this is a right invoked without question, the old Christian absolutism is only perpetuated under different conditions. The all-inclusive language of theories of universal history must be perceived by people of other religions, cultures, and world-views as a language of domination. The abstraction from *my* situation to *the* situation has always been a technique in imperialistic language control. Christian theology can remain sufficiently self-critical to avoid the techniques of an abstractive and inclusive language without abandoning hope for salvation of the totality.

3. A similar form of integrative theology of unity is advanced in Trutz Rendtorff's *Theorie des Christentums*. The concept "Christianity" is sufficiently unspecific and ambiguous to provide a framework to evaluate the specific consciousness of the age. Intended here is the collection of those values and orientations constituting the elements of tradition through which the present is shaped and in reference to which present consciousness attains articulation. Since the present character of European culture has until now been shaped by Christianity, a relevant theory of modernity must coincide with a theory of Christianity presented from the perspective of this tradition's history. All essential moments of the modern consciousness are identified retrospectively as moments in the self-apprehension of Christian con-

sciousness and vice versa. The great task of Christian theology is therefore to develop a relevant "theory of the present." Because the encompassing concept "Christianity" remains indeterminate, this theory should embrace and in turn be determined by all possible phenomena of a culture it characterizes, even contradictory phenomena. The oft-lamented secularization process is now reclaimed for the history of Christianity as a process that is possible and definable only within Christianity. Modern atheism is appropriated merely as that which Christianity negates. And because modern Christianity must embrace all phenomena of modernity, even alternate theories, such as those of dialectical theologians, specifically Karl Barth, must be interpreted as expressions of modern Christianity. Given this method of integrating everything determinate into the indeterminate and infusing the remaining indeterminates with pregiven determinations, it is difficult to discover and identify non-Christian thoughts and phenomena anywhere. Yet it is even more difficult to define what is Christian. The distinction between Church and Christianity is a feature of European modernity. It even acknowledges a Christianity without, outside, and against the Church. Conversely it forces the Church to reach outside itself. Certainly one can only integrate what already exists. Thus the "theory of Christianity" always appears *post festum*. It is affirmative, not critical. The triumph of Christianity is carried on in this method of appropriation. As one's own position is not subject to reflection, its validity is asserted ubiquitously.

4. Finally the *functionalist theory of religion* offers the most comprehensive integration of Church into society. Definitions of the nature of religion here become superfluous. Its truth is asserted universally, and its functions within the social system are analyzed for the purpose of its administration. Every social system requires a religious subsystem for internal stabilization and for legitimation in the world horizon. The system of religion is adapted to the needs of the social system. It exists to heal wounds, to make contingencies bearable, to facilitate transitions, to create a framework for meaning, to administer basic values, to allow for possibilities, and so on. The ubiquity of religious components requires that religion remain in a state of undetermined determinateness. The analysis of processes in which religion functions socially and spiritually therefore serves the aims of organized and administered religion, primarily the aims of the people who organize and administer it.

The functionalist theory of religion as well as its offspring, the functionalist theory of the Church, is a science of administration. Thus there can be no doubt that it has a system-stabilizing effect or that it can comprehend as "religious" only functions that stabilize the system. What is analyzed and administered within this theory as ritual, symbol, consolation, and conviction is nothing other than religion itself.

That this religion is defined as Christianity is sheer coincidence. Comparable processes also exist in shamanism. The functionalist theory of religion comprehends only those religious processes reducible to universal human constants. The particularity and uniqueness of the religious contents play no distinguishing role. The functional theories of Church and religion also deliberately fail both to reflect upon and submit for discussion their own function for this specific religion in this specific society. In this way Christian faith is transformed into Christianity, and Christianity is transformed into this society's civil religion. Self-critical identity problems pertaining to the origins and goals of faith are no longer recognized. Whoever measures theology by its biblical origin, whoever wants to define faith christologically, whoever remains mindful of the memory of eschatological hope is branded a member of a social sect and banished into a subculture of public religion's subsystem.

Evangelical apocalypse

In opposition to the integrative theologies mentioned above there has emerged, since the demythologization debates of the 50s, a pietistic and, as it later came to be known, "evangelical" alternative. To the degree that integrative theories reflect society's need for security, the evangelical agitations stylize society's mute fears. Complex relations, not easily clarified by reflections, are with the help of the friend-foe mentality reduced to simple contrasts. In protest against the historico-critical interpretation of the scriptures, there was formed a front "for bible and confession." For some time the name of Bultmann stood for the archenemy; to choose against him was to evince the existence of true faith. When the demythologization debates were superseded by the discussion of political theology, the name Moltmann was placed on the Index. Then, when Philip Potter became the first black secretary general of the World Council of Churches, questions of world peace and the Third World became prominent. Potter was thereby fashioned into a symbol of the enemy for the true believers. The modern symbol of fear embodied in Marx and "anti-Christian Communism" represents the eschatological Antichrist himself. The pattern of this development is as simple as it is fatal: true belief is a personal decision. Such a decision has an eschatological quality. As was said in the beginning, one decides on one's weapon only in battle, when one must confront the enemy. Thus the decisionist and confessional faith is one with the apocalyptic Armageddon for Christ against the Antichrist. It is the task of a fundamental theology to call for a decision of faith, to clarify the situation of choice and, with this aim, to unmask the long-range strategies of the Antichrist against Christ and his followers. This is the evangelical apocalypse: struggle is necessary in order to clarify an obscured situation. Thus advocates of fundamental theology are today involved in a struggle of faith against the *Zeitgeist*, in a Church struggle against the ecumenical movement, in a cultural struggle against anarchy, emancipation, liberalism, and pacifism, in a political struggle against Communism, and, all things taken together, in an apocalyptic Armageddon. The more specific characteristics of the archenemy are interchangeable. The devil has many faces. At present they include concepts of humanity, Christo-Marxism, group dynamics, and a penal law oriented to rehabilitation. Yet the war is waged not simply against people and their ideas but against the "oscillating manifestations" of the Antichrist. In this struggle all means seem permitted and all proof superfluous.

The transformation of Christianity into Manichaeanism is now perfect. Yet behind its ludicrously horrifying appearances, there lies concealed a calculated manipulation of fear and the systematic construction of a counterecumenism, a countermission, and a counterchurch to the Protestant Churches of Germany. The astonishing financial might of the evangelical movement in America clearly derives from business concerns interested in anti-Communist indoctrination of people they exploit. In the Federal Republic the evangelical movement is strongly represented in the congregational groups comprising those "true to the Church." Against the "Church convocation" it organizes the "convocation of the congregation"; against the theology of the university it organizes the anti-intellectual theology of the congregation. Thus it operates in the vacant chambers of society, chambers that have been ignored by the prevailing consciousness. Therein—and not in the movement itself—lie dangers that are not to be underestimated.

Jürgen Moltmann

Alienations and Liberations

New historical data

Diverse theological directions are distinguished not least of all by diverse approaches to tradition and appropriation of diverse historical experiences. Although the integrative theologies originate in the nineteenth-century Christian bourgeois world and although the evangelical movement continues the conservative, antirevolutionary, and antimodern resentments of the nineteenth century, the theologics now to be discussed must be linked to the advent of "dialectical theology" in the 20s and to the confessional Church's appropriation of the new experience with Church struggle under the German dictatorship. For the theologies of the Barmen Theological Declaration of 1934, the confession of the confessional Church against the German Christians gave expression to a decisive and truly epochal change in the recent history of Protestant theology and the Protestant Church. For other theologies, however, this is only an episode in the greater structures of modernity. It is my belief that the experiences of the confessional Church in Germany are of epochal significance, for in them Church, theology, and Christians discovered in what formerly had been unknown territory their freedom, their identity, and their public duty. Such experiences cannot be forgotten, even if they are repressed. They aroused hope, which indeed can be frustrated but never extinguished. Thus the theological principles of the Barmen Declaration serve as theological signposts. Through the history of error and force in the most recent period, an unbroken thread of hope appears, urging the renewal of Church and theology, the renewal of the realm of freedom, the kingdom of God. One finds it not only in the theses of the Barmen Declaration, but in the Stuttgart "Confessions of Sins" of the Protestant Church of 1945, in the Darmstadt Statement of the Brotherhood Councils (*Bruderräte*) of 1947, and in the Memorandum of the Protestant Churches of Germany on the Reconciliation with Poland of 1965.

The Barmen Theological Declaration (1934)

Thesis 1: Jesus Christ, as he is attested for us in Holy Scripture, is the one Word of God which we have to hear and which we have to trust and obey in life and in death.

We reject the false doctrine: as though the Church could and would have to acknowledge as a source of its proclamation, apart from and besides this one Word of God, still other events and powers, figures and truths, as God's revelation.

Thesis 2: As Jesus Christ is God's assurance of the forgiveness of all our sins, so in the same way and with the same seriousness he is also God's mighty claim upon our whole life. Through him befalls us a joyful deliverance from the godless fetters of this world for a free, grateful service to his creatures.

We reject the false doctrine: as though there were areas of our life in which we could not belong to Jesus Christ, but to other lords—areas in which we would not need justification and sanctification through him.

Thesis 3: The Christian Church is the congregation of the brethren in which Jesus Christ acts precisely as the Lord in Word and sacrament through the Holy Spirit. As the Church of pardoned sinners, it has to testify in the midst of a sinful world, with its faith as with its obedience, with its message as with its order, that it is solely his property, and that it lives and wants to live solely from his comfort and from his direction in the expectation of his appearance.

We reject the false doctrine: as though the Church were permitted to abandon the form of its message and order to the pleasure or to changes in prevailing ideological and political convictions.

Thesis 4: The various offices of the Church do not establish a dominion of some over the others; on the contrary, they are for the exercise of the ministry entrusted to and enjoined upon the whole congregation.

We reject the false doctrine: as though the Church, apart from this ministry, could be and were permitted to give to itself, or allow to be given to it, special leaders vested with ruling powers.

Thesis 5: Scripture tells us that, in the as yet unredeemed world in which the Church also exists, the State has by divine appointment the task of providing for justice and peace. [It fulfills this task] by means of the threat and exercise of force, according to the measure of human judgment and human ability. The Church acknowledges the benefit of this divine appointment in gratitude and reverence before Him. It calls to mind the Kingdom of God, God's commandment and righteousness, and thereby the responsibility both of rulers and of the ruled. It trusts and obeys the power of the Word by which God upholds all things.

We reject the false doctrine: as though the State, over and beyond its special commission, should and could become the single totalitarian order of human life, thus fulfilling the Church's vocation as well.

We reject the false doctrine: as though the State, over and beyond its special commission, should and could appropriate the characteristics, the tasks and the dignity of the Church, thus becoming an organ of the Church.

Thesis 6: The Church's commission, upon which its freedom is founded, consists in delivering the message of the free grace of God to all people in Christ's stead, and therefore in the ministry of his own word and work through sermon and sacrament.

We reject the false doctrine: as though the Church in human arrogance could place the Word and work of the Lord in the service of any arbitrarily chosen desires, purposes, and plans.[2]

The Stuttgart "Confessions of Sins" (1945)

It is with great sorrow that we say: Through us infinite grief has been visited upon many peoples and countries. That which we have often expressed in our congregations, we now proclaim in the name of the entire Church. For many years we indeed fought in the name of Jesus Christ against the spirit that found its frightful expression in the Nazi dictatorship; but we accuse ourselves of not having confessed more courageously, prayed more faithfully, believed more joyously, and loved more ardently.

The Darmstadt Statement of the Brotherhood Council of the Protestant Churches of Germany (1947)

1. We were given the word for reconciliation of the world with God in Christ. This word we shall hear, accept, enact, and execute. This word cannot be heard, accepted, enacted, and executed as long as we do not allow ourselves to be absolved of our sins, our fathers' as well as our own, and if we do not allow ourselves to be called home by Jesus Christ, the good shepherd, from all the false and evil paths on which we, as Germans, have strayed through our political aims and actions.

2. We went astray when we began to dream of a special German mission, as if the world could be healed by the German nature. In this way we paved the way for unchecked political power, placing our nation on the throne of God. It was calamitous that we began to base the domestic policies of our state solely on strong government, and the foreign policies solely on military expansion. Thus we denied our calling, which directed Germans to make use of given talents to serve the common interests of all people.

3. We went astray when we began to erect a "Christian front" against the new structures that had become necessary in the societal life of men. The alliance of the Church with the forces committed to conserving the old and the conventional has exacted its bitter revenge.

We betrayed the Christian freedom that allows and even commands us to alter life situations whenever the communal life of mankind requires such change. We denied the right of revolution but tolerated and sanctioned the development of absolute dictatorship.

4. We went astray when we thought it was necessary to form in political life and with political means a front against evil, light against darkness, just against unjust. In this way we falsified God's free offer of grace as extended to all by forming political, social, and ideological fronts, thus leaving the world to its own justification.

5. We went astray when we overlooked that the economic materialism of the Marxist doctrine should have reminded the Church of the congregation's obligation and promise for the lives and communal life of the peoples of this world. We failed to make the cause of the poor and the disenfranchised—in accord with the gospel of God's coming kingdom—the cause of Christianity.

6. Acknowledging and confessing this we know that as a congregation of Jesus Christ we were absolved to pursue a new, better service for the glory of God and the eternal and temporal salvation of mankind. What is required for our people and above all for the Christians among them is not the catchphrase, Christianity and Western culture, but a return to God and the devotion to one's neighbor in the strength of the death and resurrection of Jesus Christ.

7. We attested to it then and attest to it again today: "Through Jesus Christ befalls us the joyous deliverance from the godless fetters of this world for a free, grateful service to all of his creatures." We therefore beseech you: do not let despair become your Lord, for Christ is the Lord. Renounce all faithless indifference, do not let yourselves be seduced by dreams of a better past or by speculations about a coming war. Instead, become aware, in this freedom and with great dispassion, of the responsibility that each and all of us bear for the construction of a better German state, which serves justice, welfare, domestic tranquility, and the reconciliation of nations.

New theological data

The discovery of the Old Testament

During the National Socialist movement of the "German Christians" it was demanded that the Old Testament, as a Jewish book, be removed from the Church and replaced with a myth of the German people, for example, the *Edda*. Christianity would thereby have been fully perverted into a folk religion. Although in 1933 this demand frightened many Christians, it in fact only made apparent the age-old alienation of the Church from the Old Testament. From Schleiermacher through Harnack the Old Testament had long since become obsolete for liberal Protestantism:

The rejection of the Old Testament in the second century would have been a mistake and was rightly repudiated by the great Church. Preserving it in the sixteenth century was a fate the Reformation was not able to avoid. However, maintaining it since the nineteenth century as a canonical text in Protestantism is the consequence of religious and churchly paralysis. (Adolf von Harnack, 1924)

The present ecclesiastical liberation and theological renewal are characterized by the development of a new relation to the Old Testament. Christians have discovered the constitutive significance of the Old Testament for the understanding of the New Testament, recognized that Jesus was unmistakably a Jew, and comprehended that the God whom he had instructed us to call "Father" was none other than the God of Abraham, Isaac, and Jacob. After the long history of anti-Semitism Christians came to understand that like the two "testaments of hope," Israel and Christianity, belong together like siblings. The new, no longer historicoreligious but theological approach to the Old Testament is intertwined with the name of Gerhard von Rad. We owe to him and to his school the insight that the conceptual world of Israel should not be separated from the historical world, and that the legitimate form of theological discourse about the Old Testament is contemporizing recounting (vergegenwärtige Nacherzählung). The Old Testament insight into the meaning of history and narrative called into question the traditional Hellenistic logification of Christian theology and corrected its abstractions. In the Old Testament school there emerged an alternative mentality opposed to theological scholasticism: collective experiences of history are dissolved in concepts but preserved and mediated in narratives. Therein Christian theology discovered its own character as narrative theology. Christian theology influenced by the Old Testament began to develop a sensitivity for the experience of hope and the unredeemed character of this world. Through the Old Testament Christian faith once again became realistic, political, and vibrant, abandoning its gnostic fixation on "God and Soul." The majority of the new systematic approaches to theology, Protestant and Catholic, are rooted in this discovery of the Old Testament.

The discovery of Israel

Logically connected with the discovery of the Old Testament is the discovery of the kinship of Christians and Jews. That this discovery required a history of the persecution of Jews lasting centuries and required for its end the unforgivable sins of the Holocaust is something that can be acknowledged only with shame. The relation of the Church and Israel is essentially always the reverse side of the Church-state relation. From early on Christian anti-Semitism was connected with the accommodation of Christians to state power. Conversely Christians discovered their kinship with Jews in times of their own political persecution. Anti-Semitic laws were first promulgated in the Roman Empire when Christianity was made into the state religion. As a state religion Christianity was inclined to assert itself absolutely and to present itself triumphantly as the fulfillment of the hope of Israel. Yet because neither the Church nor the Christian empire are the "Kingdom of God," Christians developed a hatred of their own imperfection. The most profound basis for the Christian hatred for Jews is this Christian self-hate. It governed not only the medieval empire but also the bourgeois Christian world of the nineteenth century. As a price for emancipation the Christian state demanded that the Jews abandon the hope for the Messiah. Hence the political messianism of the "Third" or "Thousand Year" Reich was not coincidentally but unavoidably anti-Semitic. An acknowledgment of Israel's special calling and Israel's hope serves to awaken the Church from its state-churchly and church-stately dreams and to lead it to the road of its own hope for the Kingdom of God. Only in knowing that it is connected with Israel on the road to hope through history will the Church be prepared to engage in the necessary political reistance against ideological and practical imperialism. Israel's existence and its way of existing are therefore vital to the truth of the Church. Viewed from the Israeli perspective, Christianity can be understood as the preparation by people for the messianic period (*praeparatio messianica*). Since for Israel God, People, and Country form a unity, Christians are not entitled to accept positively the Israeli conception of God while despising the people, as was the case in the nineteenth century; nor to respect God and the people of the covenant while despising the country, as is the case today. The joint discussion of Jews and Christians is presently coming to a head in the question of the theological recognition of the country and state of Israel. Christians' attitude toward the states in which they live is closely tied to this recognition.

The discovery of hope

Logically connected with the contemporizing of the Old Testament and the acknowledgment of Israel is the reacquisition of the hope contained in Christian faith: "Christianity that is not altogether and absolutely eschatology has altogether and absolutely nothing to do with Christ" (Karl Barth, 1921). It is always a sign of Christianity's bourgeois domestication when eschatological hopes have disappeared and migrated to sectarians and revolutionaries. As a civil religion Christianity must extinguish the disturbing hopes of the Old and New Testament in order to become socially acceptable. Conversely, to the extent that the messianic hopes within Christian faith are reestablished, opposition and resistance will develop against this tendency toward bourgeois domestication.

It is therefore understandable that in the 60s Ernst Bloch's philosophy of hope found a receptive audience in many younger Protestant and Catholic theologians, who constructively appropriated it. "Theology of hope," "political theology," and active commitment to a democratic socialism all were influenced by Bloch. The new "political theology" of Johann Baptist Metz applied Carl Schmitt's old concept against itself, so as to make theology politically critical and to extend the claim of totality to the political. Eschatological and political theology have found a particularly resonant echo in the Latin American "theology of liberation." Since 1967 the discussion of socialism has destroyed many old alliances between theologians and, surprisingly, has called forth new ones. Proceeding from the theme of "the kingdom of God and socialism," Helmut Gollwitzer, a disciple of Karl Barth, has arrived at a position similar to that of a disciple of Rudolf Bultmann—Dorothee Sölle—who proceeded from the theme of "existential and political hermeneutics." A common social praxis has also brought together diverse theological reflections. Differences remain, however, with regard to the messianic and moral interpretation of socialism.

The trinitarian concept of God

As a civil religion Christianity can dispense with the formation of a distinct Christian conception of God. It is enough if it concentrates the general religiosity on one notion of natural theology and maintains that God is and that God is one. Thus a general and vague monotheism continues to represent even the notion of God for this Christianity. To the extent that Christianity reflects on its identity in the manner of social and religious criticism, however, it is obliged to develop a specifically Christian conception of God. What is specifically Christian is the sign of the cross. Thus a Christian doctrine of God must be conceptualized with reference to the shame, helplessness, and God-forsakenness of the crucified Christ. But if every statement about God is at the same time a statement about the crucifixion, then the Christian doctrine of God must make a break with the axiom of antiquity's philosophical concept of God, on which it had been based for so long. The "crucified God" is not unalterable, not incapable of suffering, and not a monadic unity. Reflection upon the alterability, capacity for suffering, and trinitarian liveliness of God are therefore the new tasks of Christian theology. To conceive God as a supreme substance was the aim of the scholastic doctrine of God. To comprehend God as absolute subject was the aim of the modern doctrine of God. To understand God in His trinitarian history is now a task of systematic theology, one on which Protestant and Catholic theologians are already at work. A theology that no longer finds adequate orientation in the venerable but nonliving concepts of the tradition yet does not seek refuge in the religious indeterminacy of modern theological discourse, is faced with the task of speaking about the living God with reference to the crucified God. In this concreteness it gains its breadth. In this determinacy theology becomes an open and liberating invitation to all.

Literary Criticism in Germany Today

Peter Bürger

Reception Theory as Symptom

Bourgeois society is distinguished from prebourgeois social formations in that, among other things, it destroys traditions and yet is unable to live without them. We can examine this dilemma by looking at its origins. Even for genuine republicans the abolition of religious cults in the French Revolution was a shock. They felt the loss of a certain cultural practice, the rhythmic recurrence of annual ecclesiastical rituals. Rooted less in belief than in habit, these rituals served to disrupt the daily routine of securing life's basic needs. The attempt to create a countertradition with revolutionary rituals failed.

In bourgeois society a cultural tradition is established not through public occurrences but through an individual's private appropriation of aesthetic objectifications. As such it is accessible to the social strata distinguished by property and education. The legitimation function that culture performed for the propertied class was exposed at the latest in the historical avant-garde movements. These constitute the historical presupposition for Herbert Marcuse's dialectical critique of bourgeois culture as an affirmative culture, one that both adheres to the counterfactual image of a better life and simultaneously obstructs its practical realization.[1]

Neither the avant-garde protest against the bourgeois institution of art, as one separated from life, nor the dialectical critique of bourgeois culture (formulated in exile, by the way) has radically altered this approach to aesthetic objectifications. It continued to possess a conservative character up into the 1960s. In 1960 Hans-Georg Gadamer in philosophic fashion once again gave conceptual expression to this dominant mode of cultural appropriation. In his view tradition ultimately constitutes a given condition that cannot be called into question, one the individual must simply accept.[2]

Gadamer's conservative concept of hermeneutics has been criticized by Jürgen Habermas, who demonstrates that tradition's authority owes it potency to what remains an unclarified relation to the social base, to the systems of labor and domination.[3] Habermas invokes the power of reflection to call into question the legitimacy of a tradition established in authoritarian fashion. When placed in the historical setting where the "CDU [Christian Democratic Union] State" (Schäfer/Nedelmann) appeared to be at an end and the transformation of the Federal Republic toward "more democracy" appeared within reach, these considerations could have furnished the impetus to develop a critical science of culture. Such a science would have had the task of further developing procedures for the analysis of works from the standpoint of the critique of ideology and of clarifying the connection between tradition and domination. The attempts made in this direction (in literary criticism by Peter-Uwe Hohendahl, Norbert Mecklenburg, and Jochen Schulte-Sasse, among others) have largely gone unnoticed. The events of France in May 1968 aroused hopes for revolution in young intellectuals, who often confused the rapid political developments occurring in their imaginations with those in reality.

Whereas the left was only partially successful in using the opportunity to institutionalize a critical mode of relating to cultural objectifications, the right, with the concept of reception theory (*Rezeptionsästhetik*), developed an extraordinarily effective counterstrategy. Far from taking recourse in the culturally conservative position of Gadamer, its proponents abandoned this approach together with the assumption that cultural traditions are of value in orienting life. (The term "[counter]strategic action" naturally need not reflect the consciousness of the agent; it merely serves as a graphic reconstruction of relations.) By its own account, reception theory no longer aims to interpret single works of art; instead it merely specifies those elements (narrative gaps) in a work of art, which are subsequently to be assigned meaning by different interpreters in different historical situations. Reception theorists are no longer interested in discussing with other literary scholars the substantive meanings that could be extracted from cultural objectifications for the present. Rather, dismissing such "concretizations" as always dogmatic, they dedicate themselves to what they regard as the sole scholarly task, the delineation of the possible range of such concretizations. The strategic advantage of this position is obvious: the proponents of reception theory can, without discussion, dismiss as prescientific and repudiate as dogmatic all attempts at appropriation while presenting themselves as at once scientific and open-minded (that is, free from all fixations).

A comprehensive critique of reception theory would have to expose this strategy. That the leap from the hermeneutic problematic into objectivism remains a bald assertion is just as obvious as the fact that the specification of narrative gaps represents nothing more than an atrophied stage of text-immanent interpretations. Particularly troublesome are the consequences of reception theory for the appropriation of cultural traditions. Inasmuch as it eschews rational discussion about the substantive meanings of artistic objectifications, reception theory no longer allows any determination as to how and for what reason specific works of art are to be appropriated. Whereas conservative and critical forms of hermeneutics, at least in principle, stand in dialogic relation with one another, both professing the aim of elucidating tradition so as to acquire value orientation for the present,[4] reception theory dismisses this mode of appropriating tradition in the interest of what must remain an illusory objectivity. In its seeming withdrawal to a metalevel (that of specifying structures that direct semanticization), this scholarly approach relinquishes the field of interpretation to the capricious generation of meaning supplied by individual subjects. These consequences, which reception theorists vehemently refuse to acknowledge, are especially apparent within the sphere of teaching literature. Here the political implications of reception theory also become evident: against the attempt to clarify traditions by means of a critique of ideology, one abstractly posits an individual pupil who should satisfy "his own needs." The socially mediated character of these needs is not examined.[5]

The success of reception theory should not be attributed to clever advertising techniques, as is sometimes asserted, but rather to the fact that the theory provides a pseudosolution for one stage of development in the cultural crisis of late-bourgeois society. At a time when the authority of cultural tradition is not only questioned by certain intellectual groups but is in large measure bereft of its binding character

for the rest of the educated public, at a time when a critical appropriation of tradition could define our mode of relating to cultural
objectifications, reception theory encourages (in part unwittingly) a
subjectivistic dissolution of tradition into the arbitrariness of individual
experiences. Stated differently: confronted with the possibility that
radically democratic and socialist intellectuals could lay bare the critical
potentials of bourgeois society and could provide alternatives to late-
capitalist society, a segment of the right-wing intelligentsia responds
by refusing to recognize the truth content contained in tradition

A tendency toward a dissolution of the emphatic concept of truth
is observable within the very structure of reception theory, since that
theory incorporates elements from a variety of disparate scholarly
contexts without even questioning whether such components can be
conjoined (Russian formalism, Gadamer's hermeneutics, Benjamin's
reflections on the formation of tradition, and subsequently Ingarden's
phenomenology of the work of art and Luhmann's systems theory).
The renunciation of the need for coherence implied by this view is
only the flip side of the "openness" asserted by the right against all
attempts at consistent theory formation.[6] As a matter of fact reception
theorists have already developed a defense strategy to dismiss as illegitimate questions of the consistency of their own theory formation;
they talk of a "paradigm shift," whereby a theory of natural scientific
development is unreflectively transferred to the historical-hermeneutic
sciences. Claiming to have introduced such a paradigm shift into literary
criticism, reception theorists established their doctrine as the framework
within which literary criticism must operate today. Given their premises,
placing a taboo on critique is the only natural consequence. But this
does not encourage theoretical progress and objective debate with
alternate conceptions.

The Benjamin Model

The crisis over the relation to tradition that has developed in late-
capitalist societies—and we have interpreted reception theory as a
symptom of this crisis—is by no means an affair of the right alone.
On the contrary, signs are discernible on the left indicating that the
semantic potential of cultural traditions either can no longer be appropriated or can be appropriated only with force; and signs are also
discernible that the process of appropriation is leading increasingly to

subjectivistic isolation. I would like to examine these tendencies more closely, since it is my impression that social constraints are here asserted behind the backs of individuals, who are less able to defend against such constraints since they cannot perceive them.

In view of the hardly disputable fact that Adorno "was the most knowledgeable Marxist and the one most fully in command of the subject matter" (as Habermas wrote in his eulogy), it may seem rather astonishing that an entire generation of young literary scholars has so decidedly cast its lot with Benjamin against Adorno.[7] The reasons for this are, first of all, political. As is well known, Adorno maintained that late-bourgeois society was in a "petrified" state and that the chance for a socialist revolution had irrevocably passed. In his theory Adorno is no longer interested in directing a praxis that aims to achieve social change. Instead he is content to allow ideas of a liberated society to manifest themselves in critique. By contrast, it is possible to find formulations in certain of Benjamin's later works that can be understood to affirm the possibility of revolution. Even the cultural-political positions of the two authors can be fashioned into an equally crude opposition. Where Adorno criticizes politically committed art as a submission to heteronomous ends, an attack from which not even Brecht is spared, Benjamin from the very outset stressed Brecht's artistic and political significance. Moreover, in his essay, "The Work of Art in the Age of Mechanical Reproduction," Benjamin seems to present a theory of art that accounts for artistic development in terms of the development of the forces of production.

It is not my intention here to establish that more can be drawn from the debate between Benjamin and Adorno than was adumbrated above. Instead I would like to focus on the problematic character of the fact that a significant amount of leftist literary scholarship emerging from the student movement relies not on Benjamin's rationality but, contrary to his own principles, on his authority. In literary scholarship such fixation on authority continues a bad tradition. Stated polemically: what Goethe was for the text-immanent approach, Benjamin frequently is for the materialist approach.

Two things are remarkable about this choice of authority figure. Benjamin composed his materialist writings in France as an emigrant pursued by the fascists. The situation's historical specificity is reflected in Benjamin's works, which were written with an eye to exerting an influence on his times. With few exceptions, however, Benjamin's

Peter Bürger

situation has been little discussed in the current reception of his work. What has been neglected above all is any questioning of whether Benjamin's conceptions, formulated under specific historical and bio-graphical conditions, are at all adequate to provide solutions to con-temporary problems. Nor does anyone discuss, if those conceptions are deemed adequate, what changes should be made to ensure their implementation. Even Benjamin's revolutionary messianism, for in-stance, might be traced to the hopelessness of the historical situation in which he wrote. If this is the case, then this messianism cannot be applied directly to the Federal Republic, where entirely different con-ditions clearly obtain. If it is so applied, one runs the risk of emigrating from one's own contemporary situation and becoming apolitical despite one's political position. Benjamin's adoption as a political role model contains a fateful noncontemporaneity for political identity.

No less significant in this context is a feature of the Benjamin oeuvre that has certainly also contributed to its influence: its antisystematic character. In opposition to this view, one could argue that Adorno's philosophy is itself presented as an explicit critique of systematic think-ing. It could be claimed, in other words, that here Benjamin and Adorno are actually in agreement, for which reason Benjamin's in-fluence cannot be explained in this way. Let us therefore attempt to differentiate. Adorno sees systematic thinking as a form of domination, the subordination of the particular to the universal, the extirpation of the nonidentical. In contrast he proposes a way of thinking that rescues the particular. But both antisystem and system require the same strin-gency. The sole difference is that an antisystem eschews systematic presentation. The contradictions in Benjamin's work are of a different nature; they stand side by side, without dialectical mediation. Benjamin attempted to extend the avant-garde principle of montage to the essay. Montage, however, is a combination of elements that, when so com-bined, are presumed to "flash," thereby creating something not con-tained in the elements individually. But this implies that Benjamin gave up the postulate of coherence clearly underlying Adorno's antisystem.

It seems symptomatic that Benjamin, whose thought grants ruptures and discontinuities a central role, has become the model for an entire generation of leftist literary scholars. In Benjamin's personality ruptures are contained in a highly complex and certainly vulnerable identity that attained equilibrium in the force field of Brechtian Marxism,

Jewish theology, and the Frankfurt school. Although the adoption of this identity type is impossible, the Benjamin model has clearly become the legitimizing basis for a critical practice that no longer adheres to the postulates of coherence.

Let us avoid misunderstanding. I am not criticizing the effort to develop a critical science of culture through recourse to Benjamin; I am criticizing the attempt to generate a political and critical identity by emulating him—whether through adopting his theoretical position or fixating on his objects of research, such as Baudelaire. Particularly problematic in this regard is the tendency to create an aura around Benjamin, a practice that continues the bad tradition of German literary scholarship. Inasmuch as we are indebted to Benjamin in particular for a critique of auratic tendencies in art, it might have been assumed that he deserved a more objective evaluation. The supposition that this fixation on Benjamin conceals unresolved problems in critical and political identity cannot be easily dismissed.

That these are problems of political and critical identity can be seen by examining the most recent publications issuing from the circles of literary scholars who are attempting to develop Benjamin's approach further. Although there is nothing inauthentic about the manner in which they attempt to effect this continuation, it is clear that they have not sufficiently harnessed the historical distance between Benjamin and us so as to make his position a basis for productive debate. This is evident from the frequently almost Manichaean manner in which Benjamin and Adorno, like good and evil spirits, are placed in opposition to each other. In many cases the fixation on Benjamin corresponds to a negative fixation on Adorno.[8] Benjamin thereby serves to legitimize a return to the stereotypes of text-immanent interpretations. Thus there is (again) talk of a "congenial" interpreter, and interpretation is deemed a "second-level work of art." Such talk is concerned not with the literary scholar's methods but with his ingenuity. Where a rationally proceeding and critical approach to literary scholarship has as its object of reflection the distance between the work to be interpreted and the interpreter's standards, here undifferentiated unity is the measure of interpretive success. This approach follows a tradition in existence since the time of Romanticism. It is connected with a hypostatized notion of the autonomy of art and is thus part of the institution of art as it exists in developed forms of bourgeois society. The critique of the autonomous status of art, initiated by the historical avant-garde movements and recently repeated in literary scholarship, comes to a halt before the literary scholar's perception of his professional identity. As before, the latter now seeks recognition as a noted figure through his work. Wanting his uniqueness to be acknowledged, the scholar virtually supplants the object of study. To be sure, neither the individual literary scholar nor the literary marketplace should bear the blame for this state of affairs. It is understandable that the desire for individual recognition increases as hopes for social change are revealed to be illusory. The literary marketplace, which could well also mediate collective processes of discussion, is reduced to a forum for individual self-presentation.

Criticism presupposes that it is possible to change behavior through reflection. It seems, however, that self-enlightenment cannot progress where individual identity is itself the issue. Insight into the deforming power of the market driving people into abstract competition with one another does not encourage the development of alternative modes of behavior. The fixated desire to make a name for oneself threatens to conceal the cognitive objectives in whose interest one first began scholarly work. The shrill severity of the tone not only represents the external adoption of a polemical mode of communication. It also attests to an abstract will to succeed, one that has internalized the principle of competition.

It is in their adoption of an extremely individualistic, still largely unexamined professional image that one discerns, it seems to me, one of the reasons for the identity crisis of leftist intellectuals today. This crisis becomes virulent when the individualistic professional image is fused with an abstract notion of politics, one beyond the boundaries of the Federal Republic's social reality. One wants to be both in and not in the establishment. A pseudosolution to this problem can be found in the Benjamin cult. Benjamin is an outsider, a revolutionary, and yet he is also acknowledged by traditional literary scholarship — even if, it is true, only as someone dead. Such a double identity can hardly be maintained indefinitely. In view of the growing pressure from *Berufsverbot* (professional proscription) and the massive intimidation of critical intellectuals, a resigned retreat to the traditional professional image seems the most obvious solution (interlaced, perhaps, with cryptic hopes for a revolution — hopes scarcely comprehensible to anyone but the individual himself). Otherwise, all that remains appears to be a retreat into political minigroups, whose social significance is apparent, if at all, only to our Secret "Service." The contradiction is obviously not productive, since the entire societal structure seems only to offer solutions bespeaking aporias.

In opposition to this attempt to connect the subjectivistic dissolution of cultural traditions (which reception theorists articulate) with the subjectivism emerging from Benjamin's followers, it could be argued that recent Baudelaire scholarship, oriented as it is to Benjamin, attempts a historical-critical appropriation of its subject matter. Certainly this is the case with some of the more recent literature on Baudelaire. I think it is important, however, to point out that the subjectivism here in question affects the method of interpretation at the very point where allegorical interpretation is used to wrest a socialist meaning from Baudelaire's poems. The attendant sophistication and historical erudition are admirable, but the method remains problematic.

It is common knowledge that the allegorical approach was developed in Greece when the Homeric pantheon of gods could no longer support changing notions of ethical life. Thus the scandal of the battle among the gods depicted in the twentieth book of the *Iliad* was removed by interpreting it as an allegorical expression of the conflict of natural phenomena. The allegorical method is a way of appropriating cultural objectifications while spanning the chasm between a tradition whose value is asserted authoritatively and the conceptual world of an interpreter estranged from it. This method subordinates the former to the latter, demonstrating that a rational approach to tradition has not yet been established. However brilliantly it may be carried out, the recourse to allegory indicates, it seems to me, a problematic relation to tradition. The latter is indubitably accepted as a value (the possibility that the extraordinarily high esteem enjoyed by Baudelaire today might be attributed to a process of tradition formation that requires critical clarification cannot be considered here). At the same time it is forcibly subordinated to one's own world-understanding. Much in the way that Vergil was fashioned into a Christian in the Middle Ages, Baudelaire is fashioned into a socialist today.[9] We are still far from a critical science of literature.

The Shadow of Nietzsche

The element of force in the allegorical method reappears in attempts to assert a "positive barbarism" against the cultural crisis of late capitalism, stressing the necessity of "destruction."

Peter Bürger

The stance of positive barbarism implies distrust in the face of appeals made to humanism and spirit, a dauntless plea for destructiveness and barbaric detachment, a retreat from the values of creativity and individuality. All this can go up in the smoke of an aestheticized auto-da-fé . . . , but it can also lead to the destruction of programs for cultural reconciliation, which always appear in the name of humanity.[10]

The concepts of destruction and positive barbarism are taken from or modeled on essays by Benjamin. For him they express an impotent attempt to stem the rising tide of fascist barbarism with an awareness of the need for a radical new beginning.[11] Today it is not possible to actualize these concepts without discussing their place within a society where a technocratically administered educational system has set out to wash its hands of culture and humanism. Instead of sustaining the tension between the humane contents of bourgeois culture and its nonrealization, instead of making this the basis for a critique of social reality, one now invokes—even after what took place in Germany between 1933 and 1945—an abstract "destructiveness" as an attitude vis-à-vis bourgeois culture. It is small comfort when the author, concluding his essay, assures us that "pseudorevolutionary iconoclasm is not intended." In the place of a reflection aware of its responsibilities for the present, one now encounters the daydream of a solitary individual who forgets his own impotence through fantasies of destruction.

The fascination generated by many of Benjamin's formulations is in fact the fascination for Nietzsche: the thrill of the radicalness of an utterance indifferent to the context in which it is expressed. "The destructive character is young and cheerful. . . . Proper to such an Apollonian image of destruction is the realization of how greatly the world is simplified when judged on its worthiness to be destroyed." This assertion by Benjamin could also have been expressed by Nietzsche. It is not surprising that Nietzsche's shadow threatens to become dominant at the moment when hopes raised in 1968 are sinking ever further into the past. Symptomatic of this turn toward Nietzsche, it seems to me, is an essay whose very title contains a Nietzschean echo: "Plädoyer für Verräter" [Plea for a traitor].[12] Betrayal here refers, among other things, to a liberation from "constrictive loyalty relations," as they were constituted by leftist groups at the beginning of the 70s. Evident though the efforts for liberation from imposed orthodoxies may be, the traitor metaphor becomes problematic if it designates a general disposition. For in this event the legitimate call for the subject's emancipation from heteronomous constraints would flip over into an intellectual rootlessness that is merely the abstract negation of dogmatic fixation. Tradition as a "relation to the dead, whose weight threatens to pull the living into the abyss of the past" (Nietzsche: "Man . . . resists the great and ever greater weight of the past: this oppresses him"[13]); "Denial of history . . . in order to make history" (Nietzsche: "All action requires forgetfulness"[14]). This recourse to Nietzsche's critique of history may express the cultural crisis of late capitalism: what it does not do, however, is clarify this crisis. It remains bound to an irrational concept of life that stands opposed to a rational organizing of social reality.

Subjectivity

"The situation in which the individual is vanishing is at the same time one of unbridled individualism."[15]

In order to forestall misunderstanding, let me emphasize that it is not my intention to deny the relevance of what the left today has thematized as the problem of subjectivity. It must be acknowledged that the left has long neglected this problem and thus conceded it to the right. The consequences of this can be seen, for instance, in the aesthetic struggle against naturalism. Committed to a positivist conception of reality, naturalism falls outside the domain of subjective experience and therefore can be fully appropriated by aestheticism.[16] It is the merit of the French surrealists, Breton in particular, to have recognized this problem. That this is a central problem of our time is demonstrated by such important books as Christa Wolf's *Kindheitsmuster* and Peter Weiss's *Die Ästhetik des Widerstands*.

Much as one must acknowledge the value in considering subjective factors, it is nonetheless necessary to acknowledge that the left's retreat into subjectivity is also an expression of the identity crisis of the bourgeois individual per se. Without claiming to be able to provide a sociopsychological explanation for the phenomena here adumbrated, I would at least like to suggest where such an explanation might best be found. Particularly helpful in this regard is Alexander Mitscherlich's notion of the "fatherless society." To cite Habermas's formulation: "the sociopsychological signature of the age is characterized less by an authoritarian personality than by the destructuring of the superego."[17] The decline in the significance of the father figure in childhood development has had the consequence that the individual has become incapable of developing the assured ego-identity necessary to achieve relative independence from the demands of his own drives as well as those of society.[18] In place of an ego-identity capable of mediating contradictory demands, one now finds a narcissistically cathected self that abandons itself to fantasies of omnipotence, which can never find confirmation in reality. The conflict between a narcissistically omnipotent and a factually impotent self demands reconciliation. This is achievable on a privatistic model in which private mythology replaces a system of norms admitting of rational examination. Desires for self-realization that remain fixated on a narcissistic ego-ideal threaten a further regression. This may explain the tendencies toward a dualistic mode of thinking (the Benjamin–Adorno polarity), as well as the fixation on the privatistic model of Benjamin. Since the chosen father is dead, everyone is entitled to imagine himself as the only legitimate heir. But regression is not an acceptable fate, especially for intellectuals.

That radical democratic and socialist intellectuals do not have an easy time of it in the Federal Republic is nothing new. The reasons for this are also well known: in this country there is no organized leftist movement comparable to the parties of the French left. The left's successes at the end of the 60s and in the early 70s instilled unrealistic hopes in many people for revolutionary social change. Today it is clear that those hopes were illusory. The question is how one should react to this loss of hope. The answer, I believe, is as follows. What we need is sobriety and the specification of our place in society. Instead of vacillating between the frustrations of impotence and fantasies of omnipotence, we should evaluate and use with a more responsible concern for political consequences the limited social space available. Obviously these insights are difficult to realize. *Berufsverbot* and the campaign against terrorist "sympathizers" engender fear. As long as this fear remains unclarified, the individual will fall victim to the forms of reaction imposed upon him—either through rigidification, by adhering to an abstract consciousness of his own unmistakable uniqueness, or through depersonalization, by developing contradictory identities. Even the attempt to realize a nonalienated subjectivity in or through depersonalization risks succumbing to the mistaken notion that we need only desire what society forces upon us.

Notes

1. Herbert Marcuse, "The Affirmative Character of Culture," in *Negations: Essays in Critical Theory*, translated by Jeremy Shapiro (Boston: Beacon Press, 1968), pp. 88–133.

2. Hans-Georg Gadamer, *Truth and Method*, translation edited by Garrett Barden and John Cumming (Now York: Seabury Press, 1975), esp. p. 278.

3. Jürgen Habermas, *Zur Logik der Sozialwissenschaften: Materialien* (Frankfurt: Suhrkamp, 1970), p. 283ff.

4. Jürgen Habermas, *Legitimation Crisis*, translated by Thomas McCarthy (Boston: Beacon Press, 1975), pp. 70–71.

5. Ch. Bürger, *Tradition und Subjektivität* (Frankfurt: Suhrkamp, 1980), chaps. 3 and 4.

6. I have discussed an example of the heterogeneity of theoretical approaches to reception theory in *Vermittlung–Rezeption–Funktion: Aesthetische Theorie und Methodologie der Literaturwissenschaft* (Frankfurt: Suhrkamp, 1979), chap. 6, §3, where further reference to the literature can also be found; cf. chap. 5, §2.

7. Jürgen Habermas, *Philosophische-politische Profile* (Frankfurt: Suhrkamp, 1971), p. 190.

8. An early example is H. Lethen's essay, "Zur materialistischen Kunsttheorie Benjamins," *Alternative* 56/57 (October–December 1967):225–34. And more recently the essays by B. Lindner and D. Oehler in the issue of *Text+Kritik* devoted to Adorno (Munich, 1977).

9. See, for example, D. Oehler's interpretation of Baudelaire's *Le Cygne*, in which it is explicitly stated: "The swan is the banished part of France, the militant proletariat of Paris." ("Ein hermeneutischer *Sozialist* . . . ," in *Diskussion Deutsch* 26 (December 1975):569–84; here see p. 579). For a critique, see H. Stenzel's contribution to the discussion in *Diskussion Deutsch* 29 (June 1976):299–303.

10. B. Lindner, "Technische Produzierbarkeit und Kulturindustrie. Benjamins 'positives Barbarentum' im Kontext," in Lindner, ed., *"Links hatte noch alles sich zu enträtsein . . . ," Walter Benjamin im Kontext* (Frankfurt, 1978), pp. 180–223; here pp. 219–20). See also the essay of I. Wohlfahrt, ibid., pp. 65–99.

11. Walter Benjamin, "The Destructive Character" [1931], in *Reflections: Essays, Aphorisms, Autobiographical Writings*, edited by Peter Demetz, translated by Edmund Jephcott (New York: Harcourt Brace Jovanovich, 1978), pp. 301–303; "Erfahrung und Armut" [1933], in *Gesammelte Schriften*, vol. 2 (Frankfurt, 1977), pp. 213–19.

12. G. Mattenklott, "Plädoyer für Verräter," in M. Gerhardt and G. Mattenklott, eds., *Kontext vol. 2: Geschichte und Subjektivität* (Munich, 1978), pp. 12–24. "Liberated from the fire, and impelled by the intellect, we then pass from opinion to opinion, through the change of parties, as *noble betrayers* of all things that can in any way be betrayed—and nevertheless without any feeling of guilt" (Nietzsche, *Human All-Too-Human: A Book for Free Spirits*, part 1, translated by Helen Zimmern (New York: Russell & Russell, 1964), p. 405).

13. F. Nietzsche, *On the Advantage and Disadvantage of History for Life*, translated by Peter Preuss (Indianapolis, IN: Hackett, 1980), p. 9.

14. Ibid., p. 10.

15. Theodor Adorno, *Minima Moralia*, translated by E. F. N. Jephcott (London: New Left Books, 1974), p. 149. The translation has been slightly modified (*tr.*).

16. Cf. *Naturalismus—Ästhetizismus* (Hefte für kritische Literaturwissenschaft, vol. 1, Frankfurt, 1979).

17. J. Habermas, "Technology and Science as 'Ideology,' " in *Toward a Rational Society: Student Protest, Science and Politics*, translated by Jeremy J. Shapiro (Boston: Beacon Press, 1971), p. 107. The translation has been slightly modified (*tr.*).

18. I am following the presentation provided by K. Horn in the introduction to the book he edited, *Gruppendynamik und der "subjektive Faktor"* (Frankfurt, 1972), p. 40ff., here p. 59.

Historiography in Germany Today

Hans-Ulrich Wehler

When thirteen years after the end of World War I, Karl Jaspers published his culture-critical analysis, *Die geistige Situation der Zeit*, he did not concern himself with the influence of German historical science, even though he had long been preoccupied with questions in the philosophy of history. Since he was interested primarily in transformations of epochal tendencies, this restraint was not without an internal justification, for little had changed in German historiography since the decades immediately preceding World War I.[1] If thirteen years after the end of World War II, someone had attempted a comparable assessment of the state of the West German science of history, he would still have confronted these same traditions that had been established prior to 1914 and fully sustained during the decades of the Weimar Republic, the Nazi regime, and the rebuilding phase of the Federal Republic. This longevity raises problems that require explanation, just as it poses questions about the causes and consequences of the radical change that has been underway since the early 1960s.

In retrospect it is clear that a set of novel sociopolitical conditions combined with the cumulative effect of six controversies, all resolved within the same period of time, marked an irreversible caesura in West German historiography. In the course of the controversies over German military objectives in World War I and over the Workers' Council Movement of 1918–19, transformations occurred in the long-dominant field of political history, whose consequences also altered the general climate within the ranks of historians. Concurrently the nature of National Socialism was being reinterpreted, the role of social and economic history was being passionately discussed, the dispute over the "primacy of domestic politics" was being resolved, and a theoretical debate was being staged with unprecedented intensity. All of these discussions, their consequences, and their subsequent developments come into clear focus only when contrasted with the preceding period. Hence a short review is indispensable.[2]

What was until 1960 the paradigm of the German (since 1945–49 the West German) science of history derives from the nineteenth century; several of its elements are even traceable to baroque court historiography.[3] Basic to this paradigm are concepts of state-building processes, the politics of the modern coercive state (*Machtstaat*)—particularly in terms of the "primacy of foreign politics"—and the rise of the modern nation-state. These are all concepts oriented to the modern state, to state history, and to competition among nations. They each reflect fundamental experiences with the sociopolitical processes of modernity in the course of the formation of European states since the late Middle Ages, circumscribing in this respect an important domain of past reality. Other domains, such as economic development or social inequality, were either ignored or considered only from the perspective of political influence "from above." In the period between the postrevolutionary restoration epoch and World War I—and it was during this period that German historiography took shape as a science and acquired its institutional status within all old and new universities—the explanatory model of state politics was so canonized that all other interpretive modes appeared as deviations from the "mainstream" of German historiography.

Of course, state history was never absolutely dominant. Intellectual history (*Geistesgeschichte*) pursued a vaguely formulated connection between the action-guiding influence of ideas and political activity. Cultural history either explored, in antiquated, conceptionless fashion, the material culture of everyday life or limited itself entirely to art history. Both old and recent historical schools of political economy often based their studies in economic history on the assumptions of evolution theory (as in the various stage-theories of economic growth).

On the whole, however, proponents of state-centered political history, ecstatic over the productivity of their paradigms—confirmed for decades and reconfirmed in 1871—never allowed its preeminence to be threatened. Symptomatic of this was their tendency to designate this form of political history as "general history" (*allgemeine Geschichte*). The small-German [a federal state excluding Austria and under Prussian leadership], national-political variant represented by Treitschke allowed even fewer grounds for self-doubt. This basic attitude was further fortified by the fact that the position of civil servants in public institutions had to a large degree codefined the intellectual horizon of university historians in the course of their professionalization. At the same time classical German historicism's doctrine of understanding (*Verstehenslehre*) was generally accepted as the profession's sole methodological tool. Coupled with this was a strong resistance against any attempts at systematic explanation.

In two great foundational discussions these positions were roughly defended in the following fashion. During the 1860s Johann Gustav Droysen sharply demarcated the understanding of historical individuality from H. T. Buckle's positivistic claims. And the overwhelming majority of German historians, even before the turn of the century, condemned Karl Lamprecht's efforts to forge a historical synthesis from the perspectives of cultural history and mass psychology, castigating such efforts as materialist marginalia deviating from the solely redemptive path of political history and historicism. When studies in social and economic history were pursued (and they were pursued in quantitatively staggering proportions), it was almost exclusively by those holding professorial chairs who belonged to the modern historical school of political economy. In general political history, virtually nothing existed concerning the rise of capitalism and market-conditioned class society. During the great capitalism debate, which for years engaged Max Weber, Werner Sombart, and others, historians looked on from the sidelines.[4]

In World War I neither the neo-Rankean nor the neo-Treitschkean traditions suffered any damage. Most historians saw their conceptual models confirmed by the global war of nations. They defended the putative superiority of the monarchical authoritarian state over "the West" and in particular over the Russian autocracy. They disseminated the "German ideas" of 1914 and backed the annexational military policies, which were criticized only by an astonishingly small group of clear-thinking academics.[5] Following the defeat the majority of academic historians remained committed to the traditional paradigms and underlying assumptions. Not even the "Copernican year" of 1917, which brought the Russian Revolution and the entrance of the United States into the war, could induce German political historians to reexamine, in light of the novel character of "world politics," their Eurocentric view of history and their partiality for German coercive state politics. On the contrary, an opposition to the Versailles Peace Treaty, to the "lie of war responsibility," to the unloved if not despised Weimar Republic, united many historians in a new consensus. Effective ostracism threatened those who failed to toe the line. Politically conservative, or at most right-liberal, they further argued both against "enemy foreign countries" and against the democracy that supplanted the small-German Imperial state. They remained bound by the methodological conventions, feeling even somewhat confirmed in their parochial dismissal of Western social sciences. Moreover, with respect to social origin (they came predominantly from the educated Protestant middle class), political outlook, methodological orientation, and accepted models of interpretation, the corps of historians constituted a closed phalanx.[6]

The few outsiders who merit special attention can be ordered into five types. To begin with, there was Friedrich Meinecke, who had once been fully accepted by the discipline. Simultaneously a "Monarchist at heart" and a "Republican in thought," Meinecke reacted with far more political shrewdness than many of his colleagues.[7] At the same time his history of ideas, which fed on a dissatisfaction with pure diplomatic and political history, was a source of considerable attraction, its spiritual sublimation notwithstanding. With him in Berlin, if clearly on the periphery, was Otto Hintze, the most powerful intellectual force between 1900 and 1930, a man embodying a unique combination of "academic progressiveness" and "political conservatism."[8] The work of this important constitutional and social historian, the first to display an interest in Max Weber, has exercised a profound, belated influence since the 1950s. A third outsider was the politically conservative Kurt Breysig; it was because of the vehement opposition to his comparative history of culture that Breysig was not appointed to a personal chair in sociology (at Berlin) until 1923, when he was fifty-six.

Markedly distinguished from these individuals, all of whom were initially influenced by the Borussian School, were the liberal South German Catholic Franz Schnabel at the Technical University of Karlsruhe, whose *Deutsche Geschichte im 19. Jahrhundert* first began to appear in 1929, and the Protestant Silesian (National-)Liberal Johannes Ziekursch, whose studies in constitutional history criticized Old Prussia so openly that it was only later, with the provisions made by Cologne's Mayor Adenauer for liberals in municipal politics, that he was able to obtain a professorship on the Rhine (until 1954 Cologne had a city university). Ziekursch's *Geschichte des deutschen Reiches von 1871 bis 1918* proved far superior to the conservative expositions. Hajo Holborn, Hans Rosenberg, Ludwig Bergsträsser, and Martin Hobohm represented comparable liberal positions. Throughout the entire Weimar period a left-liberal such as Veit Valentin could not obtain a university professorship. Historians like Gustav Mayer, Arthur Rosenberg (who for a time represented the Communist party of Germany in parliament), and Hedwig Hintze, all of whom belonged to or sympathized with the Social Democratic party, had to struggle with the same difficulties; they were never able to obtain anything but marginal positions. Younger historians such as Eckart Kehr, Alfred Vagts, and G. W. F. Hallgarten, who stood politically to the left of center (although not committed to any party) and who dealt with the explosive problems deriving from the history of imperialism, had virtually no chance to pursue an academic career. When in 1931 the Freiburg historian Gerhard Ritter became irate over the "pure-bred Bolshevik" Kehr, claiming that "this gentleman should habilitate—now, if possible—in Russia, where he naturally belongs," he was merely giving particularly pointed expression to common antipathies.[9]

The frightening lack of protest that characterized the historians' acceptance first of Hitler's "assumption of power" and then of the Nazi regime itself is to be explained neither by unreserved sympathy nor by effective intimidation. Of the approximately 150 professors, associate professors, and lecturers in the field of history, not one, as of January 1933, was a member of the National Socialist German Workers' party (NSDAP); but many in positions of power shared the prejudices, resentments, and aims that comprised the diffuse political ideology of National Socialism. For example, there was agreement about the need for a revision (complete, if possible) of the Versailles Treaty, combatting the war responsibility thesis, the transformation of the national coercive state, the longing for a hegemonic position in Europe, the ideology of the Reich, and the pan-Germanic (in part, even folkish) program. In view of the breadth of the consensus, most historians had little difficulty in reaching an accord with the new ruling system. It is for this reason that after 1933 there was so "astonishingly little conflict between what was represented and expected by the Nazi regime and what was taught and written by historians."[10] If, vis-à-vis the unpopular Weimar Republic, one had affirmed the newly discovered autonomy of the universities, so now one apparently could again submit without reservation to traditional state loyalty. After 1945 these historians, in defending themselves, repudiated the line drawn by Allied propaganda from Luther through Friedrich II and Bismarck to Hitler; yet in 1936 Gerhard Ritter, who was by no means unique, had on his own made the connection between Friedrich II and the Potsdam Spectacle with Hindenburg and Hitler.[11] Following the "annexation" of Austria and the war in France, an opinion poll would likely have revealed unanimous agreement among German historians that Hitler was one of the greatest politicians in German history. No significant resistance was marshaled against the early emigration of notable colleagues, against the forced expulsion or resigned departure of others into exile. On the contrary, historical science was permitted "without resistance" to be "brought into line by the Nazi regime." Because nearly all Liberal and Social Democratic historians were obliged to leave the country, the political homogeneity of the discipline was enhanced; in effect the Nazi period intensified its markedly "conservative, chauvinistic (*nationaldeutsche*) outlook." Whoever secretly harbored scruples against the initial war policies of Hitler's dictatorship could console himself with the idea of a realization of pan-Germanic dreams or a supposed renaissance of "German nativism (*Volkstum*) in Central Europe (*Ostmitteleuropa*)." In a respected journal of the discipline, *Historische Zeitschrift*, the Munich historian Karl Alexander von Müller, first party member among full professors, introduced the notorious section on the "Jewish question." Of the 339 essays published under his aegis, at least 101 reveal the depth of penetration by the Nazi "nonspirit" (*Ungeist*).[12]

Unlike what happened after 1918, the unparalleled crimes and the destruction wrought by the Nazi Reich, and therewith the end of both the short-lived nation-state and German great power politics as such, made imperative a fundamental revision of traditional historical concepts and paradigms. East of the Elbe this redirection was rigorously implemented from above. By contrast, the reaction in West Germany was noteworthy for the aristocratic reserve with which the responsibilities were initially acknowledged. In order to forestall misunderstanding, it should be emphasized that Hitler's Germany was subject to unanimous condemnation. A few historians who had been convinced of the ideology of the German Reich and the politics of nationalism, such as Herman Heimpel and Reinhart Wittram, publicly acknowledged their illusions and obtained a new right to work as university teachers. On the whole, however, an inappropriate circumspection prevailed. Just as early historicism had introduced the traditionalist search for identity in response to the issues of enlightenment and revolution,[13] so now a call was made for a return to superior and time-honored traditions. The skepticism of de Tocqueville, of Burckhardt, struck a responsive chord; a "politically and morally tamed historicism" found widespread support. The call for German "self-reflection" paralleled a well-disseminated "intellectual-historical (geistgeschichtlich) orientation." "The longing for a sublime, moral form of self-criticism and a simultaneous adherence to traditional values" typified this "initial state of West German historiography after 1945 and indicated that a drastic change had by no means taken place." The belated repudiation of National Socialism was transfigured into antitotalitarianism, which under the umbrella of the cold war entered into an unproblematic relationship with what for decades had been a pronounced anti-Communism. The behavioral and political mentality of the vast majority of historians was in full accord with the general cultural-intellectual climate of the first decades of the Federal Republic.[14]

This agreement can be traced with more precision if we look at a few specific issues. Whereas an optimistically evaluated continuity in the development of the "Western cultural complex" had previously formed one of the cornerstones of German historicism, now the concept of discontinuity, while certainly logically connected to that of continuity, was laden with great political significance, becoming the preferred explanation of events after 1933. Thus, stated in an extreme form, Hitler could be understood as a destructive eruption of existential evil into a fundamentally sound German world, a view that relieved historians of the responsibility to investigate empirically the susceptibility of German society to a dictatorial charismatic leader. A statement made about Hitler by Otto Hintze to Meinecke was circulated with much assent: "The man . . . actually does not even belong to our race. There is something altogether foreign in him, something akin to an extinct primeval race, whose nature remains arrested at a fully amoral level." The observation of this Prussian constitutional historian contained a true insight into Hitler's nature; yet all too frequently it allowed individuals self-righteously to close their eyes to the sociohistorical presuppositions of Hitler's rise and his regime.[15] Gerhard Ritter, profiting from his moral reputation as an imprisoned member of the resistance group around Goerdeler, even went so far as to trace National Socialism back to the general European problems of mass democracy, one-party rule, Führer state, industrial society, cultural decline, and nihilism. The fact that Germany was the sole Western industrial country to produce a radical, autonomously successful variant of fascism does not appear to have further disturbed him in his efforts to shield this aspect of the German past from critical scrutiny. Burgeoning doubts about the continued methodological adequacy of an historicism restricted to biography and state history induced Ritter, in 1950, to concede that "a history of the modern period that does not master basic economic categories . . . or even sociological methods would lead to pure rhetoric lacking in deeper cognitive value." This was all very well to say, but it remained mere lip service without consequence; nonetheless, this postulate does provide a basis for evaluating the extensive writings Ritter was still to publish. He was not the only one who adhered to a statism of older provenance, one that did not promote a democratic, pluralistic understanding of the state.[16]

For a short period a debate flared up over the Bismarckian politics involved in the founding of the Reich. With the exception of Schnabel's principled objections, this debate was staged wholly in terms of traditional conceptual and semantic cliché-ridden notions, before it again died out without result.[17] Controversies of equal importance were abruptly silenced before they had a chance to unfold. In a brilliant 1952 dissertation, Otto Büsch—inspired by Hans Rosenberg, then of Brooklyn College, who was visiting Berlin as guest professor—outlined how one could tackle the central problem of Prussian militarism, namely the social militarization of society. This novel approach was squelched by Gerhard Ritter, who in his wide-ranging work, *Staatskunst und Kriegshandwerk*, sought to prove the basic thesis that only occasionally in Prussia did military thinking dominate civil-political thinking. Certainly his four volumes represent the "end point of a specifically conservative view of history," which simply denied the autochthonous sociopolitical causes of the German crisis since the time of industrialization and the establishment of the Reich. Ritter reacted bitterly to the scathing criticism that this transparent apology elicited from Ludwig Dehio, first postwar editor of the *Historische Zeitschrift*. It took quite some time to kill the rumor that this dispute was responsible for

Dehio's premature and dispirited resignation from the editorial board of the *Historische Zeitschrift*.[18]

When in 1958 Hans Rosenberg published his important analysis of the Prussian bureaucracy, aristocracy, and monarchical autocracy between 1660 and 1815, which inaugurated a new chapter in German political-social history, Ritter managed to torpedo a German edition with a curtly dismissive opinion.[19] Meanwhile the history of the German resistance against Hitler was restricted exclusively to the group of July 20, 1944. Hans Rothfels, one of the few historians who returned from emigration to a West German professorial chair, developed the rudiments of this interpretation in his 1948 book, *The German Opposition to Hitler* (initially published by a right-wing American publishing company). In this view the resistance was dominated by members of the old upper stratum—the officer corps, senior civil servants, and the clergy—whereas only scant mention was made of the thousands of workers' movement members who between 1933 and 1944 risked and lost their lives in the resistance. Nearly twenty years had to elapse before a more accurate perspective was possible and, with all due respect to the courage of the men of July 20, before their partially romanticized and anachronistic conceptions were subjected to critical scrutiny.[20]

Despite the unmistakably restorative character of the 50s a few promising, if varyingly successful, tendencies were noticeable. Ludwig Dehio, still a pronounced annexationist in World War I, formulated, as a result of his own painful experience, an independent critical position from which he resolutely assailed the deformations of German power politics and even the ideological weaknesses of German historiography. Reaction on the part of members of the discipline ranged from cool to icy. The challenge contained in Heinrich Heffter's great history of German self-administration was likewise not accepted.[21]

At the same time there emerged a new form of contemporary history that drew strong inspiration from—so the formula reads—a "coming to terms with the past" (*Bewältigung der Vergangenheit*). This attracted a first generation of young historians who placed great value on cooperation with scholars working in the field of systematic political science. Karl Dietrich Bracher's 1955 *Auflösung der Weimarer Republik* [Dissolution of the Weimar Republic] still represents the exemplary model of this fusion of interests. Despite nods of acknowledgement the critique by academic historians emphasized objections from a historicist standpoint. In integrating systematic positions, the new approach generated a palpable sense of uneasiness. Although Bracher may well be the most significant West German historian of the past two decades, he was never appointed to a chair in history. The rapid academic development of the field of contemporary history and its equally speedy institutional expansion did nothing to alter the scruples held by members of the appointment commissions. The remarkable number of publications by the Commission for the History of Parliamentarianism as well as the Munich Institute for Contemporary History testify to the impressive productivity of members of this discipline. It was only relatively late, however, that these institutions were able to liberate themselves from the Procrustean bed of their restrictive commitment to the period between 1917 and 1945.[22]

Finally a stimulating discussion was also sparked by the call for a "structural history." The concept was taken from categories of the French *Annales* school; it drew attention to supraindividual connections and thus away from biography and the simple history of events. By its own account "structural history" was to penetrate the totality of historiography and not simply the most easily assimilable parts such as social and economic history. Yet the programmatic thesis remained sketchy, a precise definition of the structures worth investigating was not provided, and the concept was too vague, too formal, and too lacking in content for its claimed integrational capacity. Nonetheless this postulate represented an overdue counteraction against historical tradition and effected the transition to the theoretical discussions of the 60s.[23]

In surveying the fifteen years prior to 1960, during which time historiography remained an essentially conservative domain, it becomes apparent that until then no break with tradition had in fact taken place. Since the corps of West German historians had undergone only a structurally insignificant de-Nazification and not far-reaching reforms, since they were left to their own "capacity for renewal," it was foreseeable that the continuity of personnel would have been maintained and that the structure of the teaching staff, the subjects taught, and the pedagogical method would have remained virtually unchanged.[24]

Nonetheless, under the mantle of a carefully revised traditionalism, far-reaching transformations were underway, and these surfaced abruptly in the 60s. The advanced students and doctoral candidates, assistants, and lecturers who were active in history departments around

1960 belonged to a generation that for the most part had become convinced that National Socialism, the world war, and the collapse had conclusively discredited the traditional nationalist and idealist conceptual models. Harboring a justified skepticism about the old paradigms focusing on the actions of states and rulers (*Staats- und Hauptaktionen*), they welcomed the rapid unfolding of the social and political sciences. They viewed the offerings of these related systematic sciences as a desired adjunct to their own work and not as containing a threat of dehistoricization. Returning emigrants like the political scientist Ernst Fraenkel or the sociologist René König found a receptive audience among these individuals. An interested and approving opening to the West European and American world was for them as self-evident as was a liberal-democratic point of view. By then many of them had studied at American and English universities and were in this way decisively influenced during the formative period of their development. Study in France by contrast played only a very minor role.[25] Although representatives of this generation sought and found new orientation in disparate academic milieus, a few centers deserve special mention. For instance, the Free University of Berlin was notable for the personal magnetism of its political scientists, who had been stimulated both by Hans Herzfeld's early call for the formation of a specialty in the area of contemporary history and by the lasting influence of Hans Rosenberg. During the academic tenure of Hans Rothfels, new stimuli inspired a group of contemporary historians at Tübingen, a development that was abruptly interrupted after 1958, however. At Heidelberg Werner Conze directed his students to the many unresolved problems of social history, a field he promoted with an energetic commitment at the organizational level as well. Theoretical questions were investigated with persistence by Theodor Schieder in Cologne, who also encouraged his doctoral students to pursue sociohistorical studies. His greatest influence, however, stemmed from his wide-ranging interest in methodological questions and problems of comparative research.[26]

Gradually these academic centers produced a number of younger historians who were ready for innovation, and these were the people largely responsible for carrying on the movement since the 60s. In line with Thomas Kuhn's description of the general prehistory of paradigm shifts, anomalies were amassed after 1960 that undermined the "disciplinary matrix" of the "community of scholars" and facilitated the breakthrough of new tendencies. With the coming of age of a new generation, a highly diversified range of experiences attained expression. Somewhat surprisingly, the new currents managed to weather several academic storms without precipitating the crystallization of distinct sects or the continued isolation of groups. The subsiding of the cold war and the well-disseminated reorientation of ideas favored change, and in line with the growth of new positions and university reforms, nonconformist thought and behavior was now tolerated with a willingness that would not have been forthcoming from the older corps of professional historians.

These mutually overlapping processes significantly ruptured the development of West German historiography. Previously in the German historiographical tradition, "critical history" in the sense of Nietzsche had been practiced only by such outsiders as Franz Mehring, Arthur Rosenberg, and Eckart Kehr, and then only quite sporadically. "Often enough," Nietzsche had demanded, man

must have the strength, and use it from time to time, to shatter and dissolve something so as to live: this he achieves by dragging it to the bar of judgment, interrogating, and finally condemning it. . . . [T]hen it becomes clear how unjust is the existence of . . . a privilege, a caste, a dynasty, for example, how much it deserves destruction. Then its past is considered critically, then one puts the knife to its roots.[27]

After 1945 the time might have been ripe in West Germany as well to dissolve politically, in this Nietzschean sense, the numerous clichés of the inherited view of history and to abandon once and for all persistent models of interpretation. In fact, however, this possibility arose only after a peculiar fifteen-year incubation period.

The Fischer controversy represented a first stage in this change. In 1961 the Hamburg historian Fritz Fischer, in his well-documented, voluminous investigation of the military policies of Imperial Germany from 1914 to 1918, had shattered a consensus that since the 30s had been deemed unimpeachable. In place of the well-preserved unanimity of interpretation (repudiation of the "lie regarding Germany's responsiblity for the war" and the equal share of responsibility on the part of all the powers that had "stumbled" into war), he unleashed a vehement attack on the war-engendering and war-prolonging effects of the Imperial German policies of expansion. Overnight, historians and members of the interested public found themselves confronted with a thesis that drew unimagined parallels between Hitler's triggering of the war in the summer of 1939 and Bethmann Hollweg's policy of (mis)calculated risk in the summer of 1914. The question was thereby posed, if at the outset not very explicitly by Fischer himself, of the continuity of modern German history—and with a new explosiveness. For some time the discipline was dominated by shrill and indignant repudiation, which remained unintimidated in the face of Fischer's "hypertrophied criticism" and what some even called his vitriolic eruptions of hate ("monologue of a madman"). In the polemical assertions of Gerhard Ritter and Erwin Hoelzle, a provincial nationalism surfaced that seemed incapable of any rational consideration of the arguments. Fischer had obviously touched a raw nerve; but he did open the door to a long-overdue examination of the history of Imperial Germany.[28]

Despite the continuous attack Fischer's remarkable success remained unshaken six years later. To be sure, as a result of certain factually justified criticisms several modifications and differentiations of his theses were necessary. Moreover, comparative scholarship would still relativize much of what he considered specifically German. Finally, one must acknowledge the misleading and indefensible character of Fischer's first assertion, one clarified only in the course of acrimonious debates—namely, that in a methodical quest for world power, the German Reich had been preparing for war since 1912 and had merely translated the plans of the prewar period into action. Yet the "quietistic taboo on sacrosanct basic assumptions" was overcome. Both the history of the final years of peace and the war period of Wilhelmine Germany would have to be written differently today (as has already been done) than before Fischer's book appeared. One of the most plausible features of the new interpretation is encapsulated in the formula of a defensive act of aggression as a preventive flight forward, which characterized the willingness of the Berlin government, externally and internally pushed into a corner, to accept the risk of a hot war in the summer of 1914. This was the result of Fischer's pioneering study, which, as indicated by its general effect, promoted a more realistic assessment of the Imperial Reich.

A former theologian, Fischer was interested in making an active, rigorous contribution to a catharsis, to a purification of the public consciousness in the land of Nazi crimes. Toward this end he may have provided some impetus, though this is difficult to judge. Within the discipline, however, it is indisputable that the controversies in which he participated did have a purifying, invigorating effect, which many younger scholars even found liberating.

As regards methodological considerations, Fischer initially proceeded conventionally, reconstructing political history from actual deeds. Yet in one new edition after another and in his other writings, he placed ever more emphasis on socioeconomic factors in explaining political decisions, thereby expanding the parameters of political history. It is no coincidence that Fischer attracted unorthodox individuals as students, encouraged them to produce studies in an academic New-Found-Land and became himself the titular head of the field of critical political-social history.

That Fischer stimulated intensive investigation into the Imperial Reich is beyond dispute. Older research interests and historical analyses, which led back crablike to the roots of National Socialism, thereby found abiding support. While German history between 1848 and 1918 belongs to the best-researched epochs of modernity, the society and politics of Bismarckian Germany, owing to Fischer's efforts, have been newly interpreted from a variety of perspectives. One of Fischer's accomplishments, although occasionally overlooked in the din of the debates, should not be underestimated: he scrutinized with unprecedented intensity the mentality of the Wilhelmine ruling elite and the politically dominant classes.

Finally, Fischer irrevocably placed the problematic of continuity on the agenda of historians' debates. Long before others had adopted the theme, Fischer, with a moral zeal stemming from his ethics of conviction, introduced the discussion of this complicated matter, often in the face of spiteful opposition. At present a neoconservative critique of this continuity discussion, a discussion that after his contributions can no longer be ignored, castigates the "urge"—deriving both from the "psychological pressure of the victorious powers' criticisms and from one's own scruples (at times in a self-tormenting fashion, at times superficially)"—to "subject those politically responsible in preceding generations to the condemning tribunal of future generations."[29] Nonetheless such revealing formulations do nothing to alter the internal validity of Fischer's critique.

Fischer could occasionally appeal to several preliminary critical studies by foreign historians (Luigi Albertini and Hans W. Gatzkes, for example). By contrast, the discussion concerning the German Workers' Council Movement of 1918–19, initiated before but resolved at the time of the Fischer controversy, was notable for its explicit adoption and redevelopment of the interpretation of one who had been branded an outsider by German historiography, namely, Arthur Rosenberg. With respect to this issue as well, the ruling consensus that the only choice was between the conservative Weimar Republic and Bolshevization through the Council was again cemented in the textbooks of the 50s. The new scholarly investigations of, among others, von Oertzen, Kolb, and Rürup disrupted this schematism and—further following the line of Rosenberg—shed definitive light on the greater openness of the historical situation and especially on the democratization potential of the Council prior to 1919, when it was radicalized on many levels, perhaps as a result of disappointment. It is beyond doubt that these studies, owing to their knowledge-constitutive interests, were able to examine with new intensity the question of whether the first German republic may have possessed more secure social foundations. The results of the rapidly growing body of literature that flowed from the interpretive model delineated here have overwhelmingly stood the test of critical debate. The romanticizing mythology of the Council, which a segment of the New Left has been cultivating since 1968, may have temporarily obscured this scholarly and political progress. Nonetheless, the breakthrough to a broader, freer understanding of these epochal years can no longer be seriously disputed.[30]

At the same time a shift toward open competition among rival interpretations had become apparent in the academic preoccupation with National Socialism. If previously an elastic form of totalitarianism theory predominated, like that underlying the influential studies of Bracher and his coworkers, a "revisionist" direction now demanded recognition. In line with their pragmatic understanding of politics, the proponents of this view sought to achieve the following objectives: (1) to regard National Socialism no longer as a monolithic Führer dictatorship but as the polycracy of competing power centers; (2) to overcome the fixation on Hitler as sole or at least all-important center of Nazi politics, a view that in certain respects still accords with the ideological stereotypes of Goebbels's propaganda; and (3) with all due weight to the special role of the charismatic Führer and the Hitler Movement, to map out the limits on action in domestic and even foreign politics. Martin Broszat and Hans Mommsen, Peter Hüttenberger and Wolfgang Schieder all were instrumental in securing a hearing for the new position. Unfortunately there presently exists no general presentation based on these perspectives that comprehensively develops the revisionist position.

Moreover, Ernst Nolte, in peculiarly skewed relation to the internal scholarly debates, repeatedly propounded in various comparative studies his "phenomenological" interpretation of "Fascism in its epoch." He deserves credit for reintroducing the concept of fascism into the scholarly dispute over the historical classification of international right-wing radicalism during the interwar period, irrespective of how questionable certain of his brilliant theses have proven to be. In comparison with these currents of contemporary history, the fascism discussion, sparked in recent years by the New Left, has indeed provoked a bitter battle of concepts, with the Tibetan prayer wheels of orthodox Marxist-Leninist definitions spinning to great fanfare; the empirical yield, however, has been negligible. One learns more about National Socialism from a single chapter in a book by Bracher, Broszat, or Nolte, from an article by Hans Mommsen or Wolfgang Schieder, than from their opponents' entire ten-year critique of fascism. Even the old power elites' responsibility for the collapse of Weimar and their cooperation with the Nazi regime has since the mid-50s been clearly emphasized by certain of these authors. The moral-political impetus expressed in the revivified critique of fascism, a critique directed against the tendencies toward repression and trivialization in the restoration years of the Federal Republic, very quickly degenerated into crude attempts to invest capitalists with demonic qualities and to declare them responsible for every misdevelopment. Nor is much to be learned from the purely defensive posture that quickly rigidified dogmatically in the repudiation of "revisionism" and "Fascism theories." By this is meant the interpretation of National Socialism as "Hitlerism," which fashions Hitler's personality and politics into the sole fulcrum and rotation point. Methodologically this approach, defended primarily by Andreas Hillgruber and Klaus Hildebrand with the aid of a rather lean argumentational structure, entails a wholly personalistic traditionalism at the expense of the sociohistorical context. The underlying conception, that an overpowering Führer was in fact able to implement step by step his initially conceived program, not only overestimates the freedom of action and the operational rationality of the Nazi regime; it also explains why the "programmologues" met with justified criticism as regards the one-sidedness of their Hitler monomania and their general understanding of politics.[31]

From the mid-60s the dispute over the significance of social and economic history was carried on with increased intensity. A myriad of programmatic articles demanded a general revaluation of these fields, which had long been treated with conspicuous neglect. Likewise within empirical research a shift of interest toward a developmental history of modern industrial capitalism was postulated. At the same time use was made of the preparatory work done long ago by influential historians like Conze and Schieder favoring an unorthodox social history; indeed their authoritative judgment served as a type of escort for those participating in the dispute. One central premise now found considerably more support than before. The notion was widely accepted as a presupposition that socioeconomic changes had a unique historical influence and exercised a pervasive impact on the course of industrial capitalist development. Interests bearing on the many aspects of these total societal transformation processes were given priority. They also required theoretical explanations incomparably more powerful than those employed in traditional political history. Consequently historians were called upon to combine a historical-hermeneutic approach with systematic analysis necessary for the comprehension of supraindividual, anonymous processes and structures.

This discussion was linked to a revaluation of the major representatives of a historically oriented social science (in particular Marx and Weber), the older social history (first and foremost Hintze's), and those historians who, already having acknowledged the importance of socioeconomic problems after World War I, were pushed to the periphery or who were forced into emigration in 1933. In this way the studies as well as the influence of Eckart Kehr, Arthur Rosenberg, and Hans Rosenberg, among others, had a remarkable aftereffect and topicality that even in 1960 was still unforeseeable.

A glance at the results of the nearly fifteen-year debate leaves an ambivalent impression. On the one hand research in the area of social and economic history has been energetically set in motion. The number of scholarly publications has been constantly increasing since 1965. A good number of the productive scholars among the younger generation have addressed problems that either derive directly from social or economic history or can be treated only through a competent consideration of these dimensions. The significance of social and economic history for the study of modern history can no longer be disputed. It is now recognized to be no less integral a part of scholarly research than late medieval or early modern regional history. The charge of materialist truncation, a reproach long popular, has been rendered implausible. In this respect the proponents of social and economic history have undoubtedly gained ground. While universities were increasing the number of their positions, professional chairs were established in the field of economic history, less often in social history alone, more often, however, in the traditionally combined orientation of economic and social history. As early as 1972 both disciplines were well anchored in twenty-three of thirty-eight accredited universities. So far, so good.

On the other hand the reservoir of qualified newcomers, despite the decade of disputes (during which the priority of analysis of "Economy and Society" was constantly invoked), remained astonishingly small, even though academic job possibilities were plentiful, the attraction of unresolved problems considerable, and the opportunities for publication favorable. Obviously a long arid stretch exists between formulating interest in an attractive project and finishing the drudgery unavoidable in its execution. Moreover, it is clear that while desirable interaction between, for instance, economicohistorical and politico-historical approaches has increased, specialized research concentrating on sociohistorical and economicohistorical questions in the strict sense still leaves much to be desired.[32] Presumably social and economic history is in many places even now regarded more as special history than is state-oriented political history, with its antiquated claim to be the sole portrayer of general history.

Closely intertwined with the controversy over the status of social and economic history was the dispute concerning the "primacy of domestic politics." As early as the 20s Eckart Kehr defined the concept, without receiving much response. As a polemical counterconcept to the intractable predominance of the "primacy of foreign politics," proponents of the basic idea of a primacy of domestic politics sought to call attention to intrasocietal, socioeconomic factors and to break up the ossified clichés of political history. Between 1965 and 1975 this postulate spawned an interest clearly demonstrable through reference to a body of literature that is not among the weakest products of West German historiography. Much progress has undeniably been made, particularly within the field of socioeconomic explanation of political decision-making processes. This can be seen in a collection of historical studies that have shed revealing light on German domestic politics; it can also be traced in studies on the imperialist and armament policies of Imperial Germany, on the dissolution of the Weimar Republic, and on the rise of National Socialism. Similarly the yield has been considerable in the analysis of the domestic-political preformation of decisions in foreign affairs, particularly in the sense that the actors involved are significantly influenced by the inclination to defend the social status quo. Moreover, it has been possible, through the advocacy of the primacy of domestic politics, to force proponents of traditional forms of political history to argue for and to defend their claims. In view of their prebendary mentality, this obviously was an uncommon development, to which indeed they have responded with expressions of outrage—not, however, with the superior rational arguments that can be marshaled on behalf of a modernized political history.

Meanwhile the primacy of domestic politics has doggedly done its job. Naturally a dogmatizing of issues must be avoided. It is because of this "primacy" mentality that the problematic of the interdependency of intrasocietal and international constellations as well as the interplay of domestic and foreign politics is frequently neglected. Evidently the difficult balancing of determining factors requires subtler approaches, which are at present convincingly provided neither by political historians nor by political scientists.[33]

Mention has already been made of the fact that theoretical discussions have, with a certain necessity, developed out of efforts to justify social and economic history, their concrete research objectives, and the claims announced with the primacy of domestic politics. Active here were impulses that, resulting from problems encountered in research, prompted scholars to reflect on theoretical and methodological questions. Additionally, a general pent-up demand simultaneously became evident, one resulting from a decade of stagnation in theoretical disputes; this took the form of a self-satisfied late-historicism and a frequently vague yet pervasive sense of dissatisfaction with the ruling doctrine of understanding. Hence the third major "foundational discussion" to be observed emerging from these diverse motives was characterized by a call for more theory, a call not always conscious of its objectives. Retaining a diffuse character, it combined thoroughly diverse objectives. Questions of the philosophy of history, the function of knowledge-constitutive interests, the efficacies of various methods, and cooperation with related disciplines in the humanities were all discussed with equal thoroughness, just as the critique of misdevelopments in the past was resolutely presented.

A few points merit special emphasis.[34] Part of the debate revolved about the question of a new, topical method of historical analysis, one able to serve as a guide for all historiographical disciplines. But the view was also advanced, rather belatedly, that such a *Historik* could be established on a modernized variant of classical historicism, which allegedly had been unjustly maligned.

A unique problem area, to which the new critique of historicism also made reference, was demarcated by the call for meaningful cooperation between historiography and the social sciences. At issue was, first, the fusion of hermeneutic and systematic approaches and, second (and more important), the better solution of practical research tasks, such as problems of social inequality, industrialization, and economic business cycles and crises, which could not be properly understood with traditional historiographical tools. Some dispute arose about the qualitative criterion of "better" in the sense of theoretical clarity, stringent interpretation, the consideration of higher degrees of complexity, and sound empirical justification. Gradually there emerged the conception of a historical social science, which promised a more adequate treatment of such tasks. As regards theoretical-methodological orientation, historical social science was to link "understanding" with systematic explanation; even in this connection no one wished to renounce the achievements of historicism, because there is no turning back. This approach would combine the application or acquisition of theories, models, and ideal types with empirical rigor. It is defined by a pronounced interest in interdisciplinary and comparative investigations and must therefore strive to keep the historical totality or the whole societal context as the focal point of research. In order to be effective, historical social science must constantly interact with the results, methods, and ideas of the various social sciences, must examine and accept or reject aspects of them, must respond to stimuli or must gain reflective distance. A conceptual framework appropriate to the subject matter remains desirable, while the goal consists in formulating historical theories. It is immaterial whether one speaks of a historical social science or a social-scientific history. What is important is that the claims be realized, something for which the signs appear favorable.[35]

Recently the theoretical debate has subsided somewhat. Those with expertise in purely theoretical matters discuss highly specialized questions in their own study groups. Theoretically fortified to some degree, historians more interested in an improved analysis of real problems dedicate themselves anew to practical studies. On the whole, a sharpened theoretical understanding has emerged, which in this form had previously existed only in very particular cases. No one should want to exchange this level of reflection for the naive empiricism of positivistic pragmatism.

It is indisputable that all these transformations, which are reflected in the content and the outcome of the controversies here described, were fostered by the increase in the number of available positions between 1960 and 1975. Until 1960 the employment level in all West German universities remained fairly constant. However, the development of contemporary East European and American history has resulted in an augmentation of the personnel constituting history departments.

Several studies have indicated that in the span of fifteen years personnel in the field of academic historiography increased by a factor of four to five. Werner Conze studied published university records for the years 1950–1975 (although his figures did not take into consideration such academic centers as teachers colleges and archives). His results suggest that the number of full and associate professorial positions increased fourfold and the number of assistant positions sixfold over the period, with most of the increase concentrated in the period 1960–1975.[36] In 1978 the National Academic Advisory Council (*Wissenschaftsrat*) examined data from the Federal Bureau of Statistics showing an even more invigorated expansion. Although they did not have comparable figures for 1960, their 1976 analysis, which combined universities and multiversities (*Gesamthochschule*) in a single category, came to conclusions similar to those reached by Conze. Thus the documentation of the four- to sixfold increase in the number of positions can be regarded as established. According to Conze the findings demonstrated, among other things, that a significant change had taken place in age distribution: as early as in 1973, 45 percent of all professorial positions (*Ordinariate*) were held by persons born between 1929 and 1941. In 1976 half of all professors and occupants of middle positions would still have twenty to thirty years of service ahead of them.

Thus during the reorientation phase of West German historiography, an unprecedented expansion in the pool of academic positions provided an opportunity to pursue an academic career for those who, for a variety of reasons, had turned away from the traditional disciplines. Reform measures and the founding of new universities minimized the "hierarchical pressure" inherent in cooptation through appointment procedures; it also eased the "mechanisms of social selection."[37] The domestic-political climate of reform encouraged open debate and the acceptance of both innovation and controversial positions. Despite an increase in Cassandra calls decrying the diminishing interest in history, the production of literature has grown by leaps and bounds, largely as a result of the increase in the number of professional historians.

How are we to interpret the consequences of this growth? The conservative critique accentuates the "unsuspected dangers" stemming from the "faulty investment in personnel during the hasty and politicized phase of establishing and expanding the new university system."[38] However, we have not been apprised more precisely of the nature of this gloomy threat. A more realistic assessment provides an altogether positive general impression. In teaching and research, middle-aged and younger historians who profited from the university expansion underway since 1960 have met every test. They have accepted and upheld the approved standards of historiography. The quality of their publications has been confirmed the world over by the judgment of experts in the respective fields. With respect to theoretical reflections and intensive empirical source investigations, they need not fear any comparisons. The openness with which ideas have eclectically been accepted—be they from Weber or Marx, Hintze or Gerschenkron—has both improved theoretical foundations and expanded the horizon of interpretation. Despite sometimes stormy debates the formation of esoteric sects has been avoided. And the effective intraacademic socialization among historians, clearly unlike that among sociologists and political scientists, has sustained a remarkably high number of shared basic assumptions, methods, and traditions during the 60s and 70s, despite considerable differences in opinion. Even more skeptical senior historians were able to acknowledge this achievement; at any rate, they should find the new currents a stimulating challenge. That extreme positions do not materialize seems to be connected with the nature of historians' professional activity, which in its disciplining structure serves to dissolve stereotypical judgments and utopian assumptions. The moderate heterogeneity of the corps of West German historians, the belated yet robust injection of liberal-

democratic attitudes, the achieved pluralism of competing methodological and political positions — all these constitute a new set of attained
values. If one recalls the "special way" (*Sonderweg*) of German historiography, the present situation appears refreshingly liberalized. A link
with West European and American conditions has been achieved for
the first time within the profession.[39]

Which points of view would merit special consideration in a review
of the development since 1960? As a positive factor mention must be
made again of the general transformation within the expanded corps
of historians. Social and economic history are firmly established. The
programmatic battle cry has died down, a circumstance resulting in
an upswing in scholarly research. Noticeable progress has been made,
for instance, in the area of early modern industrialization, particularly
on the development of salaried employees, the old middle classes,
and interest associations. The social history of industrial workers has
become a new focal point, replacing the older history of the workers'
movement, which has also been energetically developed. Research
into mobility has finally begun. At the same time, however, other
important subjects such as the history of the bourgeoisie and the
university-educated middle class (*Bildungsbürgertum*) remain largely
unclarified. In various fields of inquiry within social and economic
history, the working method of a historical social science has proven
its worth. Pressing, unresolved questions that do not conform to narrow
departmental divisions have received fresh impetus from this interdisciplinary procedure.

The controversies of recent years have largely been manifestations
of a paradigm shift. The predominance of traditional political-historical
models of interpretation has been dissolved. Conceptions of a modern
political history that are compatible with an informed understanding
of conceptual and theoretical problems are discussed with astonishing
infrequency, even though a modern political history is in fact indispensable. Yet conceptually refined theses within the history of industrialization or economic growth have demonstrated their integrational
force. A topic of animated discussion today is the paradigm of a societal
history (*Gesellschaftsgeschichte*) rooted in a currently viable synthesis that
is oriented to the unity of history. Societal history in this sense aspires
to an analysis of society in its entirety, which is constituted by three
equally important dimensions: economics, power, and culture. Its synthetic capacity is to be proven in terms of its ability to accommodate

the complexity and connection of diverse dimensions of reality more adequately than do older concepts of integration. In order to fill out the wider circumference of a societal history, it is necessary to appeal to the results of the separate individual historiographical disciplines. When viewed as sectorial sciences, these separate disciplines—whether as constitutional or economic history, social history, or the sociology of social inequality—cannot fulfill the claim to synthesis. Irrespective of one's assessment, a valid task undoubtedly remains, given the present tendency in the direction of high-level specialization, to discuss and above all to examine empirically such integrational proposals. The credibility and attraction of historiography is also connected to its ability to provide a synthetic comprehensive presentation. It is of course an open question within academic discourse whether the superiority of a different concept in the extraordinarily meager number of competing paradigms can be demonstrated in argument and in fact.[40] It remains to be seen whether the representatives of a modern political, economic, or cultural history will attempt to substantiate such a claim to synthetic capacity on the part of their disciplines' leading concepts.

For the time being it must remain an open question how quickly and thoroughly recognizable weaknesses in the recent development can be eliminated or in what way outstanding problems can more satisfactorily be resolved, given that they have at times been obscured by polemical debates. For instance the relation of social and economic history to a modern political history needs closer examination. An additional challenge has been presented, as already mentioned, by the investigation of the interdependency of domestic and foreign political developments. Quantitative research still has a great deal to learn, even if the monomania of American and French proponents of this "cliometric" approach must by all means be avoided. It has been justifiably demanded that social historians dedicate themselves more persistently to the problems of daily life, however blurred the concept of daily life may still appear. Thus they have been encouraged to follow the lead of historians in France, England, and the United States who have responded to stimuli emanating from social anthropology. (For this reason the histories of population, family, urban life, women, education, and sport also deserve more intensive examination.) Until now such considerations have remained largely at the level of programmatic demands, which, moreover, have not gone beyond the catalogue of postulates proposed by Thomas Nipperdey in 1967 at the Freiburg Congress of German Historians. It remains to be seen whether in this domain a subtle neohistoricism — which gives preference to immanent interpretations deriving from the social life-world of the groups, classes, regions, and cities under investigation and which asserts a right of its own vis-à-vis dogmatic class formulas — will make itself felt just as it does among American historians who attempt to combine the fashionable "culture" trend with the notion of "history from the bottom up." It is further a task of political historians to set limits, through efforts more in touch with reality, to the threadbare and indeed mutilated historicism underlying the notion of Hitlerism. Another deficiency lies in the fact that hardly any attention is being given to a modern intellectual history, even in the sense of a social history of ideas, or a modern history of political ideas, although a cultural history that investigates cultural phenomena in terms of the relative autonomy of economics, power, and culture defined above, and that seeks to operate at the highest level of contemporary discussion, can dispense with neither. The history of science is also in desperate straits. It is perhaps less surprising that, owing to a concentration on the burdens of German history, a demanding, problem-oriented form of comparative research has only begun to emerge. At issue in this matter is on the one hand the tension between the dissolution of older traditions and the renunciation of new ways of posing questions and on the other hand the fact that a shift in research emphasis is often characterized by the one-sidedness often needed to achieve the goals of reorientation. In all cases historians, through their efforts, could provide solutions.[41]

More serious are several new dangers present since the mid-70s, which have refreshed memories of the older burdens of German historiography. In view of the uneven cyclical rhythm evidently underlying not only economic but also intellectual activity, a conservative countermovement opposed to the reform euphoria of the late 60s and early 70s was to be expected. The oft-proclaimed "shift in ideological currents" (*Tendenzwende*) has also led in the universities to irritating forms of conservative backlash, linked in its zealous transfiguration of the past with the fashionable vogue of nostalgia. Resistance against the belated advance of social and economic history has intensified. Cooperation with the social sciences has met with clear repudiation. By some it is regarded as a betrayal of the discipline itself, even if, in view of the superior quality of their analyses of long-term socio-economic, political, and cultural processes, historians have no reason to adopt a defensive attitude. Increasingly the liberal-democratic direction is being confronted with an ideological and often religious opposition built on fronts reminiscent of earlier conditions. In certain regions pluralism is being visibly restricted. Individuals who kept a lemurlike silence during the period of change now find a golden opportunity to exact their revenge. As a consequence bitter feuds have erupted in departments and disciplines over habilitations, appointments, and position extensions. A stranglehold has been placed on public, argumentative discussion. At the meetings of historians in Braunschweig (1974), Mannheim (1976), and Hamburg (1978), a telling reversal was signaled in the overly cautious reticence displayed by younger participants who, in view of the power constellations in some history departments, evidently were no longer willing to expose themselves through controversial theses.

One extreme example of the changing climate is the mean-spirited McCarthyism that has been surfacing since 1974–75. Thus, for instance, the Bonn historian Walther Hubatsch, one of the last representatives of the Borussian School and an inveterate German conservative, took aim, in some unforgettable remarks, at "modern agitating forms of argumentation" advanced under the banner of the "primacy of domestic politics." For him this "doctrine" not only signified a "flight from unpleasant reality, a narrowing of horizons, a shirking of responsibility, and a retreat into a state of dreamlike bliss in some isolated nook"; it also activated

in a tired imitation of the Marx-Engels-Lenin tradition [which has heretofore not been pursued by a single West German historian of note!] history as an arsenal in the struggle against imperialism and capitalism. In this way our considerations acquire a broader, more fundamental dimension. It is virtually impossible to calculate how much Marxist ideology is contained in certain historiographical elaborations, how much is peddled, often unconsciously, as fashionable jargon. Even scholarly reviewers [clearly an especially odious offense!] unconditionally surrender to this inclination. Thus confusion and perplexity are quite deliberately ushered into the world of concepts and their application. Yet the past is formidably immense. It can be understood only by those who seriously make the effort.[42]

Clio, grant that which can help Hubatsch!

Similarly, the Cologne historian Andreas Hillgruber has rebuked the student and assistant movement, in existence since the late 1960s, on the grounds that by "1970–71 at the very latest . . . it had become reliant on the forces of a doctrinaire Marxism-Leninism, oriented to the 'GDR Model.' " Members of the New Left, Hillgruber argued further, embarked on "a search for ideology ('a need for theory'), and indeed in the later phases a search even for indoctrination; . . . radical social reform (practically speaking: social revolution 'in installments') [represented] the sole task of the present. The dubious thesis of the primacy of domestic politics furnished pseudoscientific legitimation for such demands." Should the advocate of this conservatism, psychologically impaired by the surroundings, really be surprised when such attacks—which in one breath argue against the "theoretical needs" (Koselleck) of historiography per se, against the necessity of social-welfare-state reform politics, and against the demonstrable merits of a hysterically discredited conception of historiography—are met with resolute countercritique? Who should still be surprised that this faction steadfastly ignores the paradigmatic character of societal history, itself misunderstood as "tantamount in practice to a handmaiden of 'leftist tendential history' "?[43]

It was with similar insouciance that the Mainz historian Winfried Baumgart summarily sought to defame as neo-Marxism a theoretical position of which he disapproved.[44] His colleague at Münster, Klaus Hildebrand, using denunciatory language, likewise misunderstood supposedly "Marxist-oriented . . . theories of societal history": societal history harbors a "claim to absoluteness," plans an "octroi of exogenously defined paradigms" (?), seeks to become a "superscience," indeed—lament is made to Ranke—to erect a "dictatorship of knowledge." Moreover, from the early Marx's definition of "true theory," which, as is well known, "requires clarification and development according to concrete situations and existing conditions," Hildebrand culled, in a repeatedly slipshod form of interpretation, the command that historiography "reduce its theories exclusively to the 'true theory' of Karl Marx" (here with the imputed meaning of the one true, sole redeeming theory).[45]

Such formulations do not represent occasional derailments. Rather, they bespeak an illiberality imbued with vague suspicions lacking substantiating argument, and must be firmly opposed. *Vestigia terrent.*

A new phenomenon is visible in the right-wing conservative nationalism that surfaced in the *Propyläen Geschichte der Deutschen* by the Erlangen historian Helmut Diwald. This nationalism is novel in that it strikes a note previously heard only among ideologues of the National Democratic party of Germany or Nazi-sympathizing outsiders like David Hoggan; never, however, had a university professor embraced such a position. Apparently it is now possible to feel at home inside the borders of right-wing radicalism. Fortunately the first critical reviews — "the most scandalous thing I have had to read in a German book since 1945" (Golo Mann) — were unanimous in not dispensing with an acerbic tone.[46]

A considerably diminished explosiveness is apparent in three characteristic *Topoi* of the recent neotraditional discussion. The call for a unified national conception of history itself represents only "a historically ossified cliché" and, in view of the dependency of historical research on knowledge-constitutive interests and choice of perspectives, "cannot be scientifically grounded." The verbosely proclaimed postulate that the reacquisition of a stable identity is of the highest priority is based on a mistaken notion of identity that would only too gladly repress a critical working out of changing experiences and a productive confrontation with tensions and ruptures, favoring instead an unquestioned acceptance of traditional values and an affirmative internalization of norms. Affixed to this approach, like an ornamental arabesque, is an attack on the "modern relevantists" who, with their "patent-democratic" view of history, cling to the "magic of emancipation" (Nipperdey). The neoconservative direction in theoretical debates is matched by, among other things, the strict demand for a sharp distinction between the genesis and the validity of scholarly theses, one that would help achieve an objective, value-neutral representation. This requirement is made even though it is clear that normative predecisions rooted in the life-world (which to the extent possible should be made explicit and accessible to discussion) irrevocably influence and permeate the language, evaluation, and choice of problems. In this respect the aphorism of an English historian rings true: the historians most likely to arouse suspicion are those who "most loudly proclaim their impartiality while filling in a vacuum with their own prejudices."[47]

Compared to such accompanying manifestations of the ideological shift, the supposedly imminent danger entailed by a leftist tendential history seems a grotesque dramatization. Even though a politically significant number of middle-aged and younger historians continue to support the liberal-democratic positions of the left-middle (in the United States they would be unceremoniously included in the "liberal community"), virtually all of them are, in terms of scholarly practice, more Weberian than Marxist. To this day "proponents of Marxist principles" represent an "unqualified exception" within West German historiography. Here, too, in comparison with other West European countries, there is apparent a specifically German peculiarity for which the label "provincial" would surely be a euphemism. More prevalent is an unbiased, eclectic appropriation and experimental examination of stimuli that can be received from Marx's writings and from neo-Marxist historiography. For a variety of reasons it would be beneficial if nondogmatic West German Marxists were to participate actively in the discussions of historians, for it would then no longer be necessary constantly to refer to the stimulating studies of French, English, and American representatives of an "histoire marxisante." The climate created by the Decree against Radicals (Radikalenerlass) has clearly not been conducive to impartial debate. At any rate the thresholds of tolerance should be kept high enough so that this position could readily be included in discussions.

On a different plane are practical difficulties that, although not confined to historiography, nonetheless exist there. Teaching and administration often smother scholarly research. Compared to France, England, and the German Democratic Republic, the number of research positions is still extremely limited. This is linked to a certain German provincialism, one also apparent in the formation of focal points: non-German history is still a neglected area in West German historiography. Even the histories of Western and Southern Europe and, more properly, of North and South America, Africa, and Asia are only sporadically explored; in none of these areas has there yet occurred any discussion of fundamentals.

In view of both the ubiquitously practiced restriction on the number of positions and the integration of teachers colleges into universities, the next academic generation is paying a high price for the appointment of younger faculty members (who still have several decades of their careers ahead of them). The career possibilities of this next generation are shrinking continually. For the same reason conflicts about filling positions have been intensified. It is particularly the unorthodox scholars who are directly affected by increased conservative opposition. A new religious confessionalism fully able to implement its objectives has recalled memories of the "clerical alley on the Rhine" (*rheinische Pfaffengasse*). An effort must be made to remedy this situation as quickly as possible by means of research programs, foundation grants, expanded research facilities, and a more simplified exchange between schools and universities. Otherwise it is impossible to rule out the danger that the continuity of research will be interrupted and the ability to compete internationally impaired.[48]

Problems of a different nature, meanwhile, have raised the question of how the results of scholarly research might better be conveyed to the reading public. One prerequisite for academic progress in the social sciences is a precise conceptual framework for specialized languages. In this sense the undifferentiated critique leveled at specialist jargon contains a good deal of naiveté, which stems from unfamiliarity with the subject matter and perhaps even bald obscurantism. Nonetheless it remains an important task, albeit one involving mastery of a difficult practical art, for historians to present academically acceptable analyses in a prose less esoteric than that employed by some. This is all the more so because the tension between a theoretically oriented historiography and the expressive mode of everyday language can never be eliminated fully but only lessened. It is precisely professional historians who should not concede this transfer exclusively to the few journalists interested in the subject matter. While the latter may write with enviable fluidity, they rarely possess the scholarly work experience needed to sharpen the criteria for a balanced, independent judgment of controversial issues. A familiarity with sources is also lacking. Moreover an element of insecurity persists that stems from the necessity of forever having to accept, without their own mechanisms of control, information at second or third hand—reason enough for the historian to be more considerate of the lay reader and to strive for an unadorned, easily comprehensible style. This holds particularly for studies that aspire to broad influence and that attempt to provide the synthesis obviously so much in demand.

In spite of these heavy burdens, the positive changes should not be ignored. For the first time modern social and economic history are now integral parts of West German historiography; their absence is no longer conceivable. For the first time representatives of the liberal, social-democratic current hold secure positions in approximately twenty-five of the sixty West German universities. The opportunities for publication are more favorable than ever before. An increased number of periodicals and more than a dozen literary monograph series make available a broad forum for discussion, altogether free of traditionalist intervention. This fundamentally distinguishes the situation from the period prior to the 60s. The historical profession has in a positive sense become more heterogeneous. It must learn to live with this pluralism of competing directions in a liberal way. The left-wing middle has thus far sustained the intellectual offensive and remains willing to engage in free debate based on sound argument. The hysterical tones of some neotraditionalists, who are by no means always older historians (there is also the problem of "premature senility"), should not obscure the fact that, despite the academic and political dividing lines, discussion has remained possible. Much value should continue to be attached to such forms of regulated conflict. Since in its social function historiography has always contributed to the "rationalization of social and political conflicts and to long-term tendencies that may appear anonymous to the nonhistorian," it cannot dispense with a controlled form of argumentative discourse.[49] Conflicts are not onerous disturbances of scholarly harmony that ought to be avoided. Rather, as demonstrated by the development of West German historiography since the 60s, conflicts further scholarly progress and contribute to a freer and more critical consciousness. In view of the outstanding problems and the undeniable forms of resistance, it remains worthwhile to continue fighting for a differentiated social and economic history, for a modern political history, for consideration of cultural anthropology, and even for the primacy of a critical societal history, not least of all in order to redeem the claims connected with them.

Notes

1.Karl Jaspers, *Die geistige Situation der Zeit* (1931; 5th ed., Berlin, 1971) [English: *Man in the Modern Age* (Garden City, NY, 1957)]. I would like to make clear at the outset that the following remarks deal solely with the historiographical interest in German history since the eighteenth century. I am not competent to provide a comparable treatment of medieval and early modern history. Moreover, my intention in this survey is not to trace progress in the substantive analysis of modern history (in the sense, say, of a report on the state of research), but rather to shed light on paradigms, interpretive models, and theoretical-political transformations. Thus emphasis will be placed on dominant traditions, openly fought conflicts, and changing background conditions in the development of (West) German historiography; consideration will not be given to the silently persisting continuity in some spheres of scholarly research.

For a critique of the first draft I would like to thank D. Geyer, J. Kocka, G. Meyer-Thurow, J. Mooser, H. Müller-Link, I. Peikert, H. Rosenberg, and H.-C. Schröder. A more detailed

252

Hans-Ulrich Wehler

version with more extensive documentation can be found in H.-U. Wehler, *Historische Sozial-wissenschaft und Geschichtsschreibung* (Göttingen, 1980), pp. 13–41, 299–317.

2. The central controversies since the 1960s will be treated more fully below. For the best survey of the interests pursued here see G. G. Iggers, *Deutsche Geschichtswissenschaft* (Munich, 1971–1976 [3rd ed.]); Iggers, *Neue Geschichtswissenschaft. Von Historismus zur Historischen Sozialwissenschaft* (Munich, 1978), pp. 11–54, 97–218, 259–64; Iggers and W. Schulz, "Geschichtswissenschaft," *Sowjetsystem und Demokratische Gesellschaft* 2 (1978):955–59; J. Kocka, *Sozialgeschichte* (Göttingen, 1977), pp. 48–111; B. Faulenbach, ed., *Geschichtswissenschaft in Deutschland* (Munich, 1974), in particular Hans Mommsen's essay, pp. 9–16, 112–20, 138–46; H. Mommsen, "Betrachtungen zur Entwicklung der neuzeitlichen Historiographie in der Bundesrepublik," in G. Alföldy et al., eds., *Probleme der Geschichtswissenschaft* (Düsseldorf, 1973), pp. 124–55; W. J. Mommsen, *Die Geschichtswissenschaft jenseits des Historismus* (Düsseldorf, 1972, 2nd ed.); Mommsen, "Die Geschichtswissenschaft in der modernen Industriegesellschaft," in *Festschrift K. D. Erdmann* (Stuttgart, 1975), pp. 11–25; W. Conze, "Die deutsche Geschichtswissenschaft seit 1945," *Historische Zeitschrift* 225 (1977): 1–28; A. Sywottek, *Geschichtswissenschaft in der Legitimationskrise* (Bonn, 1974); I. Geiss, "Die westdeutsche Geschichtsschreibung seit 1945," *Jahrbuch des Instituts für deutsche Geschichte in Tel Aviv* 3 (1974):417–55; H.-U. Wehler, ed., *Deutsche Historiker*, vol. 1–5 (Göttingen, 1971–72)(in one volume: Göttingen, 1973), vols. 6–9 (Göttingen, 1980–82). As reflected in the East German critique: G. Lozek et al., *Unbewältige Vergangenheit* (Berlin, 1977, 3rd ed.); E. Engelberg, *Probleme der marxistischen Geschichtswissenschaft* (Cologne, 1972); J. Streisand, ed., *Studien über die deutsche Geschichtswissenschaft*, 2 vols. (Berlin, 1963–65).

3. The notion of paradigm is taken from T. Kuhn, *The Structure of Scientific Revolutions* (Chicago, 1962). Cf. D. A. Holliger, "T. S. Kuhn's Theory of Science and Its Implications for History," *American Historical Review* 78 (1973):370–93. Here we shall not directly consider the development in the Soviet Zone of Occupation, since 1949 the German Democratic Republic, where historiography has been subordinated to a state-ordained Marxism-Leninism. Cf. A. Dorpalen, "Die Geschichtswissenschaft in der DDR," in Faulenbach, ed., pp. 121–37; J. Kocka, "Zur jüngeren marxistischen Sozialgeschichte," in P. C. Ludz, ed., *Soziologie und Sozialgeschichte* (Opladen, 1973), pp. 491–514; Kocka, "Marxistische Geschichtswissenschaft/DDR," *Sozialwissenschaftliche Informationen* 2 (1973):39–44; Kocka "Theorieprobleme der Sozial- und Wirtschaftsgeschichte," in H.-U. Wehler, ed., *Geschichte und Soziologie* (Cologne, 1976, 2nd ed.), pp. 305–30; Kocka "Sozial- und Wirtschaftsgeschichte," *Sowjetsystem und Demokratische Gesellschaft* 6 (1972):1–39; Kocka, "Theoretical Approaches to the Social and Economic History of Modern Germany," *Journal of Modern History* 47 (1975):101–19; D. Riesenberger, *Geschichte und Geschichtsunterricht in der DDR* (Göttingen, 1973).

4. T. Schieder, "Geschichtsbewusstsein und Geschichtsinteresse in der Krise?" in *Vom Nutzen und Nachteil der Geschichte für unsere Zeit* (Cologne, 1973), p. 22.

5. Cf. K. C. Schwabe, *Wissenschaft und Kriegsmoral. Die deutschen Hochschullehrer und die politischen Grundfagen des Ersten Weltkrieges* (Göttingen, 1960); F. Klein, "Die deutschen Historiker im Ersten Weltkrieg," in Streisand, ed., vol. 2, pp. 227–48; K. von See, *Die Ideen von 1789 und 1914* (Frankfurt, 1975).

6. H. Herzfeld, "Staat und Nation in der deutschen Geschichtsschreibung der Weimarer Zeit," in Herzfeld's *Ausgewählte Aufsätze* (Berlin, 1962), p. 51, and generally pp. 49–67; B. Faulenbach, "Deutsche Geschichtswissenschaft zwischen Kaiserreich und NS-Diktatur," in Faulenbach, ed., pp. 66–85; C. Weisz, *Geschichtsauffassung und politisches Denken Münchener Historiker in der Weimarer Zeit* (Berlin, 1970); E. Kehr, "Neuere deutsche Geschichtsschreibung," in Kehr, *Der Primat der Innenpolitik*, edited by H.-U. Wehler (Berlin, 1965–76, 3rd ed.), pp. 254–68; F. Ringer, *The Decline of the German Mandarins: The German Academic Community 1890–1933* (Cambridge, MA, 1969). Informative: H. Schleier, *Die bürgerliche deutsche Geschichtsschreibung der Weimarer Republik* (Berlin, 1975). Here and there historians partial to traditional state metaphysics turned, during the period between the wars, to a resuscitated form of nativist mentality (*Volkstumgedanken*),

some even sympathizing with nativist and in part racist ideologies. A few demanded that what up to then had been political history be supplemented with a "folk history." This carried no more force than a weak undercurrent, and yet a connection was traceable from it to O. Brunner and G. Ipsen. The provincial reaction of most historians to 1918 and Weimar—typical of an amply documented parochial rigidification—was glossed over to an extraordinary degree by Werner Conze ("Das Kaiserreich von 1871 als gegenwärtige Vergangenheit im Generationswechsel der deutschen Geschichtsschreibung," in W. Pöls, ed., *Festschrift W. Bussman* (Stuttgart, 1979), pp. 383–405, here p. 391.

7. F. Meinecke, *Politische Schriften und Reden* (*Werke*, vol. 2) (Darmstadt, 1958), p. 281.

8. J. Kocka, "Wissenschaftliche Progressivität und politischer Konservatismus im Werk O. Hintze," *Neue Politische Literatur* 18 (1973):1–7.

9. Ritter's citation: *Deutsche Historiker*, p. 100.

10. R. Vierhaus, "W. Frank und die Geschichtswissenschaft," *Historische Zeitschrift* 207 (1968):619. Cf. K. F. Werner, *NS Geschichtsbild und Geschichtswissenschaft* (Stuttgart, 1967); Werner, "Die deutsche Historiographie unter Hitler," in Faulenbach, ed., pp. 89–96; H. Heiber, *W. Frank und sein Reichsinstitut für Geschichte des Neuen Deutschland* (Stuttgart, 1968); F. Grauss, "Geschichtsschreibung und Nationalsozialismus," *Vierteljahrshefte für Zeitgeschichte* 17 (1969):87–95; O. J. Hammen, "German Historians and the Advent of the National Socialist State," *Journal of Modern History* 13 (1941):161–88; E. Y. Hartshorne, *The German Universities and National Socialism* (London, 1937); V. Losemann, *Nationalsozialismus und Antike. Studien zur Entwicklung des Faches Alte Geschichte 1933–1945* (Hamburg, 1977); P. Schumann, *Die deutschen Historikertage 1893–1937* (Göttingen, 1975); W. F. Haug, *Der hilflose Antifaschismus. Zur Kritik der Vorlesungreihen an deutschen Universitäten* (Frankfurt, 1967). An obtrusively apologetic tone permeates Conze's assessment (*Kaiserreich*, pp. 393–94) of the conduct of most historians in 1933 and the first years thereafter. If today the influence of "the 1933 national advent climate," the "pan-Germanic" view of history, and the suggestion of that which "in 1933 appeared to be the 'reemergence' of the Reich" are proffered, in a way that was perhaps still possible in 1949, as supposedly adequate explanations, any vehemence in the critique of tradition since the 60s is again understandable and to some extent justified.

11. G. Ritter, *Friedrich der Grosse* (Heidelberg, 1936; Königstein, 1978 [not included in the editions after 1945]); English: *Frederick the Great* (Berkeley: University of California Press, 1968). On the other hand Hajo Holborn, who in 1933 emigrated to America, told me that at the 1938 Zurich Congress of Historians, as the German delegation marched past him in lock step, Ritter stepped out of line and, despite earlier theoretical disputes, greeted him with marked cordiality, despising as he did the cowardliness of his colleagues.

12. H. Mommsen, "Haben wir zuviel Historiker?" *Die Zeit*, June 10, 1978, p. 68. Iggers, *Neue Geschichtswissenschaft*, p. 322. Von Müller took over from the rabidly repressed Meinecke in 1935. The data on the number of articles are from H. Rothfels's unproblematic but differently interpreted statistics ("Die Geschichtswissenschaft in den 30er Jahren," in A. Flitner, ed., *Deutsches Geistesleben und Nationsozialismus* (Tübingen, 1965), pp. 90–107). Cf. H. Schleier, "Die HZ 1918–1943," in Streisand, ed., vol. 2, pp. 292–302; T. Schieder, "Die deutsche Geschichtswissenschaft im Spiegel der *HZ*," *Historische Zeitschrift* 189 (1959):1–104. An irritating apologia permeates H. Gollwitzer, "K. A. Müller: An Obituary," *Historische Zeitschrift* 205 (1967):295–322. In the first years after 1933 approximately 15 percent of professional historians were dismissed, banished, or forcibly retired: K. D. Bracher et al., *Die nationalsozialistische Machtergreifung* (Cologne, 1960), pp. 321, 506. Cf. the literature in note 10; G. G. Iggers, "Die deutsche Historiker in der Emigration," in Faulenbach, ed., pp. 97–111; B. Bailyn and D. Fleming, eds., *Perspectives in American History*, vol. 2 (1968).

13. See the revealing confession of Ranke ["Ansprache am 90. Geburtstag 21.11.1885," in *Werke*, vol. 52 (Leipzig, 1888), p. 595]: "For the most common result was indeed that the

creations of the past, threatened with being annihilated by revolutionary impulses, had apparently constituted a necessary object of study."

14. Citations: Schulin, p. 15; H. Mommsen, "Betrachtungen," pp. 126, 130; Mommsen, in Faulenbach, ed., p. 115. The establishment of professorial chairs in East European history at many West German universities was linked primarily to the ideology of the cold war; in no way, however, did it represent, as Conze asserts, a (desired?) "counterbalance to the one-sided opening to the West."

15. See T. Schieder, "Grundfragen der neueren deutschen Geschichte," *Historische Zeitschrift* 192 (1961):1–16; Schieder, "Erneuerung des Geschichtsbewusstseins" (1957), in Schieder, *Staat und Gesellschaft im Wandel unserer Zeit* (Munich, 1974, 3rd ed.), pp. 188–207 [English: *The State and Society in Our Times* (London, 1962)], as well as, e.g., the writings of H. Heimpel [*Der Mensch in seiner Gegenwart* (Göttingen, 1954), *Kapitulation vor der Geschichte* (Göttingen, 1956)], R. Wittram [*Das Interesse an der Geschichte* (Göttingen, 1958)], and A. Heuss [*Verlust der Geschichte* (Göttingen, 1959)]. Cf. Iggers, *Deutsche Geschichtswissenschaft*, pp. 328–29. Hintze: F. Meinecke, *Autobiographische Schriften* (*Werke*, vol. 8)(Stuttgart, 1969), p. 383.

16. G. Ritter, "Gegenwärtige Lage und Zukunftsaufgaben deutscher Geschichtswissenschaft," *Historische Zeitschrift* 197 (1950):21–22; H. Mommsen, "Betrachtungen," p. 129.

17. Documented in L. Gall, ed., *Das Bismarck-Problem in der Geschichtsschreibung nach 1955* (Cologne, 1971). For a critical evaluation: H.-U. Wehler, *Bismarck und der Imperialismus* (Cologne, 1969; 5th ed., Frankfurt, 1983), pp. 412–502, 511–15.

18. O. Büsch, *Militärsystem und Sozialleben im Alten Preussen* (Berlin, 1962; his 1952 dissertation at the Free University of Berlin); G. Ritter, *Staatskunst und Kriegshandwerk*, 4 vols. (Munich, 1954–68) [English: *The Sword and the Scepter* (Coral Gables, FL, 1969–73)]; H. Mommsen, "Betrachtungen," p. 138. Review of L. Dehio, "Um den deutschen Militarismus," *Historische Zeitschrift* 180 (1955):43–64. Cf. V. Berghahn, ed., *Militarismus* (Cologne, 1975); Iggers, *Deutsche Geschichtswissenschaft*, pp. 340–47; and the literature in note 15.

19. H. Rosenberg, *Bureaucracy, Aristocracy and Autocracy: The Prussian Experience 1760–1815* (Cambridge, MA, 1958), particularly pp. 229–38. Presumably the state of the social and economic history of the modern period was so much more undefined during the first half of the Federal Republic than fifty years earlier because the Historical School of Political Economy had in the interim died out and because the systematic social sciences had been "dehistoricized."

20. H. Rothfels, *The German Opposition to Hitler* (Hinsdale, IL, 1948) [German: *Die deutsche Opposition gegen Hitler* (Frankfurt, 1960), pp. 28, 47, 51–54]; Iggers, *Deutsche Geschichtswissenschaft*, pp. 344–46; H. Mommsen, "Betrachtungen," pp. 136–37. The new critical stocktaking begins with the essays of H. Mommsen, H. Graml, and others in H. Buchheim and W. Schmitthenner, eds., *Der deutsche Widerstand gegen Hitler* (Cologne, 1966). For a fair evaluation of Rothfels, who apparently had great personal magnetism but who also supported several neoconservative misdevelopments, see H. Mommsen, "Geschichtsschreibung und Humanität. Zum Gedenken an H. Rothfels," in W. Benz and H. Graml, eds., *Aspekte deutscher Aussenpolitik im 20. Jahrhundert* (Stuttgart, 1976), pp. 9–27.

21. See Dehio's essays ("Deutschland und die Epoche der Weltkriege," "Ranke und der deutsche Imperialismus," "Gedanken über die deutsche Sendung 1900–1918") in Dehio, *Deutschland und die Weltpolitik im 20. Jahrhundert* (Vienna, 1955), pp. 9–96 [English: *Germany and World Politics in The Twentieth Century* (New York, 1959)]. H. Heffter, *Die deutsche Selbstverwaltung im 19. Jahrhundert* (Stuttgart, 1950/69). Conze's present position (*Kaiserreich*, pp. 395–96) is characterized by its acceptance of the adequacy of Dehio's critique of German foreign policy and its evaluation by historians; in any case he is far more in agreement with this critique than with what until then were more comprehensive objections. It is common knowledge that Dehio shied away from a comparable critique of internal structural problems and misdevelopments.

22. See H. Mommsen, "Betrachtungen," pp. 131–38. For a survey of an important part of the research: H.-P. Ullman, *Bibliographie zur Geschichte der deutschen Parteien und Interessenverbände* (Göttingen, 1978); K. D. Bracher, *Die Auflösung der Weimarer Republik* (Villingen, 1955; 6th ed., Königstein, 1978); cf. the introduction to the review by Conze in *Historische Zeitschrift* 183 (1957). Before Bracher left Berlin for his Bonn chair in politics, his appointment (supported by historians) to Brüning's professorship of political science at the University of Cologne foundered on the vehement clerical-religious opposition whose scurrilities I followed as a doctoral candidate at Cologne.

23. For the best discussion of this topic: Kocka, *Sozialgeschichte*, pp. 70–82 and specifically p. 79; Conze, p. 17. Cf. W. Conze, *Die Strukturgeschichte des technisch-industriellen Zeitalters* (Cologne, 1957).

24. H. Mommsen, "Betrachtungen," p. 130; Conze, *Geschichtswissenschaft*, pp. 5, 11–13.

25. This generation had experienced the final phase of the war as young soldiers, as aides in antiaircraft artillery, or as members of the Hitler Youth. Their willingness, following an initial disillusionment, to accept as a model the politics and society primarily of the United States and England was rooted in a certain psychological necessity. This need did not preclude a revision of conceptions that then were perhaps too often idealized.

26. One thinks of the first Berlin group, including K. D. Bracher, G. A. Ritter, G. Ziebura, G. Schulz, O. Büsch, W. Sauer, F. Ansprenger, F. Zunkel. Apparently Conze was originally led to social history by insights drawn from his own empirical studies in agrarian and demographic history, together with interests nurtured on Ipsian historical sociology (*Volksgeschichte*). For about fifteen years, starting in 1955, he was to be its most important representative. Schieder, a key figure in West German historiography between 1950 and 1975, was one of the first to take up the many problems that have been topics of discussion since the late 60s; see, e.g., T. Schieder, "Der Typus in der Geschichtswissenschaft" (1952), in Schieder, *Staat und Gesellschaft*, pp. 172–87; Schieder, "Strukturen und Personlichkeiten in der Geschichte" (1962), in Schieder, *Geschichte als Wissenschaft* (Munich, 1968, 2nd ed.), pp. 149–86; Schieder, "Möglichkeiten und Grenzen vergleichender Methode in der Geschichtswissenschaft" (1965), ibid., pp. 187–211; Schieder, "Unterschiede zwischen historischer und sozialwissenschaftlicher Methode," in Wehler, ed., *Geschichte und Soziologie*, pp. 283–304. Schieder himself fulfilled many of his own demands: Schieder, "Europa 1870–1918," in Schieder, ed., *Handbuch der Europäischen Geschichte*, vol. 6 (Stuttgart, 1968), pp. 1–196; Schieder, "Europa 1918–1970," ibid., vol. 7 (1979), pp. 1–354; Schieder, *Staatensystem als Vormacht der Welt, 1848–1918. Propyläen Geschichte Europas*, vol. 5 (Berlin, 1977). Approximately 50 percent of the dissertations completed under his supervision were published as books; approximately 50 percent of his doctoral students became college teachers. Otto Brunner, who is often cited in connection with the development of West German social history, exercised a primary literary influence, yet formed no circle of students; see Brunner, *Neue Wege der Sozialgeschichte* (Göttingen, 1956; 2nd ed., 1968). It seems to me that the "conceptual history" persistently advocated by Conze, R. Koselleck, and Brunner will lead, even when seen from a moderate viewpoint, to a dead end and further divert attention from the unresolved real problems of social history. As Hans Mommsen has written ("Betrachtungen," pp. 140–41), conceptual history "remains stranded on the outskirts of a notion of history that takes fully into consideration socioeconomic processes"; it stands, when viewed from the perspective of a critique of ideology, in danger of "seeking a normative reference point in prerevolutionary, traditionally anchored 'societas civilis.' " Cf. J. J. Sheehan, "Begriffsgeschichte: Theory and Practice," *Journal of Modern History* 50 (1978):312–19; H. Berding, "Begriffsgeschichte und Sozialgeschichte," *Historische Zeitschrift* 223 (1976):98–110; H. Medick, *Naturzustand und Naturgeschichte der bürgerlichen Gesellschaft* (Göttingen, 1973), pp. 16–21.

27. Translation from F. Nietzsche, *On the Advantage and Disadvantage of History for Life* (Indianapolis, 1980), pp. 21–22 [slightly modified (*tr.*)]. When from the supercilious standpoint of a Heidelberg professor's preoccupation with high standards, Conze (*Kaiserreich*, pp. 399–404) pointedly criticizes

the "break with tradition that occurred around 1960" (p. 402) and denounces the "tradition-disdaining tendencies" (p. 404) in parts of West German historiography, the inner rationale of this "critical" history once again becomes clear. Moreover, poor judgment and a marked inclination to oversimplify is evident in his portrayal of the discussion since the 60s by means of specific, and of course politically charged, stereotyping clichés, which cannot do justice to the actual course of development and the present situation. These clichés will be described and assessed more precisely later in this essay.

28. H. Mommsen, "Betrachtungen," pp. 238–39. Cf. V. Berghahn, "Die 'Fischer-Kontroverse'— 15 Jahre danach," in *Geschichte und Gesellschaft* 6 (1980):403–19; Berghahn, "F. Fischer und seine Schüler," *Neue Politische Literatur* 19 (1974):143–54; J. A. Moses, *The Politics of Illusion: The Fischer-Controversy in German Historiography* (London, 1975); A. J. P. Taylor, "F. Fischer and His School," *Journal of Modern History* 47 (1975):120–24; A. Sywottek, "Die Fischer-Kontroverse," in *1. Festschrift Fischer*, pp. 19–49; I. Geiss, "Die Fischer-Kontroverse," in Geiss, *Studien*, pp. 108–98; for the most recent East German assessment: F. Klein, "Zu einem neuen Buch von F. Fischer," *Zeitschrift für Geschichtswissenschaft* 26 (1978):1109–15. For a balanced classification: W. J. Mommsen, "Die deutsche Kriegszielpolitik 1914–1918," *Kriegsausbruch* (1914):60–100.

In 1961 a noted German historian with whom I had hoped to discuss Fischer's first book responded to my query in the following way: "It is absolutely incomprehensible to me how a German historian not living in Leipzig could write such a pamphlet." An icy silence met my suggestion that it was indeed fortunate that the author in fact did not live in the GDR but in Hamburg and so could even be invited to participate in a discussion.

29. The quotation is from Conze, *Geschichtswissenschaft*, p. 14 (October 1976). Nipperdey and others (see note 47) also should consider carefully, without feeling forced to question explicitly their postulate of "justice" (which indeed cannot ultimately be contested), whether the time may be ripe to turn from a deferential treatment of preceding generations toward the option of Nietzsche's "critical" history.

30. See the overview in G. P. Meyer, *Bibliographie zur deutschen Revolution 1918/19* (Göttingen, 1978), and E. Kolb, ed., *Vom Kaiserreich zur Weimarer Republik* (Cologne, 1972).

31. See H. Mommsen, "Betrachtungen," pp. 131–38; Mommsen, "Nationalsozialismus," *Sowjet-system und Demokratische Gesellschaft* 4 (1971):695–713; W. Schieder, "Faschismus," ibid. 2 (1968):438–77; H. A. Winkler, "Die 'neue Linke' und der Faschismus," in Winkler, *Revolution, Staat, Faschismus* (Göttingen, 1978), pp. 65–117, 137–59.

Nolte himself summarized the discussion of his books: *Die Krise des liberalen Systems und die faschistischen Bewegungen* (Munich, 1968), pp. 432–58; *Der Nationalsozialismus* (Berlin, 1973), pp. 197–208.

J. Kocka, "Gegen einen Begriffskrieg," *Frankfurter Allgemeine Zeitung*, December 18, 1978.

A. Hillgruber, "Tendenzen, Ergebnisse und Perspektiven der gegenwärtigen Hitler-Forschung," *Historische Zeitschrift* 226 (1978):600–21, and the controversy between K. Hildebrand ["National-sozialismus oder Hitlerismus?" in M. Bosch, ed., *Persönlichkeit und Struktur der Geschichte* (Düsseldorf, 1977), pp. 55–61] and H. Mommsen (ibid., pp. 62–71), where the superior arguments of a leading "revisionist" are particularly evident.

The citation is from W. Schieder, "Spanischer Bürgerkrieg und Vierjahresplan," in *Festschrift W. Conze* (Stuttgart, 1976), p. 833.

32. For a discussion of the debate over social history, see among others Kocka, *Sozialgeschichte*; "Theorieprobleme"; "Theoretical Approaches"; "Theorie in der Sozial- und Gesellschaftsge-schichte," *Geschichte und Gesellschaft* 1 (1975):9–42; H.-U. Wehler, ed., *Moderne Deutsche Sozialgeschichte* (6th ed., Königstein, 1981), pp. 9–44; Wehler, "Geschichte und Soziologie," in Wehler, *Geschichte als Historische Sozialwissenschaft* (3rd ed., Frankfurt, 1980), pp. 9–44. For a continuation of this discussion to 1976, see Wehler, *Bibliographie zur modernen deutschen Sozialgeschichte* (Göttingen, 1976), pp. 31–71.

For the debate over economic history: the essays by Kocka mentioned above in this note; R. H. Tilly, "Soll und Haben: Recent German Economic History," *Journal of Economic History*

29 (1969):298-319; Tilly, "Soll und Haben II, Wiederbegegnung mit der deutschen Wirtschafts- und Sozialgeschichte" (1978), in Tilly, *Kapital, Staat und Protest in der deutschen Industrialisierung. Gesammelte Aufsätze* (Göttingen, 1980); H.-U. Wehler, "Theorieprobleme der modernen deutschen Wirtschaftsgeschichte (1800–1945)," in Wehler, *Krisenherde des Kaiserreichs* (Göttingen, 1970), pp. 291-311. The continuation of the discussion to 1976: Wehler, *Bibliographie zur modernen deutschen Wirtschaftgeschichte* (Göttingen, 1976), pp. 34–69.

33. See the Kehr collection of essays, *Primat der Innenpolitik* (1965; 3rd ed., 1976), and his dissertation, *Schlachtflottenbau und Parteipolitik 1894–1901* (Berlin, 1930; Vaduz, 1966), which had a considerable impact. Regarding the controversy: A. Hillgruber, "Politische Geschichte in moderner Sicht," *Historische Zeitschrift* 216 (1973):529-52; H.-U. Wehler, "Moderne Politik- geschichte oder 'Grosse Politik der Kabinette'?" *Geschichte und Gesellschaft* 1 (1975):344-69, also in Wehler, *Krisenherde* (2nd ed., 1979), pp. 383-403; Wehler, "Kritik und Kritische Antikritik," *Historische Zeitschrift* 225 (1977):347-84, also in *Krisenherde*, pp. 404-26; K. Hildebrand, "Geschichte oder 'Gesellschaftgeschichte'?" *Historische Zeitschrift* 223:328-57. Media: G. Schmidt, "Wozu noch 'politische Geschichte'?" *Aus Politik und Zeitgeschichte* B17/75 (April 26, 1975), and H. Rudolph, "Was ist Geschichte?" *Frankfurter Allgemeine Zeitung*, June 9, 1978.

Perhaps this is the place to mention explicitly that although in some of the debates I marched along with the troops, I have also made a real effort, without renouncing my own sympathies, to present the reader with an accurate synopsis of the content as well as the pros and cons of the disputes.

34. One can acquire an overview of the debate's various stages and positions from H. Berding, *Bibliographie zur Geschichtstheorie* (Göttingen, 1978); K.-G. Faber, "Zum Stand der Geschichtstheorie in der Bundesrepublik," *Jahrbuch der Historischen Forschung*, vol. 3 (1976–77)(Stuttgart, 1978), pp. 13–28; M. Riedel, *Verstehen oder Erklären?* (Stuttgart, 1978); T. Schieder and K. Gräubig, eds., *Theorieprobleme der Geschichtswissenschaft* (Darmstadt, 1977); J. Kocka, ed., *Theorien in der Praxis des Historikers* (Göttingen, 1977); M. Baumgartner and Jorn Rüsen, eds., *Geschichte und Theorie* (Frankfurt, 1976); and the publications of the Arbeitskreis für Theorie der Geschichte (contributions to *Historik*): R. Koselleck et al., eds., *Objektivität und Parteilichkeit* (Munich, 1977); K. G. Faber and C. Meier, eds., *Historische Prozesse* (Munich, 1978); J. Kocka and T. Nipperdey, eds., *Theorie und Erzählung in der Geschichte* (Munich, 1979); K.-G. Faber, *Theorie der Geschichtswissenschaft* (3rd ed., Munich, 1974).

J. Rüsen, *Für eine erneuerte Historik* (Stuttgart, 1976); "Historismus und Historismuskritik," in T. Nipperdey, *Gesellschaft, Theorie, Kultur* (Göttingen, 1976), pp. 59–73.

For the East German critique: H. Schleier, *Theorie der Geschichte—Theorie der Geschichtswissenschaft* (Berlin, 1975); H. J. Steinbach, *Analyse und Kritik neuester Tendenzen in der bürgerlichen einschliesslich sozialdemokratischen Historiographie der BRD*, unpublished doctoral dissertation, Berlin, 1976. Cf. T. P. Koops, "Die Kritik der westdeutschen Methodendiskussion in der *ZfG*," *Festschrift Erdmann*, pp. 225-37.

35. As regards historical social science, see Kocka, *Sozialgeschichte*; R. Rürup, ed., *Historische Sozialwissenschaft* (Göttingen, 1977); W. Schulze, *Soziologie und Geschichtwissenschaft* (Munich, 1974), pp. 178–244; Rüsen, *Historik*, pp. 6, 45–54; Wehler, *Geschichte als Historische Sozialwissenschaft*; Wehler, *Historische Sozialwissenschaft*; Wehler, *Modernisierungstheorie und Geschichte* (Göttingen, 1975); W. J. Mommsen, *Geschichtswissenschaft*, passim; Mommsen, *M. Weber* (Frankfurt, 1974), pp. 203-22. Examples of practical realization can be found in: Rürup, ed.; Kocka, *Sozialgeschichte*; *Bibliographie zur modernen Sozialgeschichte bzw. Wirtschaftsgeschichte*.

Traditionalist critique: G. Mann, "Die Alte und die neue Historie," in C. Podewils, ed., *Tendenzwende* (Stuttgart, 1975), pp. 40–58; Hildebrand, pp. 335, 350 (monopolistic tendency to repress "all disciplines of historiography"). Conze (*Geschichtswissenschaft*, p. 21): one can "clearly observe the movement of an antihistoricist swing of the pendulum toward a criticohistorical social science that is understood as having an emancipatory function. Indeed it is pertinaciously propagated with the claim of being generation-specific and future-aspiring."

36. Conze, *Geschichtswissenschaft*, pp. 18–20; Wissenschaftsrat, *Empfehlungen des Studienangebots* (Cologne, 1978), p. 97, Table 2. The figures for teachers colleges are, in this interpretation of

the subject matter, "too low." Cf. H. Mommsen's data ("Zuviel Historiker?"), estimating 700 professional historians. By contrast the United States has six times as many historians per capita; England has two and one-half times as many; and France has 800 in modern history alone.

37. H. Mommsen, "Betrachtungen," p. 147.

38. Conze, *Geschichtswissenschaft*, pp. 16, 20.

39. See Iggers, *Neue Geschichtswissenschaft*, pp. 97–218; H.-U. Wehler, ed., *Die moderne deutsche Geschichte in der internationalen Forschung 1945–1975* (Göttingen, 1978); K. Epstein, *Geschichte und Geschichtswissenschaft im 20. Jahrhundert*, edited by E. Pikart et al. (Berlin, 1972), as well as, for instance, J. Droz and H. Brunschwig's running collection of reviews in *Revue Historique*. The favorable judgment passed by qualified foreign historians on the standards of the West German historiography of the 60s and 70s should give critics something to think about. Dissertations that were still common in the 20s and 30s could not be submitted by doctoral candidates today. Nearly all good theses are published in book form, as indeed they should be.

40. As regards specific questions, see Kocka, *Sozialgeschichte*; Kocka, *Theorien*; Kocka, "Theoretical Approaches"; E. J. Hobsbawm, "Von der Sozialgeschichte zur Geschichte der Gesellschaft," in Wehler, ed., *Geschichte und Soziologie*, pp. 331–53; Wehler, "Vorüberlegungen zu einer modernen deutschen Gesellschaftsgeschichte," in *2. Festschrift Fischer* (Bonn, 1978), pp. 3–20, revised in Wehler, *Historische Sozialwissenschaft*; Wehler, "Anwendung von Theorien in der Geschichte," in Kocka and Nipperdey, eds.

Whereas the GDR history of the workers' movement, owing to its dogmatic assumptions, has been in some cases devalued to the point of total uselessness, a West German superiority has been attained in the study of the social history of industrial workers—a superiority that can be challenged only if, contrary to all expectations, H. Zwahr's splendid book, *Zur Konstituierung der Proletariat als Klasse* (Berlin, 1978), were quickly to find followers.

41. See T. Nipperdey, "Kulturgeschichte, Sozialgeschichte, historische Anthropologie" (1968), in Nipperdey, *Gesellschaft*, pp. 33–58; Iggers, *Neue Geschichtswissenschaft*, pp. 143–47; Kocka, *Sozialgeschichte*, pp. 89–91; Kocka, "Arbeiterkultur als Forschungsthema," *Geschichte und Gesellschaft* 5 (1979):5–11.

A gap is also appearing in agrarian history, where the East German research of Berthold, Harnisch, Heitz, Müller, among others, holds a clear advantage.

42. W. Hubatsch, *Kaiserliche Marine* (Munich, 1975), pp. 76–78. Regarding Hubatsch, see Iggers, *Deutsche Geschichtswissenschaft*, pp. 347–48, and K. O. von Aretin, who called him one of the "last masters of good-sounding nationalist phraseology" (*Süddeutsche Zeitung*, April 4, 1966).

43. A. Hillgruber, *Deutsche Geschichte 1945–1972* (Berlin, 1974), pp. 182–94; Hillgruber, *Deutsche Grossmacht- und Weltpolitik im 19. und 20. Jahrhundert* (Düsseldorf, 1977), p. 7, note 1.

44. W. Baumgart, *Deutschland im Zeitalter des Imperialismus, 1890–1914* (Berlin, 1972), p. 12; Baumgart, *Der Imperialismus* (Wiesbaden, 1975), pp. 99–109. Critique: G. Ziebura in *Historische Zeitschrift* 223 (1976):483–84, and *Neue politische Literatur* 21 (1976):171–81; H.-U. Wehler, "Deutscher Imperialismus in der Bismarckzeit," in *Krisenherde*, pp. 309–36.

45. Hildebrand, pp. 329, 335, 246–47, 356. A response: Wehler, *Kritik*. Marx-Engels, *Werke*, vol. 27, p. 409 (1842).

46. H. Diwald, *Propyläen-Geschichte der Deutschen* (Berlin, 1978). Reviews: E. Jaeckel in *Die Zeit*, December 1, 1978; K. O. von Aretin in *Frankfurter Allgemeine Zeitung*, January 5, 1979; G. Mann in *Der Spiegel* 49 (1978); also E. Jaeckel, *Die Zeit*, May 11, 1979.

47. H. Mommsen, "Zuviel Historiker?"; T. Nipperdey, "Wozu noch Geschichte?" in G. K. Kaltenbrunner, ed., *Die Zukunft der Vergangenheit* (Freiburg, 1975), pp. 37, 47, 56. Has it already been forgotten how often Goebbels employed the phrase "patent democrats"? See generally the essays in this anthology, which provide a wealth of conservative lamentations. C. J. Burckhardt et al., *Geschichte zwischen Gestern und Morgen* (Munich, 1974); H. Lübbe, *Geschichtsbegriff und Geschichtsinteresse* (Basel, 1977), e.g., pp. 145–54, 168–207. For a critique: Kocka, *Sozialgeschichte*, pp. 119–20, 129–31.

T. Nipperdey, "Über Relevanz," in Nipperdey, *Gesellschaft*, pp. 13–32; Nipperdey, *Historismus*; "Wozu noch Geschichte?" Likewise, if in a more robust and demanding manner, M. Rauh, *Die Parlamentarisierung des deutschen Reiches* (Düsseldorf, 1977), pp. 7–14; cf. P. C. Witt, "Wie reformfähig war das Kaiserreich?" *Geschichte und Gesellschaft* 9 (1983). E. H. Carr, *The New Society* (Boston, 1957), p. 103 (who in part cited Hancock). Also revealing are the ritualistic motions that were recently activated against Habermas by young conservatives such as Hildebrand (p. 339) and L. Gall. In "Zu Ausbildung und Charakter des Interventionsstaats," *Historische Zeitschrift* 227 (1978):553, note 2, Gall reproaches, of all people, the author of *Strukturwandel der Öffentlichkeit* (1962) for providing "little more than an account reflecting the influence of *Stamokap* [State Monopoly Capitalism] theories, even as he seeks to repudiate them."

48. H. Mommsen, "Betrachtungen," p. 152; cf. Mommsen, "Zuviel Historiker?"; "Empfehlungen des Wissenschaftsrats"; Conze, "Geschichtswissenschaft," p. 19. Cf. Conze's polemic (pp. 26–27), in which he asserts that the long-neglected social history of industrial workers, whose study he had championed, demands "greater methodological and technical exertions than the average amount that had been sufficient for advancement during the period of the quantitative leap." The veiled advertisement for a coworker evokes sympathy. Nonetheless it is hardly possible to specify what the "average amount" is; moreover, in what I believe to be a complete list of historians working in social history who obtained appointments after 1960, I can find *partout* none who were consumed by such "exertions."

49. H. Mommsen, "Zuviel Historiker?" Here one thinks of such periodicals as *Geschichte und Gesellschaft*; *Archiv für Sozialgeschichte*; *Neue Politische Literatur*; *Leviathan*; *Gesellschaft*; *Sozialwissenschaftliche Informationen*; and so on; and such series as *Industrielle Welt*; *Kritische Studien zur Geschichtswissenschaft*; *Historische Perspektiven*,, *Studien zur modernen Geschichte*; *Historisch-Sozialwissenschaftliche Forschungen*; *Studien zur Wirtschafts- und Sozialgeschichte*; *Forschungen zur Wirtschafts- und Sozialgeschichte*; *Untersuchungen zur Wirtschafts-, Sozial- und Technikgeschichte*; *Studium: Sozialgeschichte*; *Sozialgeschichtliche Bibliotek*; *Beiträge zur Geschichte Osteuropas*; *Schriftenreihe des Forschungsinstituts der Friedrich Ebert-Stiftung*; and the like. Additionally, there are series of readers such as *Neue Wissenschaftliche Bibliothek* and the *Neue Wissenschaftlichen Texte*.

It must also be emphasized that many of the discipline's journals welcome contributions from representatives of the currents mentioned earlier. The polarization of views that occasionally surfaces has not led to any complete termination of interaction, even if neoconservatives gladly avoid public disputes.

Perspectives on German Affairs

The Burden of the Past

Hans Mommsen

The Filbinger affair, the debate over the extension of the statute of limitations for murders committed during the Nazi period, and the reaction to the television film *Holocaust* have made clear that the burden of the Nazi past has not been lightened, that the historical consequences of the "Thousand Year Reich" have not been resolved. The profound effect that the film portrayal of the politics of the "final solution" had especially on the younger generation—perhaps because it reduced the inconceivably gruesome banality to a level immediately intelligible and comprehensible—has revived the critical question of the responsibility of the older generation. This is a question that had begun to disappear in the late 50s and that had been concealed behind the political polarization of the "critical left" and the democratic welfare and achievement society.

Is the new sensitivity—visible in the animated reaction to the *Holocaust* broadcast by large segments of the population, unanticipated equally by the media and the experts—an expression of an altered awareness, or is it merely another episode? The efforts, observable everywhere, of journalists to capitalize on the theme of *Holocaust* is indicative of an increased desire for information about contemporary history. It certainly also indicates an unconscious inclination to isolate this theme, to disengage it from the larger process involved in critically working through recent German history, and to cloak in moral self-criticism the political consequences this history has bequeathed to contemporary social and political reality.

There is much to be said for the thesis that the sensitivity revealed in the reaction to *Holocaust* will remain without political consequence as long as it does not succeed in focusing public discussion on the basic sociopolitical causes of National Socialist violence. For it will in no way suffice to unite the nation in an abhorrence of the Nazi atrocities and thereby derive indirect justification for the so-called liberal-democratic basic order and welfare-state realities of the Federal Republic of Germany. Yet it is just these features that characterize the basic tendency of the political public sphere as it demands more and more information about the Third Reich and a more intensive concern for the problems of National Socialism both in the teaching of history and politics and in the popular portrayals of historians. What is called "coming to terms with the recent past" (*Bewältigung der jüngsten Vergangenheit*) thereby assumes the character of mere instruction about events, whose function is to confirm distance and to isolate the clear emergence of neo-Nazi sentiments.

Neo-Nazism and Postfascism

Those responsible for civic education have long bemoaned the dearth of adequate "enlightenment" about contemporary history. One factor contributing to this lamentation was the emergence of a new, militant variant of the National Democratic party of Germany, a party that holds the respect of members of the middle class. Constituting this variant are radical youth groups who imitate, in historically authentic manner, the stylistic tools and propaganda contents of National Socialism and who, by invoking theories of right-wing terrorist extremism, have shattered the public's illusion that terrorist forms of protest are of significance only for ultraleftist sentiments. The historical and political causes of this emergence of an unusually militant form of neo-Nazi association have not yet been adequately investigated. Nevertheless some distinctions must be made regarding the background of this startling phenomenon, which should not be quantitatively overestimated.

The now unmistakable change in the form of right-wing radical protest appears to be possible only because the social taboos that were effective during the postwar decades in preventing any direct adoption of Nazi attitudes, have lost their force. Otherwise it would scarcely be possible to explain why youth of the National Democratic party in Dortmund were able to demonstrate in the manner of Josef Goebbels, encountering only sporadic protest from passers by. What is surprising is the enthusiasm with which juvenile minorities have adopted the style and propaganda contents of the Nazis. It is absurd to assume that superior historical education might remedy this situation; where the extermination of Jews is applauded, historical reality cannot serve as a terrifying *Mene Tekel*, a foretelling of destruction.

It can be asked whether this conscious assault on social taboos, whose criminal risks are fully known to the young, is not essentially apolitical. Might it not reflect a misguided need to combine social engagement with authoritarian subordination? This is in fact possible only where a mode of behavior prestructured in authoritarian fashion emerges alongside an effective loss of the authority held by ruling groups in society. The protest against the older generation in connection with the crimes of the Nazi regime, as well as the conflict of rebellious students with their typically upper-middle-class backgrounds, are a part of the same phenomenon. Both signify an unwillingness on the part of the young to deal seriously with the historical burdens of the society into which they were born.

The official repression has had a stimulating effect on the fringe neo-Nazi groups of the younger generation. The societal trend toward nostalgia and toward emotive needs for identification, manifest in the formation of escapist sects, is linked with an unreflective attachment to historical models that appear "interesting" in connection with the generally observable tendency toward rehistoricization. There are many reasons why West German society—and here the Federal Republic does not stand alone among industrial nations—is not fully able to provide, in addition to skills and orientations, sets of values that assure a minimum of sociocultural continuity. Neo-Nazi activities, abhorrent as they may appear, are certainly not the most disquieting form of the dichotomous relation of the generations. Even if alcoholism and drug abuse among the young are declining, a significant portion of the younger generation is active in creating a variety of subcultures that can be viewed as latent or manifest forms of protest against the adult world.

There is no doubt that the critical student movement contained analogous sociocultural symptoms. Yet its decline in significance by no means implies social normalization; all utopian admixtures not-withstanding, it professed the aim of public engagement, which, admittedly, was detached from the totality of social conditions and triggered authoritarian reactions. By contrast the apolitical forms of juvenile escapism presently supplanting the dying leftist subculture represent a long-term threat to a democratic system based on the capacity and willingness to participate, particularly when accompanied by structural unemployment among the young and by their repudiation of career and education. The experience of the Weimar Republic, which was burdened with the same generational dichotomy, indicates that those groups in the population who are not politically inclined, who are not integrated into political parties and associations, are precisely the ones who, under conditions of general crisis, represent a significant component of a fascist potential for mobilization.

As a result of the *Holocaust* broadcast, the social pressure to make neo-Nazi attitudes taboo has once again been intensified. It cannot be expected that this will last. It is telling that a reputable publishing firm like Ullstein/Propyläen could sell large numbers of Hellmut Diwald's *Geschichte der Deutschen* before reviewers began to protest and call attention to its indisputably neo-Nazi features (not to mention various of its other inadequacies). Similarly a lecture by Diwald, while pointing in the same direction, was delivered at the Mannheim meeting of historians without eliciting significant protest either from the profession itself or from the public at large. Publications of this kind acquire relative popularity, because they appear to present an unbiased evaluation of National Socialism and the history of the Third Reich and thereby accommodate the repression of unpleasant historical matters of fact.

At the level of mass consumption, a comparable tendency is also noticeable. Pamphlets discussing the theme of the Third Reich and World War II, published in large quantities, are always presented as objective renderings of historical reality. Their uncritical dissemination is indirectly tantamount to a positive revaluation of the politics of National Socialism. Although The Law for the Protection of the Young has restricted their sale to the counters of railroad station kiosks, legal prohibition cannot suffice without a social taboo on such publications. The relatively large circulation of the *Deutsche National-Zeitung* must be seen in the same context. The quantitative decline in the number of radical right-wing organizations says little about the extent to which ideological elements of Nazism persist or even gain ground in West German "political culture."

What makes this situation distinctive is the fact that a potential infiltration of the democratic structure from the extreme right must not be viewed solely in terms of the avowedly militant neo-Nazi splinter groups. Far more important are such groups as the Viking Youth, which, while outwardly presenting a nonpolitical appearance, fulfill the youths' needs for identification through means that contain explicitly fascist elements and teach a pseudoidealism of the Nazi variety. The fascist mobilization employed these same techniques and was similarly dependent on the political instrumentalization of seemingly nonpolitical forms of communication.

The Conflict of Generations and the Legitimation Crisis of the Political System

One of the structural weaknesses of the Weimar party system, disregarding the Communist party and the National Socialist German Workers' party, was the remoteness of its policies to the concerns of young people—the inability to bind politically the ascendant generation, whose members were certainly not among the comrades who had fought at the front. The religious youth associations were something of an exception. In the Federal Republic as well, the parties have difficulty integrating their younger members, and it is quite possible that the young—as happened in the Weimar Republic—will not be brought closer to the existing political system by means of greater organizational efforts. Certainly it would be wrong to want to start the Youth Movement anew, although clearly no youth groups exist that can accommodate social communication outside parties, associations, and churches. It would be disastrous if new subcultural forms of a passion for order were to fall victim to communal authorities charged with their administration. The vacuum that here exists offers neo- and postfascist tendencies significant opportunities for penetration, and the latent unemployment among the young heightens this danger.

The emergence of neo-Nazi tendencies among fringe youth groups indicates that the political spectrum in the Federal Republic once again seems to be opening toward the right after the extraparliamentary opposition and the student movement had since the beginning of the 60s forced a displacement to the left. The relative lack of success of the ecology parties in the state elections of 1978 (disregarding the respectable showing of the alternative parties in West Berlin) should not obscure the fact that the heterogeneous political groupings contained in this opposition movement have not been able to bring young voters back into the existing party system. The stagnation in voter movements points to a potential political isolation. The articulation of quite diversely politicized protest positions in citizens' and ecology initiatives represents, it is true, an institutionalized challenge to the parliamentary system; yet this is in every respect to be preferred to an ominous nonarticulation, quite aside from the fact that it is only through such strategies of articulation that the willingness for political participation can be stirred.

In this regard as well, the Weimar experience merits consideration. Antirepublican groups were successful in exploiting the generational conflict dominant in German society during the 20s. Even within republican parties this conflict created an increasingly antagonistic attitude among younger members, to which party leaders responded with disciplinary techniques of an organizational variety; it also intensified the retreat to the superannuated programmatic-ideological elements of tradition and led to political sterility. This conflict of generations stretched across the spectrum of political opinion and was linked to the qualitatively distinct political socialization of a age group no longer affected by the experience of the World War I. Exactly the same thing has occurred in the Federal Republic. The ways of legitimizing conditions in the Federal Republic typical of the 50s and 60s—referring to the overcoming of the fascist dictatorship, the establishment of democratic institutions (the "Freest society in the world," as it is so often called), and the rebuilding process—no longer possessed binding value for the subsequent generation, which knew the Federal Republic as the basis of everyday political life and not as a fundamentally new political construction.

The leftist student movement drew a considerable amount of its social dynamism from this conflict, a dynamism that for a time broke through the confines of academia. With the demise of the student movement and a "normalization" heartily welcomed by the right (representing a depoliticizing in the negative sense), this problem of continuity—caused by the fundamental caesura resulting from the events of World War II and embodied in political expectations and models of legitimation—was not resolved but only repressed. A cyclical countermovement has apparently been set in motion in the attitudes of the younger generation, one tantamount to an inversion of the political poles. Characteristically, protests against pro-Communist publications within labor unions find their most primitive expression among younger union members.

Analogous to the situation in the Weimar Republic, a legitimation crisis is also occurring in the Federal Republic as regards both the political system as a whole and the leading political and representative parties. The fear, prevalent in the early 60s, of an elimination of ideological standpoints and a programmatic amorphousness in political debates was initially refuted by the "critical" left and the student movement, to which the left furnished a theoretical core. Today the intermediate-range perspectives on reform have largely been scrapped. Who still speaks of the long-range program of the Social Democratic party? The constant stretching of the "liberal-democratic basic order," which in backhand fashion has become a tool for disciplining internal currents critical of democracy, cannot conceal the lack of perspective in political development—something for which the parties are certainly not alone responsible. Small wonder, then, that the political commitment of many young people has been transferred to the ecology movement, which runs counter to the interests of the associations and the parties.

The reemergence of a fundamental critique of civilization, which provides an ideological basis for the unreserved and emotional participation by many people in such events as demonstrations against nuclear power plants, is ambivalent with regard to political orientation. It is traceable to a broad ideological current of the Weimar Republic, which was continued in the resistance, especially in the Kreisauer Circle. In this new movement, now made legitimate by the concern over ecological issues, anticapitalist resentments and forms of preindustrial romanticism stand side by side and can even be combined. The Weimar experience certainly cannot be projected unreservedly upon the present situation. Nonetheless such manifestations of the dissolution of the traditional political spectrum and its political-normative priorities are symptomatic of a far-reaching crisis of legitimation.

Democratic parties are reacting to these events with a remarkable increase in the activity of grass-roots organizations, encapsulated in the slogan, "close to the citizenry"; these organizations are characterized by a high degree of positive democratic engagement. Yet the official policies of the government and thus of the party apparatus are committed to appeasement strategies that cannot meet the need for goal-directed engagement on the part of active segments of the younger generation. Structural unemployment and the question of rationalization have permitted this problem to recede temporarily into the background. But it would surely be unrealistic to expect the younger generation to respond automatically to the cessation of crisis-free economic growth with a pragmatic form of political self-effacement. The experience of the Weimar Republic, whose political irrationalism has no correlate in the political landscape of the Federal Republic, teaches that a social and political system unable to generate positive political perspectives beyond a patchwork preservation of the status quo is condemned to extinction.

As a matter of fact, in the early 20s, following a period of uprising and upheaval the ruling elites and associations had adopted a mentality characterized by a purely backward orientation. In this way the dichotomy between a diffuse mobility in the intellectual sphere, sparked by an awareness of new challenges, and a social and political leadership guided by traditional conceptions became insurmountable. The parties recalled the programs and ideological contents of the prewar period; the interest groups regarded 1913 as the Golden Age, and the celebration for the constitution invoked Reich romanticism and a statist mentality against the constitution. The Federal Republic is barred from this path by the history of the Third Reich, which, like a monolithic block, has made the road to a holy national history impassable. Besides, the self-consciousness of the Federal Republic, owing to its economic growth and political stability, is too pronounced to allow it to be placed in a direct relationship with the "unfortunate" Republic of Weimar.

Nonetheless, everywhere there appears a need to touch up the pallid models of legitimation deriving from the founding years of the Federal Republic through invocation of national traditions. Typical of this tendency is the call for a resuscitation of the "thousand-year" German history before National Socialism, for the intensification of historical instruction in the schools, so that young citizens will acquire the national identification that will protect them from a dangerous "doctrine of salvation." A blunt demand is made for a unified "picture of history" (one derived, whenever possible, from the articles of the constitution), even though this common understanding of history has never existed in Germany and, under the conditions of a pluralist society, will never exist. Obviously historical education is here understood exclusively in terms of its affirmative function; this state of affairs is entwined with the illusion that through recourse to history a sociopolitical consensus of the *juste milieu* could be established—a consensus that since the end of Konrad Adenauer's chancellor-democracy has lost favor to an all-too-narrow form of political polarization.

That an historical need for legitimation exists within all political groups is evidenced by the development of the leftist student movement. Although initially formulating an ahistorical program of protest, one derived from theories of natural law, this movement gradually adopted a view of history more aligned with its reality. The plethora of new and pirated editions of nineteenth-century socialist tracts and publications demonstrates this change, and it seems symptomatic that this outwardly differentiated conception of history, bearing the stamp of neo-Marxism, exists outside official historiography, although to some extent it has consciously accepted the challenge of Marxism-Leninism. The introverted character of this leftist consciousness of history, reflected in analytic narrowness and jargon-encumbered terminology, merely inverts the societal remoteness long typifying the dominant approach to historical scholarship, which in large measure disregards modern industrial reality, perceiving it as fundamentally ahistorical.

Transformations in Historical Consciousness and the Legacy of Contemporary History

Currently a displacement of historical interest seems to be occurring that leads away from the problematic of contemporary history and brings aestheticized points of view to the fore. The Staufer exhibition, Wallenstein romanticism, the preparation for a comprehensive exhibit on Prussia, the prize competition for the depiction of Prussian history— these all are attempts to reconstitute an interest in history shaped by the educated middle class. Yet this current, directed to an affirmative understanding of history, competes with a tendency (also felt in scholarly research) to accord increased attention to regional history and to examine it from the perspective of social history, as opposed to the more traditional perspective of the history of provinces (*Landesgeschichte*). Because regional history suspends transnational European comparisons, it bypasses the standard history of the nation-state and mirrors the waning significance of nation-state consciousness vis-à-vis both regionalist and European self-understandings.

The countervailing character of these movements is unmistakable and corresponds to the tension in the present political culture of the Federal Republic between a statist mentality and both local and regional efforts at participation. This is also reflected in the content of historical research and teaching. The sociohistorical tendency that has projected domestic problems into the foreground is confronted with a growing emphasis on foreign-policy issues and a return to personalist modes of consideration, such as those baldly expressed in the "Hitler Wave." Battlefronts in the scholarly approaches to contemporary history, supposedly long abandoned, have been reoccupied. "Totalitarianism theory," largely dismissed in scholarship both as an ideological reflex to the cold war and as a static model of explanation, is again affirmed, in opposition to a Marxist-influenced "fascism theory," as an authoritative interpretive foundation for the analysis of communist as well as fascist systems. Complaints about a surfeit of social history are connected with a revival of neo-Rankean positions.

Underlying this is the occasionally unabashed effort (as with the Antiterrorism Congress of the Christian Democratic Union/Christian Social Union) to harness the historical tradition for the legitimation of predominantly conservative conceptions geared to the politics of order. The process of the dissolution of the Weimar Republic produced an arsenal of legitimations for authoritarian strategies, which, under the guise of a "defensible" democracy, introduced the step-by-step dismantling of essential constitutional guarantees in favor of the "protection of the state." Had a "Decree against Radicals" (*Radikalenerlass*) existed in Weimar, Hitler would never have attained power—thus runs the assurance from prominent quarters. In fact, nearly the opposite is true. Simple adherence to the basic laws for civil servants would have made impossible Hitler's naturalization, achieved through his appointment to the Braunschweig governmental council. On the other hand Communists were effectively denied access to governmental service, and von Papen's bureaucratic-political measures against republicans in the Prussian administration paved the way for Hitler's movement. The bourgeois-liberal government under Heinrich Brüning stabbed the Prussian cabinet in the back when the latter, together with other state governments, took active steps to bar Nazis from high-level administrative positions.

Recently Helmut Kohl revived, as an allegedly common conviction among historians, the perversion of history according to which the

Weimar Republic fell victim to the combined radicalism of left and right and was crushed between Communism and Nazism. This view suppresses the fact that it was Hitler's alliance with the conservative power elites in Hindenburg's entourage that enabled him to assume the chancellorship. The illusory hope that they would be able to manipulate the "drummer" to institute an authoritarian regime based on the exclusion of the organized workers' movement drove the traditional elites into an arrangement with Hitler, following the miscarriage of their own attempt to establish an authoritarian regime without popular support. Similarly, no mention is made of the fateful role played by a hybrid and frequently near-hysterical form of acceptable anti-Communism expressed in the willingness of numerous bourgeois-liberal groups to entrust Hitler with the governance of the Reich. The adherence to totalitarianism theory by historians and journalists who, in their trek through the middle, have long since reached the right, and the reaffirmation of an ideology in which the role of the bourgeois-liberal tradition functions solely to secure liberty, are both characteristic of a trend toward invoking the destruction of Weimar democracy to denounce an undesired political polarization as inimical to democracy. In this connection particular attention must be paid to the tendency, prevalent in historiography, to detach the causes of the Nazi seizure of power from basic social and economic conditions and to downplay the joint responsibility of leadership groups within the military, the bureaucracy, and industry. The emphasis on the personal role of the dictator and the inner Nazi leadership clique, and the inclination to adopt personalistic interpretations of the regime, point in the same direction.

At issue are not merely academic disputes. Operating beneath the surface are political taboos that reflect the continuing force of apologetic motivations. Consider, for example, the debate over the extent to which the regime's criminal actions originated wholly or in part in Hitler's actual decrees. The hypothesis that the practical steps for the implementation of the program for the systematic liquidation of European Jewry might have been undertaken independent of the dictator's initiatives met with unanimous rejection, and criticism of this hypothesis had a decidedly emotional character.

A similar development is the wearisome debate over the responsibility for the burning of the Reich's parliament building, a debate whose focus at the very outset shifted from explanations of factual circumstances to the mythology that had already emerged on the night of the fire. The vehement polemic over the alleged proof of van der Lubbe's sole responsibility, advanced only rarely in a competent fashion, and the confounding of the factual issue with questions of alleged "trivialization" is explainable only against the backdrop of the apologetic motivations of conservatives and the vested interests of Communists. The insight that conditions make the dictator, not the dictator the conditions, is something that still has not found a place in West German historical consciousness.

The Return to the Authoritarian Conceptions of the Late Weimar Period

The *Holocaust* broadcast silenced every voice that called for the burial of the dispute over the Nazi past and a return to business as usual. Nonetheless it fortified rather than diminished apologetic tendencies. When one recalls that Robinson's study of the racial defilement proceedings in Hamburg lay for years in a publisher's files before a courageous editor pushed for its publication; when one notes that Herbert Wehner, on account of his membership in the Communist resistance, was prevented from speaking at a memorial for the victims of July 20, 1944 [killed in reprisal for the attempted assassination of Hitler], while the heirs of Nazi leaders are still legally entitled to the publication and royalty rights of their literary estates; when one recognizes that the Federal Constitutional Court, in line with the Nazi law for German civil servants, still specifically prescribes the political loyalty of civil servants; and when one sees, finally, that the media display no reluctance in presenting films about the Nazi period to a public lacking proper political sensitivity—and a wealth of further examples can be amassed—then it can hardly be said that any moral or political working through of the recent past has taken place.

In this connection mention must also be made of the common failure to appreciate the justified sensitivity of people in the countries occupied by Germany during World War II toward attempts to relativize historically the events of the Nazi period. The traumatic experience of the Nazi politics of violence and extermination is still too close to be discussed "objectively," even if this experience is sometimes exploited by fervent political interests. When he attempted to connect the Holocaust, despite its uniqueness, with outwardly comparable cases of intentional genocide, Ernst Nolte incurred unexpected wrath from well-meaning Western historians. In view of the burden placed by the Nazi legacy on all, and not simply the generation that lived through that period, it is not fitting for Germans to expose defensive feelings within the public opinion of other peoples, especially when such attitudes persist below the surface of the public sphere of the Federal Republic.

It is common to respond to discussions of events such as the pogrom of November 9, 1938, or Auschwitz with moral self-criticism, indeed with national confessions of guilt. But there is little interest in laying bare sociopolitical causes and in drawing lessons for the present; instead the explanations offered revolve around the subtle form of ideological manipulation to which the German people supposedly fell victim.

The jolt furnished by *Holocaust* did not lead to a call for a more extensive investigation of the foundations of the Nazi system, the responsibility of the social elite, or the socioeconomic as well as institutional presuppositions for the rise of fascism. Historians limit themselves to a dissemination of long dominant interpretations of the Nazi regime, although these—at least as far as the West German literature is concerned—have in a broad sense bracketed the question of the concrete implementation of the "final solution" and have been restricted to a repetition of the chronological boundaries for the period of Jewish persecution. The concept of recent historical "enlightenment" is revealing here, since it implies an unwillingness to draw political consequences. "A Nation Is Moved" [a headline in *Der Spiegel*]—with this motto the actual shock experienced primarily by the younger generation is in a backhand fashion used as proof of the "antifascist reliability" of the West German population. Political consequences will now be buried under the flood of journalistic reflections on the reaction to the *Holocaust* broadcast. With successful enlightenment about the fact that the murder of the Jews did in fact take place, the German public will return to business as usual and will conclude, from the absence of anti-Semitic currents, that "something like that" cannot happen again.

It remains to be seen whether impulses emanating from the recollection of Jewish persecution and extermination, impulses that definitely have had a special effect on the historical consciousness of the younger generation, will occasion further reflection on the basic question of the continuity of assumptions and political structures above and beyond the singular occurrence of Nazi fanaticism. Without this cultural-political and psychological-moral disposition on the part of German society, the unprecedented accumulation of cynicism, the gruesomeness, the will to extermination, and the use of violence amalgamated with petit bourgeois mediocrity, the bourgeois love of order, the pseudoidealist fulfillment of duty, and the misguided sense of nationality that constituted the Third Reich would never have attained their apparently incomprehensible reality.

Hannah Arendt spoke of the banality of evil. She saw quite clearly that the experience of National Socialism, its historical uniqueness notwithstanding, also remains a *Mene Tekel* for contemporary political structures and constellations, which by means of comparable mechanisms, techniques, and assumptions are capable of justifying oppression and slavery in the name of what is purportedly a common good. Even in Western, democratically constituted industrial societies, no one is protected from a government that, partially released from public controls and acting in concert with a capricious bureaucratic apparatus, takes steps that in Germany, under the unfavorable conditions at the end of the world economic crisis, set in motion an escalation of violence that neutralized the restabilization forces of a streamlined political system and that could no longer be arrested from within. My Lai and the Nixon administration attest to the kind of deformations possible even under exemplary conditions of public freedom of speech; and there are good reasons for questioning whether the mechanisms of a police bureaucracy, whose apparatus appears unduly inflated as a result of the purely transitory threat posed by terrorist splinter groups, are not unexpectedly discovering new fields of operation, all public and parliamentary controls notwithstanding.

There can be no doubt that large numbers of intellectuals in the Federal Republic are growing skeptical about particular deformations of the political system precisely because of the predominantly democratic attitude of the vast majority of the electorate. The West German population is characterized by a will to sobriety and by a resigned acceptance of the German situation that developed as a result of World War II. Nationalistic slogans find no following; the question of reunification constitutes no focal point for political mobilization. However, reactions in the public sphere to leftist minorities, and the psychological repercussions of terrorism in particular, have made apparent the persistence of quickly mobilizable authoritarian dispositions among large segments of the population.

Against the backdrop of a waning period of released pent-up economic growth and a dubious political-bureaucratic synchronization, a return to the political language and political conceptions of the late phase of the Weimar Republic seems to be taking place within broad segments of society. One might point, for example, to the use of the pejorative concept "trade union state" as well as to the call for a national "will to perseverance" on the question of reunification. There is a tendency toward a juridification of political decisions, the model for which can be found in the Brüning era. Even a weak turn toward recession elicits the well-known slogan against the "double bread-winner," whereby discrimination against the employment of women is intended. A temporary budgetary lull has prompted the administrative bureaucracy to adopt conservative programs that, albeit under changed economic-political circumstances, mirror Brüning's extremely problematic deflationary policies. As then, cuts are made first in the educational sphere; the abolition of pensioned retirement for university professors—an economy measure of Brüning's chancellery—survived beyond the phase of recession. With regard to the problem of terrorism, the chief federal prosecutor can speak of a feeling for justice in the population, although it is an indispensable tenet of the constitutional state that criminal prosecution and punishment not be addressed in terms of the climate of public opinion.

A wealth of examples can be amassed documenting a latent willingness to adopt the statist-authoritarian mentality that dominated the Weimar Republic from the time of the stabilization phase and that contributed considerably to the undermining of the parliamentary system. Even behind the pledges of the welfare state is concealed the well-disseminated expectation that the executive is obligated to keep the social process free of conflict.

In contrast to other Western countries, strikes and lockouts are regarded not as legitimate tools of autonomous parties in wage negotiations but as disturbances of public order. The autonomy of these parties in negotiations is frequently not viewed as an instrument that leaves the regulation of industrial relations to the parties themselves and involves the public hand only in extreme cases. Rather, a significant portion of the German population holds the view that the government is obligated to end labor struggles quickly by means of a governmental settlement. What is often overlooked is that in the long run this under-mines the institution of autonomous wage negotiation and, as in the Weimar Republic, damages the political system and its authority. This can lead to a state of affairs in which government and parliament, beyond their responsibility for necessary legal guarantees, are so sad-dled with overall responsibility for the configuration of industrial re-lations that, as in the 20s, republican institutions are overtaxed and the standing of parliamentarianism is impaired.

Education and the Public Sphere

Finally we must mention the latent animosity toward education, which threatens to reverse the euphoria over education characteristic of the late 60s and early 70s into a weariness with education; this trend coincides with changes in demographic patterns that had resulted in part from World War II and the postwar situation. It would be easy to overlook the fact that the crises that have plagued the development of the secondary and especially the tertiary sector of the educational system are one of the lasting consequences of the Nazi regime. The university sector, in terms of the numbers of both students and pro-fessors, shrank during the Nazi years to half its 1928 capacity, despite the territorial expansion of the Reich. This shrinkage compounded the stagnation permeating parts of the secondary and nearly all of the tertiary sector during the Weimar Republic. As a result it was only in the mid-60s that the construction of universities in the Federal Republic surpassed the per capita level attained in 1928; only thereafter was there a real expansion in capacity. In spite of the astonishing expansion in higher education, the number of students remains con-siderably below that of other Western industrial countries and socialist states. At the same time we must reckon at least through the mid-80s with a one-third growth in the number of students.

The motives behind the deceleration in the construction of the tertiary sector and the restriction of the secondary level are by no means rooted in economic considerations alone. Hidden in the eloquent complaints about an impending glut of university graduates lie con-cealed—in addition to vested group interests and socially sullied expectations—massive prejudices about the emancipatory function of academic training. The reproach advanced all too frequently, that the universities and in particular the humanities are removed from practice, contains, behind the pretext of a concern for the social character of the public realm, a strong mistrust of the role of intellectuals in contemporary society.

Certainly there are deficiencies in the German university system that cannot be ignored—for example, the absence of a genuine academic community, the priority of status over effective scholarly achievement, the hierarchical organization of functions that creates a situation in which younger scholars remain dependent far too long, and the limited degree of interdisciplinary academic interchange. At the same time the university only mirrors the situation of the culture as a whole. It was illusory to believe that it would be possible to institute within the socially removed sphere of the university a degree of group participation whose presuppositions did not exist in the general political culture. A legitimate protest against the authoritarian structure of German universities rigidified into a movement that, after a continuous escalation of its aims, lost all sense of proportion about the possibilities for fundamental social change and finally abandoned itself to a revolutionary strategy out of touch with reality, thereby scattering the energies for reform into a number of opposing directions.

Following the demise of the protest movement, which consistently found widespread support in the student population, a reversal set in that revived authoritarian forms of intrauniversity communication, restricted the participatory rights of students and assistants, and left as the real result of the efforts at university politics a considerable expansion of state intervention in the university domain. The phase of reform produced a few important results: the establishment of comprehensive and extension universities, the greater emphasis given to the pedagogical-didactic aspect of teacher training, greater professional security for middle-level groups, and an increased transparency in degree requirements. But at the same time there now exists a disproportionately higher degree of regimentation, and the insecurity of students and assistants regarding their professional opportunities has created a climate of resignation and social withdrawal, conducive to sterility and an ivory tower mentality.

Despite considerable effort the social isolation of the university sphere has not been substantially reduced. Moreover intellectual disputes are now being removed from the domain of university life, and one has the impression that a sort of subcultural autonomization is developing similar to the one that existed in the Weimar Republic. The university debates concerning political direction have destroyed the internal unity of the professorial corps even within individual departments. A significant number of university teachers have lost internal autonomy; they are no longer in a position to express themselves communally on central questions and to assert, with regard to the public at large, the primacy of theoretical arguments that transcend the technocratic spheres. The susceptibility to interest groups organized along political lines is demonstrated by the politics surrounding appointments in the social-cultural sciences, where academic qualifications are giving way increasingly to political, religious, and status-oriented group interests.

Conclusion

I have come to the end of my reflections. My intention was to show that the political culture of the Federal Republic, and in particular the spiritual situation in its many refractions, bears the imprint of a historical burden rooted in the lingering ideology of the "German way" as well as in inherited, authoritarian mentalities and forms of behavior. Emancipation in the intellectual sphere has not kept pace with the Federal Republic's remarkable economic, technological, and social recovery. The extension of educational opportunity and the improvement of secondary as well as tertiary sectors of education have not defused the latent animosity toward education in significant parts of German society. Knowledge is viewed largely as service-rendering. The emancipatory function of research and its role in the securing of the future are not properly acknowledged. Existing disparities are not eliminated, but are concealed by an ideology of normalization, which in truth represents an unnoticed return to the conceptions of the late Weimar Republic.

Many younger intellectuals are seeing their hopes dashed, yet can find no way to express themselves effectively. Their representation in a few spheres should not conceal their increasing isolation. It is up to the younger generation to determine whether this development leads to external accommodation and nostalgic, aestheticized flight into the private sphere or to critical commitment and participatory partisanship in the public sector. The impulse supplied by *Holocaust* can shift interest away from a harmonizing reacquisition of the historical consciousness of continuity and toward the critical working through of the historical burdens of the German political tradition. Whether this happens depends not least of all on whether those active at all levels in the educational sphere and the media seriously consider that spiritually coming to terms with the Nazi experience consists not in any one-time enlightenment, but in a persistent confrontation with the causes and operating mechanisms of fascist domination. Not mere enlightenment but active participation must be the common goal.

Terrorism and the Critique of Society

Albrecht Wellmer

Conservative politicians, social scientists, and journalists are today advancing the reproach that "leftist" ("critical," "Marxist") forms of social theory have prepared the way for terrorism. It is difficult, if not impossible, for the representatives of such theories to react in a meaningful way to such accusations should they prematurely step onto their opponents' turf and accept the defensive role of the accused fashioned for them. For instance, the charge is made that certain statements, figures of thought, or arguments emanating from Marx, Adorno, or Marcuse can be rediscovered, if only implicitly, in the proclamations of the Red Army Faction (RAF) [the chosen name of the terrorist group commonly known as the Baader-Meinhof gang]. Should he wish to prove his innocence, the social theorist so accused has no alternative but to show that the respective statements, theories, or arguments were not intended by their authors in the way in which they have (possibly) been construed by the terrorists. But once pushed into this role, he has already acceded to that epidemic criminalization of ideas and opinions in terms of which the accused is always the loser, regardless of whether he succeeds in proving his innocence. For he has agreed to submit proof of the harmlessness of his thoughts and thus, to a certain extent, has imposed upon himself the obligation to think only harmless thoughts in the future. Whoever agrees to play this game is drawn into that spiraling mechanism of terrorist violence and state repression in which only two equally unpalatable options remain open: on the one hand, an unthinking indignation or a cheap distancing; on the other hand, a senseless and, if not political, at least emotional solidarity with the terrorists. As a result, critical thought is lost along the way. If today it is made responsible for the simplifications, regressions, and delusions of terrorist consciousness, this is only because the state which in this country is being defended against terrorism is all too frequently no longer the liberal constitutional state but a status quo whose defenders evidently have reason to be fearful of critical thoughts. Incidentally, in the attempt to link social criticism and terrorism, societal conditions are, as has so often been the case in German history, again exonerated, whereas all that is objectionable is attributed to those critical of these conditions.

In what follows I want to examine the theme of terrorism and the critique of society in a way that differs from the perspective of those for whom its formulation already contains an accusation.[1] My reflections are based on the assumption that the critique directed at critical theory is intimately connected with the suspicion of "sympathizing" with terrorism that has now been fashioned for the left as a whole. Thus the theme of the following remarks is simultaneously "terrorism and the left." Since the terrorists regard themselves as "leftists" or "socialists," there is certainly reason enough not to concede the topic to the right. Yet it is difficult, when discussing this topic, to avoid the objective force of the friend-foe mentality that has increasingly come to dominate the relationship between the state and the terrorists. The more the left as a whole falls victim to a friend-foe mentality, the more this mentality leaves its mark on leftist discussions and leftist attempts at self-definition. Whoever is portrayed as an enemy of the state and a friend of the terrorists may in the end be no longer able to discern any choice other than that between a cheap distancing from terrorism and an emotional solidarity with those now victimized by their own strategy of violence. By contrast, I think it is important, apart from false distancing and false solidarity—two modes that reciprocally engender each other—that the left define its relation to terrorism rationally and not in terms of considerations imposed from without.

In what follows I submit a few critical observations on the socialist self-understanding of the Red Army Faction and other "urban guerilla" groups. Further, I make reference to the interplay, so fatal to the left, between terrorism and political reaction. Finally, I advance some considerations on the basic social causes of terrorism as well as the presuppositions underlying the propagandistic-political manipulation of terrorism by the political right. While my aim is not to defend critical theory, my analysis will be based on assumptions central to its perspective.

I

Let me begin by arguing for a thesis whose validity is in no way diminished by its lack of originality. Simply stated: There are no grounds for regarding the terrorism of the Red Army Faction and affiliated groups as a radicalized variant of leftist or socialist politics. Accordingly the left has every reason to draw a clear line of political demarcation between itself and the terrorists; this is all the more so since today terrorist strategies have consequences for the left that endanger the left's own possibilities for action and existence.

To begin with I would like to clarify the sense in which I shall speak of a clear line of demarcation between the left and the terrorists. Today a good deal of repression is contained in the means members of the left use to distance themselves from terrorism—repression, that is, of the fact that, viewed historically and genealogically, the terrorism of the Red Army Faction and other groups was at one time very much intended as a variant, admittedly a radicalized one, of leftist politics. What I am referring to, however, is not simply the existence of biographical lines leading from the New Left of the 60s to the terrorist groups; I am also referring to the fact that, as regards her motives, personal experiences, and self-understanding, a woman like Ulrike Meinhof joined the Red Army Faction *as* a socialist. We cannot afford to repress these facts if we wish to come to terms with terrorism in a way that is adequate on theoretical, moral, and political grounds. It is precisely at this level that the demand for solidarity still has significance: not the false political solidarity with groups whose actions have long since become objectively reactionary, but the solidarity with people with whom at one time we shared an element of common history—common experience, intention, and despair.

Let me now clarify the thesis according to which the individual terrorism of the urban guerilla groups is not to be understood as a radical variant of leftist politics, that in fact such terrorism actually plays into the hands of social reaction. I refer, particularly by way of the experience of the Red Army Faction, to (1) certain basic errors and delusive distortions of reality that, from the very beginning, have characterized terrorism as a desperate form of socialist practice or at least socialistically intended practice, and (2) certain mechanisms that have contributed to the fact that what once was intended as a socialist form of illegal practice has actually assumed features of right-wing violent criminality.

The first error, or rather the first illusion, concerns the transference of models developed in the context of Third World liberation movements onto conditions of highly industrialized societies organized as parliamentary democracies.[2] This can be designated the Mao–Fanon–Che Guevara syndrome. Once "imperialism" was finally recognized as the iron clamp binding together all forms of oppression and alienation as well as all the world's emacipation movements, members of the Red Army Faction were able to interpret the emancipation problems of the First World in terms of the categories of Third World liberation movements. The correct insight that social change can be achieved only where individuals resolutely commit themselves to a transformative practice evolved into the illusion that "a few dozen fighters who really begin to act and not merely talk incessantly . . . [can] fundamentally alter the political scenery," and indeed that the armed struggle of a few could bring about the "assent of the masses" to armed struggle, thereby setting in motion their emancipation.[3] Only the forcible repression of all that is to be learned from a Marxist-oriented critical theory of society concerning the possibilities for a transformation of late-capitalist societies could render plausible such a forced, short-circuited reduction of the Third to the First World. In fact, it is doubtful that the terrorists could ever have seriously believed in this aspect of their illegal struggle. I am inclined to regard it as a pseudopolitical rationalization of a despair regarding the possibility of political change, one reflected in the conviction that "under imperialism armed struggle in its illegality is the only possibility for practical critical activity."[4]

It is certainly true that the struggle of the terrorists—and with this I come to their second illusion—did lead to some "fundamental changes in the political scenery," although not in the sense originally anticipated by members of the Red Army Faction. But even in view of this disappointment, they had little difficulty finding theoretical rationalization for their commitment to the continuation of armed struggle. Now they claimed that the capitalist system must be compelled to declare openly its latent fascism; once political repression had finally attained a sufficient measure of openness and intensity, the masses would recognize their real enemies and join the forces of the armed revolutionaries. Accordingly they designated as a goal of the struggle that of "forcing the state into an open confession, into a reaction in which the structure and the apparatus of repression become visible and comprehensible, and are thus presented as the motivating condition for revolutionary initiatives."[5] The experience of the 70s was really not necessary to make apparent the illusory character of this idea; one glance at the history of fascist Germany would have sufficed.

Yet even with regard to this second illusion, the terrorists had insulated themselves against disappointment. This insulation was rooted in their understanding of "proletarian internationalism." They regarded their struggle as a part of an international war of liberation against imperialism and the multinational organization of capital. In this way they had already found support in a mass movement, the anti-imperialist struggle of the peoples of the Third World. From this perspective it is possible to view the intensification of contradictions and forms of repression in the metropolises as the product of what is in any case an inevitable "feedback reaction of the wars of liberation of the peoples of the Third World upon industrialized societies."[6] The function of urban guerillas is once again redefined: they are members of a Leninist cadre that will provide a "political-military vanguard, a political-military core" to the people for the inevitable class struggles of the future, thereby ensuring the conditions for revolutionary activity.[7] From this perspective the masses of capitalist metropolitan centers, who were initially envisioned as the real addressees of revolutionary initiatives, seem to be the potential subjects of revolutionary struggle only in the long run. For now it is no longer a question of galvanizing emancipatory processes in metropolitan centers, at least not directly, but only of participating—by residing at the heart of the enemy—in the Third World's struggle for liberation against imperialism: the demolition of metropolitan centers becomes the goal of armed struggle, and the urban masses now appear only as objects in this struggle. But under these conditions even a long-term isolation of the terrorists from the people, from the masses to be liberated, or even an intensification of repression without the ensuing emergence of a revolutionary mass base for the Red Army Faction and affiliated groups, could no longer challenge their convictions.

I believe in short that the interpretations, justifications, and strategic calculations of the Red Army Faction reveal traits of a system of delusion. This is particularly true in that assumptions both in and out of touch with reality have been amalgamated among members of the group to form a system of ideas so immune to disappointment that genuine and self-critical processes of experience are hardly possible any longer. This, I believe, is one of the circumstances—disregarding others for which the Red Army Faction was not responsible—that makes it so difficult to ascertain the truth about what really happened in Stammheim (and in other prisons).[8] Of course it has to be assumed that the extensive isolation of groups associated with the Red Army Faction, both under the conditions of illegal struggle and later in the prisons, contributed considerably to their self-immunization against corrective experience. "Theory and practice become one only in struggle"—this statement is found in a now often cited *Der Spiegel* interview with the Red Army Faction collective conducted during the period of the RAF prisoners' third hunger strike.[9] Given its context, this statement sounds as if it came from some distant fantasy world; it strikes us as a truth torn out of context and therefore leaves us nearly dumbfounded.

In the same interview one also finds the following statement: "What the Bolshevik cadre was for Lenin is today, under the conditions of the multinational organization of capital and the transnational structure of foreign and domestic imperialist repression, the organization of a proletarian counterforce, as it emerges with the guerilla."[10] I cite this sentence to illustrate once again the unreality underlying the Leninist, not to mention Marxist, self-understanding of the Red Army Faction. What in the Leninist conception of the party contradicted the Marxist theses can at least be explained through reference to the conditions in a backward and autocratically ruled country, such as Russia prior to World War I. In any case this conception was linked to the elimination of terrorist tendencies through the rise of a Marxist-oriented workers' movement, albeit one largely condemned to illegality. The problematic character of the Leninist conception—even if successful from the standpoint of pure power politics—has clearly been demonstrated, it seems to me, by the Stalinist development in the Soviet Union. But the Red Army Faction not only applied this conception, as other Leninist sects have done, to democratically governed Western industrial societies, itself already a considerable distortion of reality. It also, in almost frenzied fashion, carried out this conception— in reverse, as it were—to its logical conclusion: Western metropolises now appear as the St. Petersburg of a worldwide system of oppression, in which only the armed struggle of determined guerillas, who establish themselves as the leaders of the enslaved masses, can put an end to the tyranny of capital, itself at once omnipresent and stylized into the personality of a superczar. Only the forced amalgamation of images and models in the terrorists' fantasies can render comprehensible their conviction that a destruction of the metropolitan centers effected by means of armed struggle must necessarily lead to a better, liberated, and socialist society.

Now it is certainly true that the original core of the Red Army Faction was composed of an extraordinary group of men and women, whose self-chosen fate (I am not speaking of their end, about which I can only speculate) has evoked abhorrence and sorrow even among those never inclined to condone their actions. Owing to their biographies, their intelligence, and their ties to the student movement of the 60s, they continue to occupy a special place within the terrorist underground. This is also true because, although they long ago became unreceptive to criticism from the left, they still possessed both the intelligence and the will to explain themselves publicly, and because their actions were at least in part still amenable to political interpretation. It seems to me that not even this is true in any comparable measure for the subsequent generation of terrorists. On the contrary, one is struck with the impression that the terrorist underground, in a spectacular nosedive, has once again distanced itself from the level of reflection of the Red Army Faction founders and that their actions have increasingly assumed a subpolitcal character. This is matched by an increasing insensitivity toward the victims of violence, an increasing expansion of the category of those who can be sacrificed as victims of terrorism, an increasing restriction of political praxis to military-strategic action, an increasing restriction of political perspectives to such secondary goals as the freeing of prisoners, and, finally, the apotheosis of armed struggle into a way of life that has become an end in itself. This offers the guerilla the only possibility to preserve and act out a group identity, which has now shrunk to an antagonistic relationship toward the system—quite apart from the fact that the continuation of armed struggle provides the only chance for survival in freedom, the only chance to escape the martyrdom of life imprisonment. In a certain sense all this was already true for the old core of the Red Army Faction, but now there seems to be a "logic" to the intensification of such tendencies. The logic of an increasing loss of experience and reality is now complemented by the logic of an increasing particularization and depoliticization of action-oriented interpretations of reality. We thus observe one of the mechanisms by which a form of illegal struggle, initiated on the basis of socialist premises, assumes features of a right-wing form of violent criminality. With this I come to the second stage in my reflections.

I would like to call attention to two closely connected mechanisms, which seem to account for the fact that a form of illegal struggle conceived in a revolutionary fashion has resulted in an interplay of terror and reaction. The first concerns the psychosocial situation of the terrorists; the second the sociopolitical consequences of terrorism.

The first mechanism has been described, convincingly I believe, by Michael "Bommi" Baumann in his account of his experiences, *Wie alles anfing* [How it all began], and by Horst Mahler in a television interview. Baumann and Mahler both describe how, under conditions of illegality, conspiratorial mimicry, and increasing pressure from the outside world, the experiential and communicative gains of the anti-authoritarian phase of the student movement were lost. The isolation of the group from the outside world resulted in its being cut off from the experiences, needs, and learning processes of those on whose behalf it had decided to act. The growing external pressures and the group's survival problems had the result that the group's relation to the outside world was reduced more and more to primitive forms of strategy; people appeared as little more than character masks that were valued differently according to different strategies ("pigs," sympathizers, traitors). And finally the growing pressure from the outside world turned back on the group itself. The external loss of experience and reality was equally an internal loss of experience and communication. Thus their very life conditions forced the terrorists to assimilate the most inhumane features of the apparatus they were fighting. After having declared the naked terror that the system spreads to its periphery (Vietnam) to be the system's sole reality, they themselves adopted a form of struggle instantiating this very feature of the system: the reduction of all life processes to the spreading of terror. "Bommi" Baumann has portrayed this mechanism in particularly drastic fashion:

Although the whole point had always been to get away from Siemens, all of a sudden you are back there again. There you stand with short hair, with a suit, with everything just as you had left it, and all the people react . . . in exactly the same way; they are as callous as ever. Your have toiled all these years, done everything, and all of a sudden here you are right back where you started. . . . This is what has made everyone kaput—the psychological difficulties within the group. These things happen everywhere, but they are more easily overcome if you have a broader outward perspective. Or there were learning processes, where occasionally strangers were present with whom you could discuss things; that's the way it was in all the communes. . . . You develop only predatory instincts, and then you run around like a gunman. Of course any sharp eye could recognize you. What you are doing is madness—always running around with a gun. A man who runs around with a gun shifts his center to the weapon; your center is where you carry the gun. . . . You have only business relations with others. When you meet someone, all you say is "You've got to take care of this, you've got to rent this apartment, and in three days we'll meet here on this corner." If he criticizes you for any reason, you just say, "That doesn't interest me in the least." Either you play along or you don't play at all; it's as simple as that. You become like the apparatus that you are fighting; in the end it has caught up with you.[11]

The second mechanism to which I would like to make reference concerns the social and political consequences of terrorism. Since the terrorists have deliberately cut themselves off from the needs, experiences, and learning processes of their social surroundings, and since their strategy already contains an element of contempt for the masses who supposedly are to be liberated by them, it is little wonder that their actions have elicited responses ranging from perplexity to disgust in the vast majority of the population. In view of the weakness of republican traditions in Germany, it was easy under these circumstances to use a form of violent criminality understood as "leftist" and "social-critical" as the pretext for the criminalization of leftist and social-critical positions. Thus terrorism has furnished the legitimation for a form of political repression directed against the entire left, one now threatening the substance of the liberal constitutional state in which we have lived since the end of World War II. But the preservation of a democratic republic remains the first condition of existence for a socialist left that wants more and better things than the forms of democracy and public life possible within the capitalist systems of the present. Because the terrorists accomplish nothing aside from supplying publicly influential legitimations for the restriction of basic democratic rights, because they provide legitimations for a defamation of the entire left and its theories, and because they themselves have long since terminated all solidarity with the democratic left, one has no choice (if one still wishes to apply political categories) but to term the objective content of their action reactionary. Oskar Negt is therefore quite correct in speaking of a "pincer movement" of terrorism and reaction, one directed against the democratic republic in general and the socialist left in particular.

It may seem that I have thus far ignored an essential, perhaps the most essential, dimension in the problematic of terrorism: the moral dimension. But in fact this is not the case. Thus far I have been proceeding on the assumption that there are a priori arguments against the use of physical violence against individuals and in particular arguments against the taking of human life; the validity of such arguments should be self-evident to every socialist. Accordingly physical force, the graver and more irrevocable it is, requires a special legitimation that in particular instances suspends such arguments. That there are situations in which counterforce, including killing, can be morally justified is something that as a rule not even liberals contest. Examples would be situations in which violence is the only possible means of successfully resisting an intolerable form of oppression or an intolerable form of moral corruption. In certain situations there may even be a moral obligation to engage in a physical form of resistance or to make use of physical force. But whoever adopts violence imposes upon himself a heavy burden of proof. If it can be shown that the justification for violence derives from a system of delusion, that it is the product of illusion and self-deception, then the result must be not only a moral condemnation of violent actions but also a judgment on the "moral pathology" of the perpetrators of violence—even when their actions, as with some terrorists, assume the form of moral selflessness.

To this I would like to add that there are good reasons why I only now make explicit the moral implications of my previous remarks. Direct moral condemnation of terrorism normally reveals, no less than the justification of violence by the terrorists, features of rationalization and interested self-deception. The language of morals is also a means of domination. The moral critique of terrorism becomes pure hypocrisy when joined with the silent toleration, rationalization, or even open justification of forms of state-organized terrorism of a technologically programmed disdain for human life. The terrorists' disdain for moral norms is, however, only a reflex of the ideological function these norms perform in society. If it were possible to redirect the moral energies vented today against the terrorists in the direction of a humanization of society and thereby free those energies of their repressive and ideological character, the problem of terrorism would take care of itself. The terrorists' fundamental illusion consists in their assumption that such a redirection of moral energies and the concomitant alteration of modes of experience, interpretations of needs, and attitudes could be a consequence of their armed struggle.

II

Having characterized the terrorism of the 70s in the Federal Republic as a form of political struggle that has become pathological, I would like to make some comments on the question of where we might most reasonably look for explanations of this pathology of moral-political consciousness. I should emphasize that it is not my intention to add a new explanation to what is already a long list of attempted explanations—explanations indeed usually fashioned for purposes of political expediency. My aim is not, for instance, to show that in place of the alleged cause of terrorism—"critical theory"—other causal factors can be designated. An explanatory approach of this nature would presuppose thorough empirical investigations. It would presuppose in particular the reconstruction of the obviously different biographies of individual terrorists. Yet I believe that this sort of empirical investigation could contribute to a real understanding of terrorism only if it were linked to a proper interpretation of those problems, contradictions, and pathologies that are generated by society and that represent the social matrix within which terrorism could first arise as one of many possible forms of reaction. To be more precise, I think it is futile to attempt to understand terrorism (1) if one does not treat it as an expression of legitimation problems and system pathologies in our society, (2) if one does not explain the irrationalist, existentialist, and actionistic elements that it shares to some extent with other strategies of refusal as they are developed within the political sphere everywhere in late-capitalist systems, and (3) if one does not elucidate how the system's pathologies are reproduced in the way in which the terrorists process the experience of these pathologies.

I have already indicated why I think the most promising explanatory strategies are to be found in theoretical approaches deriving from the orbit of Marxist or critical social science. The virtue of such theoretical approaches lies in the fact that they cannot be extricated from their relation to either practical political or philosophical discourse, since they represent systematized attempts at self-understanding on the part of acting individuals about their social situation. They lead not to "value-neutral," technically exploitable prognostic knowledge, but— at least under optimal conditions—to the enlightenment and self-enlightenment of acting individuals about the significance and possibilities of their social praxis. In what follows I shall indicate very provisionally where I see the theoretical potential of critical theory and how I think it can aid us in achieving a better understanding— and thus a more thorough assessment—of contemporary terrorism.

Let us begin by looking to the legitimation problems and systemic pathologies of our society. Relying on Marx, Weber, and Lukács, Adorno and Horkheimer have already analyzed the development of capitalist societies as a process of technical and bureaucratic "rationalization" detached from the sphere of practical rationality. For them this was a process in which the increasing destruction of external nature was complemented by an increasing technical and manipulative control of the individual's internal nature as well as an increasing bureaucratic administration of social relations. This autonomization of instrumental rationality corresponds to a persistence of relations of violence even where violence does not appear in the unveiled form of terror itself—be it in the case of fascism or on the edges of democratically organized industrial societies (as in Vietnam). If one analyzes modern industrial societies from the perspective of a structural violence maintaining itself in the technical-bureaucratic processes of rationalization and under the cover of democratic constitutional institutions— a structural violence that permeates the social relations of individuals as well as their psychic constitution—then it is self-evident that individual terrorism can at best appear as an impotent form of resistance that remains subject to the logic of the system and that, to a certain extent, brings the latter to its culmination. But a theory that understands the reality of capitalist industrial societies as a tendentially totalizing network of delusion can in fact no longer account for the source of critical intentions and experiences in terms of which it would be possible to call into question the universe of instrumental rationality. If the older critical theory, beginning with the *Dialectic of Enlightenment*, can be reproached for anything in conjunction with the question of terrorism, it would have to be the fact that—in ironic agreement with the "suspicion of terrorism" critique being fashioned today for the entire left—it hardly permits the envisaging of forms of emancipatory praxis that are not already infected by the irrationality of the system against which they are directed. But in reality it is a long way from this reproach to that of the right, which, far from challenging the resignative features of critical theory, seeks to criminalize its critical content.

In line with classic Marxist forms of critical theory I want to claim, first, that the reproduction process of capitalist societies generates contradictions and crises, in terms of which the reproduction of these systems, under the two boundary conditions of the private exploitation of capital and representative democracy, appears at least tendentially problematic. In opposition to Marx, however, I assume that an analysis of the crisis-nexus of captitalist societies is not sufficient to demarcate unequivocally their "systemic limitations." In opposition to both Marx and the critical theory of Horkheimer and Adorno, I assume further that this crisis-nexus has no objectively unequivocal meaning—neither one that entails the necessary emergence of a classless society, nor one that entails the realization of a universe of instrumental reason, which closes itself off ever more effectively against practical reason.

Second, in line with recent developments in critical theory (Habermas, Offe, Castoriadis), I wish to claim that the system-threatening contradictions and crises of capitalism are no longer to be sought primarily at the level of the economic system, but instead are to be understood above all as problems of legitimation, motivation, and administration.[12] These are the contradictions and crises that today seem to represent the essential points of departure for regressive and terrorist forms of "dropping out" of society and of radical refusal. What needs to be understood is how the short-circuited manner of experiencing and processing problems and contradictions found with the terrorists is connected to these problems and contradictions. It is to this question that I now offer a few suggestions inspired above all by the analyses of Habermas.

The problems and contradictions I have in mind concern the bourgeois system of legitimation as well as the bourgeois life-form itself: (1) the democratic constitutional self-interpretation of Western industrial societies; (2) the bourgeois ethic of achievement; and (3) the forms of life that are privatistically centered on the nuclear family and on professional career.

The basic moral-political norms of the bourgeois-liberal republic no longer appear credible, first of all, because there exists no corresponding democratic-moral quality of everyday life and because they enunciate no obvious connection between political decision-making processes on the one hand and individuals' experiences, needs, and possibilities for action on the other. Thus it seems that the advancing processes of rationalization and bureaucratization both promote and impede the active participation of individuals subject to them.[13] Second, these norms seem to lack credibility both because they are frequently contradicted by the injustices and conditions of exploitation reproduced by capitalist systems and because they appear powerless against the apparatus and the destructive consequences of economic and social progress. And finally, they lack credibility because they are employed according to the needs of the ruling elites to mask and justify imperialist power relations between First and Third World countries. The ersatz ideology of economic growth and the "objective exigencies" resulting from the imperatives of economic growth can supposedly compensate for this legitimation deficiency within bourgeois-liberal democracy as long, and only as long, as problems of securing material existence and increasing private consumption remain effective as the basic focal points of political behavior. This is clearly no longer, or no longer exclusively, the case for radical minorites, countercultural movements, "dropouts," or the variously constituted forms of extraparliamentary political organization and initiative.

The bourgeois achievement ethic loses its credibility to the degree that a proportionate relation between objective qualification and professional success can no longer be structurally guaranteed and also to the degree that a proportionate relation between the adaptation to performance pressures and the possibility of a meaningful and fulfilled life can no longer be experienced.

Finally, the traditional norms of bourgeois life, privatistically oriented to family and the professional career of the husband, and the corresponding virtues of discipline and the planning rationality linked to the capacity for delayed gratification, also lose their plausibilty. And they do so to the degree that the advancing process of rationalization destroys the traditional foundation of the meaning of family and profession without generating the potential for an existentially experienced sense of meaning capable of supplanting the bourgeois form of life. This point obviously affects men and women differently in view of their differing conditions of life and socialization, especially since, with the breakdown in the legitimations for the traditional sex role division within a patriarchal society, women now recognize themselves as the oppressed and underprivileged half of society. Certainly there exists a problem of emancipation for men as well as for women, but that problem is not present in the same manner or with the same immediacy. Men still have at their disposal the socially recognized role models and identification patterns furnished in their processes of socialization; they *can* adopt these models, even if, as ever, at the price of repressing conflicts or suppressing needs. For women, however, this is true only to a much lesser degree; for the most part they are confronted today with a system of role expectations that is in itself contradictory, one in which the conflicting roles are for them often at once inescapable and unacceptable. Therefore they are provided with scarcely any role models or identification patterns that do not already incorporate structurally identity conflicts, lack or loss of social recognition, or threats to an affirmative self-image. For this reason the problem of meaning appears to women more massively and more inescapably than it does to men as a problem of emancipation, for which the existing (male) society provides no ready solutions. Any elucidation of the specific motivational background of female terrorists would certainly have to take these circumstances into consideration.[14]

Somewhat simplistically, one could speak of two "main zones" of contradiction or legitimation deficiency. The first concerns the contradiction between, on the one hand, universal norms of freedom, human dignity, self-determination and rational discourse, which are embedded in political institutions and the socialization processes of individuals; and, on the other hand, the structures of a society that continually reproduces injustice, oppression, destruction, and practical irrationality and is also cynically inclined to repudiate its own normative claims when the defense of positions of domination is at stake, be they internal or external (in relation to Third World countries). Here I am concerned with the structural contradiction between normative claims and social reality, which could be eliminated only through either the abolition of the boundary conditions of capitalist production or the complete forfeiture of the normative claims connected with it. The latter is in any case not possible as long as the universalist norms of bourgeois society are still embedded in the political institutions and socialization processes of capitalist societies.

The second main zone of legitimation deficiency pertains to the discrepancy between systemic structures and necessities and the conditions for the formation of a strong identity and a meaningful life. Here we are directly concerned with the immediate living conditions of individuals. The processes of technical and bureaucratic rationalization produced by the structure of the system destroy—together with the imperatives of economic growth—traditions, traditional forms of life and modes of orientation, and thus the last traditionalist foundations for a strong identity, without simultaneously generating the foundations for a universalistically constituted particularity, that is, the possibility of a meaningful life under the conditions of a consciousness that has become universalist. The degree of alienation, atomization, fragmentation, and uprooting that develops with the complexity of modern industrial systems, dramatically surpasses what Hegel analyzed as the "loss of ethical life" in civil society. For those traditions, historically evolved modes of life, and traditionalist models of interpretation, to which with compensatory intent conservatives are today happily appealing once again, are either destroyed or annulled by a societal reproductive nexus that long ago became entwined with state functions, that is, by economic growth and technical-bureaucratic rationalization. To be sure, this process of destruction is not necessarily a process of enlightenment, as Marx and Engels apparently still believed when they wrote:

All fixed, fast-frozen relations, with their train of ancient and venerable prejudices and opinions, are swept away, all new-formed ones become antiquated before they can ossify. All that is solid melts into air, all that is holy is profaned, and man is at last compelled to face with sober senses his real conditions of life and his relations with his kind.[15]

But this process could be arrested in its destructive consequences only if it were brought to a conclusion *as* a process of enlightenment; conservative strategies can only arrest enlightenment and intensify the repressive force of the system without, however, resuscitating traditions *as* traditions. The loss of ethical life generated by the reproductive process of industrial systems can be compensated for only through democratic forms of organization that would again bring the total societal process into an intelligible connection with everyday reality and the needs of individuals.

The two problem zones I have designated are of course closely connected. Both designate social conditions under which it is becoming ever more improbable that systemic necessities, a universalized consciousness, and the claims and needs of individuals could still be combined to make possible a simultaneously just and good life.

The pathologies of consciousness that result in this way are, it seems to me, multiple in nature. I only wish to mention a few that I believe are apparent even to an eye unschooled in sociopsychological analysis.

1. The dessication of spheres of practical rationality and therewith a reduction of practical problems to technical-instrumental ones.

2. Regression to a preuniversalist state of moral consciousness and a return to the modes of solidarity, emotional security, and meaningful life that thereby seem—spuriously—to have been rendered possible.

3. All those forms of pathology that result from the repression of conflicts that individuals can no longer resolve and of their needs and demands—at least to the extent that these fall outside the socially sanctioned interpretation of needs and the economically established mechanism for their satisfaction.

4. A new cult of immediacy, of forms of actionist and existentialist coping with life, in which the complexity of social reality is effectively suppressed and in which meaning and identity are sought at the expense of reality and are stabilized and lived out in forms of direct solidarity.

5. An inurement of a violated moral consciousness to a reality that can be perceived only as a network of total deception, as absolute evil; such moral consciousness necessarily remains abstract and can interpret reality only in the form of delusionary systems.

6. The redogmatization of a consciousness that has lost all certainties of traditional life-orientations, world-views, and identity-guaranteeing interpretive systems and that is unable to perceive any conditions allowing for the harmonization of needs for meaning-constitutive interpretations with the norms of critical rationality.

I am not able to indicate in what specific combination these pathologies of consciousness reappear in terrorist groups. Here it is important to show both that terrorism stands much closer to the notion of normality possible in this society than our professional defenders of state would like to believe and that it reflects and brings to a head the pathologies of the system against which it is directed. Were one interested in further explaining terrorism, one would have to become more specific. Thus in addition to the fact that terrorist forms of guerilla warfare in Third World countries or in Ireland have a different meaning and different roots than terrorism in highly industrialized nations—despite the now-apparent international connections—it is necessary to take into account specific cultural, social, and historical differences of the respective systems even when comparing, say, the Red Army Faction and the Red Brigade. In Germany, for instance, the emergence of terrorism seems hardly comprehensible without the background of an unmastered fascist past and without considering the fact that the republican form of government resulted not from a historical process of emancipation but from the defeat of fascism. In Germany the legitimation deficiencies of the system have something of a personal note, because they are connected with a specific legitimation deficiency of the older toward the younger generation. And this deficiency has a particularly historical note, because it is related to the problems of a political tradition in which a monarchical or an authoritarian political order has, in case of doubt, always taken precedence over individual liberties, and in which, for this reason, obedience and discipline—even in the face of state-organized terror—have always been viewed with less suspicion than the critical questioning of decayed orders and authorities.

III

Thus to speak of German conditions is simultaneously to speak of a still-unmastered past whose weight leans oppressively into the German present. Here I am referring to a continuity that, as already indicated, subsists in the Federal Republic beneath the surface of democratic institutions. This is the continuity between a republican form of government and an authoritarian past, anchored in political attitudes, modes of behavior, and traditions and, of course, in individuals. It accounts for the fact that in Germany the democratic republic is threatened from opposite ends: by the bureaucratic apparatus of domination with technically perfected possibilites for control and manipulation; and by the vestiges of an authoritarian past.

Certainly it is this continuity that accounts in part for fact that in the Federal Republic the forces of a democratic renewal are constantly being pushed into what often appears as a hopelessly defensive role. It is also a part of this continuity that in the German public's consciousness the word "terrorism" is still reserved largely for *all* forms of violent guerilla and liberation movements, regardless of whether they are the senseless acts of violence by German urban guerillas or emancipatory forms of armed struggle against exploitation, dictatorship, and torture in the countries of the Third World. At the same time state-organized terror, although it has consequences far more terrifying for the populations of the affected countries than the violent acts of scattered leftists, can always count on excusatory words from German politicians and the German media—at least as long as this terror is not practiced by Communist regimes. The German public's thresholds of sensitivity are differentiated accordingly. When on the occasion of his—admittedly, more than "uncouth"—attempt to articulate a moral-political critique of terrorism (summary: "Our road to socialism . . . cannot be paved with corpses"), "Mescalero" did not defend but in a self-critical fashion fully admitted to feeling a "secret delight" at the murder of Chief Federal Prosecutor Buback, a cry of outrage rippled through the media—even the *Frankfurter Rundschau* spoke of a "naked fascism" (May 8, 1977), and a large-scale police operation accented the public agitation.[16] The attempt by forty-eight professors and lawyers to counter the mounting hysteria over the leftist "slough of [terrorist] sympathizers" in the universities, by making the complete text of the controversial "obituary" available to a systematically uninformed public, not only failed to achieve its desired aim but actually backfired on its authors and led to one of the most harrowing episodes in the struggle against the possible or presumed "sympathizers" with terror.[17] Yet when a leading defender of the liberal-democratic constitutional state like Franz Josef Strauss proclaims his by no means secret delight with the successes of the Chilean military dictatorship in its struggle for freedom and democracy in that country, he need not fear an outraged German public—and not simply because Chile is far away.[18]

In Germany the concept of a liberal-democratic order has undergone peculiar semantic transformations—with the consequence that this order is not only associated with a capitalist economy, as in other Western nations, but is also being interpreted by means of such concepts as order, discipline, state, and security. One could even say that this concept has been semantically adapted, in a sometimes terrifying manner, to the authoritarian elements of the German tradition.[19] A corresponding political perspective obscures the contours of a terror intertwined with order, a state-organized terror, and yet is especially quick to notice terror in the immediate vicinity of a critique that recalls the unfulfilled promises contained in the concepts of freedom and democracy. In the end a freedom, or that part of it not integrated into the existing order, is for conservatives again pregnant with "terror"—as if the German problem did not consist in being terrified of freedom.[20]

The attempt to link social criticism with terrorism in fact conceals the interplay of terrorism and reaction. It goes hand in hand with the efforts to derive, from the terrorism of the Red Army Faction and related groups, legitimations for a restriction of basic democratic rights, for an intensification of political repression, and for the introduction of elements of a penal law based on opinion (and sentiment) into the German legal code. The tendency toward a step-by-step restriction of democratic liberties has in recent years led to a situation where the articulation of radical critique and the critical concern for basic democratic rights have increasingly become matters of personal risk, especially for members of the younger generation (but not only for them, as the Brückner case demonstrates).[21] Once again the readiness to conform is valued more highly in Germany than those virtues without which a democratically constituted republic must degenerate into an authoritarian state. This tendency is further characterized by the fact that even in legal decisions, and no longer merely in the rhetoric of politicians and the practice of governmental bureaucracies, sectors of the existing social order are equated increasingly with the basic core of the country's republican constitution. Thus at the official level as well, the liberal-democratic basic order is becoming ever more synonymous with the real power relations and economic structures of our society. Under these conditions every form of criticism and critical analysis that calls attention to the unfulfilled promises contained in the republican canons of basic rights and liberties becomes an attack on the constitution and thus is deemed inimical to the constitution.

The creeping criminalization of critical positions fulfills at least three distinct functions. (1) It has features of a process of repression, serving the restoration of a good conscience in the face of the pathologies of the system identified by social critics. (2) It furnishes a legitimation for the intensification of political repression. (3) It performs the task of identifying scapegoats. If the left in general and the leftist theorists in particular are responsible for terrorism, then society no longer needs to recognize in the terrorists a mirror image of its own unsolved problems; instead it can shift the blame for these problems to its critics and thus attempt to solve them by reducing the critics to silence.

The insight into the connection of terrorism and reaction, as well as the recognition that the defense of the democratic republic has today become a question of survival for the socialist left, should certainly also serve as an occasion within the left for a critical and in some cases even self-critical reflection on the *meaning* of a defense of basic bourgeois-democratic rights and liberties. With this I come to a few concluding remarks, in which I would like to indicate the sense in which terrorism should also function as an occasion for the left to clarify its own positions. I am concerned primarily with the question, basic to the Marxist tradition, of the proper distinction between the ideological and the progressive content of bourgeois-liberal democracy. The old and justified reproach regarding the latter's merely "formal" character is connected with the view that bourgeois parliamentary democracy is the political form of capitalist class domination. As Rosa Luxemburg recognized, this can only mean that it is not democratic enough, it impedes the extension of forms of democratic self-determination to all spheres of social life, including the sphere of material production, which according to the bourgeois understanding of democracy is prepolitical and thus should remain outside the sphere of the democratic will-formation. Accordingly a democracy would be "material" that could be experienced as a form of freedom permeating the social life context as a whole and thus determining the everyday life of individuals. In the Marxist tradition this has been linked to the expectation that with the overcoming of the limits of bourgeois democracy—following the abolition of capitalist forms of private property—forms of social life would be developed in which it would be possible to combine freedom, solidarity, and a no longer obstructed form of individual self-realization. I believe that we must now concede that we cannot know to what extent and in what sense a future form of social life can approximate the ideal. This problem did not exist for classical Marxism and classical anarchism, at least in the form in which it is posed for us, since both assumed (secretly or openly) that it was only necessary to overcome specific obstacles—capitalist private property, the state, or traces of alienation in individuals—and freedom would then unfold in an unobstructed fashion. Such a model derives its plausibility from situations of oppression or enslavement experienced as intolerable; included here are such metaphors as "breaking the chains." From a social-theoretical standpoint, however, this model becomes false to the extent that it purports to interpret negative conditions as the empirically necessary and sufficient conditions for social freedom, even if this happens, as in Marxist theory, only with reference to a specific phase of historical development. Either the conditions assumed to be necessary are not sufficient (abolition of private ownership of the means of production); or they are sufficient only because what is thought to inhere in them coincides with freedom itself (overcoming of alienation, of class domination, and so on). That a corresponding problem did not properly exist for Marx stems not least of all from the fact that the negative definition of the conditions for emancipation was originally incorporated into his theory in the sense of a dialectical negation of a negation—one best understood in terms of a historicophilosophical temporaliztion of the dialectic of division and reconcilation found in Hegel's *Philosophy of Right*. But Marx was never really able to work this dialectical figure into his historico-materialist theory, and it was left behind as a historicometaphysical residue.

But this implies that even the positive conditions for an anticipated future form of social freedom require specification if this anticipation is not to drift aimlessly into the void. It is certainly correct to say that such specification can itself only be the result of historical praxis—in the sense in which Marx had spoken of the "discovery" of the political form of the commune. But this merely transfers the problem to a different level, at least as long as one adheres to the notion of a theoretical clarification of emancipatory practice. For now the problem is posed in the sense that theory must have an adequate concept of already existing forms of freedom, if it wishes to anticipate emanci-pation not as a mere negation but as a "sublation" of this freedom. Mere fantasizings of future forms of freedom without a clear con-sciousness of historically achieved—however inadequate—existing forms of freedom can only lead to an abstract negation of existing reality and thus do not even correspond to the strict standards set by Marxist theory itself. But the consciousness of already existing forms of freedom is also the consciousness of those (positive) conditions under which alone social transformations could occur as processes of emancipation. It is, in other words, a consciousness of what remains a (minimal) condition for the possibility of rational freedom in a world imaginable to us.

In advancing these considerations I do not wish to plead for a restriction of practical-emancipatory fantasy; my aim is rather to criticize a false form of fantasizing revolutionary consciousness. Thus once again I return, albeit with a changed perspective, to the reproach of mere "formalism" leveled against bourgeois democracy. This reproach is raised by a segment of the Marxist left, at least that which bases itself on Lenin, in a way that differentiates it from the one mentioned earlier. According to this critique the universal and formal guarantees of rights characteristic of bourgeois-liberal democracy, in particular the guarantees of constitutional rights, are as a whole the mere expression of bourgeois class domination and are thus superfluous under conditions of socialist democracy. In the meantime, however, we have been able to amass enough historical experience to know that this view contains a fateful error, which can lead to the replacement of a formal by a material democracy tantamount in this second sense to the abolition of democracy and thus at the same time to the prevention of socialism. Against this view it has now become an question of survival for the left to develop a clear consciousness not only of the ideological and repressive content but also the progressive and emancipatory content of bourgeois-liberal democracy. This is the question that today distinguishes the democratic left from the dogmatic neo-Stalinist left. For the democratic left the defense of constitutional rights and democratic liberties within our society can never be merely a tactical question; rather, by defending such rights and liberties the left also defends its own future conditions of existence.

Political concepts cannot be detached from the historicopolitical contexts in which they originate. Nonetheless it might be time to redefine politically the concepts "left" and "right" in terms of the relation of political groups to democratic-republican forms of self-determination. One could then once and for all abandon to the right the cynicism regarding the unfulfilled promises of a democratic republic. To be sure, "leftist" terrorism would not thereby become "rightist" terrorism; but the left itself—the democratic left—could more effectively defend itself against attempts at criminalization for which the

Albrecht Wellmer

delusions and acts of violence by a self-appointed radical vanguard supply the pretexts. This, too, would contribute to a resolution of the problem of terrorism.

Notes

1. This text is based on a lecture I delivered in May 1978 at a symposium entitled "Terrorism and the Critique of Society," organized by the philosophy department of the University of Heidelberg. An abridged version was published in the *Frankfurter Rundschau* in July 1978, and for the purposes of the present publication I have revised the text once again, especially sections I and III. So as not to obscure altogether the context in which my reflections originated, I have retained the original lecture format of the text. Although the immediate occasion for the lecture has in the interim lost some of its topicality, there is little to suggest that any fundamental change has taken place in the political situation that in the past produced such occasions.

The original text of the lecture met with massive criticism, and not only from the right. To the extent that I have found these criticims justified, I have attempted to learn from them; I am not certain how successful I have been.

2. Rote Armee Faktion, "Das Konzept Stadtguerilla," in *Texte der RAF* (Lund, 1977), p. 337ff., esp. p. 355ff.

3. Kollekitv RAF, *Über den bewaffneten Kampf in Westeuropa* (Berlin: Wagenbach-Rotbuch), p. 43.

4. "Erklärung zur Sache" (January 1976), in Schwarze Hilfe, ed. *Der Tod Ulrike Meinhof: Dokumentation*, p. 121.

5. *Texte der RAF*, p. 260.

6. Ibid., p. 252.

7. Ibid., p. 253.

8. Stammheim is the federal maximum security prison, located near Stuttgart, that was constructed to house terrorists. In October 1977 three members of the original Red Army Faction core in prison there (Andreas Baader, Gudrun Ensslin, and Jan-Carl Raspe) were found dead in their cells. The official explanation for their death was suicide, but, as Wellmer indicates, this claim was viewed with skepticism by many members of the left. (*tr.*)

9. *Texte der RAF*, p. 247.

10. Ibid., pp. 253–54.

11. "Bommi" Baumann, *Wie alles anfing* (Frankfurt: [Gemeinschaftausgabe], 1976), pp. 115–28.

12. See especially J. Habermas, *Legitimation Crisis*, translated by Thomas McCarthy (Boston: Beacon Press, 1975); C. Offe, *Strukturprobleme des kapitalistischen Staates* (Frankfurt, 1973); C. Castoriadis, *Postscript zur Neudefinition der Revolution* (Berlin: MAO-Leaflet, 1974).

13. Castoriadis, *Postscipt*, p. 33.

14. An attempt in this direction is found in Ilse Korte-Pucklitsch, "Warum werden Frauen Terroristen?" *Merkur* 357 (February 1978). See also S. von Paczensky, ed., *Frauen und Terror* (Hamburg, 1978).

15. Lewis S. Feuer, ed., *Marx & Engels: Basic Writings on Politics and Philosophy* (Garden City, NY: Anchor Books, 1959), p. 10.

16. "Mescalero" is the name for a group of anarchists who fashioned themselves as "urban Indians." In 1977 a Mescalero group at the University of Göttingen published an "obituary" for Chief Federal Prosecutor Buback, who in the spring of that year was killed in a terrorist attack. In it they professed to a type of "secret delight" (*klammheimliche Freude*) over Buback's death, although, as Wellmer indicates, this was by no means intended to condone terrorism itself. (*tr.*)

17. See P. Brückner, ed., *Die Mescalero-Affäre*, 3rd ed. (Hannover, 1978).

18. *Die Zeit*, December 12, 1977.

19. Two randomly selected examples: (1) The flowing transitions between such words as "detrimental to the state" (*staatsabträglich*) and "unconstitutional" (*verfassungswidrig*) as used by politicians and the police. On account of "behavior detrimental to the state," Helmut Gollwitzer was expelled from Berlin in 1940 by the Gestapo. In Hannover the police reported the "*staatsabträglich*" behavior of a person involved in the preparation of an activity of Amnesty International to the Office for the Protection of the Constitution. See P. Brückner, D. Damm, and J. Seifert, *1984 schon heute—oder war hat Angst vorm Verfassungsschutz* (Frankfurt, 1977), p. 29.

(2) The expression "the preventive protection of the state" (*Vorverlegung des Staatschutzes*) (against internal enemies) was already (or still) used in 1951 in a parliamentary debate during the Korean War in connection with an intensification of penal law for political crimes. It derives, as R. Schmid has shown, from Roland Freisler [chief justice of the Nazi supreme court]. See Hans Schueler, "Der Justiz den Spiegel vorgehalten," *Die Zeit*, March 30, 1979.

20. Compare H. Lübbe, "Freiheit und Terror," *Merkur* (September 1977).

21. The politically outspoken Hannover psychology professor who was suspended from his university position for his part in the publication of the text of the Mescalero obituary. Brückner, incidentally, was one of the speakers participating in the symposium where Wellmer delivered the present paper. His invitation had prompted the rector of the University of Heidelberg to prohibit the philosophy department from holding the symposium on university premises; it took place in a municipal auditorium. (*tr.*)

What Is the Germans' Fatherland?

Horst Ehmke

Ecstatic over the Wars of Liberation, Ernst Moritz Arndt asked himself a question he then answered in a rhyme as much euphoric as apolitical: "Wherever the German tongue is heard, wherever God in heaven sings songs, this, brave German, is what you shall call your own." The designation of the sphere of the German language as "the German fatherland" was in view of, say, the political development of Switzerland or the Netherlands, already anachronistic in 1813. And the invocation of the dear Lord for the brave, song-singing Germans was an apolitical evasion of the question of what, after all, is or should be and could be the inner dimension of this fatherland.

With no other people has the question of a fatherland been posed so frequently as with the Germans. Never have they been certain of an answer. Germany was and is in fact a difficult fatherland. In their *Xenien* Goethe and Schiller gave the Germans the following advice: "You hope in vain, Germans, to form yourselves into a nation; develop yourselves instead, as certainly you can, more freely into human beings." In the ensuing decades there followed a development from cosmopolitanism to chauvinism, one eliciting from Grillparzer the deep, heartfelt sigh: "From humanity through nationality to bestiality"—something that today sounds like a premonition of the Nazi regime. "What characterizes the Germans," Friedrich Nietzsche mocked, "is that with them the question, 'What is German?' never dies out."

The external dimension of the "German question" has been aptly circumscribed in the notion of the "belated nation." Whereas in England, France, and the United States a politically and economically strong *Bürgertum*, or liberal middle class, had long since combined national unity with civil liberties, Germany continued to rest on the remnants of what the Thirty Years War and the Peace of Westphalia had left behind of the "Holy Roman Empire of the German Nation." The first rearrangement of the medieval empire oriented to state sovereignty was forced by Napoleon. The existence of a multiplicity of small and middle-sized states dominated by the Austro-Prussian dualism ensured that the national question would remain open.

The absence of political unity dictated that the budding feeling of German nationality would first be determined by cultural considerations—the common language of Luther, common customs, common songs, and later common literature, philosophy, and science. It is no coincidence that the concept of the "cultural nation," intended equally to bridge religious differences, developed on German soil. Only with the struggle against Napoleon were political considerations to assume a dominant role with regard to German national feeling. Thus for us as well the idea of unity was fused in a broad front with that of freedom. Yet the demand for freedom was understood—as is indicated by, say, the rhyme of Ernst Moritz Arndt—essentially in an external fashion: namely, as one directed against Napoleon. The demand for freedom from the traditional ruling powers was not equated with the "national" demand for liberty. This was a concern of the liberals.

The internal-political hope vested in the Wars of Liberation was shattered at the Vienna Congress, under Metternich, through the European restoration. The attempt of our *Bürgertum* to attain at once national unity and civil freedom—"better freedom without unity than unity without freedom," as it was claimed at the Badenweiler Festival, Pentecost, 1823 (Karl von Rotteck's famous and vilified formula)—failed conclusively with the bourgeois-liberal revolution of 1848–49. The forces of reaction regained the upper hand over a weak and politically inexperienced *Bürgertum*, which, to the extent that it did not emigrate, made its peace with the authoritarian state after 1849. The call for democracy and parliamentarianism in political life had begun to be replaced by a call for the legal-constitutional (*rechtstaatliche*) taming of the authoritarian state. The more the *Bürgertum* withdrew from politics the more resolutely it applied itself to the tasks of rapid economic and industrial development, for which the German Customs Union (*Zollverein*), established in 1834 on Prussian initiative, had already created a "small-German" framework.

After 1848–49 the national question, which had hitherto been connected with the questions of unity and freedom, passed into the hands of the conservatives, but at the cost of the question of freedom. In the period from 1866 to 1871 the question of unity was decided from above, in Bismarck's diplomatic preparations and finally in "blood and iron." What the *Bürgertum* had not been able to accomplish was apparently now achieved through Prussian power. At issue for Bismarck in this small-German solution was less the national question than the power of Prussia, or Prussia-Germany. Austria was excluded, a state of affairs that in domestic politics led to the internal division of the liberals. For a minority the establishment of the Reich appeared, in view of the European background of German history, to be as artificial as the Prussian state itself. Yet the great majority of the *Bürgertum* truly worshipped Bismarck and his success. The political right acquired a national prestige to which the *Bürgertum* submitted at the expense of the internal-political development of Germany. The domestic dimension of the establishment of the Reich, of the belated struggle for the nation-state, became the political tragedy of the German *Bürgertum* and thus the tragedy of the nation in the bourgeois-liberal period.

In the Reich wrought by Bismarckian obstinacy the *Bürgertum* left politics to Bismarck in order to apply itself all the more energetically to the pursuit of its own economic interests. Its political silence was made golden in the truest sense of the word. Even the national liberals gave up the call for parliamentarianism in the Reich; and they betrayed their own principles when in 1878, they—unlike the Catholic Center party (*Zentrum*), who had already gone through the experience of the Bismarckian *Kulturkampf*—voted for the special law against the Social Democratic party. With the fateful approval of this attack on the internal unity of the nation, the German *Bürgertum* placed itself in opposition to the democratic left, now represented primarily by the young workers' movement. In view of this failure of the *Bürgertum*, the workers' movement, having inherited many of the weaknesses of German liberalism, found itself confronted with the double task of fighting for both political and social democracy. But the *Bürgertum*, its political back already broken—hemmed in between the authoritarian state, with which it had made its hollow peace, and the emerging workers' movement—developed such a fear of the left that even now it cannot refrain from defaming the democratic left: from "comrades without a fatherland" (*vaterlandlose Gesellen*) to "freedom or socialism."

Economic dynamism coupled with political backwardness is what characterized the *Kaiserreich*. A concept of the nation, separated from the concept of freedom, was fashioned into a chauvinistic ("*deutsch-nationale*") provinciality. Nation and political freedom were placed at odds with each other, a state of affairs that simultaneously served to estrange us further from the Western democracies. As Max Weber complained time and again, Bismarck had left the German *Bürgertum*, through its exclusion from practical political responsibility, without political experience and training. And following his resignation, Bismarck was himself, curiously enough, astonished by the political vacuum that his "*Realpolitik*" had left behind in the German people. In this vacuum there could develop that megalomania characteristic of the Wilhelmine era that led Prussia-Germany into World War I. Only with the defeat of the *Kaiserreich* was the way opened in Germany for the transition from a monarchical authoritarian state to parliamentary democracy.

It was with the slogan of "the primacy of foreign policy" that German bourgeois historiography, reliant as it was on the authoritarian state, attempted to justify retrospectively the coexistence of Bismarck's diplomatic acumen and circumspection in foreign affairs with his simultaneous failure vis-à-vis the domestic dimension of the national question: the endangered external situation of Prussia-Germany, it was argued, had brought about the anachronistic conditions of domestic politics. It is worth noting that proponents of this form of historiography never once attempted to substantiate their thesis through reference to the cases of Switzerland or the Netherlands, both of which, under far more difficult external conditions, had fought for and maintained a liberal constitution.

It is indeed no coincidence that the external dimension of the establishment of the Bismarckian Reich had again been called into question. It was called into question because the domestic dimension of the belated nationhood itself remained dubious. Blood and iron do not make a nation. The political right in Germany, which had acquired great national prestige in the establishment of the Reich, had led the nation into war and to defeat. Following the war they disclaimed all responsibility and left it to the democratic left to come to terms with the consequences of their irresponsible policies. They prepared the way for Hitler by attempting to place blame on the democratic left for the consequences of their own adventuristic politics: "November

criminals," "politics of abdication." That they were able to do so with
such success is connected with the fact that for the German workers'
movement—since the establishment of the Bismarckian Reich and the
persecution of workers under the antisocialist laws—the concept of
nation appeared to be a right-wing concept, or at least a concept used
by the right against it. Thus the first German democracy also foundered
on the heritage of Bismarck's Reich. It was destroyed—and with it
the German unity that had been forged in the establishment of the
Reich—by a regime that considered itself to be finally and definitively
breaking with the European Enlightenment's belief in freedom, human
rights, and tolerance.

The politically dubious tradition of the German *Bürgertum* had also
provided the context for the book by Karl Jaspers that is the focal
point of the reflections collected in this volume. This claim may seem
surprising. For not only did *Die geistige Situation der Zeit* quickly achieve
renown as the major interpretation of our age in the concluding phase
of the Weimar Republic, but it was also highly unusual that a German
philosopher should express himself on issues of such topicality. Finally,
it is clear from this book, which appeared in 1931, that Karl Jaspers
saw in fascism as well as Bolshevism the destruction of the freedom
that had emerged from the European tradition. Nonetheless at that
turning point in German history, shortly before Hitler's assumption
of power, the book mirrored the political impotence of the German
Bürgertum.

Whoever expected to find in Jaspers's book a social-political analysis
of the hard-pressed Weimar democracy found himself instead elevated
to a higher plane: the situation of the age was not analyzed politically
but interpreted from the standpoint of intellectual history. This interpretation took the form of a grand bourgeois cultural critique of the
modern "mass" world of Western industrial societies. This form of
cultural criticism did not for an instant reflect on its own origins in
the bourgeois-liberal or, more precisely, German *bürgerliche* tradition.
Instead it presupposed the *bürgerliche* social canon of the self-reliant
individual, under the protection of marriage and the family. Measured
by this standard, the struggle of industrial societies for a social and
political constitution appropriate to them appeared as a mere history
of decline. Thus it was necessary to escape from the latter, "at a
moment of world-transformation," through an attitude of the aris-

tocracy of spirit, through a decision for selfhood in the consciousness of doom.

The danger of totalitarianism, latent in modern industrial societies, is described. Yet it is not analyzed in a manner such that the critique could become practical in the sense of the elimination of this danger. The work provides no political orientation; indeed it even reinforces the lack of orientation, since it remains altogether ambivalent regarding its relevance for the social and political disputes of those years. This is the case not only with regard to the obfuscating talk of "destiny" or of a "genuine folk," the latter being understood in terms of its opposition not only to the notion of the "masses" but to that of the Western "nations" as well. In terms of political action as well, Jaspers's invocation of selfhood remained without bearing on the real problems of the Weimar Republic. It thus remained abstract. And this is all the more so since Jaspers's thought was imbued with an arrogant skepticism vis-à-vis democracy. Not only did he consider the democratic principle of majority rule as a condition for the existence of the masses; he also stressed the necessity of a leader (*Führer*), harboring as he did profound doubts about the ability of the "human masses" to handle democracy. Accordingly the principle of equality was viewed with a skepticism that served to elevate the common anxieties and prejudices of the German *Bürgertum* into the realm of metaphysics. In opposition to the principle of equality, emphasis was placed on the nobility of sentiment, the decision for selfhood.

Measured against the metaphysical intensity of this stance, all hitherto existing forms of value attitudes were declared to be obsolete, which further heightened the lack of orientation:

The old antithesis of world-views such as individualism and socialism, liberal and conservative, revolutionary and reactionary, progressive and regressive, materialist and idealist, are no longer appropriate, even though everywhere they are still pressed into service as banners or invectives. A confrontation with world-views, as if there were several from which to choose, is no longer the way of attaining to truth.[1]

What remains is one's "own nontransferable choice" between nothingness and selfhood.

The possibility of a "new man" is then addressed by way of an example whose choice appears to be dictated by the conviction that "in war destiny speaks":

The stirring reports of the ways in which, during the last phases of the war, when our Western front was crumbling, here and there some of our men stood firm and, as self-sacrificing individuals, effected what no command could have made them do, actually and at the last moment safeguarding the soil of the fatherland against destruction and storing up for German memories a consciousness of invincibility — these reports disclose an otherwise scarcely attained reality as a symbol of contemporary possibilities. Here was the first human existence which, in the face of nothingness, was able to realize, no longer its own world, but a world which would belong to future generations.[2]

Thus, cast in philosophical jargon, what is here presented as the symbol of contemporary possibilties as such is the historical lie of the unconquered on the battlefield. The descent into nothingness is in part glorified and in part glossed over in philosophical fashion. This front experience of philosophy is politically as devoid of meaning and lacking in perspective as the tradition of the German *Bürgertum* from which it derives. In what is still its most apt characterization, Georg Lukács spoke of this phenomenon as "the Ash Wednesday of subjectivism."

The destruction of the Weimar Republic was no "destiny," but a consequence of the dubious political tradition of the German *Bürgertum*, one that also was not without influence on the workers' movement. With the destruction of the first German republic in the crimes of the Nazi regime, the German unity forged by Bismarck in 1871 was also lost.

Of decisive importance for the division of Germany following World War II, initiated and lost by the Nazi regime, was the conflict between the victors, leading to the "cold war." But one must not forget that the division of Germany was seen as necessary by our neighbors in the West as well as the East. They regarded the German Reich, "belatedly" born during the last century in the three wars waged against Denmark, Austria, and France, as a threat to European peace, and they regarded its colonial and naval policies as aggressive. Following World War II and Hitler's occupation, the partition of Germany performed for them the function of maintaining European peace. The treaty commitments, into which the Western powers entered in accord with our wish to eliminate the division of Germany, could not banish from the world this basic political state of affairs.

But the establishment of the Federal Republic of Germany and West German politics under Adenauer, rearmament in particular, were also factors in the process of the German division. As a result this policy, always accompanied by the corresponding countermoves of the East, so consolidated the division of the country that the often-invoked term "reunification" served more to conceal than to characterize the reality of this policy. It is perhaps precisely for this reason that reunification, which at the establishment of the Federal Republic had been formulated in the preamble to the Basic Law (*Grundgesetz*), the country's constitution, as a political hope and task, was fashioned into a dogma in line with the "politics of strength." This was the dogma that enabled Dr. von Merkatz, a secretary in Adenauer's second and third cabinets, to suggest in Parliament in 1953 that what was at issue in "reunification" was "the liberation of the occupied German territories"—a German nationalistic formulation of what was then the American policy of "roll-back." As this policy has failed, we need not concern ourselves here with its ramifications for foreign affairs. For our purpose it must be emphasized that—in the political tradition of our *Bürgertum*—the domestic dimension of the German partition was not at all reflected in the so-called politics of strength; instead the solution to the problem was postulated to lie in the "annexation" of the German Democratic Republic (GDR) by the Federal Republic.

The policies of the ruling coalition between the Social Democrats and the Free Democrats concerning Eastern Europe and Germany as a whole have in a laborious process brought the Federal Republic's politics back to reality. These policies have established our interest in the politics of détente, which had been set in motion by the United States and the Soviet Union. In this way they have eliminated the danger, conjured up by the Union parties [Christian Democratic Union, Christian Social Union], of the isolation of the Federal Republic in world politics. They have acquired for us increased influence and increased freedom of movement in foreign affairs. Finally these policies have initiated an easing of tensions in the relations between the Federal Republic and the GDR. For "the proof of the nation's coming of age," as Herbert Wehner formulated it in 1969, consists in the fact "that we are obliged to live with one another in a divided fashion, and yet in a way that serves the interests of peace." Moveover, it is as a result of the politics of détente that Germans in East and West can once again come together as families and friends. At the same time it has kept open the German question. Although the millions of encounters of Germans in East and West have served to consolidate the nation, they still constitute no answer to this questions.

An answer will be difficult to find. The German division has now lasted longer than the combined duration of the Weimar Republic and the "Thousand Year Reich." It is anchored in the opposing social orders of East and West. The ideological oppositions runs deep and divides not only Germany but the world. And yet Germans understand themselves as belonging together and ask about their future. There is no sense in anticipating the answer to this question in terms of the standard prescriptions of confederacy or federalism. These can be obtained too easily. What is important is rather to gain clarity about the present internal and external dimensions of the German question: Under which internal and external conditions are further steps even conceivable?

Let us begin by considering the external conditions. We cannot expect that the German question is as important for others as it is for us. This is so even for the Chinese, who in their dispute with the Soviet Union loudly declare their support for a reunification of Germany. But this is also the case for the Soviet Union, which, as was claimed by many observers in conjunction with the naming of a new Soviet ambassador to Bonn at the end of 1978, is supposed to "play the German card." This expression is as foolish as the one according to which the Americans could "play the China card." For even if the Soviet Union were prepared to abandon the GDR—and there are no grounds at all for this assumption—the security interests of the Federal Republic, Western Europe, and the United States remain such that the German question could not be solved by the Soviet Union alone.

What must we West Germans do? We must—and in this we could reach agreement not only with our compatriots in the GDR but even with the political leadership there—accept responsibility, in view of the German borders, for the consequences of the war begun and lost by Hitler. All else would result, externally, in isolating ourselves and, internally, in poisoning ourselves. In the view not only of our Eastern but also our Western neighbors recognition of the western border of Poland as it exists today is a necessary, if not sufficient, condition for progress on the German question.

Second, we must expect progress on the German question only in the context of progress on the "European question"—here, too, the Germans in East and West could reach agreement. As a European civil war World War I shook Europe's internal stability and its place in the world. Through World War II and its consequences, not only Germany but Europe as well was divided. Dismembered Berlin is a symbol today not only of the defeat of the Nazi hubris and of the absurdity of the division of Germany; it is also a symbol of the absurdity of the division of Europe. Thus progress on the German question will be able to find support, or at least acceptance, by our neighbors in East and West only as a function and component of progress on the "European question."

The German division has its own European dialectic; neighboring countries see it as serving their own interests. Yet they, and particularly the East European countries, pay for it with the high price of the division of Europe. Thus it serves the German as well as the European interest not only to maintain, with the commendable support of the other member states, the silent partnership of the GDR in the Common Market, but also to keep open, or to open up, the West European community and, correspondingly, the East European alliance for an all-European cooperation. With the entry of Greece, Portugal, and Spain as developing countries, forms of closer cooperation will in any event be more determinate for the Common Market than was the old notion of the supranational integration envisioned for the European Six (*Sechser-Europa*), and to an even higher degree than had been the case following the entry of Great Britain.

Third, we must assume, again inasmuch as there exists agreement with our compatriots in the GDR, that progress on the German question can be achieved only in conjunction with the continuation of the politics of peace and détente. It is the politics of small steps rather than big words that has made porous the border running through Germany and Europe—something that not too long ago was called the "iron curtain." It is the politics of détente that has brought the Germans in the East and West together again. The continuation of détente requires an active policy of arms control and disarmament, one that pursues, neither mindlessly nor anxiously, the goal of stabilizing at a lower level of troops and weapons a balance of power that secures peace.

From all this follows, finally, an insight that [former] President Scheel once again articulated on the twenty-fifth anniversary of the workers' revolt in the GDR: as regards the German question, nothing is to be achieved against the will of the Soviet Union, whose power in Europe emerged with the defeat of the Nazi dictatorship. As has already been indicated, this does not mean that for its part the Soviet Union is capable of solving the German question whenever it chooses. But it does mean that we Germans have to be interested in maintaining good relations with the Soviet Union.

As regards progress on the German question, internal development is indissolubly connected with external behavior, in the East as well as the West. In the Federal Republic, for instance, it was only after a long struggle that the domestic prerequisites for the politics of détente were established. The internal dimension of the German question is no less important than the external dimension, and it is even more complex. The "politics of strength" has attempted to suppress the domestic dimension of the German question by postulating annexation of the GDR. In this way nothing has been improved in a divided Germany. What is the basic situation today in the GDR and in the Federal Republic?

In the East bloc the GDR achieved a position of economic superiority, one that has since been shaken by the world economic crisis. Yet despite the external recognition it has received in conjunction with the politics of détente, its domestic situation has not stabilized. For external and internal reasons the regime of the Socialist Unity party of Germany has not succeeded—as is symbolized by the almost warlike fortification of its inner German frontier—in constructing an order that is not only tolerated but actually accepted by the population. The situation of the Socialist Unity regime is made more difficult by the fact that with regard to questions of standard of living and civil rights the Federal Republic is the point of reference for people in the GDR. It is for this reason that the German question remains a more vital concern in the GDR than in our affluent democracy. This must be viewed in connection with the fact that the GDR, where some of the traditional, nonpublic structures of society have been conserved more fully than in the Federal Republic, preserves a stronger feeling of nationality vis-à-vis its Eastern neighbors (the Soviet Union included) than is the case with the Federal Republic vis-à-vis its neighbors in the West. With regard to the Soviet Union, the feeling of nationalism is intensified by the fact that the system of Soviet Communism is perceived as an alien system.

Thus the Socialist Unity party, which initially attempted to take over the national question, has been placed on the defensive by the social-liberal coalition policies concerning Eastern Europe and Germany as a whole. Giving up, at least verbally, the goal of a unified Germany, it now proclaims, within the framework of a clear-cut policy of demarcation (*Abgrenzungspolitik*) vis-à-vis the Federal Republic, the existence of two German nations, one in the West, which is defined capitalistically, and a "socialist nation" in the GDR; this position's long-range objective is to dissolve these two nations in a comprehensive union of socialist republics. The notion of the "socialist nation" is drawn from that passage in the *Communist Manifesto* where it is stated that in the transition from the liberal-national to the socialist-international order, the victorious proletariat "must first constitute itself as a nation." The capitalist structure in the West, and thus the Socialist Unity party policy regarding the German question, remains subject to change. But even aside from this tactical question, the Socialist Unity party exhibits "national" insecurities. Thus the assurance of Honecker following the deletion of all national references from the 1974 GDR constitution: "Citizenship: GDR; Nationality: German."

Whereas in the GDR it has been the internal situation of the regime that has kept the national question alive, especially in relation to the Federal Republic, the internal situation in the Federal Republic has up to now apparently had the opposite effect. The abuse to which national values and sentiments had been subjected by National Socialism, the incorporation of the Federal Republic into the Western world (together with a considerable alteration of the traditional structure of society), the "economic miracle" and the process of European unification have, particularly for the young, relegated the national question to the background. The formula that had been so vilified during the last century, Karl von Rotteck's "Better freedom without unity than unity without freedom," has become, 150 years after the Badenweiler Festival, a West German article of faith—and this despite all oaths to reunification. Yet what is conspicuous in this stable "West German" (*bundesrepublikanische*) situation is the astonishing lack of clarity regarding the further perspectives on the German question and, in this connection, the self-understanding of the Federal Republic.

This uncertainty begins with the linguistic usage in which the dispute regarding quotation marks for the "GDR" was replaced by the no less heroic dispute involving the abbreviation "FRG."[3] It was continued at the level of judicial constructions concerning the survival or lack of survival of the German Reich, established in 1871 and destroyed by

Hitler. Only gradually has it become clear that a "re"-unification in the sense of a reestablishment of the old German nation-state does not represent a very realistic perspective for the further development of the German question. For the fathers of the Basic Law it is no disgrace that the hope they expressed with the establishment of the Federal Republic has not been fulfilled, the hope that the Basic Law would be only a provisional measure that would soon give way to a lasting solution for Germany as a whole. It was for good reason that this hope was written only into the preamble and not into the text of the constitution itself. But the Federal Constitutional Court once again demonstrated a regrettable lack of judicial self-restraint and political judgment when it derived from this preamble a legal obligation on the part of political authorities for what has been called an "eternal drive for reunification." The judicial arrogance contained in this claim is so fatuous that the critical remark—with this decision the Constitutional Court had taken on more than it could handle[4]—can be characterized only as an understatement. In his assertion, "World history is no local court," the former Finnish national president, Passikivi, makes a point that one would like to drive home to the gentlemen of the Court. Damage has been done not only to the political institutions, irrespective of their partisan composition. Damage has also been done to our political consciousness.

The resolution of the ministers and senators of culture of the states of the Federal Republic, passed at the end of 1978, regarding the treatment of the German question in school instruction indicates that on the basis of the decision of the Federal Constitutional Court no responsible pedagogical service can be rendered in this matter. It has been correctly pointed out that the decisive weakness in the resolution lies in the unclarity and confusion that surround its central point, the question of what a nation is and what the German nation is.[5] At the outset it is stated: "The German nation continues to exist as a linguistic and cultural unity." But because the concept of a "cultural nation," which to be sure has its German history, remains inadequate and blurred, the resolution goes further: "The German nation also continues to exist as a citizenry (Staatsvolk) which has no common state but whose members hold, irrespective of the separate regulations in the GDR, united German citizenship." The reduction of the nation to the "citizenry" of a state that politically no longer exists satisfied the judgment of the Constitutional Court; yet that such a concept of nationhood is politically meaningful and capable of being conveyed pedagogically is something that even ministers of culture will not be able to accept. Finally, because there is still contained in this resolution reference to the "central and eastern German territory [Raum]," one can only see a testimony to involuntary self-irony in its demand "to characterize the phenomena [sic] of the German division" in a way that is conceptually unobjectionable. In view of this official form of linguistic and intellectual confusion, it is small wonder that in the Christian Social Union's policy statement of July 1978 on the German question reference is made to the "parts of the Reich beyond the frontiers of December 31, 1937," whereby the well-meaning reader is left to guess whether what is meant thereby is Danzig or Alsace-Lorraine.

We are in fact confronted with the danger that here "a new chauvinistic spirit or at least a West German nationalism" may be developing.[6] In political discussions "national" arguments are increasingly advanced, arguments that, far from relating to Germany as a whole, are actually expressive of a Federal Republic nationalism. As a nationalism that would not eliminate but only deepen the division of the nation, this would represent—as do corresponding attempts in the GDR—the last perversion in the history of our reflection about the nation. One might argue that it would be politically unwise to endanger the identification of the citizens of the Federal Republic with their democratic state by artificially keeping open the German question. But the German question *is* open. And one can in this connection hardly speak of a West German national consciousness without adverse consequences. The existing linguistic and intellectual confusion conjures up the fear that others may be fishing in murky waters and that the national question may fall into the wrong hands once again in our history. What do we mean, what *could* we mean of substance, when today we, as Germans, speak of state, folk, nation, fatherland?

From the perspective of the *state* the situation of Germany today takes the following form. Within the territory of the former German Reich bounded by the 1937 borders there exist two states, the Federal Republic of Germany and the German Democratic Republic, restricted through the responsibility and right of the four victorious powers for "Germany as a whole" and especially for Berlin. No peace treaty was made with conquered Germany following World War II, and this left many problems and disputes unresolved. These concern the relation of the Federal Republic and the GDR to each other and to the former German Reich on the one hand; and the questions of borders with our neighbors, Poland in particular, on the other.

The Federal Republic understands itself within its territorial limits to be a successor to a German Reich that in a legal sense has not perished. It renounced the use of force with regard to the existing borders in Europe and recognized the western border of Poland. It raises no (more) "claims of sole authority to speak for Germany as a whole," but it does understand its relation to the GDR as one based not on international law but on a sui generis form of constitutional law. In the treaties with the East and the basic treaty with the GDR it has kept open its option to strive in a peaceful way to eliminate the division of Germany.

In the view of the GDR, however, the former German Reich has perished in a legal sense as well. The GDR understands itself as one of two sovereign German states, which are related to each other under international law. As has already been indicated, its initial objectives, oriented to Germany as a whole, were allowed to recede behind a rigid politics of demarcation in relation to the Federal Republic. The GDR has recognized the existing borders in the East.

Thus for all practical purposes there stand opposed in the area of the former German Reich two sovereign states with differing social orders, integrated into opposing systems of alliance; neither against each other nor against neighboring countries in East and West do they or can they raise territorial claims. The ongoing disputes over questions of constitutional and international law are also of political significance. This is so particularly with regard to Berlin and the status of Germans from the GDR under the law of the Federal Republic. But for the continued development of the German question we should not overestimate the disputed legal questions; we have been taught this by the fate of the "claim of sole authority" and the "Hallstein doctrine" connected with it.

The existence of two states in Germany allows the question of the *nation* to become in a renewed fashion the "German question." The leadership in the GDR has recently advanced the view regarding the relation of state and nation that what is at issue are not only two states but even two (new) political nations. Some have even expressed this view in the West. But the predominant German self-understanding in East and West, as has been shown particularly by the millions of conversations made possible by the politics of détente, is that although there are two states there is still, despite the political partition, only one German nation.

In discussions about the German question the concept of the nation is employed in disparate and often unclear ways. Thus recourse is made to the old concept of the "cultural nation." This concept draws on folkish elements such as common origin, common language, common song. While the concept of "people," not to be confused with the concept of "citizenry," has recourse to natural origins and connotes something common that has evolved unconsciously, the concept of the cultural nation adds the element of common consciousness, conscious commonality in literature, philosophy, and science. Thus it is primarily in cultural spheres that we find echoes of this view. Martin Walser has written:

Germany cannot be expunged from my historical consciousness. They can print new maps, but they cannot produce anew my consciousness. For this I have been a reader too long. I am aware of what transpired before something such as the Federal Republic of Germany came to be. I refuse to participate in the liquidation of history.[7]

And at the GDR's writers' congress Stephan Hermlin declared at almost the same time:

Thus I am a German writer, being whoever I may be, connected, both positively and negatively, with all that has been and continues to be written in the German language. The establishment of the GDR almost thirty years ago was one of the most important events in German history, and I can say that I participated in it. Yet this was not the end of German history but only a new chapter in it.[8]

In both statements reference is made to a commonality of language and culture, specifically a commonality of literature. In this way essential elements of a nation are touched upon. At the same time larger problems are bound up with the notion of the cultural nation. If it remains restricted to the cultural sphere, it is apolitical. But if it is politicized, it becomes politically dangerous. For this concept of nation would also apply to the Austrians, the Swiss-Germans, and those speaking German in many other European countries; from a political standpoint these people cannot be understood or claimed to belong to the German nation. For this reason, then, one must regard the concept of the cultural nation with critical distance.

Yet in our situation this does not warrant abandoning, together with the concept of the cultural nation, the concept of nation itself; nor does it warrant the construction of two German political nations. The fact that "nation" is not simply a cultural but a political concept does not justify its truncation into a concept of state sovereignty. The concept of the political is not exhausted by that of the sovereign state. The opposition of cultural nation and political nation stemming from the German tradition constitutes an inadmissible tearing asunder and thus a truncation of the political concept of the nation.

It is certainly true that the national movements of the nineteenth century aspired to the nation-state. But nations such as Switzerland, Belgium, the Soviet Union, and above all the United States—each constituting a melting pot of nationalities—preclude our regarding a state comprising multiple nationalities as an exception. As regards the relation of state and nation, we must today further consider the fact that the traditional nation-states are increasingly losing their monopoly over security and decision making, something that is leading not only to new forms of supranational and international cooperation but also to a reawakening of forms of regional nationalism within countries.

Conversely, we are aware of cases in which nation and state cannot be identified, since the people of a nation are organized into more than one state. In German history this has been the rule, the exception being the German Reich of 1871. Since 1945 we are once again in the same situation. For thirty years we have been organized into two states without anyone in the world doubting that it is the Germans who constitute the populations of the Federal Republic and the GDR.

The talk of "the Germans" as a nation makes it clear that what is meant is a concrete group of people belonging together historically, the totality of Germans in the Federal Republic and the GDR. In contrast to the state, be it identical with the nation or not, the nation is understood neither as a legal entity nor, following Herman Heller's formula for the concept of the state, as an "organized unity of action and decision" within a specific territory. Thus as regards the question of what the German nation is today, if indeed one still exists, the problems of the juridical survival of the German Reich of 1871 are no more relevant than are those pertaining to the borders with neighboring countries.

The word "fatherland" denotes two things: the region a nation settles and inhabits, and its homeland in a spiritual-political sense. As a rule the word designates the country in which one is born and raised. It is at once more and less than the state. It has no organs or powers, but as the area in which a nation lives it also must not be restricted to the territory of a sovereign state. Who would doubt that Magdeburg and Dresden as well as Dortmund and Munich belong to the common fatherland of the Germans in the Federal Republic and the GDR? With Alsace-Lorraine or Danzig the situation is different. Today Alsace-Lorraine is French, Danzig Polish. In this respect our fatherland has become smaller as a result of the lost war. Yet Danzig and Alsace-Lorraine belong to our fatherland as part of our spiritual homeland. Without the history and accomplishments of Germans in Alsace, or in West and East Prussia, our spiritual fatherland would be very much poorer. One's homeland can be taken away. Over the centuries German governments have forced German patriots to emigrate. Millions of refugees have been driven from their homeland through outside forces. It is impossible, however, to strip anyone of his fatherland as a spiritual homeland.

What still enables Germans in the GDR and the Federal Republic to constitute a nation in the political sense? What is it that allows them to live in two states and still have a common fatherland? To begin with, mention must be made of their *common history*. It is a consequence of this history that the Swiss and the Dutch, the Austrians and the Alsatians, the Lichtensteinians and the Luxemburgers do not belong to the German nation, although wholly or in part they belong to the circle of German language and culture. And by the same token it is a consequence of this history, including the establishment of the Reich in 1871 and the destruction of the nation-state by the Nazi regime, that the Germans in the Federal Republic and in the GDR belong to one another in a political sense more closely than to anyone else. And yet neither of these two states can reclaim the German nation exclusively for itself.

In addition to a common history, mention may be made of the *sense and consciousness of national communality*; as indicated by the stream of inner German visitations, these have their roots not only in the cohesion of families, but also in the commonality of historical experience and suffering. Were the Germans to lose or abandon this consciousness of communality, the German nation, the continuity of other common grounds notwithstanding, would cease to exist. Whether in this event a "Federal Republic Nation" or a "GDR Nation" would develop is another question.

Finally, the *common will* to remain a nation and to claim the right of self-determination, to which every nation is entitled, is also important. Today we are confronted with the question of whether, in addition to the existing feeling and consciousness of fellowship, we have and should have this will. One reason why Germans in the Federal Republic should maintain the cohesion and solidarity of the nation is that morally and politically we would become untrue to ourselves if with a shoulder-shrugging apologetic sigh of "fate" we were to leave the Germans over there to their own devices, Germans who after 1945 had to begin anew — and must continue to live — under much more difficult external and internal conditions. And we would be untrue to ourselves if we were to accept the German division as the last word on German history. Nor have our compatriots in the GDR, as a glance at their literature already indicates, forgotten this historical communality. Even the notion of the "socialist man," invented by the Socialist Unity regime in order to elevate itself in a dignified way above the doubts of our fascist past, has not been able to induce them to suppress our common past.

The will to *responsibility* in the face of this common past could constitute in both parts of Germany a central element in the will to remain a nation. "I love the nation," said Herman Heller, the important socialist scholar of constitutional law in the Weimar Republic, "because it is the greatest human totality for which I, through my actions, am able and willing to bear immediately experienced responsibility." From the responsibility in the face of this common past we Germans could acquire a common standard for our political behavior in East and West. A nation exists not only in the consciousness of communality and the will to commonality but also and primarily in the values constituting the "object," the "content" of this common will and consciousness. As Carlo Schmid once again demonstrated in his great parliamentary speech on the occasion of the signing of the treaty with East Germany in February 1972, the idea of the nation underlies the old European idea of a social contract. It is proper to a nation that it make certain values its own — "values of humanity," Carlo Schmid said, in the tradition of German classicism — in order to realize them in the framework of a community of nations.

The German *Bürgertum* did not actualize this dimension of the nation, just as it allowed the idea and the concept of the nation to fall into the hands of the political right. Yet in the context of European history the concept of "nation" originally had an enlightening, progressive significance. "Liberty, equality, and fraternity" and the hope for peace between nations delimit its internal dimensions. That the dialectic of enlightenment has led far beyond Germany to a perversion of the idea of the nation is no excuse for us to allow the nation to fall into the wrong hands for a second time in German history.

Within our history, too, there existed a liberal-democratic tradition of national thinking. It was so completely vanquished in the nineteenth century that President Heinemann still had to lament the neglect of this element of German history in our political education. Following the political abdication of the *Bürgertum*, the workers' movement continued the democratic tradition of Germany under particularly difficult circumstances. It struggled to extend within a democratic republic the constitutional rights of liberalism to all social strata of the populace and to anchor them in social reality. Out of disenfranchised proletarians it created citizens with equal rights, in this way thinking out to the end not only the notion of democracy but that of the nation as well. Thus it was the primary opponent of the "National Socialist German Workers' party," which was neither a national nor a socialist nor even a workers' party, but which through its crimes certainly besmirched the German name and played away the unity of Germany.

Following the collapse of the Nazi regime, German Social Democracy, proceeding from its democratic tradition, became the determining political force in the Federal Republic of Germany, even though the restoration policies of the Allies and Konrad Adenauer had, in connection with the cold war, made it difficult enough for this to be established. Today democratic socialism is gaining increasing authority and influence in the Federal Republic, in Europe, and in the world, because it has most decisively posed and attempted to answer the central political question of our society: the economic liberation of the moral and political individual, to recall Kurt Schumacher's formulation. Despite all necessary confrontations with conservative and reactionary forces, this development must not be understood in the narrow sense of partisan politics. In the Federal Republic it has led, among other things, to Parliament's passing by a large majority a law guaranteeing the codetermination of workers in the major business concerns. Since then the capitalist axiom that possession of capital alone can legitimize the economic-political power of decision and control is a thing of the past. Yet it would serve no purpose for us to declare that this development in the direction of democratic socialism expresses a consensus of Germany as a whole. We can enter into a national social contract only with the Germans in the GDR themselves, and not with ourselves in their name.

Certainly that which in the GDR is termed "real socialism" is happy to invoke the liberal German traditions, whose cultivation has been rather neglected in the political education of the Federal Republic. Yet real socialism—Rudolf Bahro has described it impressively—represents not a continuation of but a break with these traditions. No more has the antifascist position of the GDR (which, as its literature indicates, is thoroughly genuine) led to a political answer that, measured against the standards of our responsibility in the face of our common past, can have any lasting value. In the other part of Germany the old social structure was revolutionized; but the Nazi regime was thereby replaced not by a democratic but by a bureaucratic-dictatorial order. The fortifications along the internal German frontier of the "first German workers' and peasants' state" even reminded the Israeli writer Amos Elon of the "architecture of the concentration camps."

In this way the division of Germany is connected to the schism in the workers' movement that materialized in the Weimar Republic. At that time the German Communists split from the democratic workers' movement, subordinated themselves subsequently to the Russian Bolsheviks (who faced wholly different living conditions), and broke with the liberal origins of socialism. This led to their declaration, in compliance with the resolutions of the Sixth World Congress of the Comintern, that the Social Democrats rather than the Fascists were their chief opponents—a state of affairs making possible the National Socialist assumption of power.

Today the hyphenated dogmatism of Marxism-Leninism solidifies the division of Germany and Europe on the backs of the East European peoples and the Germans in the GDR. The Socialist Unity party of Germany, far from realizing socialism (the economic liberation of the moral and political individual), is in truth exorcising from the Germans in the GDR the idea and the hope of socialism. The disparity between the regime's words and deeds is so great that it has lost credibility. The great majority of Germans in the GDR can hardly judge communism any differently than the German Social Democrats did in their party resolution of February 1971 concerning the relation of social democracy and communism. Yet their repudiation of the Socialist Unity party regime does not mean that the people of the GDR want to be "annexed" to the social order of the Federal Republic. Their yearning for personal and political freedom is no yearning for a capitalist economic structure. They are proud of what they have created even under their conditions. Nonetheless it can probably be said that a consensus in the direction of democratic socialism would constitute today the content of the Germans' national social contract were our compatriots in the GDR able to express themselves freely and to make their own decisions. For this reason as well, we cannot release the Socialist Unity party regime from the competition of social orders.

As for the question of our political conduct toward the GDR as it is presently constituted, the external and internal conditions for progress on the German question are interrelated. Unfortunately, in recent times this question has been discussed within the framework of a conservative terminology, as to whether we should be interested in a stabilization or destabilization of the Socialist Unity regime (and other Communist regimes in Eastern Europe). This mode of questioning mirrors the situation of these regimes. From the perspective of world politics the countries of the East bloc—and first of all the Soviet Union— stand in competition with the West, with Japan, with China, and with the Third World; this competition is stretching their capacities to the limit and in the future will do so even more intensely. At the same time they are subject to strong internal pressure. They have to come to terms with the problem of their own economic, technical, and social development within the confines of the extremely limited flexibility of their political system. Many in the East had hoped that the importation of capital and know-how from the West resulting from the politics of détente would make possible the necessary increase in economic productivity without setting in motion deeper reforms. The effect has been precisely the opposite however: the process of reform has been accelerated. New forces of production—and new consumer desires—have been generated without there being any way for them to find realization in the encrusted relations of production. The volume of socially required information expands, and the self-consciousness of the cadre required for the overdue process of modernization also expands. True, its desire for more freedom of movement originates in its own interests, and yet it is at the same time socially justified. In this respect there exists in fact a "convergence" in the development of the industrial societies toward modernity. But this does not automatically lead to political consequences in the sense of a liberalization or democratization of the regimes.

Moreover, in East European countries and in the GDR national tendencies are emerging that, under the banner of reform Communism, aim to alter the "introduced" model of Soviet Communism, which is perceived as both foreign and inefficient. The more successful the political leadership is in modifying this model (silently, if possible) and at the same time raising the standard of living, the more acceptable it appears to the people living under their regime. Hungary is a perfect case in point. For the Soviet Union this constitutes a problem of power in its own bloc, which it must view from the standpoint of both world and economic politics. Aside from the particular regimes themselves, who could have a greater interest in their stability than the Soviet Union? Who aside from the Soviet Union must concern itself preeminently with the question: Under what conditions is stability in these countries to be attained and maintained in the future?

It would be fallacious to conclude from this situation that our interests would be served by promoting the destabilization of the Communist regimes in Eastern Europe. This is true for the left as well as the right. What else but chaos would today be its consequence, and what would be the alternative? It is agreed in the West that war itself would be no alternative, even if one day Soviet tanks were to roll in the East bloc for the next pseudostabilization.

But is this to say that our interest lies in stabilizing the Communist regimes in Eastern Europe and the GDR, irrespective of how unacceptable they are for us? By no means! What would induce us to work against the interests and convictions of the peoples of Eastern Europe and our own compatriots in the GDR? Just as the external dimension of the German and European question consists in détente, the internal dimension consists in reform. It is not only the West that is in need of social reform. The East needs it as parched land needs rain. We in the West must proceed farther along the road to democratic socialism. The East has still to find the path of reform from a bureaucratic-dictatorial regime to humane socialism. Otherwise the German and European division cannot be overcome. Herein lies the world political significance of those currents of reform Communism for which the name Eurocommunism has been adopted in Western Europe and for which the Prague Spring has become a symbol in Eastern Europe.

We must attempt to influence the external and internal conditions of the German question in such a way that the GDR and the East European countries could implement reforms that would serve their own interest. This would be in agreement with the stipulations of the Helsinki accords (to which they were signatories), which called not only for good neighborly relations but also for human rights in Europe.

East and West must discuss between themselves the issues not only of peace but also of reform. This is particularly the case in the country where Karl Marx and Friedrich Engels were born. Just as the past of socialism is not to be separated from the development of Germany, so the future of the German nation is not to be separated from the development of socialism. To pursue German politics from the perspective of democratic socialism is to attempt to give German history after the catastrophe a meaning, a human meaning.

Notes

1. Karl Jaspers, *Man in the Modern Age*, translated by Eden and Cedar Paul (Garden City, NY: Anchor Books, 1957), pp. 158–159. The translation has been modified (*tr.*).

2. Ibid., p. 216.

3. See H. Berschin, "Ein Geisterreich wie Utopia?" *Der Spiegel* 50 (1978):68ff.

4. T. Oppermann, "Staatliche Einheit oder innere Freiheit?" *Europa-Archiv* 21. (1978):681ff.

5. K. H. Janssen, "Chauvinismus in der Schule," *Die Zeit* (December 8, 1978):5.

6. Ibid.

7. "Über den Leser—soviel man in einem Festzelt sagen soll," *Literatur-konkret* (Fall 1978).

8. "Das Vorrecht der Dichter, vernunftlos zu träumen," *Frankfurter Rundschau* (October 3, 1978):13.

Unconcluding Reflections

Germany—A State of Flux

Dieter Wellershoff

Something that used to be self-evident has vanished, has dissolved, and has bequeathed to memory a word. This word is "Germany," the land of the Germans, a word without application. Whenever during the past few weeks I tried to think about Germany in order to write about Germany, a sense of impotence set in, a faint dizziness, a cerebral anemia, a numbing emptiness that left me in dazed, directionless expectancy. After a few minutes I would have to get up, move around, shake it off, and occupy myself with something else.

Germany. Something reverberated in me, yet it was something murky, shapeless, beyond reach, like a language that had become incomprehensible. This happened at various places: in my summer home in England, in a hotel room in Berlin, in my study in Cologne.

One day I wrote a sentence in which I tried to clarify the nature of my difficulties. I wrote it down in the middle of a blank page, as a substitute for all the other sentences that should have appeared there and that had now been obliterated by it: "Germany no longer exists." That was it. Nothing more needed to be said.

Nonetheless, I remained anxious. I had to elaborate on this sentence, to provide an explanation for it. Thus I wrote: "There is the Federal Republic and the GDR, there are the former Eastern provinces of Germany, which now belong to Poland and the Soviet Union, but Germany itself no longer exists. Nor will it ever exist again." It sounded as if I wanted to drum something into myself that I could not comprehend, would not grasp, although it is easy enough to understand

and remember this simple sentence: Germany no longer exists! And this means that the German nation as well is about to vanish.

I was born and raised a German. Today I am a citizen of the Federal Republic of Germany, at least so my passport says. I feel odd about this designation. It contains about the same emotional resonance as does the German Automobile Association, a combination in which the word "German" is like a burnt-out cinder, cooled off and no longer able to generate energy. I am a member of the German Automobile Association and a citizen of the Federal Republic of Germany. It is strange to connect things in this manner. There is something improper about it, and yet it indicates the synthetic character of the political concept, "citizen of the Federal Republic of Germany." This is too long, too formal. It is an artificial conjunction of a guiding concept and an attribute that has little meaning and sense of its own and that cannot counter what convenience simply shortens away. Citizen of the Federal Republic. This suffices; in it everything essential seems to be said. If one confronts this combination with a demanding, questioning assertion such as "I live," only the concept "Federal Republic" has the strength to respond. It designates what is most important: "I live in the Federal Republic." From this one can envisage something. By contrast, "Germany" is scarcely audible, an echo that, following the factually more powerful guiding concept, no longer attains proper expression and is for the most part forgotten.

And when I speak of the other people who live in this country with me, I call them Federal Citizens (*Bundesbürger*). This sounds to me as if I were speaking of the members of a club to which I belonged without passion or deeper commitment. I approve the club's statutes, pay my dues, flip through club circulars to keep informed about club life, take part regularly in the election of its governing bodies and other committees, express my opinion from time to time on controversial issues, appreciate the privileges I enjoy as a member and am therefore even willing to pledge my critical loyalty and my support to the club.

I think this is a lot, since I am in this way at least able to live. Yet it is an alliance of interests, not the emotional bond that a Frenchman feels for France, and Englishman for England, or a Spaniard for Spain. It is not love or a self-evident inner sense of belonging, and by no means is it identification. A love for Germany that has lost its object and yet is nontransferable prevents me from experiencing this state, understood initially as a provisional arrangement, as anything more than an acceptable framework for political life. And this love also prevents me from taking what remains of this considerably shrunken country for the lost totality. Germany has become intangible, a murmuring of voices from the past, a multifarious historical recollection that is fading away. For trips abroad I attach a "D," as in *Deutschland*, to the body of my car. But these self-adhesive, plastic stickers hold badly and keep falling off.

On what could a German national identity still be based? The German language is spoken in four different countries. And the political dismemberment of its territory retroactively dismembers our common history as well.

Yet the rupture that destroyed old institutions had merely been brought to a conclusion by the political dissolution of Germany. It had already occurred earlier, when the course of the War shifted. It only became conspicuous during the collapse in 1945.

A defeat is certainly not just a military event. It also occurs within the minds of men, as a collective loss of meaning. As soon as it became evident that the War was lost, more and more soldiers began asking themselves why they should continue to risk their lives. Why die or be wounded at this point? For whom and for what? Once such questions began to form—unexpressed at first, within the hidden consciousness of many individuals or at most in secret conversations—it seemed curious that their answer had been apparent for years. One shared in the power and successes of the collective and thereby felt elevated and strengthened. Outside the collective one was nothing. And opposition was unthinkable for the majority. The symbols of power— the maps of conquered territories, the fanfare, the special announcements, the weapons, the decorations, the heroic idols, remote authorities, the rituals celebrating all this—served as the foundation for a delusive identity linked to a promise of invincibility. These could not sustain the devastating repudiation that came with the defeats. The staggering power, which for years could send its armies into battle, had suddenly lost its motivating force, something it conceded when it tried to make its soldiers maintain their positions with threats of execution by firing squad. Such threats were useless. They destroyed the last vestige of positive identification. The armies, even when they still cohered externally, dissolved into masses of individuals whose only thought was of survival.

Yet this was only the first phase of disillusionment. The mass trauma of total defeat was soon followed by the horror and shame over the pits full of corpses in the extermination camps. There no longer existed any grounds on which to object to the nation's annulment, nor any rights to which one could appeal. Nearly every German had fought on the side of the murderers, and thus an entire nation had been burdened with unbearable guilt. Only when dissolved into seventy million individuals could the majority demonstrate that they were not directly involved in the crimes. All Germans were guilty. But what, after all, does it mean to be German? One was Herr Müller, or Schulze, a little fellow-traveler perhaps, a simple soldier, possibly wounded, disabled, exiled, or bombed-out—in other words, also a victim.

This was an easy way out of one's involvement in the collective guilt. Yet this path was open only because it corresponded to an experience. The collective catastrophe had shown everyone how impotent the individual was in the face of the event. Who could really have changed or prevented anything? Situations in which a courageous loner or a small group of determined individuals managed to throw a monkey wrench into the event that was rolling over everything, while dramatically compelling, were extremely rare and of no historical importance. Thus how could the responsibility of all these powerless individuals be lumped together into that of the huge, collectively guilty subject, the nation? The nation had become an invisible, intangible abstraction. It was no longer to be seen, it no longer manifested itself— neither through symbols nor through representations, neither in festive occasions nor in the journalistic-oratorical business of providing meaning. The stiff figures in the dock at the Nuremberg trial, presented by the papers in drab group photos, were already the remote, emasculated, dollishly lifeless actors in a movie, which fortunately was no longer being shown and which one recalled with horror in order immediately to give complete attention to the present. The present, which for every German began with the necessity of securing a handful of potatoes somewhere, a few lumps of coal, and of patching a leaky roof, also began with the pleasure one took in this limited, purely practical life, a life to which one was from then on determined to adhere, unseduced by ideas and slogans. Present history began with this retreat into privacy.

Two funerals represent the War and its end for me. In 1940 on behalf of our school, my classmate Franz Brendgen and I traveled to the funeral of our class teacher, who had died from the effects of a wound. He had been a reserve officer, was drafted at the very beginning and had served in the wars against Poland and France. Now, with pithy speeches and his company's gun salute, he was laid to rest in a flag-draped coffin. At that time, the high point of our military success, ceremony was still the rule.

On the way back Franz said to me or I to him (I can't remember exactly, since either of us could have said it): "I hope this war will last long enough so that we, too, can become soldiers." We both wore uniforms, as Hitler Youth junior branch leaders from neighboring towns. By the campfire, with the hoisting of flags, during memorials commemorating heroes, we sang a song together whose ceremonial pathos sent shivers up and down our spines:

Holy fatherland in peril,
Your sons rally 'round you.
Before strangers rob you of your glories,
Germany, we shall fall, one and all.

Germany was a rich, mythic fabric whose threading wound from the sagas of Germanic heroes through the Staufer Kaiser to Bismarck and Hitler. All that gave life luster bore these names. Yet Hitler irritated us. He did not fit the image of what is heroic and German. I believe that any unknown man in civilian clothes who looked like him, with his stringy forelocks and small mustache, would have seemed to us not merely foreign but even suspect, un-German. And yet this was indeed the Führer before whom we marched twelve abreast. There he stood, a diminutive figure on an elevated platform with his arm outstretched. For all of us he was a man possessing incomparably transcendent rank and was therefore entitled to appear a bit peculiar. He was beyond all criticism.

Our veneration and admiration was given to fighter pilots, para-chutists, tank commanders, submarine crews, and the "invincible" German infantry, which in the weekly newsreel pictures was always on the attack or else, covered with dirt and sweat, was pursuing the fleeing enemy in lock-step march. "I hope this war will last long enough." This was scarcely imaginable, since victory followed upon victory. We, the ones born late, were thus deprived of the greatest experience one could have: to be a soldier in an army that conquered the world. Later we were smiled at compassionately, yet with some distance. For we were not involved.

But the War continued and the tide began to turn. Under attack from English and American bomber battalions, German cities were turned into heaps of rubble; in Stalingrad the German army capitulated; Rommel's African corps was driven out of Africa; and at night I would surreptitiously listen to a German voice on an enemy radio station commenting on all of these events as signs of an inevitable German defeat. This voice made me lonely. It intruded on my closed world from without and, with cold irony and with startling figures and announcements, shook my belief in the outcome of history. Franz and I and our entire generation had been given our historical chance after all. But by then we had already stopped speaking of it.

We saw one another after the War, which had left us both injured. I had only received a leg wound and in the winter of 1944–45 was placed in the infirmary. Franz, however, was shot in the head. He walked with a cane and suffered from dizziness and other maladies. It was a wonder that he had survived the injury. We talked for a long time to renew our acquaintance, engaging in the sort of conversation so common at that time. He told me of the complete astonishment he felt at the moment of the bullet's impact and how, under his ringing steel helmet, he kept thinking with fainting consciousness: "Oh, so that's how it is? Oh, so that's how it is!" A bullet had answered the question he had always secretly asked himself; it had ripped away the entire heroism swindle of our youth.

A few weeks after our conversation Franz was dead. He died from the effects of his wound, as had our class teacher in the first years of the war. Yet at the grave there were no gun salutes and no lowered flags, no solemn vows and no ceremonial speeches. There was only shock and mourning. All the sacrifices and sufferings of this war had been not only in vain but meaningless and false as well. Not only had we lost; we had fought for a vile cause.

For me this "Oh, so that's how it is!" has become a short formula for critical recognition, a formula for growing up. But it presupposes error, the possibility of delusion, false appearance. While perhaps not a gunshot, this "Oh, so that's how it is!" is like a blow to a head that refuses to comprehend the obvious.

Another recollection from school is in order here. It bears witness to the impenetrability of ideologized consciousness. Our history teacher had what for us was a rather incomprehensible partiality for Roman history. There was German history of course and, most important, the German present. This we would have discussed with greater involvement. But our history teacher stuck to the Roman Republic and the Senate and also to the Caesars. Who was Nero? Who was Caligula?

We already knew that it was our teacher's habit to question us in this way, and we answered promptly: Nero, the adopted son of the emperor Claudius, upon whose removal became emperor himself, ruling from 54 to 68. He surrounded himself with attendants, took the burning of Rome as an opportunity to persecute Christians, committed suicide. Or: Caligula, son of Germanicus, Roman emperor from 37 to 41, ruled autocratically and gruesomely, killed by the Praetorians. Our history teacher listened to these litanies and said in an impatient, contemptuous tone I remember distinctly: "Caligula, he was a little idiot." It seemed to be his whim, and we imitated it when we were alone. We roared with laughter when one of us sat down behind the desk and asked, "Who was Caligula?" and the person asked replied hastily, "A little idiot, sir." These are the comical aspects of school that former students tend to recall so happily. Of course soon thereafter we had little time to think about such things. Only much later, when I had already been a student at the university for some time, did the question, "Who was Caligula?" occur to me again. And instantaneously I knew the answer. "Hitler." Our teacher had always been speaking of Hitler. Nero, it was him. Caligula, it was him. A megalomaniac, a deluded paranoid, gruesome, neurotic, possessed with fixed ideas — what then had been burning Christians were now Jews in the gas chamber: Hitler, a little idiot.

Yet we were certainly the biggest idiots—from a foolishly trusting need for community and for a meaning to life that transcended everyday existence and assigned everyone a place in the greater totality. What other possibilities were there for self-definition? Petit bourgeois families, schools, offices, factories—was this life, was this one's identity? This was no model, no plan, all this was far too limited. The language of drums and banners carried us away from the tedium—into a bloody transcendence. Meaning is the greatest opiate; millions have died from it. But a single, thorough detoxification treatment is enough for a lifetime. I am glad to have undergone one.

By contrast, the capacities of the victorious powers to provide meaning were not exhausted. Despite the expulsion of Germans from the east, despite the bombing of Dresden and Hiroshima, one could remain a Russian, and Englishman, or an American without shame or guilt. Their collective experience was entirely different from the German's. I comprehended this with astonishment and surprise in the 50s, when I traveled to England for the first time. On the trip across the Channel I listened to a radio program commemorating the anniversary of the air battle over England, in which Hitler's invading air force had been annihilated. The orator, a clergyman, said, as if it were a metaphysical certitude, "God flew at our side." At one time something similar had appeared on the belt buckles of German soldiers: "God with us." It turned out to have been a grotesque deception. Obviously the victors had more difficulty in leaving such morale-building slogans behind. Even in defeat there are special opportunities for insight.

The French stood in closer relation to the Germans, for they knew defeat, knew life under occupation, and had also experienced the veiled character of political convictions as they were exposed in changes of power. These experiences were similar to those of the Germans, who with the French were disposed to a theoretical fascination with so-called extreme situations. They called it the philosophy of existence. For this philosophy, freedom consisted in proceeding from nothingness or, as it was also said, in "abiding" in it. What could at that time be experienced was existence. One of the more advanced students explained it to me in the following way: Existence is what remains once you have lost everything that belonged to your social personality. You have a house, it burns down; you have a family, they're shot; you are driven from your homeland; you lose your arms and legs; you become blind—and yet you still have the firm, unshakable conviction that everything lost was external. This irreducible core is existence.

From today's perspective this is an odd train of thought. Yet those first postwar students, who from the prison camps entered the universities wearing tattered, dyed uniforms, jackets and coats cut from blankets, who, living in unheated shacks, possessed nothing, not minor comforts or an imaginable future—these survivors of the decimated generation, only now beginning to comprehend their survival, could recognize something of themselves in this philosophy. One was surrounded not by a rational, well-ordered world, not by universal ideas, not by comfortable middle-class possessions, but by a freedom born of a brush with death. This was the appropriate philosophy for the zero hour, as the War's end was termed by many. Of course there can never be a zero hour in history, but that we did not know. People wanted to start from scratch, with a clean slate not yet inscribed with new illusions. Existentialism was a heroizing individualistic variant of this zero-hour mentality, an intellectual shudder following the collective dance of death.

Despite the hunger and poverty the atmosphere was not depressing but charged with a newly liberated, long pent-up lust for life. One could slumber without fear, speak one's mind, and so begin to think again. It was a time of daily discoveries. We had lived in a spiritual vacuum, in a cultural neutral zone, whose closely watched borders had finally been removed. Now all at once everything descended upon us: modern literature, art, philosophy, film, theater, and, above all, a vital stimulus that taught us a new way of outer and inner movement— jazz. It was a new civilization with new life-stimuli and new forms of social interaction. Jitterbug and boogie-woogie expelled the marching gait from our limbs, and it was obvious not only in mind but also in body, in vital self-feeling, that the political framework of this new life could only be democracy. The right to self-determination and the right to privacy were closely connected and could easily be confused. This was attached to an emotional backdrop disposed to historical abstinence, reacting to ideas and potential world-political involvements and responsibilites with intense antipathy.

"Count me out" was the maxim of the survivors, who at that time in Germany shed their uniforms with the determination never to wear one again, not even an inner uniform, no collectively ordered world-view, no ideology. They were later called "the skeptical generation." Even so, many of these skeptics still cherished one last national dream: the hope for a neutralized Germany which—open to the world— would recall its best cultural traditions: its music, its philosophy, its poetry, and all that for them symbolized the true Germany. This Germany had lost its distinguishing characteristics during the years of barbarism, and now, in the lee of history, was to stand again, through the voluntary renunciation of power, as a land of humanity, peace, sublime inwardness, where the old bourgeois cultural ideal of the "beautiful soul" could finally flourish collectively.

Instead the cold war erupted between the victorious powers. What remained of Germany was carved up and, according to the spheres of influence, integrated politically, militarily, economically, and ideologically into opposing power blocs—and indeed, here as there, with special requirements of loyalty and obedience. In short, Germany was molded into the future model provinces of the hostile superpowers.

The division of Germany was historically already contained in the contradictory alliance of the victorious powers, which had been forged essentially for military reasons and which was soon dissolved following Germany's defeat. After the occupation forces had in the summer of 1945 defined the four zones of occupation agreed upon in Yalta, and after, scarcely a year later, the Soviets closed their borders to the three Western zones, unique developments began in East and West that furthered the steadily progressing division. This became clearer with each passing year. The fact that in 1949 the preamble to the Basic Law of the Federal Republic still read, "The entire German people is exhorted to realize in free self-determination the unity and freedom of Germany," not only postponed the attainment of this goal to the unforeseeable future but also gave the Basic Law the character of a rhetorical substitute for a policy of reunification that was now too great a risk and that perhaps was hopeless.

Of course the foreseeable still had to be denied for awhile. This was the psychological function of the Hallstein doctrine, which defined the establishment of diplomatic relations with the German Democratic Republic by any nation to be an unfriendly act against Bonn. This attempt to isolate the GDR internationally was, from a long-range perspective, an impotent denial of reality—as untenable, for instance, as the aggressive semantic rules of Springer-Presse, which for a long time spoke of the "Soviet Zone of Occupation" and then, in a transitional period, of the "so-called GDR." I remember that among adherents to the Hallstein doctrine there were those who believed or pretended to believe that the GDR and the entire East bloc, including the Soviet Union, would, after a period of isolation, collapse under the weight of internal difficulties and contradictions. It was a form of political superstition whose believers eagerly compiled multicolored reports on the social and economic problems of the East bloc, above all on the chaos and lagging productivity in the planned economy, yet neglected all the other factors, like power relations and the integrating force of ideology.

In fact the gap between the increasingly affluent Federal Republic and the GDR widened each year. Any fair comparison of systems, however, must also consider the special difficulties confronting the GDR. Probably the most threatening problem was the departure of thousands of people, including many well-trained specialists who, until the erection of the Berlin Wall, were fleeing to the West. Without doubt the wall was a necessity if the GDR was to achieve stability. So in the long run the development of the Federal Republic did not work to the detriment of the GDR; this was also the time of its own development. Today two German states and societies stand in opposition to each other, reciprocally strengthening each other's reality while remaining in competition. A reunited Germany has long since become an undreamable dream, forbidden to every intelligent human being.

This had to be learned by my generation and by our older citizens. The younger people grew up with it. Yet this learning process has actually gone astonishingly well.

In my college days we still sang a carnival song, "We are the Natives of Trizonesia," by which we meant: a colonized people living in gay abandon. Then we became Federal Citizens, involving at first superficial changes but later fundamental transformations. Meanwhile, students of those first postwar years are now between the ages of fifty and sixty, and when occasionally I again see college friends and acquaintances, they are typically school principals, professors, editors, media department heads, high government officials or politicians: the pillars of society.

I am a writer and an editor in a publishing house. I am not aloof; I belong to this group. The surprise I sometimes feel about this fact is not mine alone.

Two days ago I was at a reception in one of the new bedroom communities outside Bonn. Actually they are no longer so new: the garden shrubs have already attained full luxuriance. The host had been a fellow student. In the meantime he had served as an ambassador to various Asian countries and was now the head of the cultural division in the foreign ministry. A meeting like this has the effect of a time-lapse photograph, but one that denies our sense of having had an interim history. It was more a trick that transported us from the then and there to the here and now, where, increduously, we shook hands.

At this reception I spoke with the wife of another German ambassador. She is a native Swede, and her husband comes from a family that had participated in the resistance against Hitler. When she first came to Germany, she felt that it would be a great task to work with her husband to bring about Germany's reacceptance in the community of nations. Yet today they are regarded abroad (they are stationed in an African country) as representatives of the greatest European industrial power, and this is a transformation she is hardly able to comprehend.

This is the course through which history has run, remarkably direct and unwavering. What is surprising is that all unfolded as was to be expected. In this country nothing stood any longer in the way of total technological and economic mobilization. Bombs had prepared a place, and the erosions of defeat had further removed the remaining debris. But what was to be done with the millions of expatriates and refugees? They certainly could not live in our shrunken territory as a nation of shepherds and farmers, fulfilling what the Morgenthau plan had dreamed. Rather, things proceeded rapidly in the opposite direction. Once again a situation had emerged comparable to the early state of industrialization, when flight from the country drove a huge proletarian reserve army into growing industrial cities. It was worthwhile to invest in or give credit to these masses, who were eager, schooled in self-denial, and initially concerned only with survival; and this the Americans did, on account of the hastily accelerating competition of their system with that of the Soviet Union.

The so-called German economic miracle was a logical consequence of this original situation. Everything moved onward and upward. The progression could be observed on all the graphs, and nearly every Federal Citizen could attest to it. They had begun in hunger and homelessness, and year by year they reached new levels of consumption. Finally they even acquired something like a new collective identity. Ludwig Erhard, the first minister of the economy and second chancellor of the Federal Republic, even physiognomically a symbolic figure for this process, explained it when he said: "We are somebody once again." This meant: by means of economic might and proper political comportment, a country with a stable currency and balance-of-payments surplus had gradually brought itself back onto the international negotiation table; and it also meant a population that had attempted to close the wounds of the past, as if filling construction pits, and that had experienced economic growth as a new fantasy of omnipotence that was to compensate for everything it had lost (and barely remembered). Growth annulled the memory of the war and its consequences—growth as a relentless retreat forward. "More, more," cried the little Häwelmann, hero of an old children's story, a child who in dreams tried to overcome his fears and his smallness. "More, more," thought this population, which in the depth of its buried fears really did not want to believe what had actually happened.

In the years of want, when people stood waiting in lines in front of grocery stores in order to pick up at least their weekly rations, they had created for themselves a material criterion of peace. "Peace," so they said, "is when the butcher asks, 'Do you mind if it's a little bit over?' " This peace came suddenly. And now for decades this gospel of peace has been preached like a commandment of this society by every branch of the advertising industry. More consumption, more achievement, more success, more prestige, more happiness.

"We are somebody once again." Once again this revealing phrase. It gives expression to a forced self-satisfaction, an inverted inferiority complex. One sees the social climber who, still breathing hard from exertion, falls into his new lounge chair, stretches out his legs, and pops open a bottle of beer. "We are somebody once again." This sentiment came from the hearts of the people and vindicated their middle-class advancement mentality, just like that other phrase coined by the first chancellor, Adenauer, whose autocratic style of government relied upon the fears of the population. "No experiments," said he, and the majority thought: No, not under any conditions; we want to hold onto what we have achieved and to keep going in the same direction.

"No experiments." "We are somebody once again." A call to order and a pat on the shoulder. The history of a society's consciousness is articulated and espoused in successful phrases; they reveal what is and is not politically possible.

Dieter Wellershoff

Much was not possible. Fear resulted in a hysteria or paralysis of thought, and for the Federal Citizens the source of this fear was the East. From there they felt threatened at all levels, terrified by the prospect of military occupation and military infiltration. Soviet tanks could overrun the entire tiny country within three days without meeting serious resistance, so people thought. And the groundwork for such an undertaking would have been laid by secret intelligence activities, by ideological infiltration and the terror of the Fifth Column. Everything would happen overnight, and all resistance would be pointless.

In contrast to the citizens of other European nations, those of the Federal Republic possessed little confidence in their own society's power of resistance. They had, after all, learned that one could do anything with people, and that nothing was reliable. They had lost the collective self-confidence that constitutes a nation's psyche and that may be, in fact, one of the life-promoting illusions of the collective unconscious, comparable perhaps to a normal child's feeling of security at home.

The Federal Citizens did not feel secure in their shrunken, emasculated country. And they had imaginings appropriate to this situation. A paranoid propensity for fear and a tendency toward schematizing conceptions influenced political decisions and determined elections. The expatriates from the eastern provinces, and the stream of refugees from the GDR, which subsided only with the erection of the wall, have time and again inflamed this frightened and confrontational attitude vis-à-vis the East. Yet this attitude was based on old structures deeply rooted in the collective inner life of the Germans. These became evident when in 1944–45 the Red Army penetrated the territory of the Reich and triggered a gigantic people's march, which prefigured what later were the streams of expatriates, returnees, and refugees; indeed this was only its first phase. In the West, however, the advancing allied armies triggered no comparable movement of people. Instead the population remained in their houses, hoisting white flags. And the army behaved similarly during the military collapse. In the West one surrendered to the Americans and the English, while in the East the troops engaged in rearguard actions, attempting to withdraw to the West in the face of the Red Army; when this was no longer possible, they dissolved into large and small groups of refugees, each determined to reach the American and English lines at any cost. Without any question they chose as their protectors the Western Allies, thereby already indicating something of immeasurable significance about the type of political life that was to be possible in this country. The last rumor to circulate among soldiers at the collapse of the Oder front in the spring of 1945 was equally portentous. It said: the Western troops have joined forces with the Americans and the English and are now coming to help us beat back the Russians.

With its notion "Bolshevik subhumanity" Nazi propaganda had created a terrifying image of the enemy that still had an effect. It built on the old horrific specters that had been fixed in people's minds in 1917–18, if not much earlier. In this way fear of revolution was linked with an archaic xenophobia about people from the East, an unknown people to whom was attributed a threateningly unpredictable mentality. This fear was heightened by the expectation that the Russians would seek revenge for the severity of the Russian war and its immense devastation, as well as for the Nazi crimes committed in the occupied regions of the Soviet Union. Such collective feelings never arose with regard to the Americans and English, even though the German population had already long suffered under their air attacks and even though the Red Army was still far from the borders.

Thus the structures of the future were already visible. Nonetheless, without Stalin's imperialist power politics, which transformed Eastern Europe, now occupied by the Red Army, into a Soviet Union satellite in which eastern Poles and eastern Germans were driven from their homeland in a westward expansion of Soviet territory; without the impending split of the victorious powers within the Control Council Presidium and at the conference tables; without the incipient cold war, dramatically intensified by the Berlin Blockade and the hot Korean War; without what henceforth was the reciprocally coerced and escalating confrontation of the former Allies—without all this, the Germans' fears, now firmly entrenched, would probably have dissolved, and Adenauer's maxim "No experiments!" might not so easily have shunted aside the notion of a reunited, disarmed, and neutralized Germany that could serve as mediator between East and West.

What a complicated, hypothetical sentence I have just written; its conditionality signals its unreality. If this and that had not occurred, it all would have happened differently. The unrest that still stirs over the question of the possibility and desirability of a different course of history has diminished over time under the normative force of factual reality. Everything is as it has become. Everything has its logic and, when seen from a distance (for it is already distant), looks natural. Were all those who acted as they did therefore in the right? Did no one make a mistake, misunderstand reality? The opposite is unprovable, for history happens only once, and alternative experiments do not occur.

It is demoralizing to think this way, but it does provide some solace. Growing distance from events always gives tranquility. Everything is the way it is, nothing can be undone or altered after the fact. This insight sanctifies the factual and allows lost possibilities to disappear from consciousness. History is also the past simplified, giving the impression that there was only one possible future, not the alternative futures of untraveled paths, which now of course are barred.

Political action, defined by Bismarck as the art of the possible, is therefore also always an attempt to avoid possibilities, to prevent them, to make them impossible. And this process occurs inwardly as well, defining our perception of the situation. When, following the estab-lishment of the Federal Republic and its nascent integration into the West, the Soviet Union not only responded in like manner by estab-lishing the GDR but also developed, between 1950 and 1952, a series of all-German initiatives, people in the West saw this as merely a maneuver and a dangerous trap.

It struck us as particularly unforunate that in the proposals made by the GDR and the Soviet Union, the issue of free, internationally supervised all-German elections, demanded as a first step by the Par-liament of the Federal Republic and the Western Allies, was placed in the background. The Eastern proposals envisioned, as a first stage in the realization of a possible reunification, proportionately constituted all-German councils, which were to deliberate on all further steps. In the West this was not even given consideration, however, for everyone was aware of the possible consequences. In the Soviet Zone of Oc-cupation the Social Democratic party had fallen victim to the Com-munists' embrace and had perished in the Socialist Unity party. And in 1948 in Czechoslovakia Communists gained control of the police, and through the justice department outmaneuvered and liquidated the bourgeois politicians with whom they had previously shared power. This was what people feared when they entertained the idea of an all-German council in which representatives of the GDR would be included in equal number and empowered with the same authority as representatives of the Federal Republic.

Naturally such a council would not have been representative of the will of the population, not only because the GDR controlled a smaller territory and constituency, but also because free elections in the region of the GDR definitely would have had at that time a pro-Western outcome. Because this was common knowledge, however, it was also clear that all-German free elections could not be instituted as a first step in reunification and that an all-German policy could exist in the interim only by proceeding and negotiating on the basis of the existing power relations. Since the Federal Republic, as the larger part of Germany, strengthened Western power more than the GDR strengthened Eastern power, it might have been possible to create conditions under which the establishment of a neutralized, unified Germany, a type of Austrian solution, would have seemed more desirable to the Soviet Union than the unequal division that obtained.

Yet this was difficult and delicate and presupposed security on both sides. But the Soviet Union must have been fearful that an alteration of the German situation would have had unforeseeable repercussions for its East European border states, whereas in the West fear of the Communists was reaching its first peak. But, most important, the Germans' sense of national identity was weakened. It had been corrupted by the Nazi past and exhausted by the War. As a source of motivation for political action it ranked far below the need for security. It was difficult to make credible and to enact an independent, risky German policy with regard to East and West. This perhaps explains what happened, but it does not repudiate the reproach that could later occasionally be heard from foreigners, such as the French: You Germans have permitted the division of your own country and therefore have accepted it historically.

Yes, but were we not thinking ahead? Were we not the better Europeans? (In contrast, the French, for instance, were deluded still by old notions of national greatness and sovereignty and tended to regard European politics as an instrument for French hegemony, as if they were forced to heal the wounds suffered by their national self-esteem in the last war by restoring past grandeur.) Were we not obliged to rethink things fundamentally? Perhaps we had reached that point in history when it was time to look beyond the concept of the nation-state and to strive for a European confederacy. After the balance of power between European countries had collapsed so catastrophically in two world wars, it was urgent to seek out forms of integration that would make future European wars impossible.

In the meantime world-historical developments also pointed in this direction. The old European superpowers, Great Britain and France, watched their power bases disappear through decolonization. And since Germany, the third European power, had lost the War, the dualism of the two superpowers, the United States and the USSR, could serve as a basis for the construction of a new world-historical order. The European states were demoted to the rank of allies, dependent and in need of assistance. If they were ever to regain a world-political significance, they would have to harness in some form their economic and military potential. To be sure, the first possibility was only a united Western Europe. Yet perhaps by means of the integrational force that such a construction certainly possessed, there might one day result an even larger Europe. There were certainly many East Europeans who hoped for this. And the reunification of Germany, which now constituted an alternative to the European policy, would in the end also have been contained in that policy.

These were the speculations and hopes surrounding the notion of a united Western Europe. They enabled West Germans more easily to leave their national past behind. In this notion they perceived the potential for constructively overcoming that past in a now-timely leap to a higher stage of historical development, which could perhaps render forgotten what had been lost.

Yet all this was more the Federal Republic's founding rhetoric than political reality. The East-West conflict was the dominant structure and held European politics in its grip. In view of the military superiority of the Soviet Union, the largely demilitarized West European nations expected the United States to guarantee the inviolability of Europe by means of nuclear weapons. Yet this guarantee covered only specific circumstances. In the event of a limited attack with conventional weapons it would perhaps appear inappropriate and would therefore not be honored. Hence the United States demanded that its allies in Western Europe establish their own defense efforts to offset the threatening superiority of the Soviet Union by means of conventional weapons. Moreover, the Soviet Union detonated its first atomic bomb in 1949, foreshadowing an atomic stalemate that would trigger a new arms race in the sphere of conventional forces. It proclaimed the era of limited wars, in which the highest stage of risk—atomic conflict—was to be avoided.

When in 1950 the North Koreans' invasion pushed to the wall the South Koreans and their small American protective force, this was viewed as a paradigm for the dangers hovering over Western Europe. At that time Churchill demanded before the Council of Europe in Strasbourg the establishment of a European army that would include a German contingent. Adenauer viewed this situation as an opportunity to consolidate and achieve equal status for the West German substate. Yet a European defense community, which for some time had been conceived as the cornerstone of European integration, did not materialize. In 1954 it foundered in the French National Assembly. The idea of military cooperation was saved, however, and transformed into the larger framework of the Western Atlantic Alliance.

The East-West split and the division of Germany were thus completed. NATO and the Warsaw Pact, the Federal Armed Forces and the People's Army thereafter stood face-to-face in combat-ready fashion; the mutual recognition of their respective spheres of power assured a precarious peace.

In order to prevent surprise attacks, large numbers of rival bombers were constantly in the air, carrying live atomic bombs in the direction of their assigned targets, waiting for a code signal to fly on, and turning back again at the border. This phantom battle took place above our heads day and night. Then long-range missiles were developed, and the atomic overkill capacities of both sides were buried in unassailable underground bases or were hidden beneath the ocean in atomic submarines. This is the logic of a deterrence strategy, which protects its population only indirectly, through the detour of an automatic counterattack, thus removing the possibility of winning a nuclear war through surprise attack and replacing it with the contemplation of world annihilation. And it is in this way that we continue to live. What we deem improbable is perhaps only unimaginable. In any case the danger became extremely real when in 1962 American aerial reconnaissance discovered launching pads for short- and intermediate-range missiles in Cuba, and an American naval blockade forced the return of Soviet transport ships carrying additional material for an expansion of the rocket base. At that time I was driving through the GDR to a writers' congress in West Berlin, and slogans agitating against the

United States could be read on every overpass. Later in Berlin I learned that the Soviet ships had turned around and that the danger of a third world war had passed.

Such periods of tension had also occurred during the relative relaxation of tensions that followed Stalin's death in 1953, for the fundamental conflict remained. That the Soviet Union now defined its foreign policy in terms of peaceful coexistence was a strategic corrective resulting from internal and external necessities and only moved the conflict to another level. The revelations about Stalin's terror not only endangered the international prestige of the Soviet Union, above all in their European border states and with Communist parties; they also indicated internal dissatisfaction and stirred in the Soviet population long-suppressed desires for reform, desires for a life with less deprivation and less control. A new generation of elites had grown up for whom a renunciation of every form of consumerism could no longer be justified through reference to the world-political situation and the goals of their own society. At the same time it had become clear that the doctrinal competition with the capitalist system would last for some time and that the Third World presented a new arena for indirect confrontation, in which above all questions of economic and industrial performance would play a decisive role. As a result the Soviet Union had to make an effort to manage its economy in a less ideological manner and, by way of cautious liberalizations, to present a friendlier international face. Only in this way was it able to reestablish itself internally, to emerge from its isolation and, for example, attain influence at the United Nations, where it could place itself in opposition to U.S. imperialism as the champion of small countries.

Yet in its own domain of authority, crisis situations were always resolved by means of force. This was the case with the 1953 rebellion in the GDR, with the initially successful 1956 people's rebellion in Hungary, and with the 1969 violent occupation of Czechoslovakia, then on the path of reform. Yet it is also characteristic of the division of authority or spheres of influence that in 1956, when the Soviet Union was militarily engaged in Hungary, the French and English took advantage of the opportunity for a colonial police action on the Nile. Everyone cleared out, or attempted to, and no one intervened. Such were the rules of the game that had hitherto prevented the great conflict. This was the case later in Vietnam, where American forces confronted Soviet arms but not Soviet troops. And it was also the case in the Middle East, where it was not the soldiers of the world powers but their weapons systems that were in combat.

The Third World has become the occasion and battleground for these conflicts. This displacement has made peace possible in Europe, where the conflict is deadlocked in a guarded border dividing Germany and in the Berlin wall. It is a forced tranquility. And yet it serves as the point of departure for an illusion-free politics, which in the interests of humanity attempts to establish better communication between the two German states, a small lessening of the paranoid rigidity long confronting Germans. Painful though it was, the effectuated demarcation was the price paid for the difficult beginnings of a cautious easing of tensions.

The bird's-eye perspective of a summarizing account allows the historicity of events to become apparent. It generates a continuity of meaning that the occurrences described did not possess for those living through them. What was being played out nationally and world-historically was not something individual Germans necessarily experienced as their own drama. Some event might temporarily have caught their attention that they subsequently forgot. They suffered periodically from new historical necessities, then the situation returned to normal. Politics, especially world politics, was staged above their heads. They rarely felt affected by it directly, and demands on political actors had an essentially negative character: they were to ensure no new war, no revolution, and no economic crisis. All else seemed left to an individual's luck, industriousness, or ingenuity. For most people democracy meant more the right to privacy than the duty to cooperate in the shaping of social life.

Anyone not supported by idealistic illusions might see in this little cause for exasperation. Not moral appeals, but only clarified self-interests can induce people to look beyond their own life and engage in public affairs. As society becomes more complex, it becomes correspondingly more difficult to show convincingly how extensively and early in life individual and common interests intertwine. As long as everything seems to run smoothly, one gladly believes in the harmonizing gestures of those in power and feels embraced in the totality of events.

During the 50s and the first part of the 60s economic growth veiled social contradictions and injustices, since nearly everyone, if in different ways, benefited from it and since the state could adequately meet the needs of competing interest groups with its continually growing budget. This relegated politics to the status of a background phenomenon; the average citizen's participation involved at most his single and statistically insignificant vote on election day. Voting was a ceremonial gesture that, once fulfilled, allowed each citizen to return all the more calmly to his own affairs. During the War everyone had been both compulsory participant and victim. Now one became a quiet shareholder in the social process. Trusting in its progressive tendencies, one let oneself be carried along, remaining all the while in one's own circumscribed private domain. The only problems that really mattered were those to which solutions could be found within one's own sphere of action and did not have to be sought via circuitous political routes or in some later transformation of society. Should one rent an apartment or build a house, change employers or wait for promotion, get divorced or remain together—these were the decisions that preoccupied people. Anything more than that, anything that was not manageable or "achievable," was considered too remote. One wanted to live in the here and now, in the fabric of a society whose further flourishing was presumed and naively projected into the future. Everything had gone well and would continue to go well to the degree that everyone took care of himself. As long as economic growth continued and as long as help wanted advertising filled many pages of newspapers, there also seemed to be enough social welfare to handle the hardship cases, the victims and the losers in the general competitive struggle.

Compared to the forced politicization of everyday life in totalitarian states, which only conceals widespread escapist attitudes, I far prefer this privatization of life. Even though I know that important problems should only be solved collectively, I still do not want to be commanded to march and assemble. Ideological unanimity by no means implies a collective capacity to act; instead it is a superfluous, dysfunctional fetter that by implication concedes motivational weaknesses while at the same time providing no way to overcome them. Ideology obstructs the inflow of information and generates empty ritualistic behavior, making it necessary to proceed all the more cautiously. Any manual on employee motivation would construe this as the consequence of poor management. It is therefore merely poignant and no comment on governmental effectiveness that the Federal Republic's one attempt to institute a national holiday so clearly demonstrated the states's inability to embody and provide meaning: the Federal Citizens have taken June 17, the so-called Day of German Unity, as but a welcomed added opportunity for automobile outings and other recreational activities.

If one wishes to know them better, one must observe the Federal Citizens during their leisure time, in the long lines of cars that on summer weekends seek to escape the congested industrial regions; and, elsewhere throughout Europe, observe those casually chic tourists with their detailed maps and expensive cameras, who plug into and pull out of their vacations all that can be felt, seen, or bought. Now they have been in many countries, know their way around, and have shed the insecurity that, as their critics alleged, they often disguised in a demanding, insolent form of behavior. They have learned that initially they were accepted only for their money, but this is for them no longer problematic; rather it gives them a solid sense of self. For they obtained their money not in handouts but through their own hard work. One's success is apparent less at home than in the international exchange value of one's currency.

This has augmented the compensatory value of the annual trip abroad. Who really wants to take a vacation in the Federal Republic, in this country destroyed by industry, cut up by highways, with its badly built, shapelessly proliferating cities, with its towns rearranged by and interspersed with supermarkets, leisure areas, and new apartment complexes? One's own country is a workplace, offering at most a nearby recreation center, equipped with safari parks, ski lifts, and excursion restaurants. On its chemically purified fields bordered by asphalt-paved streets, no blossoms flower and no butterflies hover. The once highly praised forests are now dreary plantations of wood, for the most part cultivations of spruce. The spruce has become the typical tree of this country, which has no history and no patience. It grows rapidly and can still be chopped down by those who planted it—a cheap mass commodity, which sells quickly and turns a quick profit. It is the tree in the landscape of economic means, extended to the last nook and cranny, a consolidated, drained, infrastructurally planned, totally controlled country.

Here and there one can still sense something of what was once the country's manifold beauty. Yet visible everywhere are excavators, steamrollers, and cranes preparing a new street, a supply depot, another

industrial settlement. This country was settled by the automobile culture. Because there is no longer any limit to mobility, even far-flung
valleys and distant hillsides exhibit similar structures. There are two
terrifying books of photographs by Jörg Müller, one documenting the
progressive destruction of a landscape and the other the altering of
a city. From the time-lapse perspective of successive pictures, the
economic history of the Federal Republic appears as a history of
advancing inhumanity.

The Federal Citizens have accepted this and for the most part are
still willing to do so. After all, what has been destroyed were features
in the common inheritance, and this, it is assumed, does not affect
one's own interests. One is fixated on the compensations: consumer
pleasures, trips, the annual flight to alluring beaches and bathing
resorts, to white hotels. The fact that even the Mediterranean will
soon "stink away" and die is another matter. This is something that
one tries not to believe. But already some people are jetting to the
beaches of the Third World. Upon their return home the hordes of
vacationers, now inside the German border, can press the pedal to
the floor. Time's up. This will already have been announced in the
factory and at the office by the obligatory boastful picture-postcards.
Soon after their arrival, the sender will himself return, perhaps sighing
a bit.

Yet no one ever wished for anything else—only more. It never occurred
to people that one could wish for anything else. As a result, this society
felt offended and dismayed when, in the second half of the 60s, the
youth protest movement made apparent the huge deficit of meaning
that could not be offset by consumerism, cars, and vacation trips. At
that time the Grand Coalition of the Christian Democratic Union and
the Social Democratic party served to annul the possibility of an effective
parliamentary opposition, and in response an extraparliamentary opposition came into being. It comprised student groups and intellectuals
of differing provenance, writers, teachers, social workers, and activist
ministers, who met in Republican Clubs and who, in the struggle
against the State of Emergency Ordinance, sought to construct a new,
critical public sphere. Imaginative demonstrations, street theater, happenings, and political appeals unfurled a scenario of spontaneous democracy, which induced a few enthusiasts to believe that a revolution
was at hand. Yet when demonstrators shouted through loudspeakers

to the citizens or to the avidly courted workers, "Declare your solidarity, join in the march!," nothing happened, save perhaps for the raising of a few threatening fists.

These protests themselves served as an argument favoring the Ordinance, for the majority felt their life-style attacked and security threatened by the protesting minority. I myself delivered a speech during that famous May of 1968 at the New Market in Cologne and a few days later in the main auditorium at Cologne University, which seems typical of protests at that time. I titled it, "The Idyll Grows Malignant." In response to the threatening escalation of domestic governmental force, the speech called for more democracy. Like most speeches, it was delivered to an audience sharing the same convictions and so had little mobilizing force. For the majority wanted to be protected, insulated in their consumer bliss, which the speech denounced as pure quietism. Let me cite two characteristic passages:

What lies ahead of us, what perhaps can still be prevented, is the emergence of a dictatorship within the communal body of our democratic system. This dictatorship lies dormant, yet can immediately be made operational. It can happen that you fall asleep in a democracy and awake under a dictatorship! The transition will have been legal. Then you might receive notification that you are obliged to serve. You no longer have a right to strike. You will no longer be allowed to change or temporarily leave your place of residence. However, you could be carted off. You are not allowed to assemble or demonstrate. Your letters are opened, your calls tapped. All news is screened. You might have to join the armed forces and be deployed against groups who are said to constitute a threat to authority. Or else you yourself might belong to such a group and see the police and then even the military advancing against you. And the calm that will then be established, the stillness in which you are not allowed to move, will be the logical consequence of a policy that began and was pursued with the motto, "No experiments!" No experiments, that's what the majority has asked for: society as a comfortable, industrious idyll in the style of *House Beautiful*, in the style of glossy advertisements—everyone in the TV easy chair enthralled by the charm of the announcer. And if that is disturbed, if this calm does not last, then a state of emergency is declared. Then the calm is reestablished.

This State of Emergency proviso was meant to protect the liberal-democratic basic order, which it can suspend. But I fear that for the majority the object of protection is this pseudoidyll, the state of social stagnation with which their understanding of democracy is vaguely yet inextricably intertwined. . . .

This state, this society is characterized by delayed and diluted reforms. In spite of our great opportunity after the War to construct a modern, forward-looking society, we still have an antiquated educational system, universities in need of restructuring, insufficiently democratized labor relations, a penal code requiring reform, moral authorities like the *Volkswartbund*, money for barracks but not books, no real equal treatment for women, a city-planning policy concocted by real-estate brokers, no preparation for tomorrow since today we must stumble into every predictable structural crisis.

This mindlessness, this confused, creeping, or restorative practice — this is the real state of emergency that must be faced. And it will make itself ever more noticeable, even if the State of Emergency Ordinance is employed to suppress it. Yes, what is at issue here is a defense mechanism. The State of Emergency Ordinance is a bad conscience arming itself.

I believe that for my generation such thoughts had their beginning in the conclusion of the War, which we understood to be the starting point for a free, democratic society. The generation that had been reared in the Federal Republic and was now studying at the universities substantiated their demands differently. They had grown up with economic security, often in relatively liberal households, and now demanded from society more freedom, happiness, justice, and community. Herbert Marcuse's thesis that the growth of the forces of production renders social repression superfluous was the optimistic assumption that seemed to allow for the integration of protest into a general movement upward. After a food-clothes-house-car-travel fad, by which the Federal Citizens had measured their economic ascendance, why not now an emancipation fad? After hard work, why not become a spare-time hippie? It was good to be relaxed; one had to develop one's sensitivity, one's sexuality, one's expressive capacity, one's articulation. This was an appropriate adjustment to what had meanwhile been achieved, as if moving into a bigger and better apartment could generate more discussion and self-unfolding.

There have been visible gains in emancipation, above all a democratization of manners, increased sexual freedom, and even first steps toward a liberation of women. Everything else has been enveloped by institutions and has died out, has been encapsulated in cults or assumed the form of criminal terror. Society keeps going as before. Yet the vitality, the naive optimism, the belief that things could go on like this forever has been lost.

Warnings of a deadly furture darken the horizon. Are we threatened by an ecological catastrophe or, in response, a new world of scarcity, of control, and of distribution struggles? Ever since 1972 when the Club of Rome published its first report on the limits to growth, there has been no end to the terrifying predictions and tidings of woe. Entirely different tables and graphs now profile the future. In a few generations mankind will lie in agony if it continues to follow its present course and if industrial economic exploitation maintains its accelerated pace. The fossil fuels, developed over many millions of years, will soon be exhausted. Air pollution, water contamination, the destruction of the ozone layer protecting us from cosmic radiation, the disintegration of the ecosystem, the extermination of more and more varieties of flora and fauna, the accumulation of radioactive waste—all this will, in the accelerating, deadly final lap of the technological-industrial civilization that now begins to span the entire globe, build toward a complex catastrophe, from which there will be no recovery but at most a wretched survival for the remnants of unrecognizable humanity in a hopelessly destroyed world.

This future is no longer distant but is rather already visible; its features surround us and fill our newspapers. Stranded oil tankers pollute our coastlines. In twenty years the Mediterranean will be a gigantic cesspool: 40,000 tons of deformed fish were netted in one year near Marseilles alone. More and more industrial products are found to be carcinogenic. Industrial accidents like the one near Seveso in Northern Italy (where an entire region will not be habitable for years) are expected every day and on a less catastrophic scale are already a part of our daily news. A new ecological crime of the greatest magnitude, the clearing of the Amazon jungle without good reason, was recently conceived through a combination of Brazilian megalomania and American business acumen. It is readily apparent that the earth's last natural landscapes are falling victim to technological-industrial civilization.

Since the beginning of the 70s, this has been the panorama through which the future presents itself. The old and oft-dismissed warnings of conservative cultural critics have in a new and irrefragable fashion suddenly become topical and have shaken faith in progress and in the further development of the forces of production. Industrial progress and economic growth—the cornerstone of all capitalist and Marxist promises of happiness—now portend collective death.

An increasing number of people are disturbed by these views. Yet the silent majority will not allow itself to be affected by them, and the political institutions—parties, trade unions, government, and of course industry—are apparently unable to draw the proper conclusions. Any measure that might limit economic growth and endanger our standard of living would be unpopular. An elimination of or restriction in the compensations we receive for our labor and social alienation would expose a vacuum in the meaning of life no less horrifying than total devastation. How could we live without these daily satisfactions? Economic growth and consumer pleasures supplant all other spheres of life. It no longer seems possible collectively to furnish life with meaning. Should everyone return to religion and take consolation in the beyond? Better to go on as before.

The ecological problem is a problem of humanity's survival. But it is first a crisis in the foundations of industrial societies. Their preeminence, privileges, their affluence, their self-perceptions have been morally called into question, yet in the not too distant future they will surely be challenged on factual grounds as well. More and more, their position in the world will become viewed as one of institutionalized force, which in the long run cannot be defended. At the same time life in industrial societies will, as a consequence of growth, itself become ever more onerous, debilitating, and destructive.

The urgent need for change is countered by the complexity of the problem. The industrial societies must reevaluate their world relations and at the same time change their own costly life-style. Moreover, they must develop alternate forms of technology, as well as methods of production and transportation, that are less of a burden on the environment and that conserve energy and raw materials. These structural changes, described of late as qualitative growth, should if possible take place without far-reaching social crises. New social inequities should not arise from them, nor should there emerge authoritarian controls and planning bureaucracies throttling the individual's freedom of movement.

No one knows how this is to happen. For this reason there has only been haphazard problem-solving, a little patchwork in pollution control and some scant aid for developing countries. This has nothing to do with fundamental change. The nature of the contradictions involved is illustrated by way of a simple example. It would be important to counteract the tendency to scrap consumer goods prematurely— something that could be achieved by improving their durability and their capacity for repair. But wouldn't a reduction in consumerism entail growing unemployment, diminishing spending power, shrinking productivity, a decline in taxable income, and ultimately the collapse of the system?

Now, taken in and of themselves, without considering possible countervailing forces, these are of course irrational fears. Nonetheless, they are not altogether unfounded. Until now societal steering has been possible only by reason of continued economic growth. Even a positive rate of growth, such as an annual increase in productivity per work hour, would immediately become a problem without corresponding increases in levels of production. If new markets are not found for these additional commodities, then the increased productivity will result in unemployment, making it necessary to reorganize all of society's available labor through retraining courses and a reduction in work hours. Because these processes are complex and hardly lend themselves to direction, and because they give rise, at least initially, to conflicts and inequities, no one puts much stock in their humanizing potential. Continuous economic growth has always seemed the best solution to these problems, even when the social cost has been increased stress and more pollution. The majority of the population has always thought this way. What counts is what one can buy, not what is already there: air, water, and time. There is a destructive element in this attitude, which becomes all the more obvious as it is extended into the future. Thus Carl Amery is perhaps correct when he laconically asserts, "After 2010 or 2050 the apocalypse will be wholly predictable."

Destructive tendencies and anxiety-producing experiences that cannot be mastered are collectively repressed. One denies them, reinterprets them, places their burden on others, constructs alibis and defense mechanisms, withdraws, hides, becomes cynical or illusionary. I think that all the tensions, fears, and aggressions that have been troubling German society ever since the so-called ideological shift (*Tendenzwende*) at the beginning of the 70s are symptoms of a disturbed collective identity. Terrorism, juvenile crime, the growing numbers of drug addicts and, above all, alcoholics and suicides, can with spectacular events and numbers provide testimony to this. Yet more indicative is the privatized, psychic misery which, while manifesting itself everywhere, has not become publicly discernible, as if it could not believe in its right to exist and could not be, so to speak, normal.

A psychiatrist told me that he and his colleagues are having to deal ever more frequently with a new type of patient. It is a person who generally "functions" but is enervated in his life-impulses. He keeps going but sees no sense in it. The available satisfactions mean little to him, the efforts required to achieve them appear too great. He doesn't know what he is suffering from. It is a diffuse picture characterized by fear, lack of drive, depressive irritation, and changing body symptoms. He has already tried everything—tranquilizers, macrobiotic diets, group therapy, political radicalization. What's the point? He just doesn't know. And the therapist cannot tell him anything that he somehow doesn't already know himself. He nods, but he is bewildered. Although he can talk, he has nothing to say. He is prematurely a psychological invalid, crawling in the sand. His inconspicuousness conceals his typicality.

He is no longer a marginal figure. In him one sees the reflection of a society that, while providing little motivational inspiration, nonetheless makes people dependent by shaping their needs. Parents, as agents of an achiever and consumer society, also contribute to this process. Having no time for their children—although plenty for their jobs, the competitive struggle, and their own self-fulfillment—they assuage their feelings of guilt by spoiling them with presents. They convey to their children that whatever one can get is a mere surrogate, and yet that one has a right to it and that it is needed. And perhaps they evoke as a counterreaction a desire for truth and authenticity that casts about for something to believe in and allows itself to be lured by capricious promises of salvation until even they are perceived as mere surrogates. And then the only remaining choice is between depression and adulthood.

Of course most people still manage to find their way. And many of them overcompensate for their insecurity by appearing even more resolute. They cram, grovel, and sweat from exam anxiety, toe the line, and strive for nothing more than what society has deemed desirable. Every third citizen in the Federal Republic now has a car, and every street in every city is packed. Is this cause for alarm or celebration? According to the Allensbach Institute for Public Opinion, during the last three years our citizens' optimism has once again increased. Sixty percent look to next year with hope.

It is no different with me. Whenever I thumb through the paper and read about Iran, Turkey, and the Middle East, I am glad to be living here. I also hope that the necessary changes do not occur through privation and catastrophes but result from thoughtful deliberation and economic surplus. For only then can sufficient freedom and individuality be maintained in new social structures to make life in them worthwhile. I know these are big demands and, when measured by world poverty, maybe even elitist. Yet it does say something for this state and society that such demands can be developed within them.

Sometimes I think that my generation had a favorable beginning. It gained an identity at the end of the War, in what seemed to be an open world. I studied without thinking that I was preparing for a career. It had not yet been possible to reestablish convincingly a social world with professions and careers and pensions and other societal "givens." This was less troublesome than being a member of an established society endowed with all sorts of securities and yet not knowing whether one would find a job. It was easy to be poor then. That was no reason to be ashamed. In the 50s, however, with the growing and more perceptible social differences, shame became more noticeable. The next step presupposed more affluence and signaled, as it were, its vulgarization. This was the development of a counterculture characterized by a Bohemian seediness and a disdain for consumerism, which itself has since become a familiar theme in commercial advertising.

It is odd to recall such things and, with the feeling of standing squarely in the present, to find still within oneself so many vivid pictures of a past now foreign.

I live in Cologne, a city I saw burning as I traveled past it in a train. I carried my suitcase through its ruins to a streetcar, which took me to Bonn, my place of study. All that has become hazy, because I live here. The present is so prominent that it tends to screen all else out. I asked my youngest daughter: "How old am I in your eyes, if you can recall times past?" "As old as you are right now," she said. This is the illusion with which we live and which must be overcome by historiography and recounting. The mere fact that one recognizes it as an illusion is an advance in knowledge. This country provides me with manifold opportunities.

This summer I traveled to Poland with my wife and daughters, to what was once Pomerania, my wife's home. We visited the houses and gardens that formed the scenery of her childhood, feeling slightly like intruders and belonging there no longer. An old German lady, a refugee from Western Prussia, who had been left here by chance, showed us around and we sensed our otherness: we were Federal Citizens and she, in her poverty and her desolation, represented a part of the German past that had not been adapted to the new structures.

On this trip I had another daydream. I appeared as myself, age nineteen, in a filthy uniform. Together with a comrade whose name and face I cannot recall, I was pulling a handcart loaded with arms, ammunition, and food that had been randomly snatched from deserted houses. To make faster progress we took to the autobahn in the direction of Stettin. We were surrounded by other fleeing soldiers from many different troop regiments. Like us, they came from the collapsed Oder front and were skirting Berlin in a broad arch, in order to escape to the West by way of Mecklenburg. It was April 1945. We moved amid what for me was an unequaled welling up of spring, nature's incongruous dissent to the universal destruction of the world. Now I was driving with my family on the same autobahn through a German state, a foreign country for us; we drove in a former east German province on the Baltic, now part of Poland. It was summer 1978, early August, yet the primacy of the present began to waver. We parked in a pine tree forest and unpacked our Federal Republican picnic. Next to us stopped a military convoy with soldiers from the People's Army of the GDR, who were as old as I was then. They glanced at us but were probably not allowed to talk to us. We drove on, pine forests to the right, and to the left, farther out in gently moving lines, corn fields ripe for harvesting — a landscape that I love very much and which, for whatever reason, is more familiar to me than, for instance, southern Germany.

Driving through that area, seeing it again and yet not really recognizing it, was like being in an unsettling twilight zone of time. Does one know this village, this forest edge? Does it not conceal another picture? Suddenly a village emerged at the side of the autobahn, out of peaceful inconspicuousness, in whose pond the daydream apparition of myself was, along with many others, bathing his tired feet; at that moment Soviet tanks, appearing on the outskirts of the village, began firing, and everything convulsed into panicked screams and chaos. It was a turmoil encased in shadows, an explosive firedamp of recollections. Then the broad corn fields reasserted themselves on both sides of the road. Calm reclaimed the picture, the daydream faded, and the present became normal. These fantastic historical transformations appear even more bizarre when one imagines the ability to peer into our present for a moment. From the fall of 1943 to the summer of 1944 I was in infantry training on the Virgin Heath in Berlin. It was a wide tract of land, interspersed with hills and shrubs, bordered in part by the city, in part by a distant forest edge. During a military exercise one is often alone for hours. One squats in a foxhole waiting for the beginning or the end of an exercise and slips into daydreams. And if the eighteen-year-old soldier I was at the time had possessed this future perspective, he would suddenly have seen not the heath tract but the planed surface, the runway and landing strip of Berlin's Tegel airport. Large, strange airplanes from foreign and domestic cities would have landed before his spellbound gaze, and from one of them would have descended an older man, in whom the eighteen-year-old, in keeping with the rules of this play of thoughts, would have recognized himself. His mind's eye would have followed this phantom of his own future through a divided city. He would have watched this older man leave the streetcar at the Friedrichstrasse station and, with a crowd of others, pass a complicated border control.

And now he is in the other part of the city, in the old Prussian town center with its beautiful classicist buildings, insofar as they have survived. On the Schinkel watch sentries march in goose step across from the Opera House. Their uniforms and helmets bring to mind both the German and the Red Army. The man momentarily waits, then moves on in the direction of Alexanderplatz. Here everything is new, socialist city planning; bare, somewhat rambling, in modern functional architecture approximating Western tastes. There, in a room on an upper floor of the Hotel City Berlin, he meets Eugenia, his Russian translator. She is Jewish, a little older than he, editor of a journal for literary theory published in Moscow. And he is a writer; he will write an article for her journal. They talk about it. The next issue will be an international symposium on problems of the novel, and he is to write the German contribution.

They stand at the window and look down on the city below, and Eugenia begins to tell how she experienced the German siege of Leningrad and the icy winter of hunger when dead bodies lay on the streets everywhere. A sailor in the Soviet Navy, she had come to Berlin with the victorious Red Army; there she worked for the Soviet Military Administration and lived for years and made many German friends.

She talks; he listens. And he is determined to write the other side of the story, his story, the present essay. It should contain something of the heady feeling that overwhelms anyone in this country when surveying its recent history. These ever-changing living conditions, collective problems, premonitions, possibilities, and perhaps even something enduring prompts a theme: how, from the erosion of the old meaning-engendering myths and ideologies, more realistic behavior and perhaps even a dialogue can arise. So much new meaning emerges only in retrospect. The eighteen-year-old there in his foxhole, who a few weeks later was sent to the eastern front with a company of youths of the same age, only thirty of whom, months later, were neither wounded nor dead—this daydreamer with his future gaze could not possibly have understood this scene from the present perspective. The metamorphosis would have been incomprehensible, reassuring perhaps only in one respect: that he would live so long.

Even now, from my standpoint today, I desire no gaze into the future, only wakeful foresight. For I still want to participate in the history to come; I do not want to leap over it abstractly. I want to participate, however, with a skeptical and yet hopeful feeling for the unceasing, enduring historical change upon which we must depend.

Contributors

Karl Heinz Bohrer is Professor of Literature and Modern German Literary History at the University of Bielefeld. He is the author of *Die Ästhetik des Schreckens* (1978) and the editor of *Mythos und Moderne* (1983). Bohrer was born in Cologne in 1935.

Peter Bürger is Professor of French and Comparative Literature at the University of Bremen. He has written extensively on aesthetic theory and literary methodology, including the recently translated *The Theory of the Avant-Garde*. Bürger was born in Hamburg in 1936.

Horst Ehmke is Deputy Leader of the Social Democratic faction in the German Parliament and Professor of Public Law at the University of Freiburg. Ehmke was born in Danzig in 1927.

Jürgen Habermas is Professor of Philosophy at the University of Frankfurt. His most recent books to appear in English are *Philosophical-Political Profiles* and *The Theory of Communicative Action: Reason and the Rationalization of Society*. Habermas was born in Düsseldorf in 1929.

Johann Baptist Metz is Professor of Fundamental Theology at the University of Münster. A Catholic priest, Metz has been active in promoting a notion of political theology rooted in the social base. He was born in Bavaria in 1926.

Jürgen Moltmann is Professor of Systematic Theology at the University of Tübingen. He is author of *Trinity and the Kingdom of God* (1981). Moltmann was born in Hamburg in 1926.

Hans Mommsen is Professor of History at the University of Bochum. He has written extensively on nineteenth- and twentieth-century social and political history, focusing particularly on the workers' movement and National Socialism. Mommsen was born in Marburg in 1930.

Wolf-Dieter Narr is Professor of Political Science at the Free University of Berlin. He contributes regularly to the German periodical *Leviathan*, of which he is one of the editors. Born in 1937, Narr was raised in Würzburg.

Claus Offe is Professor of Sociology and Political Science at the University of Bielefeld. A set of his recent essays has been translated in *Contradictions of the Welfare State* (The MIT Press, 1984). Offe was born in Berlin in 1940.

Ulrich Preuss is Professor of Public Law at the University of Bremen. He is author of *Die Internalisierung des Subjekts* (1979). Preuss was born in Marienburg (now part of East Germany) in 1939.

Dorothee Sölle is Professor of Systematic Theology at New York's Union Theological Seminary, where she teaches for one semester a year. A member of Christen für den Sozialismus, Sölle is active in the West German Peace Movement. She was born in Cologne in 1929.

Hans-Ulrich Wehler is Professor of General History at the University of Bielefeld. He has written extensively on modern German history, historiography, and historical social science. Wehler was born in 1931.

Dieter Wellershoff is a writer and editor in Cologne. His most recent work is the novel *Der Sieger nimmt alles* (1983). Wellershoff was born in Neuss am Rhein in 1925.

Albrecht Wellmer is Professor of Philosophy at the University of Konstanz. His research currently focuses on the problems and prospects of critical theory. Wellmer was born in Westphalia in 1933.

Index

380

Index

Index